THE EUROPEAN UNION SERIES

General Editors: Neill Nugent, William E. Paterson, Vincent Wright

The European Union series provides an authoritative library on the European Union, ranging from general introductory texts to definitive assessments of key institutions and actors, issues, policies and policy processes, and the role of member states.

Books in the series are written by leading scholars in their fields and reflect the most up-to-date research and debate. Particular attention is paid to accessibility and clear presentation for a wide audience of students, practitioners, and interested general readers.

The series editors are **Neill Nugent**, Professor of Politics and Jean Monnet Professor of European Integration, Manchester Metropolitan University, and **William E. Paterson**, Founding Director of the Institute of German Studies, University of Birmingham and Chairman of the German British Forum. Their co-editor until his death in July 1999, **Vincent Wright**, was a Fellow of Nuffield College, Oxford University.

Feedback on the series and book proposals are always welcome and should be sent to Steven Kennedy, Palgrave Macmillan, Houndmills, Basingstoke, Hampshire RG21 6XS, UK, or by e-mail to s.kennedy@palgrave.com

General textbooks

Published

Desmond Dinan **Encyclopedia of the European Union** [Rights: Europe only]

Desmond Dinan **Europe Recast: A History of European Union** [Rights: Europe only]

Desmond Dinan **Ever Closer Union: An Introduction to European Integration (3rd edn)** [Rights: Europe only]

Simon Hix **The Political System of the European Union (2nd edn)**

Paul Magnette **What is the European Union? Nature and Prospects**

John McCormick **Understanding the European Union: A Concise Introduction (3rd edn)**

Brent F. Nelsen and Alexander Stubb **The European Union: Readings on the Theory and Practice of European Integration (3rd edn)** [Rights: Europe only]

Neill Nugent (ed.) **European Union Enlargement**

Neill Nugent **The Government and Politics of the European Union (5th edn)** [Rights: World excluding USA and dependencies and Canada]

John Peterson and Elizabeth Bomberg **Decision-Making in the European Union**

Ben Rosamond **Theories of European Integration**

Forthcoming

Laurie Buonanno and Neill Nugent **Policies and Policy Processes of the European Union**

Mette Eilstrup Sangiovanni (ed.) **Debates on European Integration: A Reader**

Philippa Sherrington **Understanding European Union Governance**

Also planned

The Political Economy of the European Union

Series Standing Order (outside North America only)
ISBN 0–333–71695–7 hardback
ISBN 0–333–69352–3 paperback
Full details from www.palgrave.com

The major institutions and actors

Published

Renaud Dehousse **The European Court of Justice**

Justin Greenwood **Interest Representation in the European Union**

Fiona Hayes-Renshaw and Helen Wallace **The Council of Ministers (2nd edn)**

Simon Hix and Christopher Lord **Political Parties in the European Union**

David Judge and David Earnshaw **The European Parliament**

Neill Nugent **The European Commission**

Anne Stevens with Handley Stevens **Brussels Bureaucrats? The Administration of the European Union**

Forthcoming

Simon Bulmer and Wolfgang Wessels **The European Council**

The main areas of policy

Published

Michelle Cini and Lee McGowan **Competition Policy in the European Union**

Wyn Grant **The Common Agricultural Policy**

Martin Holland **The European Union and the Third World**

Brigid Laffan **The Finances of the European Union**

Malcolm Levitt and Christopher Lord **The Political Economy of Monetary Union**

Janne Haaland Matláry **Energy Policy in the European Union**

John McCormick **Environmental Policy in the European Union**

John Peterson and Margaret Sharp **Technology Policy in the European Union**

Handley Stevens **Transport Policy in the European Union**

Forthcoming

Laura Cram **Social Policy in the European Union**

Jolyon Howorth **Defence Policy in the European Union**

Bart Kerremans, David Allen and Geoffrey Edwards **The External Economic Relations of the European Union**

Stephen Keukeleire and Jennifer MacNaughtan **The Foreign Policy of the European Union**

James Mitchell and Paul McAleavey **Regionalism and Regional Policy in the European Union**

Jörg Monar **Justice and Home Affairs in the European Union**

John Vogler, Richard Whitman and Charlotte Bretherton **The External Policies of the European Union**

Also planned

Political Union

The member states and the Union

Published

Carlos Closa and Paul Heywood **Spain and the European Union**

Alain Guyomarch, Howard Machin and Ella Ritchie **France in the European Union**

Forthcoming

Simon Bulmer and William E. Paterson **Germany and the European Union**

Phil Daniels and Ella Ritchie **Britain and the European Union**

Brigid Laffan **The European Union and its Member States**

Luisa Perrotti **Italy and the European Union**

Baldur Thorhallson **Small States in the European Union**

Issues

Published

Derek Beach **The Dynamics of European Integration: Why and When EU Institutions Matter**

Forthcoming

Thomas Christiansen and Christine Reh **Constitutionalizing the European Union**

Steven McGuire and Michael Smith **The USA and the European Union**

Also planned

Europeanization and National Politics

The Council of Ministers

Second Edition

**Fiona Hayes-Renshaw
and
Helen Wallace**

palgrave
macmillan

First edition 1997
Second edition 2006

Published by
PALGRAVE MACMILLAN
Houndmills, Basingstoke, Hampshire RG21 6XS and
175 Fifth Avenue, New York, N.Y. 10010
Companies and representatives throughout the world

PALGRAVE MACMILLAN is the global academic imprint of the Palgrave Macmillan division of St. Martin's Press, LLC and of Palgrave Macmillan Ltd. Macmillan® is a registered trademark in the United States, United Kingdom and other countries. Palgrave is a registered trademark in the European Union and other countries.

ISBN-13: 978–0–333–94866–8 hardback
ISBN-10: 0–333–94866–1 hardback
ISBN-13: 978–0–333–94865–1 paperback
ISBN-10: 0–333–94865–3 paperback

This book is printed on paper suitable for recycling and made from fully managed and sustained forest sources.

A catalogue record for this book is available from the British Library.

A catalog record for this book is available from the Library of Congress.

10   9   8   7   6   5   4   3   2   1
15   14   13   12   11   10   09   08   07   06

Printed and bound in China

Outline Contents

Detailed Contents

List of Tables, Figures and Boxes

Tables

Figures

Boxes

Preface

This volume provides a wide-ranging overview of the Council of Ministers of the European Union (EU), detailing both its current operations and its evolution over time. The starting point was the first edition, published in 1997. In the intervening years, there have been two significant developments as regards sources of information and analysis on the Council and its inner workings. First, detailed material that was unimaginable when we prepared our first edition has become accessible under the Council's new 'transparency arrangements'. As a result, we are now able to present a much more thorough account of how the Council, its committees and working parties operate. Where previously we had to play detective and to rely on interviews, conversations and anecdotes provided by insiders, in this edition we are able to provide much greater precision and many more sources for others to follow up.

One important innovation in this edition is the inclusion of material on recorded voting in the Council. With the help of Wim van Aken, to whom we owe a huge debt of gratitude, we have constructed what we believe to be the most comprehensive data set on explicit voting in the Council. Wim collected, collated and then carried out a statistical analysis of data we received from several sources. An overview of the results of this analysis is presented in Chapter 10, and interestingly confirms qualitative evidence dating from the period before the Council released information on explicit voting. The data set is available on the Palgrave website at www.palgrave.com/politics/hayes-renshaw for the benefit of the wider community. We also plan to produce some further analysis of this data ourselves.

Second, there has been an explosion of new analytical literature on the Council. This is a result not only of the increased data available to the researcher, but also of a much greater interest among academics in developing systematic analytical approaches, models and theories that seek to explain how the Council works, and how its operations fit into the broader EU institutional framework. Thus, in the more empirical parts of this volume, we have been able to draw on excellent studies by other authors and, in Chapters 10 and 11 in particular, have been able to locate our own study in the wider context of this now rather rich analytical literature. This is an exciting development in the field of EU studies, which has opened up many opportunities for scholarly debate and lively argument. The subject takes on even more interest given the current controversy about how the institutional system can or should develop in the future enlarged EU, and the fact that protagonists in the debate are always making assumptions and propositions about how the Council operates, or might operate in the future.

This volume has taken rather longer to complete than expected, partly because of competing demands on our time, and partly because there always seemed to be another imminent, significant event in the life of the Council or of the EU, whose effects we felt should be included in our account. On the latter criterion, however, there will never be a best time to finish, such is the evolutionary nature of the Council and of the EU. Our coverage extends to the period of the June 2005 European Council in Brussels, and hence includes an account of the provisions of the disputed Constitutional Treaty (CT), as well as some early insights into the EU-25 as enlarged in May 2004. Our hope is that this extensively revised and rewritten version will provide a kind of reference book for teachers, students and practitioners interested in this very important part of the EU's decision-making processes. The associated website (www.palgrave.com/politics/hayes-renshaw) contains further information for the interested reader.

Many colleagues have contributed in one way or another to this volume. In particular, many 'insiders' have patiently allowed themselves to be interrogated, some of them several times, as we have worked our way round the subject. We cannot name every individual who helped us, but we are grateful to them all. We have benefited in particular from the unstinting generosity of Hans Brunmayr, the Director-General of DG F in the Council Secretariat, and his colleagues, Gabrielle Weise and Marta Leon Melero. They are responsible for making the transparency arrangements work smoothly, but they have helped us far beyond the call of duty. François Head in the Press Office also deserves our thanks for responding speedily to many requests for detailed information. We have of course spoken to many people in the various permanent representations and EU institutions while preparing this book, but Fiona Hayes-Renshaw would particularly like to thank Noel White, Michael Forbes, Declan Kelleher and Peter Gunning from the Irish permanent representation, who gave generously of their time to speak to her, as did Guy Milton in the Council Secretariat. David Neligan and Sam Tarling, both now retired from the Council Secretariat, also shared their considerable experience with us. In the Commission, we would like to thank Una O'Dwyer, Paolo Ponzano and Jerzy Glucksman, among others, and in the EP Secretariat, Michael Shackleton.

Various other friends, family members and colleagues have helped us in manifold ways. Steven Kennedy has been, as always, an encouraging, patient and persistently thoughtful publisher at Palgrave, smoothing the way and keeping us going. Neill Nugent has provided helpful comments on the manuscript. Many colleagues have commented on parts of the draft at various stages. Magda Herbowska heroically carried out some bibliographical research for us. Daniel Renshaw provided expert technical support with graphic material. Angelika Lanfranchi helped us to assemble the final version of the manuscript. Harriet Wallace added some shrewd comments in the closing stages. We are grateful to them all.

Finally, Fiona Hayes-Renshaw would like to say a special thank you to the Renshaw and Hayes families for their forbearance and unflagging interest in this seemingly endless venture. In particular, Andrew, Daniel, Jessica and Ben Renshaw have been a real support in their various and much valued ways.

FIONA HAYES-RENSHAW
HELEN WALLACE

List of Abbreviations

ACP	Group of African, Caribbean and Pacific states
AD	administrator (administrative grade official)
Agfish	Agriculture and Fisheries Council
AOB	any other business
AST	assistant (non-administrative grade official)
BATNA	best alternative to no agreement
Benelux	grouping of Belgium, the Netherlands and Luxembourg
BEPGs	broad economic policy guidelines
BM	blocking minority
CAP	common agricultural policy
Cariforum	Forum of the Caribbean ACP states
CATS	*Comité de l'article trente-six* (Article 36 Committee)
CCA	Committee on Cultural Affairs
CD-ROM	Compact disc – read-only memory
CFE	Convention on the Future of Europe
CFI	Court of First Instance
CFSP	common foreign and security policy
Cocor	*Commission de coordination du Conseil des ministres* (Coordinating committee of the Council of Ministers)
COMCEN	Communications Centre
COPS	*Comité de politique et de sécurité* (Political and Security Committee)
CoR	Committee of the Regions
Coreper	*Comité des représentants permanents* (Committee of Permanent Representatives)
CR	Czech Republic
CREST	Committee on Scientific and Technical Research
CRPs	Council's (internal) rules of procedure
CSDP	common security and defence policy
CT	Constitutional Treaty
CTEU	Consolidated Treaty on European Union
DEU	Decision Making in the European Union research project
DG	Directorate-General
DPR	deputy permanent representative
DSG	Deputy Secretary-General
EC	European Communities/Community *also* Education Committee

ECB	European Central Bank
Ecofin	Economic and Financial Affairs Council
ECJ	European Court of Justice
Ecowas	Economic Community of West African States
ECSC	European Coal and Steel Community
ECU	European Currency Unit
EEA	European Economic Area
EEAS	European External Action Service
EEC	European Economic Community
EFC	Economic and Financial Committee
EFTA	European Free Trade Association
EMU	economic and monetary union
EP	European Parliament
EPC	European political cooperation *also* Economic Policy Committee
EPSCO	Employment, Social Policy, Health and Consumer Affairs Council
ERDF	European Regional Development Fund
ESC	Economic and Social Committee
ESDP	European security and defence policy
EU	European Union
EUMC	European Union Military Committee
Euratom	European Atomic Energy Community
EUSA-US	European Union Studies Association of the US
EYC	Education, Youth and Culture Council
G7	Group of the finance ministers of the leading industrialized democracies (Canada, France, Germany, Italy, Japan, the UK and the USA)
G8	Group of the political leaders of the G7 plus Russia
GAC	General Affairs Council
GAERC	General Affairs and External Relations Council
GAG	General Affairs Group
GATT	General Agreement on Tariffs and Trade
GCC	Gulf Cooperation Council
HRCFSP	High Representative for the Common Foreign and Security Policy
IDEA	electronic directory of the European institutions
IGC	intergovernmental conference
IIA	inter-institutional agreement
IMF	International Monetary Fund
JHA	justice and home affairs
JICS	Joint Interpretation and Conference Service
MC	Military Committee
MDG	Multi-disciplinary group on organized crime
MEP	Member of the European Parliament

MFA	Ministry of Foreign Affairs
NAC	North Atlantic Council
NATO	North Atlantic Treaty Organisation
NGOs	non-governmental organizations
OECD	Organisation for Economic Co-operation and Development
OJ	Official Journal of the European Communities
permrep	permanent representation
PoCo	Political Committee
PR	permanent representative
PSC	Political and Security Committee
QM	qualified majority
QMV	qualified majority voting
R&D	research and development
RELEX	External Relations (*Relations extérieures*)
SCA	Special Committee on Agriculture
SCIFA	Strategic Committee on Immigration, Frontiers and Asylum
SEA	Single European Act
SG	Secretary-General
SG/HRCFSP	Secretary-General/High Representative for the CFSP
SGP	Stability and Growth Pact
SITCEN	Joint Situation Centre of the EU
SMEs	small and medium-sized enterprises
TACs	total allowable catches
TEC	Treaty establishing the European Community
TENs	Trans-European Networks
TEPSA	Trans-European Policy Studies Network
TEU	Treaty on European Union; Maastricht Treaty
ToA	Treaty of Amsterdam; Amsterdam Treaty
ToN	Treaty of Nice; Nice Treaty
TTE	Transport, Telecommunications and Energy Council
UK	United Kingdom
UN	United Nations
UNICE	European Union of Employers' Confederations
USA and US	United States of America; United States
WEAG	Western European Armaments Group
WEU	Western European Union
WP	Working Party
WTO	World Trade Organization

Chapter 1

Introduction

The Council of the European Union (see Box 1.1) was fathered by the 1951 Treaty of Paris, and born of the 1957 Treaties of Rome. Since the transformation of the European Community (EC) into the European Union (EU) in 1991, the spotlight has been trained even more firmly on the Council, which operates at the core of the EU's institutional system. Today, the Council is not just the forum for negotiating and legislating on traditional Community business, but is also the key institution as regards the newer areas of more 'intergovernmental' work – that is, the common foreign and security policy (CFSP), the associated European security and defence policy (ESDP) and the large agenda in justice and

---

Box 1.1   *An abundance of Councils*

The Council of Ministers is often confused with two other bodies having similar names, but very different forms, compositions and functions. To add to the confusion, the Council itself is known by several different names.

The Council of Ministers, also referred to as **the EU Council** and **the ministerial Council**, is the main legislative authority of the European Union (EU), and is composed of ministerial representatives of the (currently 25) member states. The treaties refer merely to **the Council**. Following the coming into force of the Treaty on European Union (TEU) in 1993, the Council decided to designate itself **the Council of the European Union**. Legally speaking, there is a single Council, which can take decisions on any issue coming within its remit. In practice, it meets in nine distinct configurations.

The first 'other body', **the European Council**, is the supreme political authority of the EU. It is composed of the heads of state or government of each of the member states and the President of the Commission, who meet about four times a year usually in Brussels to provide the strategic guidelines and political impetus for the EU. It also acts in effect as a higher level of the Council of Ministers, by attempting to settle those issues on which the ministers have been unable to reach agreement.

The second 'other body', **the Council of Europe**, is an organisation entirely distinct from the European Union. It was founded in 1949, is based in Strasbourg and has a current membership of 45 countries. Much of the work of this intergovernmental consultative organization is concerned with human rights, education, culture and cooperation in such fields as the environment and the fight against drugs.

---

home affairs (JHA). Over the years the European Council, meeting at the level of heads of state or government, has become more and more important, operating increasingly as the senior branch of the Council.

The EU never stands still. Its basic institutional system is persistently under review and subject to changes, intended and unintended, both by explicit redesign and by evolutionary processes. The most recent example of explicit redesigning is the Constitutional Treaty (CT), which was agreed by an intergovernmental conference (IGC) in June 2004, but ran into difficulties during the ratification process in 2005. The CT was prompted by an array of proposals from the Convention on the Future of Europe (CFE), which reached its final conclusions in July 2003, having commenced its work in February 2002. Among the most controversial issues in the IGC were the provisions on the operating rules of the Council, which in turn became the fodder for arguments in the ratification processes for the new treaty, especially in those member states holding referendums. In a parallel process, the Council and the European Council have regularly introduced specific 'non-treaty' reforms to improve their own functioning. These have co-existed with evolutionary processes, as new policy tasks have generated new modes of operation, and successive enlargements of the EC and then the EU have increased its membership, with major impacts on the dynamics of the Council (see Appendix 1).

But what kind of institution *is* the Council? It is the main source of EU legislation, though it shares legislative power with both the European Commission and the European Parliament (EP). It exercises executive power under the treaties, yet the Commission is also in part an executive body. It is a more or less permanent negotiating forum and recurrent international conference, yet its primary members are ministers drawn from the member states, who are paid their salaries for their work in national governments. It makes reports to the EP on its actions and is in constant dialogue with the Commission, yet its members are account-able much more directly to national parliaments and national electorates. It is the focus for a large, multinational press corps (of about 1,000 accredited correspondents in Brussels, rising to close on 4,000 for some meetings of the European Council), through which ministers address their domestic publics.

For some commentators and practitioners, the Council is the blockage to European political integration, often obstructing bright ideas from the Commission or the EP, and allowing narrow and parochial national interests to prevail over collective European interests. For others, the Council is the saviour of common sense and 'feet-on-the-ground' politics; it repeatedly rescues the member countries and their citizens from ambitious and extravagant European proposals, and heavy-handed government from 'Brussels'. For the analyst, the Council and its processes embody the recurrent tension in the construction of the EU between the 'supranationalists' and the 'intergovernmentalists'. But it is also the organ that locks the leading politicians from the member states, and their officials, into permanent discussion about their evolving cooperation and about a shared and enlarging policy agenda. Indeed, it is this image that is the most vivid for practitioners.

The Council's operational weaknesses, which have become increasingly apparent over time, have given rise to discussions about its future evolution and role. This debate has seen the supranationalists pitted publicly against the intergovernmentalists in an apparently ongoing process of treaty reform since the early 1990s. For the intergovernmentalists, everything depends on strengthening the Council and the European Council to bear the weight of the whole EU edifice. They seek to establish these institutions as the supreme decision-makers, and the EU as the visible servant of the member states. For the supranationalists, everything depends on limiting the European Council and the Council to their shared role as the representative forum for the member states, balanced by the vesting of authority in the collective institutions intended to serve the Union's overall interests – the European Commission, the EP and the European Court of Justice (ECJ). Yet this is too stark a contrast. The Council, as we shall argue, embodies a sense of collective purpose, collective commitments and collective ideas. It is the forum for reconciling the distinctive purposes and powers of the member states with the needs for recurrent and disciplined joint action.

This volume surveys the roles, functions and processes of the Council and its relationships with other EU institutions and the member states. It sheds light on the varying analyses, both explicit and implicit, of the Council as an institution and what these tell us about European political integration more broadly. It sets out both the formal and, crucially, the informal pictures of the Council in operation. This volume also portrays changes in the behaviour of the Council over time, taking into account treaty changes, internal reforms, political cycles and shifts in the degree of confidence invested in independent decision-making at the EU level.

It is an oddity of the intellectual history of the EU that the literature on the Council has been so sparse; Sherrington (2000) and Westlake and Galloway (2004) are notable exceptions. Too much of the story is available only from the media, through which national politicians strive to give their own differing versions of negotiating successes and defeats. References to the Council, in both the academic literature and more popular commentaries, are commonly full of *lacunae*, often contain errors about basic facts, and generally lack nuance. Part of the explanation lies in the historical secrecy surrounding so many of the deliberations of the Council. We lack detailed and authoritative accounts over time of meetings, voting records and how business is actually transacted, leaving too much to be read into the resulting texts and anecdotes.

Ground-breaking rules on 'transparency', first agreed in 1992 in the aftermath of the first negative Danish referendum on Maastricht and extended over the intervening years, have gradually yielded up more detail and more 'facts', and have opened up some parts of some Council sessions to the public. Yet the Council still operates to a large extent behind closed doors, posing a major challenge for would-be analysts.

Another reason for the sparseness of academic analysis of the Council is that it is not, or is not perceived to be, the most innovative of EU institutions. The Commission, the EP and the ECJ all broke (and continue to break) new ground as institutional experiments, their innovative features commanding sustained academic interest. The Council seems a more familiar beast in two senses. First, its attributes resemble the traditional features of conventional international organizations. Second, it is as much an excrescence of the member states as the result of institutional innovation at the European level. Rightly or wrongly, the Council has largely been seen as an unglamorous institution, the flag carrier of the old state-based politics of Western Europe rather than of the new politics of European transnational integration.

This judgement understates both the relevance of the Council to the wider process of European political integration and the distinctiveness of its modes of operation. As will be argued in subsequent chapters, the Council has many idiosyncratic features; and it has generated new ways of transacting business and building agreement among the member states. The controversies, which for many outside observers are the hallmark of its operations, are themselves revealing of deeper issues about how to manage the political and economic interdependencies within the European family. The member states have certainly not withered away, and their stubborn resilience is striking. Yet the limits to their autonomy are daily revealed in the deliberations of the Council. All the more important, then, that we understand better the European institution through which states have struggled to conserve their influence over joint decision-making.

What is the Council?

Both executive and legislature

An initial problem in describing the Council is to establish its core functions and roles. Within the political systems of the member states it is relatively easy to identify the main institutions in the political process – that is to say, the executive, the legislature and the judiciary. It is usual for the executive and the legislature to be distinct, or at least for executive and legislative functions to be separable. In the EU system, no such simplicity of description is possible, and there is no clear separation of powers. The Council and the Commission share executive functions, while the Council and the EP share legislative functions. The Council thus acts in both legislative and executive modes. Moreover, as we shall see from examining treaty changes and evolving practice over the years, the balance between the Council and other organs of the EU has not been at all stable (see www.palgrave.com/politics/hayes-renshaw).

Both European and national

The Council is established under the various treaties governing the EU as a collective organ of the new European system of governance. It has distinct responsibilities *vis-à-vis* other institutions under Community law. It is required to behave on behalf of the entire membership of the Union within the internal affairs of the EU and also in relation to the world outside. Yet in a way it is only a collective gathering of the component member states. The members of the Council are, first and foremost, national politicians who think of themselves as, and indeed have been elected as, national politicians. When meeting in the Council they are, up to a point, expected to take on collective responsibilities, in spite of the deep ambiguity as to whom they represent and to whom they are responsible.

The treaties mainly refer to the 'member states', as if these in turn were monoliths, with distinct interests belonging to the political territories from which they are drawn. Occasionally the treaties refer to the member 'governments' – that is, the current political executives of the member states. These may speak for the whole of the territories from which they come, but as governments they also (or sometimes instead) speak for the political family or families from which they are drawn, and the particular constituents or clients to whom they are tied. In some member states these may in turn represent a cross-section of the political spectrum, while in others they may be partisan, primarily serving the prevailing political groups in power.

The national dimension of the Council and its sub-structures is visible in the role of the Committee of Permanent Representatives (Coreper, from the abbreviation in French) and the national permanent representations (permreps) of the member states in Brussels. The officials who comprise the permreps, under instruction from their home governments, are charged with feeding the latter's views into Council deliberations. Yet they also act in effect as ambassadors of the EU back in national capitals, educating and persuading home-based colleagues about the limits of the negotiable in Brussels (see Chapter 9).

Both multi-issue and sectoral

The Council currently meets in nine specialized configurations to deal with sector-specific issues (see Chapter 2). The Agriculture Council is the best-known and most long-standing example, while the Economic and Financial Affairs Council (Ecofin) is another that has traditionally carried great weight. This segmentation of decision-making brings together representatives from the member states who are immersed in the politics, the economics and the technicalities of each sector. Yet they are present on behalf of the member states and not only of the specific interests or constituents being addressed. Cross-sectoral aggregation, adjudication or mediation depend on bargaining and coordination between the sectoral forums. Historically, both the General Affairs Council (GAC), composed of foreign ministers, and the European Council, composed of the heads of state or government of the member states, have attempted to coordinate overall policy and priorities, with varying degrees of success (see Chapters 2 and 6, respectively). In Seville in June 2002, plans were agreed to distinguish the work of policy coordination from the oversight of external and foreign policies. The Constitutional Treaty reinforced this trend, proposing that the European Council determine the list of specialist configurations. But coordination begins at home, a process managed in different ways and with varying degrees of efficacy by individual member states (see Chapter 9).

Both a forum for negotiation and a forum for decision

The issue of transparency as applied to the Council vividly illustrates its split personality. On the one hand, the Council performs key executive and legislative tasks for the EU which, in a system of governance composed of liberal democratic countries, implies that its work should be exposed to scrutiny. Yet it is also within the Council that the participating ministers hammer out often difficult and tense agreements. Most of their time is spent poring over the details of texts as, separately and together, they strive to put them into a form with which they can all live. In the course of such negotiations, the participants often want to speak in unvarnished terms and to deploy arguments that they would not repeat so easily in a more explicit and public form. Ministers and their officials build coalitions, exercise leverage and do deals, benefiting from the veil of secrecy that largely cloaks their actions – just as ministers within cabinets do in national governments.

While many of the bargains are struck in the corridors and in informal discussions, they are pulled together in the formal sessions of the Council, as agreements are turned into texts for subsequent official publication, and as appropriate votes are cast. Inevitably, therefore, there is a tension between openness and confidentiality. Predictably, too, 'games' are played as individual participants deploy tactical manoeuvres and develop their negotiating strategies. The EU's transparency rules as applied to the Council presume that a distinction can be drawn between the Council acting in negotiating mode, perhaps excusably in private, and acting in legislative mode, sometimes now in public (see Chapter 4).

Much of the more recent academic literature on the Council, and indeed more broadly on EU decision-making, has been about bargaining behaviour, increasingly drawing on game-theoretic modes of analysis and heavily influenced by assumptions about 'rational' strategies and coalition behaviour. A distinctive feature of this volume is that we bring to this debate some newly collected empirical data on voting behaviour in the Council, which, interestingly, tests, and indeed contests, some of the more theoretical literature. Elements of this broader theoretical debate will be addressed throughout this volume, and especially in Chapters 10 and 11, as will commentaries on the impact of ideas and beliefs on willingness to agree. We should also note that a few efforts have been made to develop lines of analysis to compare the Council as a legislature with other legislatures, for example, the work of Fritz Scharpf (1988, 1994a, 1994b) and Wolfgang Wessels (1992), mainly comparing German federal policy-making with the EU's quasi-federal policy-making processes.

Legal definitions and basic decision rules

In any discussion of the legal basis for the operation of the Council, three points need to be borne in mind about the inherited system:

- The treaties are unusual in comprising institutional descriptions, constitutional lines of orientation and policy directions, each and everyone of which defines the roles and powers of the Council.
- The treaties have not drawn hard and fast lines between the powers of the member states and the powers of the EU, though the continued development of subsidiarity may tend in this direction.
- The legal rules tell only a part of the story, since much depends on informal rules, codes of conduct and accumulated practice.

Treaty-based formal rules

Under the Treaty of Paris of 1951, which created the European Coal and Steel Community (ECSC) with a predetermined life-span of fifty years – it died on cue on 23 July 2002 – the predominant institution was to be the High Authority, an embryonic government with rather strong, and to a degree autonomous, powers of decision. The Special Council of Ministers, established under Articles 26–30, was there to add to and to endorse the decisions of the High Authority. The tension between the supranational and the intergovernmental was there, but with the balance tipped towards the supranational. One interesting feature was the weighting of votes according to the proportions of coal and steel produced by the member states, an effort to relate political strength to economic power.

By the time that the Treaties of Rome were signed nearly six years later, the drafters had drawn back from so explicit an emphasis on supranationalism. Instead, the institutional framework for the European Economic Community (EEC) and the European Atomic Energy Community (Euratom) hedged bets about the relative weight of the Council and the Commission. Depending on how they are judged, these treaties either set up a 'tandem' or bicephalous executive that required constructive partnership between these two key institutions, or else opened up a competition between the two for predominance. It was only much later that the EP began to occupy significant political space.

None the less, some features from the Treaty of Paris were incorporated in the subsequent design of the Council (see Box 1.2), in particular:

* voting opportunities, sometimes by qualified majorities, sometimes by simple majorities, as well as the unanimity requirement for certain kinds of decision;

Box 1.2   *Key features of the Council*

Key points about the Council are that it:

* Represents the member governments in the European Union (EU);
* Is managed by a rotating presidency and supported by an international secretariat;
* Meets about 65 times a year, usually at its headquarters (the Justus Lipsius building in Brussels), but is convened in Luxembourg during the months of April, June and October;
* Is legally a single body, but meets in different configurations according to the subject under discussion;
* Is reliant for the preparation of its work on a pyramid of committees and working parties;
* Operates in up to 21 different languages simultaneously;
* Meets mostly in secret, although some parts of its meetings are televised and direct access to many of its working documents can now be attained via the Internet; and
* Individual members are indirectly accountable through national political processes.

In policy areas subject to the 'Community method':

* With the Commission, decides the policy agenda and responds to Commission proposals by negotiation;
* Legislates for the EU, usually in tandem with the European Parliament (EP);
* Produces regulations, directives, decisions, recommendations and opinions;

$\longrightarrow$

- presidency arrangements, shared among member governments and extended from three months to six months in turn – that is, long enough to get their teeth into the management of business;
- limited powers to amend the proposals from the Commission, for which Council members had to be unanimous; and
- a pre-arranged agenda, defined by the policy articles of the treaties.

In addition, the Rome Treaties recognized the reality that the Council would not consist just of occasional meetings of ministers. Already in the ECSC, the base of the Council had broadened to include a preparatory committee of senior national officials and expert groups, known as Cocor (the *Commission de coordination du Conseil des ministres* – see Chapter 3). The Treaties of Rome, in Article 151 (EEC) and 121 (Euratom), paved the way for what later became Coreper. Thus was laid the foundation of what was to develop into a myriad of committees

- Has recourse to voting, either by unanimity or qualified majority or, unless otherwise specified, by simple majority; and
- Establishes mandates for the Commission to negotiate on behalf of the EU in certain areas.

In certain other policy areas (for example, the common foreign and security policy (CFSP) and the related European security and defence policy (ESDP), justice and home affairs (JHA) and the monetary aspects of economic and monetary union (EMU)):

- Largely reserves control of the agenda, proposals and policy implementation to itself, with some power of initiative allowed to the Commission;
- Produces common strategies, joint actions and common positions in the context of the CFSP;
- Produces framework decisions and common positions in the context of JHA;
- Exercises limited collective representation through the presidency;
- Receives limited collective support from the Council Secretariat; and
- Operates mainly by consensus.

Additional features

- May meet in conference, either for limited cooperation, or when acting under international law;
- May meet 'informally', with no formal agenda or conclusions;
- Can take decisions by means of a written procedure;
- Increasingly subject to direction from the European Council; and
- Provides an arena through which the member governments can attempt to develop convergent national approaches in fields where the EU does not have clear collective policy powers.

at various levels to prepare the sessions of ministers and to follow up their directions (Hayes-Renshaw, 1990a).

In the mid-1960s, an effort was made to tidy up the institutional framework of the three separate European Communities. The Treaty establishing a Single Council and a Single Commission (known as the Merger Treaty) was agreed in 1965 and came into force in 1967, creating a single institutional structure for the three Communities. (The EP – at that time known as the Assembly – and the ECJ served all three Communities from the outset.) The Merger Treaty's implications need to be read with care. Broadly, it reflected the spirit of the Treaties of Rome rather than that of the Treaty of Paris, in so far as it sought to balance the powers of the member states against those of the Commission, and in Article 4 it formally established Coreper. Because the suggestion of making a single treaty had been rejected, the 'single' Council continued to operate in somewhat different ways and with different rules, depending on which treaty provided the relevant policy-making competences. This explains why subsequent rounds of treaty amendment had to include variations in the light of the specific provisions of each of the basic treaties. The new Constitutional Treaty would pull all of these into a common frame, searching for greater clarity and simplicity.

The budgetary treaties of 1970 and 1975 altered the legal responsibilities of the Council. On the one hand, the establishment of the Community's 'own resources' empowered the Council collectively to determine expenditure more expansively. On the other hand, the EP gained status as part of the joint budgetary authority, thus forcing the Council to share powers over appropriations, although not over revenue-raising.

In 1985, an IGC met to consider reforms to the treaties, with regard to both policy powers and institutional rules. In the preparatory meetings of the Ad Hoc Committee on Institutional Reform (usually known as the Dooge Committee after its Irish chairman), which tabled proposals to the IGC, discussions took place about whether or not a consensus could be found for extensive institutional reforms, including proposals to limit recourse to the Luxembourg compromise (designed to ensure that no member state would be outvoted on an issue of perceived national importance – see below). The IGC resulted in the Single European Act (SEA), which was formally adopted in 1986 and came into force in 1987. The SEA incorporated two main treaty changes that affected the Council. First, the opportunities to reach decisions by qualified majority vote (QMV) were extended, especially under Article 100 of the Treaty of Rome dealing with harmonization relevant to the single market. Second, the powers of the EP were extended into the legislative sphere under arrangements for 'cooperation' with the Council. Another less remarked feature of the SEA was the addition of a number of protocols and declarations inserted at the insistence of individual member states. In addition, the SEA 'codified' European political cooperation (EPC), bringing it partially and conditionally within the institutional framework of the treaties and making the Council (of Foreign Ministers) its main manager.

The impact of these changes is explored in subsequent chapters. Voting, or the acceptability of voting, subsequently became more common. The Council found itself having to pay much more attention to the EP in the legislative process. In addition, the Commission, benefiting from a new consensus on policy and a period of greater enthusiasm for European policies, was also able to regain prestige and leverage *vis-à-vis* the Council.

The Maastricht IGC, leading to the 1992 Treaty on European Union (TEU), took the SEA reforms a little further, at least in some respects. The TEU introduced a new 'pillar' structure. The first pillar comprised the three main Communities (ECSC, EEC and Euratom), within which the roles of the main institutions were maintained, though adjusted. The second pillar, covering the CFSP (and broadly imitated in the third pillar, dealing with JHA) adopted a different institutional and legal design, in which the Council's role was explicitly predominant. Spanning the three pillars was the light superstructure of the new EU, its guiding institution being the European Council, incorporated at last into a treaty text.

As regards the first pillar, the prior 'balance' between the Commission and the Council was preserved, although the opportunities for using qualified majority voting were extended. But the old 'balance' between the Council and the EP was tipped towards the EP, which acquired more substantial legislative powers of 'co-decision'. The rotation of the presidency was adapted, away from alphabetical order to one that sought always to have a larger member state in the so-called *troika* (the grouping of the current, preceding and succeeding presidencies in the area of political cooperation). The provisions for economic and monetary union (EMU) inserted an endorsement of the policy being taken forward by only some of the member states. The long list of protocols and declarations attached to the TEU introduced a plethora of national singularities with regard to particular policies. The most notable was the protocol relating to the 'social chapter', under which the then eleven assenting governments agreed to develop policies and legislation using the provisions of the treaties, without the participation of the British. This endorsement in the TEU of such unusual singularity was taken further in the decisions reached at the Edinburgh European Council of December 1992 concerning Denmark's voluntary self-exclusion from some policy activities.

The innovation of the second and third pillars was to designate the Council as the key body, in tandem with the European Council. While the Commission could make proposals, member governments also had a legal right of initiative. The Council was not required to share powers with the EP, nor were its decisions subject to interpretation by the ECJ. The European Council was formally charged with providing general political guidelines for the EU as a whole. In part, this simply ratified what had become practice since the European Council was created in 1974, an agreement then without a treaty base, but one that, in effect, reflected the limitations of the Council proper. In part, the TEU was also agreed in a form that challenged heads of state and government to take a more active responsibility for making the EU system function effectively.

In the mid-1990s, some of these issues were revisited in the negotiations that led to the signature of the Treaty of Amsterdam (ToA) in 1997. The main policy change was to strengthen the role of the EU in the field of justice and home affairs, and to incorporate into the EU the Schengen Agreements (governing the abolition of border controls on people). This had two main consequences: one was to add a substantial new set of policy commitments to both the first and third pillars; the other was to adopt explicit protocols that kept Britain, Ireland and Denmark outside some of these commitments. This development was underlined by the inclusion of clauses on 'closer cooperation', designed to make it easier for policies to be adopted by only some members of the Council. In addition, the EP won an expansion of its power of legislative co-decision.

However, the ToA left some business unfinished, in particular with regard to the impact of the further enlargement of EU membership. Another IGC was convened, culminating after some acrimony in agreement in December 2000 on the Treaty of Nice (ToN). This rewrote the rules for voting in the Council by changing the weightings of member states and altering the definition of majorities. A core issue was the distribution of influence between larger and smaller member states, a concern accentuated by the imminent accession of many small new members. Nice was, however, just playing for time, an incomplete and unsatisfactory outcome, which was in turn a trigger for the decision to establish the Convention on the Future of Europe, which started work at the end of February 2002.

The Constitutional Treaty, finally adopted in July 2004, went much further with its proposed changes, both with regard to the Council and the European Council specifically, and more generally regarding the overall institutional architecture. Although its eventual implementation was in question following negative referendums in France and the Netherlands in May and June 2005 respectively, it documents the package of reforms then acceptable to the political representatives of the member states. Some of the key elements in the CT relating to the Council and the European Council are summarized here, and more details follow later in the volume. Thus the European Council was established firmly as an organ in its own right, taking decisions either by 'consensus' or by QMV, with an explicit representational role in foreign affairs and with a 'permanent' (but non-voting) president to be elected for a two-and-a-half-year term, renewable once. The Council ('of Ministers') had generic legislative, executive, policy-making and coordinating functions, with an explicit recognition for the first time of the existence of different configurations, and the Council was required to meet in public when deliberating and legislating. An EU Foreign Minister (a Vice-President of the Commission), appointed by the European Council and acting as chair of the Foreign Affairs Council would conduct the CFSP, thus working simultaneously within both the Council and the Commission – a radical institutional innovation. The voting rules for QMV were reformed to rest on a double majority of 55 per cent of at least 15 member states (72 per cent in the absence of a proposal from the Commission or the new Foreign Minister), and 65 per cent of the population of the Union.

Other formal and informal rules

In addition to the relevant treaty articles governing the Council's powers and operation, its own decisions on the same matters need to be examined and understood. These include the Council's internal rules of procedure (CRPs) and decisions from Council and European Council meetings. Occasional 'inter-institutional agreements' (IIAs) between the Council, the Commission and the EP are also relevant. These will be discussed later in this volume, and a note on sources can be found in Appendix 2 to this volume.

Informal rules then determine how the legal rules operate in practice. For a long time the most important of these was the Luxembourg 'compromise' of 1966 (reproduced in Box 10.1 in Chapter 10), under which it was asserted by the French government of the day that member states should be able to block decisions that would threaten 'very important interests' (widely, but incorrectly, referred to as 'vital national interests') on issues otherwise eligible for resolution by majority voting. To all intents and purposes, the European Council has operated virtually exclusively on the basis of informal understandings, symbolized to this day by the absence of formal records of its meetings (see Chapter 6). EPC started as an informal process until its codification in the SEA, and its transformation into the CFSP under the TEU. The 'third pillar' of Maastricht, encompassing JHA, similarly formalized the well-established informal practice of meetings between national officials and ministers dealing with justice and home affairs. The Ioannina 'compromise' of 1994 (reproduced in Box 10.2 in Chapter 10) is another case in point, driven by the British concern about the allegedly adverse impact of new members on qualified majority voting. The Council agreed to be patient with dissenting minorities that were significant, but below the threshold technically empowered to block agreement. The significance and implications of these informal rules will also be discussed later in this volume, in particular in Chapters 2 and 10.

Who constitutes the Council?

The Council under the treaties consists of persons delegated by the member states. The words suggest a single body, and for some purposes this is in fact the case, since the Council can take decisions on any topic for which the treaties empower it to act. But, like the work of the EU, the reality is more complex. In practice, the Council meets in different configurations, depending on the subjects being addressed – agriculture, internal market, monetary policy, external trade, foreign policy, education, environment – the list is seemingly endless. It is natural that member governments should normally send to Council meetings ministers with the relevant specialist responsibilities. These different configurations are discussed in Chapter 2.

Though the Council is often described as the Council of Ministers (so much so, indeed, that we have used this term as the title of our book), this is not in fact its correct legal title, since the treaties refer merely to 'the Council'. Following the coming into force of the TEU in 1999, the Council took a decision to call itself the 'Council of the European Union' (published in OJ L 281, 16.11.93, p. 18). It should be noted that the CT opted for the designation 'Council of Ministers' in recognition of its composition and also perhaps in an effort to distinguish it more clearly from the European Council. In practice, the Council, when taking final decisions, normally consists of ministers from the member states; indeed, the TEU (in Article 203) specifically refers to 'a representative of each Member State at ministerial level, authorized to commit the government of that Member State'. But practice varies, not least since the boundary between senior officials and ministers differs from one member state to another (see Box 2.1 in Chapter 2).

In practice, 'the Council' consists of a pyramid of meetings, from working expert to ministerial level. A small number of senior level committees exists (see Figure 3.1 in Chapter 3), the most important being Coreper, and more may be formed when a new area of policy comes under active negotiation in the EU. At working-group level, middle-ranking officials and experts meet to work through draft texts and to prepare the deliberations of senior officials and ministers. These are described in detail in Chapter 3, but the most important points about them are:

- these various committees are similarly composed to the ministers' meetings – that is, by people delegated by the member states;
- they do not have independent decision-making power, except in so far as they exercise the authority of the Council; but
- in practice, these committees are the last actual arbiters in Council negotiations of roughly 70 per cent of the legislative output (see Chapters 3 and 10).

One further preliminary remark on the composition of the Council should be made here. The Commission is not itself a member of the Council, but it generally takes part in Council sessions at all levels. Indeed, the CRPs specify the Commission's normal right to take part, just as the various treaties specify that much of the Council's agenda is determined by the drafts and timetable of the Commission in developing policy proposals. Thus the Commission is in some respects an additional 'member state' within the Council, especially for traditional Community business. It has the power of text, although not of vote, sometimes claiming to speak to the concerns of the EU as a whole, sometimes voicing its own institutional interest. Sometimes the Council excludes the Commission from its sessions; for example, when discussing appointments to EU institutions or finalising its internal budget. How the relationship between the Council and the Commission works is crucial to the conduct of Community business, as is explained in Chapter 7.

What does the Council do?

The Council is a busy organization, as Box 1.3 demonstrates. It represents the interests of the member states. In conjunction with the EP, it establishes the legislation of the EU. It takes many important decisions about the development of Community policies. It shares decisions with the Commission and the EP on the development of the Community budget, as regards both income and expenditure. It is the main forum for developing collective policy on new issues that have not been put firmly under the authority of the Community. It acts as an entity *vis-à-vis* other EU institutions. It represents the EU *vis-à-vis* other international organizations and third countries (including in 2005, in seven Association Councils and five Cooperation Councils), with the Council presidency providing its collective voice. On some issues a conference of ministers from the member states is constituted, a practice akin to that of a more classical international organization. Thus it negotiates the accession of new members or establishes conventions (under international rather than Community law) among the member states, sometimes with the participation of non-member states. The Council also provides opportunities for ministerial representatives of the EU's member states, either completely informally over lunch or dinner, or in special informal meetings, to discuss areas of shared concern, even though they may not (or not yet) be directly subject to Community competence.

'The Council' is thus a shorthand term for a huge number of multilateral and multilingual meetings, as varying groups of ministers and officials from the member states meet recurrently with their opposite numbers from the Commission and periodically with opposite numbers from third countries. Its representatives (usually in the person and name of the presidency) conduct discussions for the Council with various

---

Box 1.3   *Council activity and output, 2003*

- Signed a Treaty of Accession in Athens on 16 April with Cyprus, the Czech Republic, Estonia, Hungary, Latvia, Lithuania, Malta, Poland, the Slovak Republic and Slovenia.
- Provided administrative and legal backup for the Convention on the Future of Europe (CFE), whose conclusions were presented to the Thessaloniki European Council in June, and for the subsequent intergovernmental conference (IGC), which commenced in Rome on 4 October.
- Drew up its first annual operational programme (presented by the Greek and Italian presidencies for 2003) and its first multi-annual strategic programme (presented by Ireland, The Netherlands, Luxembourg, the United Kingdom, Austria and Finland, covering the period 2004–6).
- Adopted a Code of Conduct aimed at improving the efficiency of the preparation and conduct of its proceedings (now included in the Council's internal rules of procedure (CRPs) as Annex IV).
- Concluded an inter-institutional agreement (IIA) with the Commission and the European Parliament (EP) on better law-making.
- Reached agreement on the location of the seats of various European Union (EU) agencies.
- Agreed on a substantial reform of the common agricultural policy (CAP).
- Oversaw the implementation of several military and civilian crisis management operations.
- Adopted 196 definitive legislative acts (154 of them by consensus).
- Took 101 decisions by means of a written procedure.
- Prepared the work and implemented the decisions of six European Councils.
- Ministers held 77 formal Council meetings and 11 informal ones.
- Coreper met 134 times (64 times at the level of the Ambassadors and 70 times at the level of the Deputies).
- 4,333 working party meetings were held.
- Participated in 16 Association and Cooperation Council meetings.
- Dealt with 2,830 applications from the public for access to documents.
- Concluded 103 co-decision procedures with the EP (38 of which were concluded after the first reading, 50 at the end of the second reading and 15 after a process of conciliation).
- Made 148 declarations on matters relating to the Common Foreign and Security Policy (CFSP).
- Held 12 open debates and 32 public deliberations.
- Responded to 669 questions from the EP (334 in written form, 32 orally with debate and 303 during question time in the course of the monthly EP plenary sessions).
- Signed 140 international agreements with third counties or organizations.
- The Council Secretariat drafted 28,417 documents, and circulated 91,812.

interlocutors, within the EU most importantly with the EP, and externally with all those from outside who have active relationships with the EU (see, for example, Box 5.3 in Chapter 5). The output of the Council consists of formal and final decisions on legislative acts that are recorded in the OJ, common positions to discuss with the EP, suggested amendments on work in progress, negotiating mandates, declarations of policy and positions (especially for CFSP), and resolutions about possible future policy or concerted national policies. Its own deliberations are documented in its minutes, often with addenda from individual governments.

Sometimes the Council acts alone, but more often its work is tied into that of other EU institutions and bodies (see Box 1.4). When acting in its legislative capacity, the Council has different responsibilities and powers, depending on the subject area under discussion and the relevant decision-making and voting procedures prescribed by the treaties (see Box 1.5), such that simplifying generalizations are dangerous. It should also be noted that there is no single clear view shared by all member states of what the Council does or should do. Indeed, the political territory of the Council is often the subject of dispute with other institutions (most commonly with the EP and the Commission, but occasionally too with the ECJ), in which individual member governments sometimes take contrasting views.

How does the Council work?

The Council works through an ongoing process of bargaining and negotiation. Every session at both ministerial and official level consists of negotiation. The whole system depends on a crucial assumption that there is give and take between the positions of the member states, and that, whatever the starting positions of the members, there is both scope for those positions to evolve and a predisposition to find agreement. Thus atmospherics, mutual confidence and reciprocal trust are important ingredients. Some sense of shared objectives about both the past and the future is a necessary condition for agreement, bolstered by the disciplines of Community law, which make it quite hard for member governments to renege on their commitments to each other. Moreover, the fact that the EU deals simultaneously in so many areas of policy makes it possible in principle for negotiations to embrace a wide variety of topics and thus be subject to cross-trading. Irrespective of the voting rules, the reflex within the Council has largely been to operate by consensus.

Specific 'decision rules' determine when and how matters should be brought to a head. From the outset, the treaties provided scope for voting by various forms of majority, in particular QMV (with weighted votes) and simple majority. Voting has in practice been rare, and this for three main reasons, further details of which are contained in Chapter 10. First, there has always been a predisposition to operate on the basis of consensus, because the participants have found it more comfortable and comforting. Even since QMV became an embedded option, votes have been formally taken at ministerial level on only about 20 per cent of eligible decisions, often with abstentions

Box 1.4 *Decision-making procedures in the European Union*

Name of procedure	Origins/legal basis	Powers of institutions	Examples of areas of application
Co-decision	• Article 251 TEC (Treaty establishing the European Community) • Introduced by the Treaty on European Union (TEU) • Procedure simplified by Treaty of Amsterdam (ToA) • Scope extended by ToA and Treaty of Nice (ToN) • Would become the 'ordinary legislative procedure' if the Constitutional Treaty (CT) were ratified	• Council and European Parliament (EP) participate as co-equal legislators • Two readings each (the first not subject to deadlines), followed if necessary by a process of conciliation • If no agreement at end of conciliation phase, proposed act is dropped • Council acts by qualified majority in most cases, by unanimity in a small number of cases	• Internal market • Free movement of workers • Some aspects of free movement of persons • Culture • Transport • Education and vocational training • Consumer protection • Environment • Research
Cooperation	• Article 252 TEC • Introduced by the Single European Act (SEA) • Scope reduced considerably by ToA	• EP granted a second reading • If no agreement after EP's second reading, Council can adopt act only by unanimity	• Economic and monetary policy
Assent	• Introduced by the SEA and the TEU in a certain number of cases • Scope extended by ToA and ToN	• Council and EP are co-equal: both must agree in order to adopt an act • Both have right of veto • EP decides by simple or absolute majority, depending on issue	• Association agreements • Adoption of Structural Funds and Cohesion Fund regulations • Provisions concerning the uniform electoral procedure

Consultation or advisory opinion	• Standard legislative procedure introduced by the Treaties of Rome • Council required (since Isoglucose case in 1979) to await EP's opinion before taking a decision	• One-stage consultation between the Council and the EP • Council must request and examine EP's opinion on a Commission proposal, but is not obliged to follow it • If Commission amends its proposal to take into account EP's opinion, Council may only amend it by unanimity	• Amendments to the statute of the European Central Bank (ECB) • Membership of the European Union (EU) • Common agricultural policy (CAP) • Liberalization of services • Citizenship • Harmonization of indirect taxation
Budgetary	• Article 272 TEC • Qualified and clarified by inter-institutional agreements (IIAs) and evolving practice	• Council and EP are joint budgetary authorities • EP has final say with regard to 'compulsory' expenditure (e.g. CAP) • Council has final say with regard to 'non-compulsory' expenditure • EP may (by majority of its members and two-thirds of votes cast) reject the draft budget and request a new one	• Annual EU budget

Box 1.5 *Classification of decision-making procedures in the Treaty establishing the European Community*

Voting rule in the Council	Participation of the European Parliament	Participation of other bodies	Example
QMV	Co-decision		*Art. 12*: rules prohibiting discrimination on grounds of nationality
QMV	Co-decision	Consultation of the Court of Auditors	*Art. 280(4)*: fight against fraud affecting the financial interests of the Community
QMV	Co-decision	Consultation of the Economic and Social Committee (ESC)	*Art. 172 §2*: research – adoption of the measures referred to in Articles 167, 168 and 169
QMV	Co-decision	Consultation of the ESC + consultation of the Committee of the Regions (CoR)	*Art. 175(1)*: environment – Community action in order to achieve the objectives referred to in Article 174
QMV	Cooperation		*Art. 99(5)*: multilateral surveillance
QMV	Cooperation	Consultation of the European Central Bank (ECB)	*Art. 106(2)*: measures to harmonize the denomination and technical specification of coins
QMV	Assent		*Art. 107(5)*: amendment of the protocol on the statute of the European System of Central Banks and of the ECB
QMV	Opinion		*Art. 37(2)*: common agricultural policy (CAP)
QMV	Opinion	Consultation of the ESC	*Art. 172 §1*: research, setting up of joint undertakings
QMV	Opinion	Consultation of the CoR + consultation of the Employment Committee	*Art. 128(2)*: employment policies, guidelines which member states shall take into account

QMV			*Art. 26*: fixing of common customs tariff duties
QMV		Consultation of the ECB	*Art. 59*: movements of capital – adoption of strictly necessary safeguard measures where movements of capital to or from third countries cause serious difficulties for the economic and monetary union (EMU)
QMV		Consultation of the ECB + consultation of the Economic and Financial Committee (EFC)	*Art. 114(3)*: composition of the EFC
QMV		Consultation of the ESC	*Art. 75(3)*: abolition of discrimination in the transport sector
Unanimity	Co-decision		*Art. 42*: internal market – social security measures for Community migrant workers
Unanimity	Co-decision	Consultation of the CoR	*Art. 151(5)*: culture
Unanimity	Assent		*Art. 300(3)*: association agreements and other agreements establishing a specific institutional framework, having important budgetary implications and entailing amendment of an act adopted under the co-decision procedure
Unanimity	Assent by qualified majority on a proposal from the Parliament		*Art. 190(4)*: European Parliament elections in accordance with a uniform procedure
Unanimity	Assent	Consultation of the ECB	*Art. 105(6)*: specific tasks of the ECB

↑ Unanimity	Assent	Consultation of the ESC + consultation of the CoR	Art. 161: Structural Funds and Cohesion Fund – definition of aims, objectives and organization
Unanimity	Opinion		Art. 19(1): citizenship – right to vote and to stand as a candidate
Unanimity	Opinion	Consultation of the Court of Auditors	Art. 279: adoption of the financial regulations*
Unanimity	Opinion	Consultation of the ECB	Art. 111(1): exchange-rate system for the European currency unit (ECU) in relation to non-Community currencies
Unanimity	Opinion	Consultation of the ESC	Art. 157(3): industry
Unanimity	Opinion	Consultation of the ESC + consultation of the CoR	Art. 175(2): provisions of a fiscal nature, measures concerning town and country planning and land use, measures affecting energy supplies and biodiversification
Unanimity			Art. 88(2): decisions on the compatibility with the common market of state aid having regard to competition
Unanimity		Consultation of the ECB	Art. 123(5): abrogation of a derogation granted to a state outside the single currency and other measures necessary to that end
Unanimity		Consultation of the ESC	Art. 144: assigning to the Commission tasks in connection with the implementation of common measures, particularly as regards social security for migrant workers

Note: * Changed to QMV under the Treaty of Nice.

Source: Note on legislative procedures from the Praesidium to the Convention on the Future of Europe, CONV 216/02, pp. 22–3. Note that some special procedures, such as adoption of the budget, discharge of the budget and some appointments are not included in this list.

rather than negative votes (see Table 1.1). Second, the Luxembourg compromise, whatever its legal force, provided disincentives to voting. However, third, voting was always possible and practised on certain issues. Indeed, on some issues, such as the annual budget appropriations and agricultural price-fixing, it has long been the normal decision rule and subject to strict deadlines. Voting became more frequent in the late 1970s and 1980s – that is, well before the SEA extended voting for the internal market and some other policy areas. Generally speaking, commentators and practitioners have taken the choice between unanimity and QMV to represent a critical choice between a more inter-governmental and a more supranational model for the EU. As we shall see, the reality is more complex and practice has been more blurred.

From the mid-1980s onwards, two factors combined to make voting more common. First, the extension of decisions subject to QMV under the SEA and the heavy subsequent legislative programme on the internal market prompted member governments to accept the possible recourse to votes much more often and to reconcile themselves more readily to being specifically outvoted, mainly on more technical issues. Second, the third enlargement in 1986, which brought in Spain and Portugal, crossed a threshold beyond which reliance on consensus-building became more problematic. Under the threat of explicit voting, rather than the implicit building of majorities under consensus rules, behaviour changed, coalition patterns altered and power relationships shifted. As we shall see in Chapter 10, active and publicly revealed voting in the Council is concentrated in a few key policy areas, and some member states are much more ready to cast explicit negative or abstaining votes than others.

Voting, when it occurs, follows much preparation of positions in the various committees and discussions that precede the final decision. The Council does sometimes take a very long time to reach a decision, but it can on occasion act with remarkable speed. Two outstanding examples are, first, the incorporation in 1990 of the former German Democratic Republic into the then European Communities (Spence, 1991) and second, the rapid agreement on a European arrest warrant in the imme-diate aftermath of 9/11. One question to be borne in mind is whether the passage of time spent in moulding agreement in the Council is functional or dysfunctional with regard to the quality, quantity or efficacy of decision outputs. (See Box 2.5 in Chapter 2 for a discussion of decision-making speed in the EU.)

The nature of the Council's operations frequently makes it hard to define in which kind of mode the Council is acting. In the past, this has not been all that pertinent. However, growing concerns about the democratic deficit in the EU and the need for greater transparency have led to increasingly insistent calls for the Council to legislate in public. Systems have been put in place to increase the transparency of the Council's deliberations when it is acting in legislative mode, but these

Table 1.1 Voting (or lack of voting) in the Council, 1999–2004

	1999 No.	1999 %	2000 No.	2000 %	2001 No.	2001 %	2002 No.	2002 %	2003 No.	2003 %	2004 No.	2004 %
Definitive legislative acts adopted	199	100	191	100	187	100	195	100	196	100	229	100
Subject to and adopted by **simple majority**	–	–	1	0.5	–	–	–	–	3	1.5	2	0.9
Subject to **unanimity**	67	33.7	55	28.8	57	30.4	56	28.7	57	29.1	69	30.1
of which												
Adopted by unanimity	66	33.2	54	28.3	56	29.9	52	26.7	56	28.6	69	30.1
Adopted by unanimity with abstentions	1	0.5	1	0.5	1	0.5	4	2.0	1	0.5	–	–
Subject to **qualified majority voting (QMV)**	132	66.3	135	70.7	130	69.6	139	71.3	136	69.4	158	69.0
of which												
Adopted by QMV without negative votes or abstentions	104	52.3	115	60.2	100	53.5	106	54.4	98	50.0	124	54.1
Adopted by QMV with abstentions	4	2.0	4	2.1	10	5.4	17	8.7	9	4.6	10	4.4
Adopted by QMV with negative votes and abstentions	24	12.0	16	8.4	20	10.7	16	8.2	29	14.8	24	10.5
Adopted by consensus	**170**	**85.5**	**169**	**88.5**	**156**	**83.4**	**158**	**81.0**	**154**	**78.5**	**193**	**84.3**

Source: Data provided by the Council Secretariat.

discussions tend to be set pieces, with the real negotiations now taking place away from the negotiating table and out of sight of the cameras (see Chapters 3 and 4). This should not surprise us; the negotiation of such issues as fishing quotas or financial allocations from Community funds are technically legislative decisions, in that they eventually appear as legal texts, but it is hard to imagine national representatives agreeing to resolve such potentially politically sensitive issues as these or, for example, negotiating mandates with third countries, in open session.

Devices to oil the Council machine

As has already been indicated, the Council is a busy and complex organization, now more than ever in need of mechanisms to facilitate its work. Two are of particular importance. First, the Council presidency (the subject of Chapter 5) has acquired increased importance over the years, and now carries the weight of considerable expectations as to the enhanced responsibilities it might bear. However, further enlargement and uneven performances by 'old' member states have led to some doubts about the capacity of all governments to be effective in the chair. The discussions in the 2002–3 CFE generated a good many proposals for alternative presidency arrangements (discussed in Chapter 5), but in the event the subsequent IGC only agreed on changes for the European Council and the Foreign Affairs Council.

Second, the General Secretariat of the Council has established itself as an increasingly important part of the institutional infrastructure of the Council. As Chapter 4 shows, it not only provides logistical and administrative support as well as legal guidance for the Council and its members, but in some areas senior officials have moved beyond these rather traditional functions and have acquired a substantive role in Council negotiations. This is connected especially to extended responsibilities for the Secretariat in the areas of the CFSP, the ESDP and JHA, where it has become involved in operational activities. In fulfilling these various functions, the Secretariat and its officials make an enormous contribution to the preparation of the work, and the proceedings, of the Council.

A wider question hangs in the debate as to how far the Council – some would argue an inner grouping in the Council – has acquired a collective identity and sense of permanency as a political driving force for the EU as a whole. Some say that the Franco-German tandem has long provided the engine, others that the impetus still often comes from the founder-member governments, and that, in any case, informal power and leverage are certainly extremely important. This question is relevant for our understanding of how the Council has developed so far. It is also pertinent to the debates about a 'variable geometry' or 'multi-speed' version of European political integration, now included in the treaties as 'enhanced' (or for CFSP 'closer') cooperation, and to the debate on whether a 'hard core group' does or should steer the Council (Deubner, 1995; Wallace and Wallace, 1995; Stubb, 2002).

With whom does the Council interact?

The Council interacts perpetually and simultaneously with other EU institutions and with the political life of the member states. Its members thus always look, Janus-like, in two directions: in towards the EU and its institutions, and out towards the member states. In the early decades of the EC, by far the most important relationship for the Council was with the Commission, our subject in Chapter 7. At that time, this innovative bicephalous executive-cum-legislature predominated in EC decision-making, with a continuous tension between the two institutions, and the EP at the margins. Meanwhile the ECJ enjoyed its own sphere of action which rarely brought it into contact with the Council, except when it reached landmark decisions that substantially altered the Council's own interpretations of its functions and sphere of decision.

From the mid-1970s onwards, the relationship between the Council and the Parliament became increasingly important. The first factor to account for the shift was the granting of budgetary powers to the Parliament in the early/mid-1970s, eventually making the two institutions the 'joint budgetary authority' and giving the EP the last word in establishing the budget. Second, direct election gave members of the European Parliament (MEPs) more ambitions as regards their own powers and made them less dependent on the goodwill of national parliaments, parliamentary parties and governments. Thus they set about flexing their muscles, not only to increase their leverage over the Commission, but also to try to hold the Council to account. Third, the spasmodic extension of the EP's opportunities to amend Community legislation under the SEA and all subsequent treaties, complicated though the details are, has now made the EP an active and much more effective intervener in the legislative and scrutiny procedures. The CT further refined and simplified these procedures. As a result, the Council now has to pay much more serious and regular attention to the EP than hitherto, as is explained in Chapter 8.

Rather less clear is the extent to which the Council is engaged in contact with other political forces and institutions at the European level. It is commonplace for both commentators and practitioners to dismiss the relationship with the Economic and Social Committee (ESC) and the Committee of the Regions (CoR) as marginal, even though the Council has to note their opinions on certain policy proposals, as Box 1.5

indicates. Yet the regional (sometimes federal) and local government levels of policy and politics have had an impact on the work of the Council and the EU more generally. Some member states have rather highly developed systems of regional government, some with devolved legislative powers, and all have structures of local government. Increasingly, led by the German *Länder* and the Spanish autonomous communities, regional authorities have established a strong presence in Brussels so as to gain direct access to EU institutions, as well as, or in counterpoint to, their links at home with central governments. However, their actual level of influence is harder to gauge.

More importantly, pressure groups, large firms, lobbyists and consultants have always been active in Brussels and have become much more visibly and numerously so since the 1980s. Though such groups have no formalized relationship with the Council, their influencing efforts pervade the atmosphere in which the Council works, even if largely through the pressure exerted on individual governments (see Chapter 9). The permanent representations of the member states, as well as national administrations, are the targets of lobbyists, and 'explanatory material' is sometimes circulated within the Council Secretariat. In some cases, even the European Council may be the direct and achieved target of lobbyists.

Always crucial to the Council's activities and the self-definition of its members have been the links with the member states. For day-to-day purposes there are two main and generally complementary channels for these links – the permanent representations in Brussels and the coordinators of European policy based in national capitals. As will be shown in Chapter 9, the governments of the member states are compelled to provide continuous coverage of EU work, and to attempt to reconcile national and EU interests in the development of bargaining positions for the Council.

To whom is the Council responsible?

It is hard to define clearly to whom or to what the Council is responsible. There was always ambiguity in the constitutional design of the EC about the lines of accountability for Community decision-making and legislative authority. Hence the system has depended on a form of 'dual legitimation'. On the one hand, the Commission – as a proto-executive – was made accountable in principle to the EP and not to the Council. On the other hand, the Council was not made formally accountable to anyone under the treaties, though it is hemmed in by increasing rules to report to the EP and to work with it. The members of the Council are responsible to their own cabinets, parliaments and electorates. What this has meant in practice has varied considerably from one member state to another. Increasingly, the debate has focused on how to tighten the lines of responsibility and accountability at the member state level, and on whether and how to give national parliaments an assigned role in the EU process. Here, however, the CT did not include an agreed collective approach.

Looking behind the scenes and into the corridors

Like any political institution, the Council can be understood only by analysing its informal as well as its formal operations, practice as well as theory, working reality as well as convenient veneer. Subsequent chapters show the variety of practice and the dangers of over-simplification. They also reveal an institution susceptible to changes in political atmosphere arising from successive enlargements, from additions to policy competences and from the competition among member states for influence and for the definition of core goals. Since the early 1990s, the competition between national and Community arenas has heightened visibly, as a result of the debate over subsidiarity and increased attention to sensitive areas of policy such as the CFSP, the ESDP and JHA, but also EMU and economic reform.

In the interstices between the national and the European levels of decision-making, those who simultaneously are guardians of national policy and negotiators of EU policy play 'two-level' games (Putnam, 1988). In practice, they have to bargain in two arenas simultaneously, no mean task given the range of considerations to be taken into account. Of course, this provides opportunities for 'political manipulation' between the two levels, always a challenging temptation for professional politicians and negotiators. Views differ on quite what these opportunities amount to. Robert Putnam's line of analysis, further developed by Evans *et al.* (1993), points to the conclusion that, on balance, it is the international arena that stands to benefit in that, behind the cover of international pressures, national politicians can sometimes be more innovative and risk-taking than when operating in a purely national context.

However, not all commentators would agree with this. George Tsebelis (1990), for example, argued that the need for politicians to satisfy domestic interests can lead them to be apparently 'irrational' at the European or international level, in order 'rationally' to deal with domestic pressures and domestic bargaining. These 'nested games' are an important feature of the politics of EU bargaining. In any event, in a period of questioning by national electorates of European integration, it is to be expected that domestic pressures may weigh even more heavily than before on Council members, although we should not necessarily expect all member states to exhibit the same behavioural or tactical traits in the way they handle bargaining in the Council.

The considerable political salience of EU policy issues makes them worth fighting over in domestic politics, and hard to hide from political scrutiny. At least four forms of political tussle within member states bear on behaviour in the Council:

- arguments within the governing party or parties over the definition of policy and bargaining positions;
- arguments between the government and the opposition over what 'national' policy should be on European issues;
- arguments between the national parliaments and national ministers over European proposals and policies; and
- competition between sectoral interests and pressure groups as they seek to gain influence over national policy.

Change and reform

Over the five decades of its existence, the Council has adapted continuously:

- its procedures and decision rules have been altered considerably, both by formal amendments to the legal rules and by informal codes of conduct;
- the volume of business transacted and outputs achieved through the Council has steadily expanded within sectors and across areas of public policy;
- successive enlargements have necessitated adaptations of bargaining behaviour, changed the character of the coalitions in the Council and altered the way in which the policy agenda is defined and pursued;
- domestic factors, both political and economic, from within the member states have increasingly intruded on the work of the Council, reflecting partly the nature of the subjects on which the Council takes decisions and partly lines of resistance to integration;
- the degrees of trust, cohesion and conflict between Council members have varied over time, with periods of greater mutual confidence interspersed with periods of considerable tension, affecting what is negotiable and what is not; and
- the relationships of the Council with the other institutions have altered. Broadly, the Council has gained ground at the expense of the Commission, and the EP has gained ground from the Council.

Since the late 1990s, the issue of self-reform has been high on the Council's agenda. In 1999, the outgoing Secretary-General of the Council and the head of the Council's Legal Service produced an internal report detailing its many shortcomings and proposed remedies. The Trumpf–Piris Report formed the basis for what became the

Helsinki Conclusions of December 1999 and, following further discussions, the Seville Conclusions of June 2002. The aim was to enhance efficiency in view of enlargement and to respond to a mood of criticism of the Council's organisation and working methods. Some of these issues were picked up by the 2002–3 CFE and the subsequent IGC, while others were left to more informal processes of reform; they will be alluded to in the relevant chapters in this volume.

Several themes run through this study of the behaviour and practices of the Council, providing an explanation for its often idiosyncratic modes of operation:

- *Efficiency and effectiveness*   It will be argued that the Council has a surprisingly good record in terms of its institutional performance but that, by the late 1990s, it was reaching the limits of its effectiveness, hence the concentration on reform.
- *The competition for institutional predominance*   The CT, like its predecessors, did not resolve the issue of institutional competition, but rather brought new dimensions to the competition.
- *Negotiation is endemic*   This is the recurrent and characteristic mode of reaching collective decisions in the Council, with consensual behaviour deeply embedded, but dependent on the preservation of mutual trust and conducive working methods.
- *Diffuse power relationships*   These have been a core and stabilising feature of the process, in that the Council, as moderated by influences from other institutions, has not been dominated continuously by any particular member state on states. This special form of multilateralism is, however, under increasing challenge, given the tensions between larger and smaller member states, between older and newer members, and between the more accommodating and the more querulous members.
- *National polities versus transnational governance*   The Council expresses the recurrent tension between these two strands of contemporary European politics, an excellent barometer of the fluctuating patterns of European political integration.

Part I

Who Does What?

Chapter 2

National Representatives Decide: the Ministers in Council

This chapter describes the upper reaches of the Council of the European Union (EU) – those meetings of ministers through which decisions are confirmed, negotiated and authorized. Most of what follows focuses on the Council as it has operated under the Treaty of Rome establishing the European Economic Community (EEC) and in the wake of subsequent treaty reforms, up to and including the Treaty of Nice (ToN), together with those proposed by the Constitutional Treaty (CT). Occasional reference is made to the Council's distinct operations under the Treaty of Paris establishing the European Coal and Steel Community (ECSC), which ceased to apply in July 2002.

Composition

The EEC Treaty provision governing the composition of the Council was short and to the point, stating merely that the Council 'shall consist of representatives of the Member States' and that 'each Government shall delegate to it one of its members'. It was left to successive versions of the Council's internal rules of procedure (CRPs – see Appendix 3 for the areas covered in the 2004 version) and subsequent treaties to flesh out the details. (The rules governing the composition of the Council are currently laid down in Article 5 of the CRPs and Article 203 of the Treaty establishing the European Community (TEC).) Essentially, three nuances have been added to the original provision: first, national representatives are now required to be of ministerial level and authorized to commit their governments; second, they may be accompanied by officials who assist them; and third, the Commission is normally invited to take part in meetings of the Council, as are representatives of the European Central Bank (ECB), in cases where it exercises its right of initiative.

Several points arising from the above should be noted:

- The texts refer to 'ministerial' level, but the definition depends on individual member states. Practice differs on both the level of minister (senior, junior or regional) and on the scope for senior officials (who may be political appointees) to act as ministers. In a sense it does not matter, so long as it is clear that the relevant representative can commit his or her government and, as the CT required, is authorized to cast its vote.

- Political status and the salience of individual issues are important in determining who attends meetings; the larger member states have a greater tendency to send less senior ministers.
- Since 2000, the Economic and Financial Affairs Council (Ecofin) has regularly included the ECB President in its meetings.
- The provision in the CRPs permitting the representation of a Council member unable to attend has been most relevant to very small member states, especially, historically, Luxembourg.
- The rule that any member of the Council may vote on behalf of one other member makes the quorum half (or just over half of) the total membership (thirteen in the EU-25).
- The Commission is invited as of right to all meetings of the Council, except in a few cases where the Council is discussing internal matters, or issues in which the Commission has no role to play (for example, the Council's internal budget or appointments to one of the EU's institutions or bodies).
- The rule that 'officials' may assist ministers begs a question as to definitions, given that the boundaries of the public service vary from one member state to another, as does the boundary between the public and private sectors in the management of certain markets.
- The issue of numbers (and related questions of efficiency) were a recurrent source of debate even before the 2004 enlargement, after which smaller national delegations at Council meetings became the norm, because of restricted space and new rules governing the payment of attendance expenses for delegates (see below).
- Officials from the Council Secretariat attend all meetings of the Council, seated beside and behind the president, in fulfilment of the Secretariat's task of 'organising, coordinating and ensuring the coherence of the Council's work' (Article 23.3 of the CRPs).

Sectoral differentiation

For legal purposes, the Council is a unitary body. As such, it is entitled to take decisions on any issue subject to the treaties, irrespective of which ministers happen to be representing the member states at a given point in time. Hence, Lord Carrington's irascible demand as he saw the agenda of the meeting he was about to chair: 'Who the hell has put pig-iron on my agenda?' (Neligan, 1999, p. 86). The December Agriculture and Fisheries Council, traditionally the last one to meet every year, is regularly required to adopt non-agriculture and non-fisheries decisions (see Box 2.1), but the practice is not confined to this configuration alone. For example, the Justice and Home Affairs (JHA) Council of 19 November 2004 adopted the decision that finally appointed the President and members of the Barroso Commission, who took up office three days later. (The fact that this task fell to the JHA Council rather than the General Affairs Council was a delicious irony, given that it was the rejection by the European Parliament (EP) of the proposed JHA Commissioner that had delayed the appointment in the first place!)

In practice, different specialized configurations of the Council have emerged in response to the rhythm and volume of business in different policy arenas. Table 2.1 shows this range and how it has developed over the years, first through a process of expansion, and later by means of fusion. Until recent times, the pattern was to establish new specialized configurations of the Council in line with the development of active policy arenas at the EU level, and the expansion of Community competences through treaty reforms. This increased specialization also reflected changing fashions in public policy and shifting EU priorities, such as the emergence of the environment as an arena of European Community (EC) activism from the early 1970s, the shift into legislative overdrive around the internal market programme in the 1980s, the creeping concern about immigration and cross-border crime in the early 1990s, and heightened fears about international security a decade later.

But expansion gave rise to inefficiency and a certain lack of coherence, and an agreement at the Seville European Council in June 2002 on the regrouping of Councils resulted in a reduction in the number of configurations, first implemented under the Danish presidency in the second half of the same year. Some continue to argue for a more radical reduction in the number of configurations, while insiders maintain that the minimum possible number has already been attained, and that some formations are already a little contrived. The CT identified only two configurations – the General Affairs Council and the Foreign Affairs Council – and left it to the European Council to determine the rest.

Each configuration of the Council has a rather well-defined and substantial area of responsibility. This is augmented by an idiosyncratic character defined by its policy remit, culture and frequency of meetings, as well as the influence of the personalities involved (see Westlake and Galloway, 2004). Some of the new configurations have a much more permanent character than others. Historically, this has been especially the case for those covering General Affairs and External Relations (GAERC), Ecofin, and Agriculture and Fisheries (Agfish). In recent years, however, we can also discern an explosion of business in JHA and the potential importance of the new Competitiveness Council (created in 2002), which groups business on the internal market, industry and research.

Box 2.1   *The Agriculture and Fisheries Council, 21–22 December 2004*

Representatives of various levels of seniority ...

Delegation	Level of representative
Presidency (NL)	Minister
Austria	Deputy Permanent Representative
	Director General
Belgium	Minister
	Flemish Minister
Czech Republic	Minister
	State Secretary
Cyprus	Minister
Denmark	Minister
	State Secretary
Estonia	Minister
	Deputy Minister
Finland	Minister
France	Minister
Germany	Federal Minister
	State Secretary
Greece	Minister
	State Secretary
Hungary	Minister
	State Secretary
Ireland	Minister
	Minister of State
Italy	State Secretary
Latvia	Minister
Lithuania	Minister
	State Secretary

⟶

General Affairs and External Relations (GAERC)

The rather awkwardly-named GAERC has, since 2002, replaced the General Affairs Council (GAC), long viewed as the most 'senior' of the Council formations. Usually composed of foreign ministers, it meets at least once a month and has two major areas of responsibility, as both its name and Box 2.2 indicate. The decision taken at the Seville European Council in June 2002 to transform the GAC into the GAERC was a response to repeated criticisms of the rather natural tendency of the foreign ministers to concentrate on the increasingly numerous foreign policy aspects of their remit, to the detriment of their role as Council coordinator (see, for example, Gomez and Peterson, 2001).

→

Luxembourg	Minister
	State Secretary
Malta	Minister
The Netherlands	Director General
Poland	Deputy State Secretary
Portugal	Minister
Slovakia	Minister
Slovenia	State Secretary
Spain	Minister
Sweden	Minister
United Kingdom	Secretary of State
	Parliamentary Under-Secretary of State
Commission	Commissioner (Agriculture & Rural Development)
	Commissioner (Fisheries & Marine Affairs)
	Commissioner (Health & Consumer Protection)
	Commissioner (Development & Humanitarian Aid)

...take decisions in several policy areas...
The Council adopted the Regulation on total allowable catches (TACs) and fishing quotas for 2005 and the Regulation on deep-sea species for the years 2005 and 2006.

Other non-agriculture and non-fisheries items were approved (as A points) in the following policy areas:

- External relations;
- European security and defence policy;
- Development cooperation;
- Justice and home affairs;
- Trade policy; and
- Economic and financial affairs.

Source: Council Press Release 354 (15873/04) available on the Council's website (www.consilium.eu.int).

These criticisms increased in the mid- to late 1990s, amid calls for a specialist Coordination Council composed of Ministers for Europe at deputy prime ministerial level. In the event, the foreign ministers succeeded in retaining responsibility for both coordination and external policy, but they now (as Box 2.2 indicates) hold separate meetings, with distinct agendas for the two areas of activity. The meetings are either scheduled on two consecutive days, or else on a single day with separate sessions in the morning and the afternoon, or with the second meeting starting immediately after the first has ended. General affairs issues are dealt with first (or on the first day) and foreign policy issues, which usually constitute the larger part of the agenda, afterwards (or on the second day). Meetings of Association and Cooperation Councils, in

Table 2.1 Changes in Council configurations and numbers of meetings

1980		1990		2000		2004	
Configurations	No. of meetings	Configurations	No. of meetings	Configurations	No. of meetings	Configurations	No. of meetings
Agriculture	14	Agriculture	16	Agriculture	11	Agriculture & Fisheries	10
Budget	3	Budget	2	Budget	2	Competitiveness ((Internal Market, Industry & Research)	4
Development	1	Catastrophe Protection	1	Culture	3		
Ecofin	9	Consumer Affairs	2	Development	–		
Education	1	Culture	2	Ecofin	11	Ecofin (including Budget)	11
Energy	2	Development	4	Education & Youth Affairs	2	Education, Youth & Culture	3
Environment	2	Ecofin	10	Employment & Social Policy	6	Employment, Social Policy, Health & Consumer Affairs	4
Fisheries	7	Education	2	Environment	–		
General Affairs	13	Energy	3	Fisheries	3	Environment	4
Justice & Home Affairs	1	Environment	5				
		Fisheries	3				

Configuration		Configuration		Configuration		Configuration	
		General Affairs	13	General Affairs (+external relations)	13	General Affairs & External Relations	26
		Health	2	Health	2	Justice & Home Affairs	9
		Industry	4	Industry & Energy	3	Transport, Telecommunications & Energy	5
		Internal Market	7	Internal Market, Consumer Affairs & Tourism	5		
		Justice & Home Affairs	1	Justice, Home Affairs & Civil Protection	6		
		Research	2	Research	2		
Social Affairs	2	Social Affairs	3	Transport & Telecommunications	8		
Transport	2	Telecommunications	2				
Others	3	Tourism	1				
		Trade	1				
		Transport	4				
15	**60**	**22**	**90**	**16**	**77**	**9**	**76**

Box 2.2   *Areas of Responsibility and sample agenda of the General Affairs and External Relations Council (GAERC)*

General Affairs

- Preparation of and follow-up to European Council meetings (including coordinating activities necessary to that end);
- Institutional and administrative questions;
- Horizontal dossiers which affect several of the EU's policies; and
- Any dossier entrusted to it by the European Council, having regard to economic and monetary union (EMU) operating rules.

External Relations

- Common foreign and security policy (CFSP) issues;
- European security and defence policy (ESDP) issues;
- Foreign trade;
- Development cooperation; and
- Humanitarian aid.

Agenda of the 2621st and 2622nd meetings of the Council of the European Union (General Affairs and External Relations)
Brussels, Monday 22 November and Tuesday 23 November 2004

Session on General Affairs (Monday 22 November 2004)
2621st Council meeting

1. Adoption of the provisional agenda.
2. Approval of the list of 'A' items.
3. Resolutions, opinions and decisions adopted by the European Parliament at its periods of session in Brussels on 13–14 October 2004 and in Strasbourg on 25–28 October 2004.
4. Preparation of the European Council (Brussels, 17 December 2004).
5. Financial framework for 2007–13.

Session on External Relations (Monday 22 and Tuesday 23 November 2004)
2622nd Council meeting

1. Adoption of the provisional agenda (*Note: no 'A' items*).
2. ESDP.

→

which representatives of the EU member states and the Commission meet representatives of the third countries bound by such agreements, are normally scheduled in the margins of the External Relations segment of the GAERC (see Box 2.2).

The 2002–3 Convention on the Future of Europe (CFE) proposed a clearer separation of foreign affairs from general coordination by

3. Middle East peace process.
4. Iran.
5. EU–China relations.
6. Ukraine.
7. Belarus.
8. ATHENA-Review 2004 : Financing of EU rapid response.
9. Africa:
   (a) Ivory Coast;
   (b) Great Lakes;
   (c) Sudan;
   (d) Somalia; and
   (e) AOB/Guinea-Bissau.
10. Orientation debate on the effectiveness of the EU external action;
11. The EC and the member states contributing to the 2005 MDG (Multi-disciplinary group on organized crime) stocktaking exercise.
12. Follow-up to the International conference on population and development.
13. Monterrey follow-up.
14. Annual report 2004 on EC development policy and external assistance.

In the margins of the Council

22 November 2004

Military Capabilities Commitment Conference (MinDef)	09.00–10.30
Steering Board European Defence Agency (MinDef)	11.00–12.00
WEAG Ministerial Meeting (MinDef)	12.15–12.45
Civil Capabilities Commitment Conference (25) (MFA)	09.30–10.30
Civil Capabilities Commitment Conference + 5/6 (MFA)	10.30–11.00
Troika Defence with 6 (MinDef)	15.00–16.00
EU-Western Balkans Forum	18.30–19.10

23 November 2004

Cooperation Council with South Africa	16.00–17.30

assigning the latter specifically to deputy prime ministers but, because of a lack of agreement at the subsequent intergovernmental conference (IGC) on this point, it was not included in the CT. Instead, the latter provided for a General Affairs Council (responsible for 'consistency' as well as for preparing and following-up on European Council sessions) and a Foreign Affairs Council (dealing with external action), without specifying which ministers should take part in each configuration.

Economic and Financial Affairs and Budget (Ecofin)

Ecofin brings together ministers of finance and/or economic affairs, normally on a monthly basis within the EU, but it also meets at the margins of other international meetings. The member governments are locked into a shared discussion of macroeconomic issues, as they concert positions in other forums for international policy coordination, notably the Organisation for Economic Co-operation and Development (OECD), the International Monetary Fund (IMF) and the Group of Seven (G7), as well as, more recently, those dealing with economic stabilization in the post-communist countries.

Ecofin is a high-status configuration of the Council, in part because its members are among the most senior individuals in national cabinets, but also because of the importance of macroeconomic and monetary issues in the EU. The finance ministers are influential domestically because of their central role as regards the national budget and because they are largely unused to being subordinate to cabinet colleagues other than – sometimes – the prime minister. Ecofin ministers have common interests and common enemies (the markets or spending ministries), which engender a club-like atmosphere when they meet. They have shown a marked reluctance to report to the European Council through the medium of foreign ministers (GAC or GAERC), and have won the right to attend European Council meetings when economic and monetary matters are being discussed, a point of increased importance after the creation of economic and monetary union (EMU) and the euro regime.

Ecofin has modes of operation that are more informal and more secretive than in most other configurations of the Council. These traits echo features common to national policy-making on similar issues and reflect the fact that much of Ecofin's work is not legislative, but rather involves policy coordination. The members of Ecofin are particularly fond of informal meetings, which are normally scheduled for April and September every year. Insiders comment that much useful business is transacted at these meetings, if only in the form of free and frank exchanges of information which facilitate agreement at a later stage in official proceedings.

Another complication is that, since the establishment of EMU, the daily conduct of monetary policy is in the hands of the ECB, while the Stability and Growth Pact (SGP) is subject to discussions in Ecofin or the European Council, and the economic side of EMU still depends on coordination among member governments rather than on direct EU powers. The latter is also true of some other areas of financial and fiscal affairs, where progress inside Ecofin has been constrained by the requirement of unanimity (which, incidentally, was maintained in the CT). In 2004, this was leading to calls for some taxation matters to be dealt with by 'enhanced cooperation' involving only some member governments.

A very important and initially informal sub-group of Ecofin is the Euro Group, consisting of the economic or finance ministers of the member states belonging to the euro zone (those that have adopted the euro as their currency) – numbering twelve at the time of writing in 2005. Its habit has been to meet on the evening before the formal monthly Ecofin session, with the other Ecofin members being informed of the outcome of the Euro Group's discussions at lunch the following day. A lively debate continues as to whether or not the Euro Group should be formalized and endowed with distinct responsibilities. Two reasons are advanced for doing this: first, to prevent full EMU members from being encumbered by those outside the euro, and second, to add specific policy powers and obligations to complement the single monetary policy. Following the original acceptance in the Treaty on European Union (TEU) of differentiated roles for euro members, the CT added that the Council should be able to adopt measures specific to euro members with only these latter able to vote, and included a short Protocol (No. 12) governing meetings of the Euro Group.

Since 2002, Ecofin now also subsumes the Budget Council, composed of the national ministers responsible for public expenditure. It operates at both ends of the policy spectrum, from the broad shaping decisions on overall resources and revenue-raising to the fine print of detailed budget heads and programme evaluation. Its importance on the former has, however, diminished, partly because of interventions from the European Council and partly because of the introduction in the late 1980s of multi-annual financial perspectives incorporated in inter-institutional agreements (IIAs) that largely deal with adjudication between the institutions (see Chapter 8).

The rhythm of the Budget Council's meetings is determined by the annual budgetary procedure, which is concentrated mainly in the second semester of each year. Consequently, two-day meetings of Ecofin are scheduled for July and November every year, the first day being reserved for Ecofin business, and the second for the budget. The work of the Budget Council is heavily circumscribed by procedural rules, set out in the budgetary articles of the treaties, the Financial Regulations and IIAs. It is locked into a distinct set of relationships with the Commission, the EP and the Court of Auditors, and was the first Council forced to recognize the EP as a constraining interlocutor. It was also the first Council configuration whose preparatory body reached decisions on the basis of implicit qualified majority voting (QMV) as a matter of routine. This was and remains the case in the preparatory sessions of the Budget Committee, composed of senior officials (the 'tough guys') from the national finance ministries, with the effect that ministers now play a less direct part in the annual budgetary process than was previously the case.

Agriculture and Fisheries (Agfish)

The Agriculture Council was the first specialized Council configuration to acquire a quasi-autonomous character in the early 1960s. The specialized policy community dealing with agricultural support was very quick to assert its policy-making authority as the common agricultural policy (CAP) developed, and it has retained a rather firm grip on policy over the years. There are pluses and minuses to this strong sectoral control. The strength of the Agriculture Council, and the pyramid of decision that it crowns, is that it comprises an expert, well-informed and 'ear-to-the-ground' grouping (Jones and Clark, 2002). Its members tend to have more in common with each other, in spite of national differences, than with their colleagues in national cabinets, with whom they compete for resources and priority. It is a clear target for farmers' organizations and for food distributors, traders and processors. It constitutes an intimate and self-reliant policy circle with a distinct 'functionalist' character.

These strengths have the corresponding weaknesses of encapsulation, vulnerability to capture or clientelism, and imperviousness to external influences, such as consumers, taxpayers, third country trade concerns and so on. The Agriculture Council now also includes the Fisheries Council, and it meets at least once a month throughout the year. As we shall see in Chapter 10, this is the Council that makes the most active and explicit use of the QMV provisions.

Competitiveness (Comp)

The Competitiveness Council has, since 2002, brought together within a single configuration all the main areas of microeconomic policy relating to both the internal market and the so-called 'Lisbon Strategy' (entailing soft coordination on socio-economic issues – see Chapter 6). It does not, however – or at least not in 2005 – include the network industries, handled by the Transport, Telecommunications and Energy Council (TTE), or the social and employment issues that relate to the Lisbon Strategy, which are the province of the Employment, Social Policy, Health and Consumer Affairs Council (EPSCO). Horizontal issues are normally tabled at the beginning of the meeting, followed by more sector-specific items, grouped according to policy area.

While insiders speak of a certain nascent *esprit de corps* within this new Council, it remains to be seen how it will settle down, since a great deal depends on how ministers from the member states, the Council and the Commission drive forward the competitiveness and economic reform agendas. An energetic investment in this policy agenda would require that this Council become a more regular and productive forum, not only in generating legislation but also in providing a mechanism for dialogue and exchanges of national experiences of reform (Sapir *et al.*, 2004). Much depends, too, on the seniority of the ministers sent to the meetings, and on the degree of fragmentation of responsibility for its component policy areas among national ministers and within the Commission.

Justice and Home Affairs (JHA)

It is in the field of JHA that the Council has seen the most impressive growth of activity in recent years (see Table 2.1), stimulated by the provisions of the Treaty of Amsterdam (ToA) in this field and then further galvanized by the impact of 9/11. Meetings are creeping up to almost a monthly rhythm with long agendas, comprising both proposals for decisions with legislative impact and coordination of national policies across a range of arenas. Already by 2003/4 it was estimated informally that some 40 per cent of the documents going through the Council (official and ministerial levels combined) related to JHA, representing an extraordinary mutual involvement of domestic ministries with historically much less experience of European or international cooperation. Monar (2004) reports a total of 500 decisions reached in the Council on JHA matters between 1 May 1999 and 31 December 2003, some ten per month, constituting a doubling of the rate prior to the ToA. It should also be noted that the JHA Council remains marked by the pillar structure of the TEU (the CT had proposed that if be abolished) and hence has to take parallel decisions on related matters that depend on different treaty provisions.

Other configurations

Apart from the formations mentioned above, the Council may also meet in four other configurations:

- Employment, Social Policy, Health and Consumer Affairs (EPSCO) is a grouping bearing the hallmarks of fusion for the sake of it, rather than because of a widespread congruence of interests or shared problems. Insiders are of the opinion that the fusion of the employment and social policy Councils has been rather profitable, but are less convinced that health fits well in this grouping.
- Education, Youth and Culture (EYC) is another example of enforced fusion. In practice, this Council configuration (and its agenda) is effectively divided between the three policy sectors, with education and youth issues sometimes being treated together.
- Transport, Telecommunications and Energy (TTE) is in one sense an obvious grouping of the components of the trans-European networks (TENs). In practice, however, the overlap between the three areas is negligible, and they continue to meet, in effect, in their old configurations, with the relevant ministers taking their places at the negotiating table as 'their' items are reached on the agenda.
- Environment is the only Council to survive the fusion process as a single entity.

Other groupings

So far we have described the Council as a body through which formalized policy and legislation emerges. Not everything is quite so cut and dried, however. The extension of the European level of governance and habits of ministerial meetings have prompted gatherings of various kinds that do not quite constitute full Council sessions, but have a Community aura about them. Three main types will be mentioned here: conferences, second and third pillar arrangements under the TEU; and partial groupings of member states.

First, some ministerial meetings have been 'conferences' – that is, gatherings not wholly bound by EU rules and codes of behaviour, and usually subject to a unanimity decision rule. So, for example:

- In the context of enlargement, the representatives of the member states meet 'in conference' to discuss terms and conditions and to negotiate these with each candidate.
- Most famously, treaty reforms are negotiated in 'intergovernmental conferences' (IGCs).
- Some decisions, for example on the sites of the institutions, have been reached by representatives of the member states meeting in conference, rather than by the Council *per se.*
- In areas with no Community competence yet established, ministers have met in conference to agree common and coordinated programmes, such as for education during the 1970s and early 1980s. Similarly, informal meetings of interior ministers paved the way for the development of JHA, initially consolidated under the 'third pillar' of Maastricht.
- When the chosen instrument for policy coordination is a convention under international law rather than an EC instrument, the representatives of the member states also meet in conference.

Second, the TEU added some important new features to the work of the Council, most famously under the so-called second (covering the common foreign and security policy-CFSP) and third (JHA) pillars, where the European Council was attributed an important part in defining the agenda of cooperation (see Chapter 6), while the Commission, EP and European Court of Justice (ECJ) were granted limited roles. The language of the TEU slipped somewhat ambiguously between references to the member states reaching decisions and the Council as the vehicle for deliberation and decision. The nature of the output included 'concerted and convergent action', 'common positions' and the possibility of 'joint action' (TEU, Articles J.2 and J.3, K.1 and K.3).

Third, the TEU (in Articles J.4 (5) and K.7) also permitted 'the establishment or development of closer cooperation between two or more Member States...in so far as such cooperation does not conflict with, or impede' that envisaged under the TEU. This acknowledged the reality of bilateral agreements (and the trilateral Benelux), the Nordic Council, Western European Union (WEU), the North Atlantic Treaty Organisation (NATO) and Schengen (the agreement on removal of border controls). This endows such partial groupings of the member states with a specific recognition and permits a choice between possible institutional frameworks in the same policy arenas. The ToA extended the reach of JHA, by incorporating the Schengen Treaties (though not for all member states), and provided a framework for moving decision-making from more intergovernmental procedures into more classical Community procedures. The special protocols for Denmark, Ireland and the United Kingdom (UK) enable the Council to take decisions that would not apply to these three, unless and until they 'opt in' to Schengen, subject to the unanimous consent of prior Schengen members. New member states have no option but to be included within Schengen, subject to having appropriate domestic provisions in place.

The ToA also added explicit provisions for 'enhanced cooperation', according to which eight of the member states (then half plus one) could agree to intensify policy cooperation, subject to some limits to protect the interests of non-participants. The ToN extended the scope for enhanced cooperation in all areas of the Council's work (Stubb, 2002). The CT clarified the intended future arrangements for this in Article I-44 and Articles III-416-423.

Frequency and intensity of meetings

Table 2.1 shows the frequency of Council sessions by configuration and over time. Three broad clusters have emerged over the years – namely, intense, recurrent and occasional. Council sessions are *intense* in policy arenas either where the main thrust of policy is set at the EU level (such as the CAP), or where a very significant part of the policy arena depends on more or less continuous interaction with EU colleagues (as in the foreign policy arena). Ministers engaged in such intense sessions and the preparation that accompanies them may see their EU counterparts as frequently as (or even more often than) their national colleagues. This intensity pervades the daily lives, frames of reference and work patterns of the participants. It encourages a dense form of collegiality and collective identity, such that a reference to 'we' or to 'our' policy is as likely be to a collective EU position as to a national position.

Councils with *recurrent* meetings are either those where there are repeated bursts of collective business, or those where there is a predictable regularity of meetings. The difference between the two depends partly on the nature of the policy arena. Some policy arenas – for example, the single market – are more subject to legislation than others, or are more affected by transnational factors, as in the environmental field. Recurrent Council sessions define in a significant way the parameters within which the relevant national ministers operate. They need to be knowledgeable and informed about the Community rules that affect their areas of responsibility, and alert both to opportunities for collective agreement and also to irritating or constraining Community obligations. There is a continuity and predictability to their involvement in the Council that spreads beyond the formal meetings and occasional informal gatherings.

The third category, of *occasional* involvement, is a very mixed bag. It covers areas where the logic for transnational policy development either is not particularly compelling or has been controversial (for example, in the areas of health, education, tourism or consumer protection), as well as areas where policy activism is sporadically in and out of fashion for one reason or another (for example, energy or transport). Understandably, proceedings in such Councils are stiffer and more wary, ease of communication less evident, and solid output more sparse. In the past, each such area had its own occasional Council sessions, but the new effort to rationalize the Council configurations has, in theory, done away with visibly separate sessions. However, we should note that, in some of the fused configurations, what often happens in practice is that a sequence of distinct sessions takes place, with a rotation of different ministers and delegations according to the items on the agenda. That being said, some member governments may field a single minister who has to cover subjects outside his or her normal brief, and may therefore rely more heavily on officials to assist with details.

Council sessions do not simply consist of meetings in Brussels (or Luxembourg or the presidency member state – see below). Ministers have to prepare for meetings: they may have to engage in lengthy and sometimes contested discussions at home on what their bargaining positions should be; and they may also spend time in 'pre-negotiation' with the Commission, or other member governments, or national or European parliamentarians. No one has produced estimates of the ratios of time spent per Council session, but it almost certainly adds up to at least two or three times the length of the sessions themselves. All in all, therefore, the heavy and repeated engagement of many national ministers in the Council reveals a pattern of transnational involvement that marks the EU out from other forums for negotiation between governments.

Organization of meetings

Regular formal meetings of the Council take place in Brussels, but in April, June and October every year they are convened in Luxembourg, as provided for in Article 1 (3) of the CRPs. This is the result of a delicate agreement on 'sites' for EC institutions, brokered during the negotiation of the Merger Treaty in the 1960s and confirmed as recently as 1997 (in Protocol No. 12 to the Treaty of Amsterdam). In Brussels, the ministers gather in the Council's headquarters, the purpose-built Justus Lipsius building which, by a coincidence that may be interpreted as symbolic, is located geographically between the Commission's principal seat (the Berlaymont) and the building that houses the European Parliament in Brussels. For duly substantiated reasons, by unanimity, and in exceptional circumstances only, the Council or Coreper may decide that a formal meeting of the Council be held elsewhere.

Several informal sessions of the Council are organized by every incoming presidency, normally taking place in that country in an effort to distinguish them from the formal scheduled sessions. There are other differences too. Informal sessions are so classified because they have no papers, no minutes and are not supposed to deal with regular agenda items or to take decisions. Views and experience vary on their utility, and several attempts have been made to reduce their number, with little discernible effect. An internal Council note of 1989 sought to restrict them to seven per presidency, but most presidencies since that date have ignored or re-interpreted these guidelines, despite reminders from the Council Legal Service about the rules governing their conduct. So, for example, sixteen informal Council sessions were held in 1999, while the 2005 UK presidency alone scheduled thirteen such meetings for the second half of that year. In an effort to follow the letter rather than the spirit of the rules governing informal gatherings of the members of the Council, 'seminars' or 'conferences' may be organized by the presidency, to which ministers with responsibility for particular policy areas are invited.

The logistical organization and substantive preparation of formal Council meetings is the responsibility of the Council Secretariat and the presidency, working in tandem (see Chapters 4 and 5, respectively). As regards the scheduling of meetings, the availability of rooms and interpreting services is a real constraint. Each presidency produces a draft timetable of meetings up to a year in advance of taking office (the CRPs stipulate seven months), in the knowledge that unfolding events may require flexibility in the run-up to and throughout their watch at the helm. When they meet, the ministers sit around large tables, which may be rectangular, round or elliptical in shape, depending on the room assigned for the meeting. Whatever the shape of the table, the presidency and Commission delegations are always positioned opposite each other, and the national delegations sit in the pre-ordained order of the presidency rotation (see Figure 2.1). For the arrangements during the first half of 2006, see Hayes-Renshaw (2006). The national delegations move one place to their left once every six months, as the new president takes the chair (see Chapter 5 for more details).

The meeting rooms in Justus Lipsius have been altered to accommodate the new members who joined in 2004, and to incorporate

Figure 2.1   *Places at the Council Table, 2006–2007*

July–December 2006		January–June 2007	
Presidency (Finland) + Council Secretariat		Presidency (Germany) + Council Secretariat	
Finland	Romania*	Germany	Finland
Germany	Austria	Portugal	Romania
Portugal	Bulgaria*	Slovenia	Austria
Slovenia	Estonia	France	Bulgaria
France	UK	CR	Estonia
CR	Malta	Sweden	UK
Sweden	Slovakia	Spain	Malta
Spain	Netherlands	Belgium	Slovakia
Belgium	Luxembourg	Hungary	Netherlands
Hungary	Latvia	Poland	Luxembourg
Poland	Italy	Denmark	Latvia
Denmark	Greece	Cyprus	Italy
Cyprus	Lithuania	Ireland	Greece
	Ireland		Lithuania
Commission		Commission	

Notes: CR = Czech Republic; UK = United Kingdom.
* Following the signature of their Accession Treaty on 25 April 2005 until the actual date of their accession, Bulgaria and Romania are entitled to send non-voting observers along to meetings of the Council and its preparatory bodies.
   On 1 January and 1 July every year, each national delegation moves clockwise one place to its left, as the new president takes his or her place at the head of the table. The delegation of the presidency member state always sits on the president's right, and the Commission delegation always sits opposite the presidency. The above seating plan applies to all levels of the Council hierarchy (that is, the ministerial Councils and all preparatory bodies) for the period indicated.

new technology designed to facilitate transmission, negotiation and voting. New Council meeting rooms have been built, existing rooms have been modified and new rules governing numbers have been implemented. Each of the twenty-five national delegations now has only one or two spaces at the Council table itself, sometimes with two directly behind it for senior officials, while 'assisting officials' are assigned a maximum of three seats further back. The presidency, the Commission and the Council Secretariat each have two seats at the main table and three directly behind it. In some meeting rooms, additional interpretation booths have been built to cater for the new official languages, and tele-guided cameras have been installed to transmit the proceedings on to screens in the meeting room and a nearby *salle d'écoute* and, where necessary, to broadcast certain parts to the public.

The standard practice is for the presidency to start with a few words to orient discussion, to report on the state of play on the dossier so far, and then to ask the Commission to speak to what is normally the Commission's text. There used to follow a more or less systematic *tour de table*, in which each member state's representative could state a broad position and indicate specific issues of concern, a time-consuming procedure, even supposing each minister talked for only five minutes. Efforts have been made in recent years to dispense with this practice, and a provision to this effect has even been included in an annex to the CRPs, under the rubric 'Working methods for an enlarged Council' (see Appendix 3). Sometimes, *tours de table* take place only on so-called 'questionnaire' issues, designed precisely to get a view from each government; otherwise delegates are asked to speak only if they oppose a proposal. Thereafter, the discussion moves more freely around the table. National representatives must request and are called upon to speak by the presidency, a necessity in order to have the use of micro-phone and interpretation. Meetings may be adjourned for longer or shorter periods for more informal discussions, or for ministers to refer back to their delegations for consultation, or to their capitals for advice.

Two further points regarding physical factors should be made. The first concerns the constant hubbub and coming and going in Council sessions. Of necessity, the meeting rooms are large, since, even with national delegations consisting only of one minister and one official, a minimum of 60 people would be present. This number includes the presidency, the Commission delegation and officials from the Council Secretariat, but does not take into account the large number of inter-preters looking on from their glassed-in booths ranged around the sides of the room. Numbers may ebb and flow as the succession of agenda items demands a changeover of experts to assist the ministers. Whispered conversations within and sometimes between delegations form a back-drop to the more formal exchanges through microphones and interpreters. It demands real powers of concentration and stamina for the participants to listen carefully, as well as to speak, not to mention to observe and interpret the 'body language' of other participants.

The second physical factor also has a direct impact on the process of negotiation in the Council, and stems from increased numbers. The size and shape of the tables now required to accommodate the members of the Council means that eye contact between all of them is now physi-cally impossible. The use of tele-guided cameras transmitting to TV screens in front of each minister may help in identifying who is speaking at a given point in time, but will do nothing to reintroduce long-lost intimacy into the proceedings. Indeed, Council meetings today are more akin to assemblies than to the round-table discussions that occurred in past decades.

Agendas, texts and minutes

Provisional agendas for individual Council meetings are produced by the presidency in advance (the CRP text – Article 3 (1) – says at least fourteen days ahead of time), and subject to unanimous confirmation at the start of each session. The provisional agenda indicates, by means of an asterisk, those items on which a vote may be requested by the presidency, the Commission or a member of the Council. The Secretariat aims to send papers sixteen days before meetings, but the reality is both less and more flexible.

In practice, most of the agenda is in any case determined by earlier rounds of discussion, by external deadlines for decision or, since 2003, by the annual operational programme of Council activities. The latter is derived from a multi-annual strategic programme that is drawn up jointly by the six member states due to exercise the presidency over the forthcoming three years. The operational programme is presented to the European Council in December every year by the next two presidencies in line (see Chapter 5). But events have a nasty habit of creeping up and changing agendas at the last moment, especially for foreign ministers. In this sense, agenda-setting is comparable to what obtains in national cabinets or councils of ministers in the member states.

Council agendas are normally split into two sections. The first consists of so-called 'A' points, which the ministers are merely required to endorse. These are items that have already been substantively agreed by officials, and now require definitive adoption by the ministers. The second section contains so-called 'B' points, which remain to be thrashed out by ministers. 'A' points can always be reopened as 'B' points, if a minister has a change of mind or position, more easily so than within many national systems. Some items also appear as 'false 'B' points', when the essence is in fact agreed, but one or more member states wish to go through a ritual statement of a contrary or distinct position, normally for relay back to their home country.

In the first edition of this book (published in 1997), we quoted hearsay evidence from Council insiders that around 85 to 90 per cent of business was transacted by ministers as 'A' points, with approximately 70 per cent having been in effect settled at working group level, and another 15 to 20 per cent by Coreper, leaving some 10 to 15 per cent for substantive discussion by ministers as 'B' points. Current insiders believe that these figures still hold true in general terms, although there may be some variation between policy areas. The Council's transparency rules now allow us to test this hypothesis, however crudely, by tallying the number of A and B points entered on provisional Council agendas published on the Council's website. The results of such an initial analysis for a restricted period of time are presented in Table 2.2.

The vast preponderance of the agenda consists of text-based discussion – that is, exchanges of opinion about the details of texts intended to emerge as formal decisions of the Council, or about Commission communications intended to provoke a dialogue. These range from the intricacies of legislative drafts, through the figures and conditions set for spending, and the fine print of negotiating mandates with third countries, to the formulation of joint declarations on any issue within the orbit of the treaties. The bulk of the discussion is at the level of detail, fine distinctions between words, and variations of national positions.

Three points follow that constitute particular characteristics of the Council. First, the focus on texts lends to Council proceedings a legalism and recourse to established precedents that should not be underestimated. Delegations need constantly to be sensitive to what is legally possible or desirable, and to have regular access to interpretative legal advice during meetings – hence the attendance throughout the meeting of at least one official from the Council's Legal Service (see Chapter 4). Concerns about the legal consequences are one important

Table 2.2   *Proportion of 'A' and 'B' points on Council agendas, October–December 2004*

Council configurations (no. of meetings)	No. of A points	No. of B points	Total
Agriculture and Fisheries (3)	65	24	89
Competitiveness (1)	4	12	16
Economic and Financial Affairs (4)	53	26	79
Education, Youth and Culture (1)	22	17	39
Employment, Social Policy, Health and Consumer Affairs (2)	23	20	43
Environment (2)	18	20	38
General Affairs and External Relations (8)	117	46	168
Justice & Home Affairs (3)	78	22	100
Transport, Telecommunications and Energy (3)	31	27	58
Other – Heads of State or Government (1)	0	1	1
Total (28)	411 (78%)	115 (22%)	526 (100%)

Notes: the data for this table were obtained from draft Council agendas posted on the Council's website in advance of the meetings in question; no distinction is made between different types of A points (for example, between legislative and non-legislative acts).

factor in explaining the often contorted character of Community decisions, although efforts have been made in recent years to rectify this weakness (see, for example, the IIA of 22 December 1998 containing common guidelines for the quality of drafting of Community legislation (OJ C 73, 17.3.1999, p. 1).

Second, it was not generally common in the past for ministers to spend much time on a general debate of principles or overall policy, except at informal sessions or during lunch or dinner. Thus, recent transparency rules requiring the televising of such debates (see below and Chapter 4) challenge established patterns of work in the Council, where public pressures are beginning to induce a different mode of discussion.

Third, it has traditionally been hard for the Council to distinguish between acting in negotiating mode and acting in legislative mode, since negotiation is so heavily concentrated on the details of legislative texts. This partly explains the early reticence about opening up parts of Council sessions to public scrutiny of its role as legislator, and disagreements with the EP over the definition of the final legislative phase of Council deliberations (see Chapter 8). It should also be noted that the idea of an explicit Legislative Council that would, as a matter of course, meet in public, was finally not included in the CT, despite having been proposed by the CFE.

The decisions of the Council are made public shortly after each meeting in the form of a press release (prepared by the Council's Press Office – see Chapter 4), which includes a truncated summary of the discussions that have taken place. Official minutes of individual Council meetings are prepared by the Council official(s) who attended the session, and normally appear about two weeks later on the Council website. They are not intended to be a detailed record of discussions; rather, they represent staging posts in the development of the debate and sometimes give evidence, for consumption within the governments of the member states, that ministers have really done their stuff and pulled their weight in Council deliberations. The unilateral declarations that are often appended are either for home consumption in national capitals, or else intended to qualify a member state's understanding of what has been agreed. Such declarations do not, however, have legal force. It follows that the minutes are a very thin record of what in fact happens in the Council. They have been much emphasized in the discussion of transparency, although their release does not infact provide a rich yield of information to EU citizens.

Voting and the relative power of member states

The treaty drafters made it clear from the outset that they intended the Council to use three decision rules: unanimity; weighted majorities; and simple majorities. This intention has been reaffirmed with each treaty reform, although the balance has changed completely (see Box 2.3). The number of areas subject to unanimous voting has constantly been

Box 2.3   *Council voting rules under various treaties*

	Simple majority	Unanimity	Qualified majority
Treaty of Rome – EEC (1957)	Default rule; Procedural issues	Most issues	To be introduced progressively
Single European Act – SEA (1986)	As above	Fewer issues	Extended scope to approximation of laws for establishment of the internal market. Potential for use in other policy areas
Maastricht Treaty/Treaty on European Union – TEU (1992)	As above	Some 1st pillar issues; 2nd and 3rd pillar issues	Extended scope in 1st pillar. Possibility of use for follow-up decisions in 2nd and 3rd pillars
Treaty of Amsterdam – ToA (1997)	As above	Possibility of 'constructive abstention' in CFSP	Extended scope in 1st pillar and for some aspects of 2nd and 3rd pillars. Introduced possibility of 'emergency brake' in 2nd and 3rd pillars
Treaty of Nice – ToN (2001)	As above	As above	New rules governing make-up of qualified majority (triple majority). Small extension in scope. Removed 'emergency brake' from justice and home affairs (JHA)
Constitutional Treaty – CT (2004)	Procedural decisions + specific pieces of legislation in which it has been established (for example, anti-dumping regulation)	Retained for small number of areas only	Default rule 'Emergency brake' retained for common foreign and security policy (CFSP). New rules regarding construction of qualified majority (double majority)

reduced, while weighted or qualified majority voting has become the decision-making rule for many of the most important EU policies. Simple majority voting has been the default rule, a fact that explains the occasional oddity of simple majority voting in the European Council. The CT would have made QMV the default rule. The upshot of the current voting rules is that voting – or at least the possibility of voting – has become much more common in the Council.

Formally, votes are taken only in ministerial sessions, although Coreper is empowered (by Article 19(7) of the CRPs) to vote on procedural issues. Implicit indicative voting can, and does, occur in senior preparatory bodies such as Coreper, or even in some working parties. Sometimes, ministers abstain from voting. When the procedure rests on unanimity, the tally depends on those voting, with abstentions in effect counting as endorsements. Technically, therefore, unanimity can be obtained with only Luxembourg assenting explicitly and all other member governments abstaining, but so extreme a case has never occurred. Where the procedure is subject to majority vote, an abstention counts as a 'no'. Chapter 10 charts the emergence of QMV as the principal voting rule in the Council, and analyses its effect on the behaviour and attitudes of the ministers and their officials in the Council. Here, we need only register the current situation, as presented in Table 2.3, which shows the current and projected (under the ToN) weighting of votes for each of the member states under QMV, as well as the formal thresholds to be reached for majority votes in order to adopt a measure, and for blocking minorities to obstruct agreement.

Perceptions about the relative power of individual member states have boiled over on several occasions in recent years into heated discussions over figures – specifically, the number of votes to be attributed to each member state and the precise thresholds for the attainment of qualified majorities and blocking minorities. Underlying the discussion of relative power is the question of whether it is a theoretical or a practical problem. A good deal of the academic discussion of the assumed practice and impact of voting has been preoccupied with developing and debating formal models of voting behaviour rather than with the empirical evidence, not least because of the historical paucity of the latter. The Council's new rules on transparency now mean that firm data on voting behaviour is available from the late 1990s onwards, against which to test hypotheses and anecdotal evidence. This we do in some detail in Chapter 10.

The main points we should retain here are:

- There is a heavy reliance on consensus, even in those cases where QMV is the rule.
- Of agreed decisions, less than one in five is contested.
- Even when decisions are contested, the number of blockers normally falls far short of a blocking minority.
- The most frequently contesting states tend to be Denmark, Germany, The Netherlands, the UK, Sweden and Italy.
- Contestation is most common in the areas of agriculture, fisheries, the internal market, transport and public health.
- The countries least likely to vote 'no' are Belgium, Finland, Ireland and Luxembourg.
- Among the larger member states, France and Spain abstain or vote 'no' rather less often than the others.

Table 2.3 *Weighting of Council votes for qualified majority voting under the Treaty of Nice*

Member states	No. of votes
France Germany Italy United Kingdom	29 each
Poland Spain	27 each
The Netherlands	13
Belgium Czech Republic Greece Hungary Portugal	12 each
Austria Sweden	10 each
Denmark Finland Ireland Lithuania Slovakia	7 each
Cyprus Estonia Latvia Luxembourg Slovenia	4 each
Malta	3
Total	**321**
QM threshold[*]	**232**
BM threshold	**90**

Notes: [*] In order for a qualified majority (QM) to be achieved, the 232 votes in favour must be cast by a majority of the member states (13 in the EU-25). Any member of the Council may request verification that the member states constituting the qualified majority represent at least 62 per cent of the total population of the EU. In order to ensure that such calculations are made on the basis of current data, the total population figure for each member state is calculated and published on an annual basis, along with the figure representing 62 per cent of the total (see Council Document 12712/04 for the figures in use until 31 December 2005).

When Bulgaria and Romania become full members of the EU, they will be attributed 10 and 14 votes, respectively, under the Nice rules. The total number of votes will then be 345. A qualified majority will require 255 votes in favour from 14 member states, and 91 votes will be required to attain a blocking minority.

For previous voting weights and qualified majority and blocking minority thresholds, see Table 10.1 in Chapter 10.

- The countries least likely to abstain are Finland, Greece and Ireland.
- There is no clear behavioural distinction between older and newer member states, or between the more integrationist by tradition and the more critical.
- There is no systematic evidence of big and small, or of old and new, member states voting together.

The principal implication of the foregoing for the proceedings of the Council to date is that, no matter which voting rule was being adhered to, there has been a tendency to continue discussion or negotiation until such time as all views have been taken on board and accommodated in one way or another, a process that occurs in different ways at all levels of the Council. Clearly, this consensual reflex has had implications for decision-making speed (see below), and special devices have been introduced in an attempt to aid the process of reaching agreement, as well as to deal with the issues arising from the Council's multilingualism (see below and Chapter 4). It is as yet too early to say whether this consensual reflex will continue, or to obtain to the same extent, in the enlarged EU, given the amount of time required for the reconciling of such a large number of views.

Language, atmosphere and special devices

The consequences of multilingualism

Language is important in the Council for several different reasons. First and most obviously, the Council is a multilingual forum always operating through simultaneous interpretation and from translated texts. All the EU's official languages are deemed to be co-equal in status, and negotiating texts for the ministers are routinely produced in each of the official languages (although problems with the recruitment of sufficient and sufficiently qualified interpreters and translators in the wake of the 2004 enlargement has resulted in an amended regime; see Chapter 4). Each participant in the Council of Ministers has the right to speak and to listen in his or her own language, and to demand that meetings be suspended if interpreters are missing or translations of texts unavailable. This constraint adds a certain formality to meetings, makes the telling of jokes to lighten the atmosphere a risky invitation to confusion, and means that participants do depend on, and use, headphones and microphones. It is hard to cut into the discussion in the way that is possible in monolingual meetings.

Some special devices and practices have become established in order to deal with the problems encountered as a result of this multilingualism. Much of the interpretation is done by relay from one of the better-known languages. Council participants from some language groups are more ready to speak and work on texts in foreign languages than others, typically Danish and Dutch speakers, and interestingly, most of the member states who joined in 2004, who display an overwhelming preference for working in English. Anglophones and francophones typically insist on speaking their own languages and, increasingly, so do native German speakers.

In practice, English and French are the most used languages, with English already being in the ascendant prior to the 2004 enlargement, and expected to increase thereafter. Participants from most other countries have in the past been willing to rely on having last-minute changes to the texts made in just these two languages, or to continue meetings with limited interpretation. However, there is no evidence of improving language skills at ministerial level (officials appear to be more ready to take language courses than their political masters and mistresses!). It should also be noted that the original language of draft texts is normally English or French, but very often not composed by native speakers. There is thus a clumsiness and approximate or quaint character to much of the language of debate, for which there is a surprisingly high tolerance.

Second, the EU has invented a language of its own, a kind of 'Euro-speak' or 'Euro-jargon' that permeates all texts and all discussions. This can emerge in several ways. Sometimes it is simply convenient shorthand for some complicated body of understanding common to all experienced participants (for example, *'acquis communautaire'*, or 'subsidiarity'), often derived from French as the initially predominant working language. Sometimes a word or phrase acquires a distinct meaning in the course of negotiation to summarize the core of an emerging deal – 'cohesion' and 'transparency' being good examples. Such vocabulary will then find its way into final texts, often much to the mystification of those outside the negotiating chamber. Sometimes a phrase adopted somewhat arbitrarily in the course of a negotiation, perhaps to avoid confusion in translation, or emanating from a pertinent ECJ judgement (for example, 'direct effect' or 'proportionality') will become the preferred shorthand for a more complicated point, or for a body of EC law and jurisprudence. Thus 'mutual recognition' and 'home country control' emerged as apparently key principles for developing the single market.

Whatever the reasons for the development of this 'Euro-speak', it has clear consequences for participants in the Council. It serves to underpin and to project shared understanding: 'cohesion' was included somewhat by chance in the text of the Single European Act (SEA), only to emerge as a principle and a point of bargaining reference for ministers from the less prosperous member states. 'Euro-speak' separates the experienced from the inexperienced, with the result that new ministers need, and take time, to settle down in the Council, as do new member governments. It also separates insiders from outsiders, whether the outsiders are citizens of the member states or interlocutors from third countries.

Third, the multilingual enjoy real operating advantages in the Council. They can compare texts and discourse between languages and can invent new formulations or self-interested amendments with greater ease. They can engage in informal and *ad hoc* discussions bilaterally with a wider range of other national participants. They can gain access to more direct information about their partners' negotiating positions, and they have the advantage of being able to speak more bluntly to domestic audiences – not many other ministers understand Danish or Portuguese, but almost everyone understands some English! Thus, though the EU Council is constrained by the multiplicity of languages, it has developed compensating devices that encourage 'we' feelings. This has also been the aim of several accepted practices introduced to deal with what are often overwhelmingly large numbers of people in the room.

Opportunities for frank discussion

Should the perceived need arise, Council sessions may break into 'restricted' or 'super restricted' session in an effort to reduce formality and to assist the process of negotiation. In the former case, ministers retain one adviser each, sometimes also with an 'invisible deputy', and in the latter they are on their own, with one Commission member and the Secretary-General (SG) or Deputy Secretary-General (DSG) of the Council, also accompanied by an adviser. In both of these cases, speech and arguments may become fiercer and tempers may be lost more easily, but ministers may also become more direct and more honest about their basic preoccupations. Moreover, deprived of the finesse and expertise of their more technically specialized or numerate advisers, ministers may opt for more political solutions to problems – and the said advisers may then spend weeks working out what was in fact agreed, as was the experience of Coreper in the wake of the Nice European Council in December 2000.

Meetings thus consist of highly formalized sessions with large numbers of participants, interspersed with rather more restricted groups, and meals and corridor discussions. Ministerial lunches and dinners can be important parts of the negotiating process, both for hard talking on items on their formal agendas that will be formalized when the official session reconvenes, and for the discussion of issues that are not tabled or the subject of formal proposals. Typically, often rather long mealtime discussions have been built into the structuring of debate for meetings of foreign ministers, finance ministers and European Council sessions, with a deliberate division of business between the informal topics and the more official agendas. But similar informal discussions are also part of the fabric of the other specialized Councils. For those Councils that meet very frequently (such as the Agriculture and Fisheries Council), the debates over meals provide opportunities for tough talking and the devising of compromise. For the Councils that meet infrequently, or where habits of meeting have only recently been established, mealtimes offer valuable opportunities for the building of personal contacts and confidence.

It will have become evident that ministers meeting in the Council quickly find themselves caught by a commitment to continue meeting or to reconvene in order to resolve outstanding differences and to reach agreement. The whole atmosphere, whatever the disputes and conflicts between positions, is oriented towards finding formulas for agreement, even if this requires working through the night, or through the week, should the need arise. Thus it is possible for sessions to go on into the night, to be prolonged for several days, or to be reconvened in successive weeks. Another procedure used to break log-jams is the presidency 'confessional', when Council presidents hold individual discussions with some or all member states in an effort to establish their bottom lines (see Chapter 5).

The device of 'marathon' meetings, first adopted to deal with issues about the seat of the institutions and the settlement of agricultural product prices in the early 1960s, became an established feature of EC bargaining in subsequent decades. Its invention rested on two assumptions: first, that there was an underlying and shared commitment to sit at the table until agreement was reached; and, second, that if ministers became tired enough, they would yield ground and accept that the forest was more important than the individual tree. More recently, marathon sessions have gone out of fashion and few sessions exceed their anticipated length (usually one or two days), partly because so many regular meetings are scheduled. Agriculture and budgetary issues remain exceptions, along with topics driven by an internal or external deadline.

Output and speed

The image of the Council at work has often been one of an institution that is ponderous and clumsy, with a disappointing level of output in relation to the time and effort committed. Indeed, much of the attention given to the SEA and the 1992 programme, which was viewed as marking a critical change, rested on the view that a breakthrough had occurred in expediting and speeding up Council decision-making and thus increasing its output. Like most such images, it is an oversimplification and, in some ways, a distortion of reality.

On the brute issue of volume of legislation, the EU has always been marked by legislative activism, with bouts of hyperactivity (see Figure 2.2, covering the decade since 1994). A mere glance at the growing size of

Figure 2.2   *Legislative output of the Council, 1994–2004*

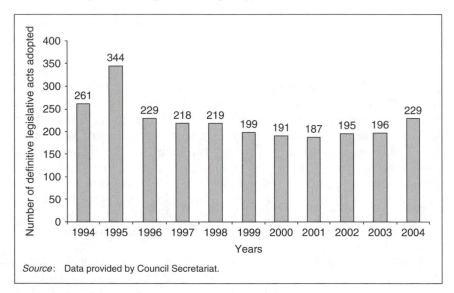

Source: Data provided by Council Secretariat.

the relevant volumes of the *Official Journal [OJ] of the European Communities* (now *the European Union*) provides testimony to this, even before the mid-1980s. The old image of slow decision-making rested more on the limits to legislative progress in some areas, notably the internal market before the SEA.

Output varies in volume and character between areas of policy, and thus between configurations of the Council. Nor does the Council only make legislation. It spends much of its time dealing with agreements with third countries and policy coordination. Here, the volumes of such agreements and the records in the *Bulletin of the EC* (now *EU*) have also shown a history of activism. The growth and diversification of EU spending programmes has been another important consumer of Council time and energy. Much time is spent on interaction with other EU institutions, notably (but not exclusively) with the Commission and the EP. The Council is also event-responsive, a factor that accounts for an exponential growth in the volume of business dealing with the rest of Europe since 1989.

The volume and rate of legislation increased markedly in the late 1980s because of the internal market programme. The original 'Cockfield list' of 300 measures, subsequently reduced to 282, accounted for much of the output, though we should note that some issues (for example, veterinary, phyto-sanitary and food standards issues) often stubbornly eluded agreement. Success with the internal market also encouraged legislative activism in other areas. However, from the mid-1990s onwards, the volume was substantially reduced (Council of the European Union,

1995), with the Prodi (1999–2004) Commission vowing to 'do less and do it better'.

In addition to crude evidence of output we also need to examine the 'speed' factor. Here we can call on an early statistical study by Sloot and Verschuren (1990), and more recent evidence gathered by Golub (1999) and Maurer (2003a). The evidence in Box 2.4 reveals a picture, even before the application of the SEA, of a steady increase in decision-making speed. It also shows that the introduction of new legislative procedures with the EP has had an impact on the figures. It appears from the figures that it now takes on average under two years to progress from Commission proposal to Council–EP decision under the co-decision procedure. Note that this is not slow by comparison with national legislative procedures.

Coordination between Councils

We have drawn attention to the sectoral organization of the Council, reinforced by the specialized preparatory committees, as we shall see in Chapter 3. Here we examine how coherence between sectors is achieved, how coordination is provided and how cross-sector mediation is developed. This is not only a practical matter, but also raises a fundamental point about the nature of the EU model of governance. After all, at the very least, the EU is a multi-sector regime and, in the eyes of some, it is a potential polity. It is certainly unusual among transnational and multilateral organizations in dealing simultaneously with so wide a range of policy arenas. From early in its history it has been suggested that the EC was unusual in encouraging 'package deals' among different policies, in permitting (or even inducing) 'spillovers' from one issue area to another, and in distributing the gains and costs of economic and political integration, not only across member states, but also among different groups or constituencies within the member states. Indeed, a crucial point in the debate between realists and neo-realists on the one hand, and neo-functionalists or supranationalists on the other, has always been located close to this point of analysis.

The broad analytical point, as it relates to the dynamics of EU bargaining, will be addressed in Chapter 11. Here we confine ourselves to the more mechanical question of the extent to which cross-sectoral processes can be observed, to counterbalance the clear importance of intra-sectoral processes of bargaining within the Council. In the past, the overwhelming emphasis was on accumulating sector-specific agendas within increasingly specialized configurations of the Council, by and large reflecting the administrative organization of the member governments. This gave considerable scope for 'package deals' within sectors, and for the aggregation of, and adjudication between, specific interests or constituencies within each of those sectors.

Box 2.4   *Decision-making speed in the European Union*

One measure of legislative efficiency in the European Union (EU) is the speed with which decisions are taken – that is, the time-lag between the presentation of a Commission proposal and its adoption by the Council or, increasingly, by the Council and the European Parliament (EP). Decision-making speed is affected by several factors, including the type of decision in question, the applicable voting rule, the initial degree of consensus among the decision-makers, the complexity of the relevant decision-making procedure, and the number of people involved.

The cooperation and co-decision procedures, by attributing a greater role to the EP, were widely expected to render decision-making more complex and more protracted. Similarly, it was expected that enlargement of the EU would slow-down the decision-making process, because of the need to accommodate a greater number of interests and opinions.

Relatively few statistical analyses of decision-making speed have been undertaken over the years, particularly with regard to the early decades of Community decision-making, and those that have, have been criticized by subsequent analysts (Golub, 1999; Schulz and König, 2000). Such analyses are not always directly comparable, concentrating as they do on varying, often overlapping, time-periods, including in their analysis different types of decisions and decision-making procedures, and presenting their findings in inconsistent ways. However, each of the studies undertaken indicates the same general trend: an underlying increase in the speed of EU decision-making over time, despite the addition of complicated, time-consuming procedures and increased numbers of participants.

The main findings on decision-making speed covering different time-periods and decision-making procedures are as follows:

Pre-cooperation procedure
Between 1975 and 1986, the percentage of proposals adopted by the Council within 22 months (668 days) rose from 74.8 per cent (in 1975) to 87.4 per cent (in 1986), indicating a steady increase in decision-making speed, even before the application of the Single European Act (SEA – which introduced the cooperation procedure and more widespread use of qualified majority voting)

What is harder to identify is either the scope for, or the mechanisms to facilitate, cross-sectoral linkage. At the formal level of the Council, three opportunities emerged:

- 'jumbo' Councils occasionally brought together in the same meeting ministers from the member states who were responsible for several issue areas simultaneously in play; this experiment has now been replaced by the new composite Council configurations;
- coordination by the foreign ministers, since 2002 meeting in a separate General Affairs session of the GAERC; and

(Sloot and Verschuren, 1990). Golub (1999) claims that, on the basis of data he collected and analysed at the end of 1996, the median time-lag fell from 1,177 days (38.7 months) in 1974 to 236 days (7.7 months) in 1978.

Under the cooperation procedure
According to a reply to an MEP's question in 1997 (Richard Corbett, question number 39/97), the average length of time for acts to be adopted under the cooperation procedure was 734 days (24.1 months) (Maurer, 1999). This increase in lag-time confirmed the widely-held view that more complicated decision-making procedures (that is, those attributing a greater role to the EP) were likely to be more protracted. Golub (1999) claims that, between 1987 and the early 1990s, the average time-lag was between 400 and 600 days, although these figures were expected to rise once pending proposals had been included in the data set.

Schulz and König (2000) maintain that the median time-lag for all regulations, directives and decisions proposed and adopted in the period 1984–94 was 156 days, with the median rising to 392 days in the final two years of this period.

Under the co-decision procedure
To date, the average length of time for acts to be adopted under the co-decision procedure is as follows:

	1991–8	1993–9	1999–2004
Without conciliation (about 80 per cent of the total)	646 days (20.8 months)	634 days (20.8 months)	541 (17.8 months)
With conciliation (about 20 per cent of the total)	876 days (28.8 months)	815 days (26.8 months)	894 (29.4 months)
Overall average	737 days (24.2 months)	710 days (23.3 months)	618 days (20.3 months)

Sources: 1991–8 Maurer (1999); 1993–9 EP Conciliation Committee delegation (1999); 1999–2004 data supplied by the EP Conciliation Secretariat.

- coordination by the European Council – of the three by far the most important, but activated for only a limited range of highly salient or politicized issues (see Chapter 6).

Otherwise, the Council has to rely on its regular processes. Chapter 3 sets out the extent to which the preparatory committees coordinate the work of the Council; Chapter 4 explains the contribution of the Council Secretariat; and Chapter 5 discusses the coordination functions of the Council presidency.

Subsidiarity and transparency

In the early 1990s, subsidiarity and transparency became the new buzz-words in the EU. The problems arising from the negotiation and ratification of the TEU, accentuated by the shock of the first negative Danish referendum of June 1992, indicated a wide sense of unease and electoral disaffection. European politicians were forced to acknowledge the need to present the whole process better to public opinion. Views varied (and still do) over the nature of the remedies for the democracy or legitimacy deficit, and to what extent the problem was short-term or long-term. Two devices – subsidiarity and transparency – were seized on as immediate potential antidotes, and seen by some as being closely interrelated aspects of the need for 'nearness' and 'openness' – originally Danish phrases that had percolated into Euro-speak.

The drive to develop subsidiarity, as reformulated in the TEU, has had a direct bearing on the work of the Council. After all, it is the Council that has to agree to all extensions of Community authority at the expense of the member states, and the Council collectively can always refuse such extensions of competence. None the less, the Council is now enjoined by its own pronouncements to pay close attention to subsidiarity in all of its activities.

Transparency, on the face of it, looks a more straightforward device, and one that has been developed by the Council as a new mode of operation and a signal of sustained good intentions. Its origins can be traced back to Denmark and the debates that preceded and accompanied the Maastricht negotiations. It was taken up by other governments, also under pressure from their own electorates, and sensitive to the need to try to get the Danes back on board in order to rescue the TEU, which led to a declaration on transparency attached to the conclusions of the Edinburgh European Council of December 1992 (published in the *Bulletin of the EC*, 12/92, December 1992). This stated in essence that:

- there should be 'open' debates in the Council on major issues, made 'public' through closed circuit television relay to the press office in the Council building;
- voting records should be published, together with any 'explanations of vote' by individual governments;
- the results of Council deliberations should be better publicised (through existing information channels) and more accessible to those who asked to see them; and
- legislation should be made clearer and simpler for the citizen to understand and, as far as possible, codified – that is, put into a consolidated form relating to particular topics.

So the question became not *whether*, but *how*, to improve transparency. It was not so hard to state that the Council and the Commission would do their best to increase transparency; in any case, the Commission had always been relatively open in its provision of information to outsiders. At the level of practice it was to prove much harder for the Council, partly because of its deeply embedded habits of secrecy, and partly because it was not self-evident which parts of Council activity could be opened up to more public view. What unfolded was a classic case of 'muddling through', during which it became clear that the Council was caught between intention and practicality, between clashing cultures of openness and secrecy, and poised on the edge of a wider discussion about the nature of the Council as an institution. The upshot was a compromise, as the eventual texts show (see Chapter 4 for more detail). It cannot be denied that much progress in the pursuit of greater transparency has been made, as is evident from the Council's website (www.consilium.eu.int), but the debate is destined to continue.

The 2002–3 CFE provided a clear opportunity for those prepared to contemplate fundamental changes to the way in which the Council operates. It therefore proposed the creation of a horizontal Legislative Council, whose proceedings would occur in public. Hailed by some as the answer to prayers for greater transparency and increased coordination, but dismissed by others as an academic idea that would not work in practice, it was one of the first victims of the subsequent IGC. Instead, the CT opted for further incremental moves to open up the Council, which were the subject of an exchange between the Council and the Ombudsman in the summer of 2004. Article I-24 (6) CT provided that: 'The Council shall meet in public when it deliberates and votes on a draft legislative act. To this end, each Council meeting shall be divided into two parts, dealing respectively with deliberations on Union legislative acts and non-legislative activities.'

We can thus observe the development of the Council at ministerial level in paradoxical ways. On the one hand, it has established an array of procedures and practices that have made it remarkable as a means of pressuring ministers from member governments into a process of sustained collective decision-making. Indeed, the resilience and inventiveness of the Council in response to events, to changes in context, and to criticism, show a surprising adaptability. The results in terms of sustained output, even efficiency, are not to be understated. But on the other hand, propositions abound for further reforms of the Council, not only at ministerial but also at other levels, suggesting a range of sources of dissatisfaction with the character and results of its work. We discuss such reforms throughout this volume and in the concluding chapter.

Chapter 3

Officials Prepare the Ground: the Preparatory Bodies

Critics of the European Union's decision-making procedures commonly focus on the amount of pre-negotiation that takes place among officials at levels below that of the Council as evidence of a lack of accountability in the system. Yet the process evident at the European level mirrors what happens in each of the member states. Just as, at national level, committees of officials meet prior to cabinet meetings or councils of ministers to prepare their deliberations, so groups of national officials meet in advance of European Union (EU) ministerial meetings in order to reduce the number of issues to be discussed in the limited time available to the elected national ministers in the Council. Within the Council hierarchy, such preparation has become the preserve of a number of high-level committees composed of senior officials from each of the member states, who in turn oversee the work of a large number of specialized working parties (WPs), also made up of national officials.

Every working day, hundreds of national officials attend meetings in the Justus Lipsius building in Brussels to discuss the details of the dossiers before them, reporting directly or indirectly to their respective ministers on the outcome of their deliberations. They concentrate in the main on the technical aspects of the dossiers, since the ministers have neither the time, nor frequently the expertise, required to discuss them in the necessary detail. The ministers can thus focus in their meetings on those issues where agreement is dependent on a more political input. However, even 'political' decisions need to be prepared in advance, so that the ministers can concentrate on the solutions that have the best chance of being accepted by the greatest number. Consequently, the EU's preparatory bodies act as filters for the issues which will eventually be debated at Council or European Council level, identifying areas of agreement and disagreement through preliminary discussions. Their operating methods at all levels are governed by the provisions laid down in the Council's internal rules of procedure (CRPs), most specifically those contained in Annex IV (Working Methods for an Enlarged Council) of the 2004 version of these rules (see Appendix 3). In addition, and perhaps more importantly for a real understanding of how these bodies work, a number of informal rules and conventions have emerged over the years, and now dictate how preparatory business is conducted within the Council.

The preparatory bodies can be distinguished by several key factors which affect their position *vis-à-vis* the Council and one another:

- *permanent or ad hoc*: the group may be in virtually permanent or at least regular session as the result of a clear and direct legal basis or, at the other extreme, be created specifically in order to discuss a particular dossier or issue area, and then disbanded. Generally speaking, the more permanent and established the group, the greater its influence in the Council system;
- *membership*: the group may be composed of very senior officials from a national ministry, or more junior desk officers with detailed expertise in a particular issue area. As a general rule, the more senior the officials in the national administration, the more influence the group will be able to exert *vis-à-vis* not only the other preparatory bodies but also the Council itself;
- *frequency of meetings*: groups may meet very frequently and regularly (for example, weekly or monthly), or may be convened only as and when necessary over a given time period. Normally, the more frequently the group meets, the more likely it will be to exert influence, although the seniority of its members may also be a factor;
- *scope of activity*: the group may be involved in one policy area alone, or may coordinate the work of a number of groups in different policy areas. Clearly, the wider the remit of the group, the greater its influence in the system;
- *reporting route to the Council*: reports of the group's work may go directly to the relevant Council, or may be reviewed by another intervening level, with the former being viewed as the more influential.

The Council Secretariat maintains a 'List of committees and working parties involved in the Council's preparatory work', which it updates as necessary, sometimes several times a year. A list published in June 2005 (Council document number 10198/05) contained a total of 283 distinct bodies covering all areas of the Council's work (see Table 3.1). These preparatory groups range from horizontal coordinating bodies to issue-specific working parties, and a clear hierarchy exists among them (see Figure 3.1). At the top is the Committee of Permanent Representatives (Coreper), a distinctive body in terms of its composition, scope of activity and status in the system, while the base of the hierarchy is

Table 3.1 *The Council's committees and working parties, 2005*

	Number of committees or working parties	*Number of sub-groups*
A Committees established by the Treaties, by intergovernmental decision, by Council act, and groups closely associated with Coreper (see below)	18	5
B General Affairs	17	2
C External Relations/Security & Defence/ Development	36	2
D Economic & Financial Affairs	9	8
E Justice & Home Affairs	22	4
F Agriculture & Fisheries	26	80
G Competitiveness (Internal Market, Industry, Research)	17	17
H Transport/Telecommunications/Energy	7	0
I Employment/Social Policy/Health & Consumer Affairs	4	0
J Environment	2	3
K Education/Youth/Culture	4	0
Total	162	121

Note: Group A consists of the following committees:

- Committees established by the treaties:
    - Permanent Representatives' Committee (Coreper – *Le Comité des représentants permanents*)
    - Economic and Financial Committee (EFC)
    - Employment Committee
    - Article 133 Committee
    - Political and Security Committee (COPS – *Le Comité de politique et de sécurité*)
    - Article 36 Committee (CATS – *Le Comité de l'article trente-six*)
    - Social Protection Committee

- Committee established by intergovernmental decision:
    - Special Committee on Agriculture (SCA)

- Committees established by Council act:
    - European Union Military Committee (EUMC)
    - Committee for Civilian Aspects of Crisis Management
    - Economic Policy Committee (EPC)
    - Financial Services Committee
    - Security Committee

- Groups closely associated with Coreper:
    - Antici Group
    - Mertens Group
    - Friends of the Presidency Group
    - Ad Hoc Group on Financial Perspectives

- Counsellors/Attachés:
    - Counsellors/Attachés

Source: Council Document 10198/05, 27 June 2005.

Figure 3.1 *Hierarchy of the Council's preparatory bodies*

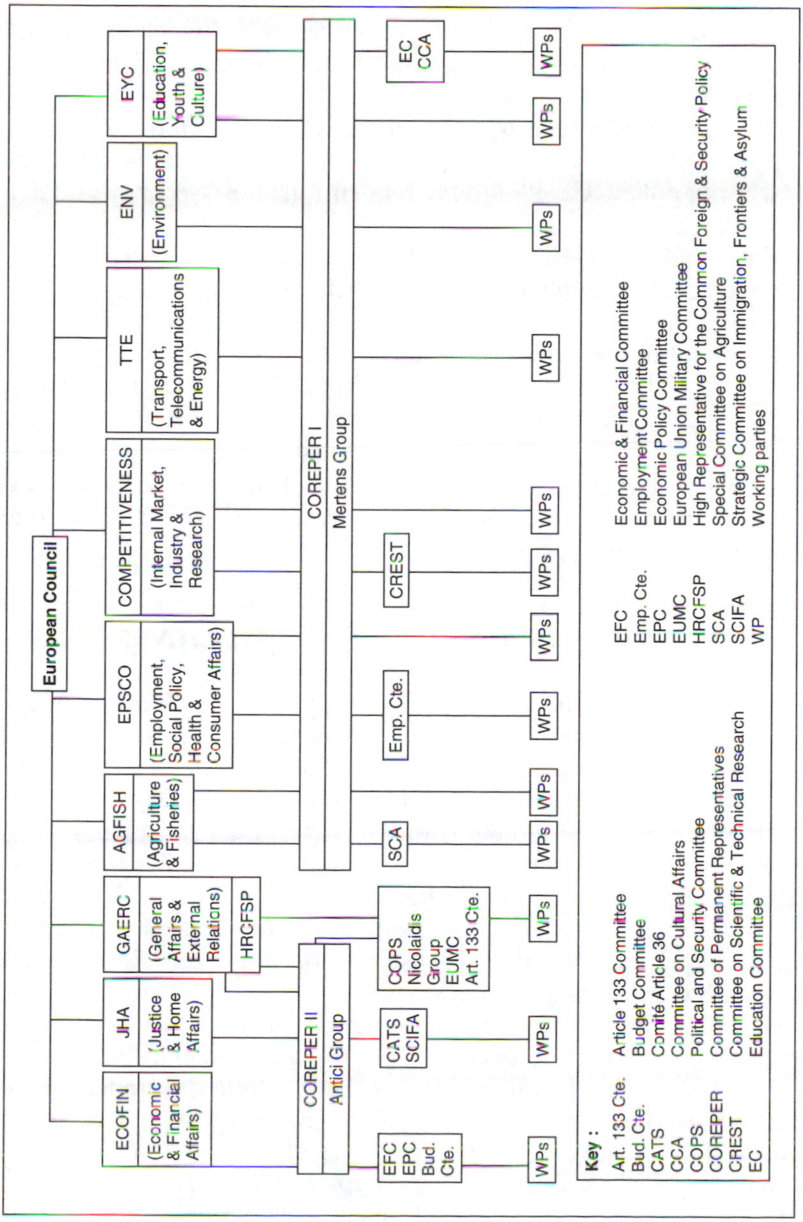

Key :

Art. 133 Cte.	Article 133 Committee
Bud. Cte.	Budget Committee
CATS	Comité Article 36
CCA	Committee on Cultural Affairs
COPS	Political and Security Committee
COREPER	Committee of Permanent Representatives
CREST	Committee on Scientific & Technical Research
EC	Education Committee
EFC	Economic & Financial Committee
Emp. Cte.	Employment Committee
EPC	Economic Policy Committee
EUMC	European Union Military Committee
HRCFSP	High Representative for the Common Foreign & Security Policy
SCA	Special Committee on Agriculture
SCIFA	Strategic Committee on Immigration, Frontiers & Asylum
WP	Working parties

composed of some 250 technical working parties. The middle ground is occupied by about ten senior committees dealing with specific issue areas, of which the most important and distinctive are:

- the Economic and Financial Committee (EFC), which prepares items on the agenda of the Economic and Financial Affairs Council (Ecofin);
- the Political and Security Committee (COPS – *Comité de politique et de sécurité*), which prepares issues relating to the common foreign and security policy (CFSP) and the related European security and defence policy (ESDP);
- the Article 36 Committee (CATS – *Comité de l'article trente-six*), which deals with justice and home affairs (JHA) issues;
- the Article 133 Committee, which assists the Commission in the negotiation of external trade agreements; and
- the Special Committee on Agriculture (SCA), which prepares the meetings of the ministers of agriculture.

This chapter examines the composition and functions of each of these bodies in turn and assesses their importance for the decision-making process as a whole.

The Committee of Permanent Representatives (Coreper)

If asked to identify the individual or body that 'runs Europe', members of the general public would probably opt for high-profile figures such as the High Representative for the CFSP and the President of the Commission, or media-conscious bodies such as the European Council and the European Parliament (EP). However, EU insiders and informed observers would be more likely to nominate the members of Coreper, a publicity-shy body which will celebrate its half-century in 2008. Coreper is unique among the preparatory bodies not only because of its composition and longevity, but also because it fulfils a horizontal function in an otherwise vertically segmented system.

Having gained the reputation among insiders as 'a locus of continuous negotiation and *de facto* decision-making' and 'the place to do the deal' within the Council hierarchy (Lewis, 2002, 2006), Coreper's previous position as the Council's most senior preparatory forum has been contested in recent years by the emergence of other high-level, specialized preparatory bodies. Despite (or perhaps because of) this development, various reform proposals and successive treaties (including the Constitutional Treaty – CT) have reaffirmed Coreper's central and coordinating role in the Council hierarchy and the EU's decision-making process. (Cynics might attribute this emphasis on Coreper's importance to the fact that many of the members of Coreper have been directly involved as their governments' representatives at the intergovernmental conferences (IGCs) that have preceded these treaty revisions.)

Origins and development

The 1951 Treaty of Paris establishing the European Coal and Steel Community (ECSC) provided for a Special Council of Ministers, which in turn created a '*Commission de coordination du Conseil des Ministres*' (Cocor) to prepare its work. Because of Cocor's undoubted contribution to the work of the ECSC Council, a broadly similar body was provided for in the 1957 Treaties of Rome establishing the European Economic Community (EEC) and the European Atomic Energy Community (Euratom). There was one crucial difference, however, in that it was agreed that the members of the new preparatory body would be resident in Brussels, where the Council was to hold most of its meetings. At the inaugural meeting of the Council of Foreign Ministers in January 1958, a joint Committee of Permanent Representatives for the two new Communities was formally established, and the first meeting of Coreper took place the next day. (By early 2005, the committee had held more than 2,000 meetings.)

The decision to designate the members of the new committee as the permanent representatives of their member governments was to have profound implications for the status and working methods not only of the committee itself but also of those who sat on it. The standing nature of the committee (it can, if necessary, be convened at very short notice) and its members' residence in Brussels, in close proximity and constant contact with colleagues from the other member states and the EU's institutions, ensure that both Coreper and the opinions of its individual members are taken seriously in Brussels as well as in the national capitals

Composition

Early in the discussions about the permanent nature of the new committee, it was agreed that the members would have diplomatic status. Accordingly, each member government appointed a senior official with the rank of ambassador from its Ministry of Foreign Affairs (in the case of Germany, the Ministry of Economic Affairs, as the then lead ministry on European issues) to serve as that country's permanent representative, and provided them with a number of officials to assist in the fulfilment of Coreper's preparatory duties. National permanent representations (permreps), headed by the permanent representatives (PRs), were established in Brussels, and today they constitute a vital link between each member government and the EU (see Chapter 9 for more details).

Given the significance of the EU for each of the member states today, the post of national PR in Brussels is perceived to be one of the most important and prestigious in each national diplomatic service. It is also an extremely demanding post, because, in order to be effective, the members of Coreper must be multi-talented: they require the ability to master the minutiae as well as the broad political sweep of a wide range of dossiers, a detailed knowledge of EU treaties and procedures, and a very developed sense of what will and will not be acceptable at both national and European levels. Experience is vital, so it is not uncommon for the PRs to have served in Brussels previously, and many remain in the post for extended periods. Some ambassadors will have already served a term as deputy permanent representative (DPR), while others may have spent time as an official in the national permrep, and virtually all will have been responsible at some stage for EU issues in their national capital.

The PRs are assisted in their preparatory functions by deputies, who are also very senior officials, often of ambassadorial level, and frequently having the rank of minister plenipotentiary. They are drawn from the national ministry of foreign affairs or one of the technical ministries, depending on how EU affairs are handled in the member state concerned. Like the PRs, the DPRs tend to have long experience and extensive knowledge of the EU system as a whole, and of Coreper and its working parties in particular.

From the earliest days of the Committee, the ambassadors acknowledged that they could not take full responsibility for the preparation of all the dossiers on the Council's agenda, which ranged from the very general to the highly detailed, and the very technical to the highly political. They therefore decided to concentrate on certain dossiers likely to be less readily conducive to agreement except at the highest (that is, ministerial or even prime ministerial) level, and entrusted the remainder to their deputies. This division of labour was formalized in 1962, since which time Coreper has met at two levels: that of the ambassadors – Coreper II – and that of the deputies – Coreper I. (This counter-intuitive numbering of the two levels refers to the way in which items were grouped on Coreper's agenda in the early days of the Communities, with the deputies dealing with items in Part I and the ambassadors concentrating on items in Part II; see Noël, 1967, p. 231.)

The two levels now operate virtually independently of one another, each being responsible for its own areas of Community activity (see below), and each reporting directly to those sectoral Councils whose work they have prepared. Consequently, the members of Coreper I are no longer deputies in the strict sense of the word, although they may be called upon to stand in for their ambassador in his or her absence. (The long run of all-male PRs was broken in 2001, with the appointment of a woman to the top position in the Irish permrep, and the same individual went on to become the first female president of Coreper during the Irish presidency in the first half of 2004. By the following year, she had a number of female colleagues in Coreper II, including the Luxembourg ambassador, who presided over the committee in the first half of 2005. The first woman to be appointed to Coreper I was an Austrian, in 1995.)

The appointment of very senior officials to the highest posts in the national permrep in Brussels imbues them with an authority they can wield in two directions. First, they tend to have fairly direct access to their respective prime ministers and foreign ministers, with the result that they are viewed seriously in Brussels as trusted interlocutors for their national governments. Second, their views are respected in the national capital, not only because of their senior position in the national administration, but also because their central position in the Council system gives them intimate links with representatives of the other member states, and with those of the other EU institutions. As a result, they are acutely aware of which lines of argument have the best chance of being accepted by their EU colleagues.

Each of the ambassadors and the deputies has appointed a senior personal assistant (often at Counsellor level), to take care of the procedural and some of the substantive aspects of their work. The Antici Group, which was named after its first chairman, Paolo Antici, was originally created (towards the end of the Italian presidency in the second half of 1975) in order to assist the ambassadors in preparing meetings of the European Council, but has since taken over responsibility for dealing with the procedural, and some of the substantive, aspects of Coreper II's work. The parallel body for Coreper I is known as the Mertens Group. Together with their opposite numbers from each of the other permreps, as well as officials from the General Secretariat of the Commission and the Council Secretariat (including the Legal Service), these officials meet on a weekly basis in advance of Coreper I and II in order *inter alia* to agree minutes of meetings, to coordinate schedules and to settle the order in which agenda items will be taken at forthcoming Coreper and Council meetings. These meetings are also used to provide advance warning about the positions the members of Coreper will be taking on particular agenda items, as well as what the presidency expects to achieve from the discussion on each item. Sometimes, they get involved in more substantive debates, as for example discussions on the language regime to be applied in the enlarged EU (see Council Document 10174/03).

Who attends meetings of Coreper? The national delegations at Coreper I and II meetings consist of a permanent core and a shifting population. The head of delegation (be it the ambassador or the deputy) is also its spokesperson, and normally attends throughout. If for some reason they need to absent themselves, the Antici or Mertens official may take their place and speak on their behalf. A small number of advisers provide background information and expertise on the items under discussion. Numbers at the meeting are in a constant state of flux, as officials come and go, transmitting messages, providing background information on items under discussion and monitoring the progress of the meeting. A typical Coreper meeting in the EU-25 is attended by a minimum of about 60 people and often over 100, space permitting.

Coreper is chaired by the representative of the member state currently holding the presidency of the Council – the PR in the case of Coreper II, and the DPR in the case of Coreper I. When it exercises the presidency, a member state is required to field two chief delegates for every meeting – one to chair the meeting, and one to head and speak for the national delegation. The onus of the presidency falls particularly hard on the PR and the DPR of the state in question, since the permrep becomes the member state's nerve-centre in Brussels for the six-month period (see Chapter 5).

The DPR has the additionally onerous task of leading the Council delegation in most trialogue meetings with the EP in the context of conciliation under the co-decision procedure (see Chapter 8).

The Commission delegation to Coreper I and II meetings is headed by senior officials from its General Secretariat, responsible for relations with Coreper, who attend throughout and speak on behalf of the Commission. They are accompanied by a shifting population of officials of varying levels of seniority from the relevant Directorates-General (DGs) with responsibility for the dossiers under discussion, and by officials from the Commission's Legal Service.

Officials from the Council Secretariat also attend the meetings, in the role of note-takers, assistants to the presidency, and legal and procedural advisers. With the exception of the officials from the Council's Legal Service, who may be called upon to clarify a legal point, they rarely address the meeting as a whole, although they may hold whispered consultations with the presidency, advising on procedural or textual questions.

Functions and working methods

What does Coreper do? Essentially, as the treaties and the Council's rules of procedure (CRPs) baldly state, Coreper is the principal body responsible for 'preparing the work of the Council and for carrying out the tasks assigned to it by the Council'. Coreper's preparatory function applies to every item on the agendas of all Council and, by indirect extension, European Council meetings, unless Coreper decides otherwise. The CRPs (in Article 19) also require Coreper to ensure the consistency of the Union's policies and actions, and the observation of certain principles and rules, thereby imbuing it with responsibility for horizontal coordination. In addition, Coreper is partially responsible for overseeing the follow-up to European Council conclusions, for representing the Council in bodies such as Association and Cooperation Councils and, most notably (since the introduction of the co-decision procedure by the 1992 Maastricht Treaty on European Union – TEU) in conciliation committee meetings with the EP. Article 19 of the current (2004) CRPs goes into far more detail than before on the actual input of Coreper, documenting more than four decades of accrued practice.

The preparation of Council agendas has both administrative and substantive aspects. At one level it requires agreement on when and in what order items are to be discussed by the ministers, while at another it involves the coordination and oversight of the work of some 250 working parties whose job it is to discuss, and as far as possible to reach agreement on, the dossiers before them. Coreper adopts the conclusions of the working parties and engages in a substantive discussion of the issues the working parties have been unable to settle, for whatever reason. Acting as a filter, Coreper indicates where agreement has been reached, highlights problem areas and, where possible and in accordance with the CRPs (currently Article 19.2), offers a range of solutions, thereby reducing the number and complexity of the issues to be discussed by the ministers (Tortora da Falco, 1980).

As a general rule, and at the risk of over-simplification, we can say that Coreper intervenes on issues that have proved too political for agreement to be reached at the level of the working parties, and too technical for discussion by the ministers. As with all rules, however, exceptions are not uncommon, since ministers can be greater masters of detail than the members of Coreper (witness their annual protracted negotiations on total allowable catches of fish). The object of prior preparation by the working parties and Coreper is for ministers to concentrate on a small number of particularly difficult dossiers during their regular meetings, while routine or less contentious matters are taken care of at the appropriate lower level.

In the first edition of this book, we expressed the view of Council insiders (now much-quoted) that some 85 per cent of all issues on Council agendas were essentially agreed in advance of ministerial sessions. A decade later, the indications are that little has changed, although we would caution against drawing hard and fast conclusions from these statistics. Dossiers, particularly the more complex ones, tend to move up and down the Council hierarchy, with the different levels whittling away at problem areas until such time as overall agreement has been reached. It is therefore difficult to attribute complete responsibility to any particular level for final settlement; rather it is a case of a symbiotic relationship between the various components of the Council hierarchy.

One aspect of Coreper's preparatory work that has changed significantly in the past decade is the degree to which it now takes the views of the EP into account. This is, of course, particularly true for issues subject to the co-decision procedure, where any advice to the Council on the position to be adopted must be informed by the attitude of the

EP, which is now an equal legislative authority with the Council in these areas. Indeed, it has been suggested (Bostock, 2002, p. 224) that, rather than facing in two directions like the twin-faced god, Janus, to which it has been likened, Coreper has now acquired a third face, directed towards the EP. While there is still some resistance within the ranks of Coreper towards the position it now finds itself in *vis-à-vis* the EP, there is no denying that much more time and effort is expended than previously in following the progress of co-decision dossiers as they work their way through the EP. At the same time, multiple contacts of a formal and informal nature are employed to reduce the distance between the positions of the two institutions (see Box 8.1 in this volume; Laffan and Shackleton, 2000; Farrell and Héritier, 2003; Shackleton and Raunio, 2003).

The aim of these ongoing contacts at various levels, where possible, is to avoid dossiers having to be discussed in the Conciliation Committee, which is jointly chaired by a Council presidency minister (and a vice-president of the EP), and in which the other member states are represented by the members of Coreper. (It should be noted that they are entitled to vote on behalf of their member governments in these meetings.) This increased contact with the EP has affected the deputies more than the ambassadors because of the division of labour between them, which sees the deputies dealing with the vast majority of dossiers subject to the co-decision procedure. Thus, of the eighty-two conciliation dossiers concluded in the period from July 1999 to December 2003, seventy-nine were dealt with by the deputies, and only three by the ambassadors. It has been estimated (Bostock, 2002, p. 223) that as much as 50 per cent of the deputies' meeting time is now spent on co-decision, either in brokering agreement at the early stages of the process, or in preparing for and engaging in conciliation (see also Chapter 8).

How does Coreper work? The short answer is: through meetings, meetings and more meetings! Both Coreper I and II normally meet on a weekly basis for at least one day each, sometimes two. Both committees usually meet on Wednesdays, but much depends on scheduled Council meetings, since the ambassadors and deputies are required to attend (as advisers to their respective ministers) those Council meetings that fall within their area of competence. The members of Coreper II normally also represent their ministers at Cooperation and Association Council meetings, both of which are chaired by the minister from the presidency member state and usually held in the margins of External Relations Council meetings. The vast majority of the ambassadors' and deputies' time is therefore spent either at or preparing for meetings.

Responsibility for the preparation of the work of the various Councils is divided between the ambassadors and the deputies, the general rule being that the latter deal with the more 'technical' issues (such as the internal market), while the ambassadors concentrate on the more 'political' ones (such as JHA issues). This distinction between technical and political matters is obviously nebulous, since many matters are a combination of the two, and indeed there are very few technical matters that do not have at least some political implications. A decision to transfer responsibility for preparing certain files from one part of Coreper to the other is sometimes taken by an incoming presidency, or by the ambassadors themselves. Generally speaking, and in cooperation with any other relevant senior preparatory bodies, the ambassadors prepare the work of the General Affairs and External Relations Council (GAERC), Ecofin and the JHA Council, with the deputies taking responsibility for the other six Council configurations (see Figure 3.1).

A single agenda for the weekly Coreper meetings is prepared by officials in the Council Secretariat, in cooperation with the presidency. Those items to be dealt with by Coreper I are listed first, followed sequentially (in a separate document) by those that will be dealt with by the ambassadors (see www.palgrave.com/politics/hayes-renshaw). Each of these documents is divided into two parts: Part I containing those items that have been the subject of agreement at the level of the working parties, and Part II consisting of items that need to be discussed by the members of the Committee. Following discussions in Coreper, agendas are prepared for the various Council meetings, again grouping items into two sections: those items already the subject of agreement and those needing to be discussed by the ministers (the so-called 'A' and 'B' points – see Chapter 2).

Far from imbuing the members of Coreper with a power of decision for which they are not directly accountable, the 'A' and 'B' points procedure is a sensible solution to the problem of ministerial overload. True, a large proportion of dossiers (some 85 per cent, according to insider estimates) are adopted by the ministers as 'A' points without any discussion at their level (or at least not at that particular meeting), but a number of safeguards exist to ensure that democratic control is exercised. First, the members of Coreper do not operate independently: they negotiate on the basis of instructions that have been drawn up or cleared by their capitals, and they act as the mouthpieces of their governments. The extent to which they can influence these instructions may vary between individuals and dossiers (see Chapter 9), but Coreper members do not normally approve any measure in Brussels unless they are sure that the resulting agreement will be endorsed by their governments. To do otherwise would be to lose credibility in Brussels or in the national capital, a dismal fate for a member of Coreper, where reputations are founded on the perceived ability to deliver in both directions.

Second, measures are deemed to have been adopted only when they have been the subject of a vote (implicit or explicit) at a meeting of the Council of Ministers. Every minister has the right at any time to request that an item appearing as an 'A' point on a Council agenda be withdrawn and reopened for discussion as a 'B' point at a subsequent meeting. Such a demand is rare, because most 'A' points are either non-contentious or else merely the final stage in a process that has seen a dossier move up and down the Council hierarchy, gathering inputs from every level. Coreper therefore has no autonomous decision-making power, and in that sense is not a substitute body for the Council of Ministers.

No voting as such takes place in Coreper, except on procedural issues (as indicated in Article 19 of the CRPs). However, negotiations on substantive issues are conducted in the committee, with eventual voting behaviour very much in mind. Whatever the voting rule that applies to the matter under discussion, the members of Coreper are empowered to indicate which side their minister would be on were the matter to come to a vote in the Council, thereby helping the presidency decide how best to proceed. Where the matter under discussion will be subject to the rule of unanimity in the Council, an attempt is made to reach unanimous agreement in Coreper. Where a qualified majority is required and consensus proves impossible to achieve, discussion tends to continue until such time as either a clearly defined majority or else a blocking minority is discernible, and the matter is sent to the appropriate level, be it up to Council for a political steer or back to the relevant working party for more detailed discussion.

In addition to formal meetings and working meals, the members of both levels of Coreper also meet regularly on a more informal basis: in the corridors, for lunches and dinners, at diplomatic functions, and in non-work-related social situations. The presidency practice of inviting the members of Coreper and the Antici Group with their spouses for an informal non-working weekend in the presidency member state in advance of European Council meetings further reinforces the relations between them. Spending so much time in one another's company in what Bostock (2002, p. 218) has termed their 'prolonged collective martyrdom', the members of Coreper develop a marked *esprit de corps*, characterized by mutual trust and responsiveness, which tends to develop into a consensus reflex and aids the process of negotiation in which they are constantly engaged.

Clearly, the members of Coreper have dual tugs of loyalty, which they claim to find neither competitive nor contradictory (Lewis, 2002 and 2006). Each is rooted in a national system, conscious of and sympathetic to both the official and the unofficial reasons underlying the national position on all issues, and committed to doing everything possible to make these views understood and respected by their colleagues from other member states. Yet the very fact of spending so much time with these colleagues has the effect of educating each member of Coreper in the ways and interests of other member states.

As a result, they are conscious of the need to reach agreement at EU level, and predisposed to look for compromise solutions that will take as many interests into account as possible.

Given its demonstrated importance for the process of EU decision-making, why is so little known about Coreper? One obvious answer is that much of what it does is routine and deeply boring to most observers. After all, the most politically interesting issues are normally discussed in the Council. Another is that reports of Coreper meetings are not available to the general public, with the dual result that their discussions are generally shrouded in secrecy and the members of the committee operate in almost total anonymity. Most tellingly, as with all bodies that engage in intricate negotiations, Coreper works most effectively out of the limelight, and is therefore understandably keen to preserve its shadowy profile. Academic interest in Coreper, although slow to materialize, has increased over time, in parallel with the committee's (and its members') perceived importance in the process of European integration. (For an in-depth analysis of Coreper in different periods, see Noël, 1967; Noël and Etienne, 1971; Hayes, 1984; Hayes-Renshaw, 1990a; de Zwaan, 1995; Lewis, 1998a, 1998b, 2002, 2006; and Bostock, 2002)

And what of the future of Coreper? Opinion is divided. There are those who believe that the erosion of Coreper's central position by such bodies as the EFC and COPS is likely not only to continue but also to increase as the Council's agenda expands to include ever more specialized policies, areas subject to soft coordination and areas of activity from which certain member states have opted out. Others maintain that the ongoing widening and deepening of the EU intensifies the need for a senior coordinating body such as Coreper, capable of combining political and bureaucratic skills either to reach agreement below the level of the Council on troublesome dossiers, or to propose a number of alternative solutions to outstanding problems on which the ministers will be required to decide.

Officially, Coreper's central position has been emphasized on numerous occasions in recent years, and detailed in official documents such as the CRPs and revising treaties. Unofficially, Coreper members express disquiet that some specialist policy areas have slipped out of their control, and that detailed preparation by other senior bodies leaves them with little 'value added' to contribute on some other issues. Common sense dictates that the policy generalists in Coreper cannot be responsible for detailed preparation in all areas of Council activity. Where they can make a significant contribution, however, is in ensuring cohesion across the Council configurations and utilizing their pronounced political and institutional sensitivity to broker agreements acceptable to their ministerial masters, where this has proved impossible to achieve at the level of the working parties.

The 2004 enlargement was an important test of Coreper's ability to conduct 'business as usual' while absorbing a significant number of new members into what is, in effect, a permanent process of negotiation. Early indications were promising on the whole, despite an initial feeling of a loss of cohesion because of increased numbers. There was some muted criticism as the new members adapted to the EU method of decision-making, although some at least felt that most of the problems arising were more the result of a lack of coordination in the national administrations than an unwillingness to conform to what was, for many of the newcomers, a profoundly different way of conducting business.

If the provisions relating to the Council in the CT were to be implemented, they would also have an impact on Coreper and the way in which it fulfils its functions within the Council hierarchy and with the other EU institutions. Such changes could conceivably serve as an opportunity for Coreper to return to doing what it does best: using its political and institutional sensitivity to maintain the flow of work within the Council hierarchy, while ensuring coordination between the various Council configurations, thereby regaining its original position at the hub of the decision-making process.

The Political and Security Committee (COPS)

Origins and development

The Political and Security Committee (PSC in English, but usually referred to as COPS, the acronym of its French name) is the 'lynchpin' of the CFSP and the associated ESDP. The term comes from the presidency's report to the Nice European Council of December 2000, which gave the green light for the transformation of an interim body (in existence since March 2000) into a permanent one. But the origins of COPS may be traced back still further, to the creation in the mid-1970s of a Political Committee (PoCo) in the steadfastly intergovernmental context of European political cooperation (EPC). Light institutionalization was the order of the day, the process was driven by the presidency, a small EPC secretariat provided administrative backup, and PoCo – which was composed of the political directors of each of the national ministries of foreign affairs – met about once a month in the presidency member state to prepare the foreign ministers' discussions on EPC matters, which took place outside the treaty framework.

The 1992 TEU formally established and institutionalized the CFSP and brought it within the EU's 'single institutional framework'. What this meant in practice was that the EPC secretariat was merged into the Council Secretariat, the foreign ministers discussed CFSP matters in the General Affairs Council (GAC) and Coreper became more involved in the preparation of their discussions. It also had the effect of transferring PoCo's meetings to Brussels, and they were also attended by officials from the national permreps in an attempt to facilitate coordination between European Community (EC) and CFSP matters. The defence component of the CFSP was addressed only in the late 1990s, but decisions and institutions followed rapidly.

At the Helsinki European Council of December 1999, an agreement was reached on the voluntary commitment of military forces to carry out the so-called Petersberg Tasks (now encompassing joint disarmament operations, human and rescue tasks, military advice and assistance tasks, conflict prevention and peace-keeping tasks, tasks of combat forces in crisis management, including peace-making, and post-conflict stabilization). At the same time, the need for new political and military bodies and structures to guide and oversee such operations was acknowledged. In particular, the need for a more permanent body than PoCo, capable of meeting very regularly and, if necessary, at short notice, was acknowledged. Based on guidelines agreed at Nice in December 2000, PoCo as such was disbanded and COPS was born (see Council Decision 2001/78/CFSP).

Composition

COPS is composed of a senior official (following initial caution on the part of some member states (Howorth, 2003, p. 20) now often of ambassadorial rank) from each of the national ministries of foreign affairs, typically with long experience of political cooperation both at home and abroad. They are resident in Brussels and based in the national permreps, where they oversee a small, specialized staff, including some military personnel. The committee meets at least twice a week and may convene at the level of political directors, who also meet informally a number of times during each presidency.

The position of chair of the committee is normally undertaken by the representative of the presidency member state. However, because of Denmark's treaty-based opt-out concerning the ESDP, the Danish representative in COPS was replaced by a Greek colleague during the Danish presidency in the second half of 2002 whenever ESDP matters were discussed. The guidelines on COPS agreed at Nice in December 2000 also allow for it to be chaired by the High Representative for the CFSP (HRCFSP) 'especially in the event of a crisis'. The High Representative frequently attends COPS meetings to brief, and be briefed by, its members.

The Commission is fully involved in COPS' work, with senior officials from DG External Relations attending all meetings. The External Relations Commissioner attends frequently, as do other interested Commissioners. The Commission has a non-exclusive right of initiative in the area of the CFSP, but no voting rights; none the less, its views on the CFSP and the ESDP are fed into the debates.

When issues relating to the ESDP are under discussion, the members of COPS may be joined by the chair of the EU Military Committee (EUMC), a body set up to advise COPS on military matters following a decision at the Nice summit. It has a permanent chair, selected by and from the members of the committee for a renewable period of three years. The EUMC is composed of the Chiefs of Defence of each of the member states, represented by their military representatives, who are resident in Brussels. They meet once a week, and act on the basis of guidelines drawn up by COPS.

Functions and working methods

The main functions of COPS are laid out in Article 25 TEU, which provides that it shall:

- monitor the international situation in the areas covered by the CFSP;
- contribute to the definition of policies by delivering opinions to the Council at the request of the Council or on its own initiative; and
- monitor the implementation of agreed policies.

The day-to-day monitoring of foreign and security policy business brings COPS into close and regular contact with the HRCFSP, the External Relations Commissioner and (since the creation of the new post in March 2004) the EU's Counter-Terrorism Coordinator, as well as with the EU's political partners, both bilateral (for example, Russia and the United States (USA)) and multilateral (for example, the North Atlantic Treaty Organisation (NATO) and the United Nations (UN)). Senior political visitors to Brussels – for example, a minister from a Balkan state or the Deputy Secretary-General of the UN – are invited to address the members of COPS or to have lunch with them, in a permanent process of information-gathering and discussion about the international political situation and the EU's potential response to it.

Policies are defined by the General Affairs and External Relations Council (GAERC) on the basis of opinions put forward by COPS, either at the request of the Council or on its own initiative. The impetus may come from one of several sources – the presidency, one or more member states, the Commission, the European Council or the High Representative for the common foreign and security policy (HRCFSP). Once a policy has been agreed by the Council, COPS is responsible for ensuring that it is properly implemented. Since the coming into force of the Treaty of Nice (ToN) on 1 February 2003, COPS has been granted the additional power to take operational decisions to implement crisis management operations under the ESDP.

This devolution of decision-making power is purely pragmatic; it is designed to avoid delays in decision-making in situations where time may be of the essence, and where waiting for the next scheduled Council meeting to take a decision is simply not an option.

In fulfilling its functions, COPS is assisted by a small number of specialized working groups. The EUMC (which has its own dedicated working party) has already been mentioned. In addition, COPS can call on the services of a Committee for Civilian Aspects of Crisis Management and a Politico-Military Working Party, which meet regularly to discuss specific aspects of COPS' work and report to it on the outcome of their deliberations. The procedural aspects of COPS' work are discussed and prepared every Wednesday by an Antici-like group known as the Nicolaidis Group. It was first established on an *ad hoc* basis under the Danish presidency in the second half of 2002, and subsequently formalized (and named after its then chairman) by means of a procedural decision taken by Coreper II in April of the following year, during the Greek presidency (Council document 8441/03).

COPS itself meets for two full days every week in the Justus Lipsius building in Brussels. Meetings are normally scheduled for Tuesday and Friday, but in the week preceding a GAERC session, the Friday meeting may be moved to the Thursday in order to allow for more time to prepare the ministerial session. In addition, COPS meets early on the day of an external relations formation of GAERC, and the members attend the GAERC with their respective ministers. On days when no formal COPS or GAERC meetings are scheduled, the members may be involved in meetings or lunches with visiting dignitaries or officials, with representatives of the other EU institutions or member states, or with scheduled meetings with the members of the North Atlantic Council (NAC).

Underpinning all this activity is a constant process of consultation of, and coordination with, officials from each member's respective capital. However, it should be remembered that a regular and intensive meeting schedule in no way guarantees a common approach or a role for COPS. During the Iraq crisis of 2002–3, for example, the committee 'was kept entirely at arms' length' (Howorth, 2003, p. 18).

And what of COPS' relations with Coreper? It was only to be expected that relations between the two committees would be strained, at least initially, for a number of reasons. From the outset, Coreper was anxious to be recognized as the more senior body, not only because of its age and experience and the seniority of its members, but also because of its position at the hub of the decision-making process. COPS was keen to carve out a niche for itself as the privileged gatekeeper for the GAERC with regard to the CFSP and the nascent ESDP, but was required to report to the foreign ministers via Coreper. Once turf-battles had been fought and questions of relative status settled, the two bodies settled down to a generally cooperative working relationship, though not without the potential for 'creative tension' (Bostock, 2002, p. 230). It is unclear how COPS would be affected under the arrangements fore-seen by the CT in the area of foreign policy, in particular the appoint-ment of a Union Minister for Foreign Affairs.

The Article 36 Committee (CATS)

Origins and development

The committees known as CATS (*Comité de l'Article Trente-Six* – Article 36 Committee) and SCIFA (Strategic Committee on Immigration, Frontiers and Asylum) are the direct descendants of what was known (until the late 1990s) as the K.4 Committee. The latter was established by Title VI of the 1992 TEU to coordinate intergovernmental cooperation in the fields of justice and home affairs under the aegis of the so-called third pillar of the European Union. The 1997 Treaty of Amsterdam (ToA) created a distinction between the free movement of persons on the one hand and the establishment of a so-called area of freedom, security and justice on the other. This resulted in the reorganization of the EU's cooperation in justice and home affairs, with issues relating to the free movement of persons (visas, asylum, immigration and judicial coopera-tion in civil law matters) being moved to the first pillar, and a new committee, SCIFA, being created by Coreper to ensure coordination of the preparatory work in these areas. Intergovernmental cooperation under the third pillar now applies only to police cooperation, customs cooperation and cooperation on criminal law. Following the consolidation of the TEU, Article K.4 became Article 36, resulting in the coordinating committee's present name.

Composition

Article 36 provides only that the committee consist of 'senior officials' from each of the member states. In practice, the members are mainly drawn from the national ministries of justice, although some come from the national interior ministries, depending on how such matters are dealt with in the member state in question. The Commission is required to be 'fully associated with the work' of the Committee, and Commission officials attend all meetings of the CATS, which is convened about once a month. The CATS is chaired by a representative of the presidency member state, and officials from the Council Secretariat (Directorate-General (DG) H dealing with JHA issues, and the Legal Service – see Chapter 4) provide the necessary administrative, procedural and legal support for its work.

Although not unfamiliar with intergovernmental cooperation, JHA officials' experience of European integration is much less ingrained than that of many of their colleagues in the national administrations, particularly those in the foreign, agricultural and finance ministries. As a result, there was a certain initial reluctance to move beyond informal dialogue and exchanges of information to a more formal, institutionalized process of common actions and harmonized legislation. However, inside observers now speak of the growth of a harmonization reflex in certain areas and, where this is unrealistic or unnecessary, given the very different judicial backgrounds and criminal law systems with which the members of the committee and working parties are familiar, a recognition of a need to cooperate and coordinate to the extent possible.

The preparation of JHA issues for discussion in Council constitutes a complex hierarchy of its own (see Nilsson, 2004, p. 133). The splitting of JHA between the first and third pillars under the ToA provided the opportunity for a much-needed pruning of the preparatory bodies in this area, which had been criticized for containing too many levels. The CATS now oversees the work of about a dozen specialized working parties, each composed of one representative from each of the member states and an observer from the Commission, chaired by an official from the presidency member state, and supported by officials from the Council Secretariat. These working parties meet as and when necessary in order to discuss issues to be agreed upon by the Council.

Functions and working methods

The CATS is first and foremost a coordinating committee, in that it organizes and regulates the work of the bodies that report to it. In doing so, it also fulfils the two other functions outlined for it in Article 36. First, it contributes to the preparation of the Council's discussions on police and judicial cooperation in criminal matters, by reviewing the work of its specialized working parties and reaching agreement, where possible, on the issues to be decided by the ministers in the JHA Council. Second, it presents its opinion to the Council, either on its own initiative or at the request of the ministers.

The CATS reports to the JHA Council via Coreper II (the ambassadors), an indication of the importance attached to this policy area by the member states. Coreper has the final view of all matters appearing on the agenda of the JHA Council, despite attempts being made, in the days of the K.4 Committee, to bypass the permanent representatives, the pretext being their lack of expertise in the area and the intergovernmental nature of JHA coordination. However, Coreper quickly reasserted its claim to superiority in ensuring central coordination and coherence, an argument that gained greater weight after the transferral of parts of

JHA coordination to the first pillar, and the division of the coordination function between the CATS and SCIFA.

The permanent representatives' lack of expertise in the area has been offset by the secondment of JHA advisers from the national ministries of justice or home affairs to the permreps in Brussels (see Chapter 9). These JHA counsellors attend meetings of the working parties and CATS, and keep their ambassadors informed about JHA issues across the first and third pillars. They also meet as a group to prepare discussions in Coreper, and their permanent presence in Brussels enables them to meet at short notice – for example, if last-minute coordination is required just before a Coreper or Council meeting. It has even been suggested that they may have more influence on the decision-making process than the CATS (Monar, 2002, p. 196).

The Economic and Financial Committee (EFC)

Origins and development

Economic and monetary union (EMU) has been a long-term objective of the EU since its inception as the European Communities in the 1950s. To this end, the Treaty of Rome, in Article 105(2), provided for a Monetary Committee (MC) with advisory status, whose job it was to review on a regular basis the economic and financial situation of the member states, and report back to the Commission and the Council. The TEU provided in Article 109c (later replaced by Article 114 of the Treaty establishing the European Community – TEC) that the Monetary Committee's chief task would be 'to promote coordination of the policies of the Member States to the full extent needed for the functioning of the internal market'. With the movement to the third stage of EMU on 1 January 1999, under the provision of the same Article 114 TEC, the Monetary Committee was dissolved and replaced by the EFC. The latter is therefore technically a relatively new committee, although it draws on the very considerable track record of its predecessor. None the less, the EFC has had to find its place in the new institutional and policy structure of EMU, including the Euro Group, and to develop a relationship with the European Central Bank (ECB). This task has been facilitated by the seniority of both its members and its masters, as well as by the very important tasks it has been assigned.

Composition

The EFC meets in a number of different compositions (Korkman, 2004, p. 97). At its most senior and broadest level, it is composed of two representatives from every member state (a senior official from the national ministry of economic affairs or finance and the vice-governor of the national Central Bank), plus two from the Commission and two from the ECB, as laid down in two Council Decisions published in the Official Journal (OJ L 358, 31.12.1998, p. 109, and OJ L 5, 1.1.1999, p. 71). On other occasions, it may be composed of treasury officials and representatives of the Commission and the ECB. Each of the full members has a deputy, and they meet as a group to prepare the work of the full committee, while Euro Group business is prepared by a Euro Group working party composed of representatives of the members of the Euro Group, the Commission and the ECB.

The EFC is unusual among the Council's preparatory bodies in two main respects. First, the chairmanship of the full committee does not follow the normal rotation system as generally practised throughout the rest of the Council. Instead, a chair is elected from among the members for a renewable term of two years. The resulting benefits of continuity and coherence have led to the suggestion that the EFC model could serve as an example for other Council preparatory bodies. Second, the committee is serviced not by the Council Secretariat, but by a specialized secretariat based in the Commission, and answerable directly to the chairman of the EFC. This rather unusual arrangement among Council preparatory bodies is viewed by insiders as being highly practical, because it allows the committee to draw on the considerable expertise and specialized resources of the Commission's DG Economic and Financial Affairs, commodities that are not readily available in the much smaller Council Secretariat. It also has the effect of precluding the exertion of control by Coreper over the preparation of the EFC's macroeconomic business. The Council Secretariat is represented in the EFC by the Director-General of DG G (Economic and Social Affairs), who attends all its meetings, as well as those of the Euro Group.

Functions and working methods

The EFC has three main tasks:

- reviewing and reporting on the economic and financial situation of the member states and of the Community;
- examining and reporting on the movement of capital and freedom of payments within the EMU; and
- contributing to the preparation of the work of Ecofin with regard to macroeconomic policy, specifically by developing (in cooperation with a number of other committees) the broad economic policy guidelines (BEPGs) that are debated and adopted every year by the European Council, and by monitoring the implementation of the Stability and Growth Pact (SGP).

The EFC may also deliver opinions, either on its own initiative or in response to a request from the Council or the Commission. Euro Group business is discussed in the EFC over lunch.

The EFC therefore constitutes the apex of Ecofin's preparatory structure for agenda items relating to policy coordination, while Coreper prepares issues touching on a Community competence. The full EFC normally meets once a month, in advance of the monthly Ecofin gatherings, but its meetings are not publicised in advance and no account of its discussions is made available publicly afterwards. The committee operates in three languages (English, French and German), but English is becoming increasingly dominant. The seniority of the EFC's members, the domestic importance of the ministers to whom they report and the importance of the issues it discusses all contribute to the elevated status enjoyed by the committee. Indeed, this is evident from the fact that, unlike his/her counterpart in Coreper, the chairman of the EFC regularly addresses the ministers in Council on behalf of the committee.

The EFC's relations with Coreper are rather ambivalent. A certain amount of institutional rivalry exists between them, with the EFC appearing to resent the requirement that, for reasons of coordination, issues go to the Council and the European Council via Coreper and the GAERC. However, this rivalry is coupled with an understanding that each has its respective role to play in its own specialized sphere. Thus the members of the EFC are senior experts in their complex policy field, with an intimate understanding of their colleagues' positions and with the ear of their respective ministers. Coreper, on the other hand, is adept at institutional niceties and consequently much better able than the EFC to ensure that economic and financial issues subject to the Community method are efficiently and competently dealt with. It remains to be seen to what extent the Euro Group will acquire a distinct, formal identity at ministerial level, and what the consequences of such a development would be for these two committees.

The Article 133 Committee

Origins and development

Formerly known as the Article 113 Committee (after the 1957 Treaty of Rome article that provided the legal basis for its creation), the Article 133 Committee deals with international trade policy issues, and constitutes the vital link between the Council and the Commission in external trade and tariff negotiations. The change in the committee's name occurred after the coming into force of the ToA on 1 May 1999, under which treaty articles were renumbered, but no substantial changes to the committee's composition or functions were introduced. The Article 113 Committee had come into existence at the end of the transitional period in 1970, and had been preceded by the Article 111 Committee, whose members and functions were almost identical.

The scope of Article 113 was not clearly defined in the EEC Treaty and, in the early years of the committee's existence, was a source of controversy between the Commission and certain member states (as opposed to the Council as a body), because the powers and prerogatives of each institution had not been clearly spelt out. With time and experience, however, the two institutions learned to work together harmoniously for the most part, and a *modus vivendi* has been reached between the Article 133 Committee and Coreper.

A recurring issue has been the extent to which EU competence might be extended in the trade field to cover the range of issues addressed by the World Trade Organization (WTO). In the discussions over what became the ToA, it was suggested that EU competence might be extended to cover not only goods but also services, as well as some transversal issues (such as intellectual property) that had otherwise been treated as 'mixed competence' issues. The issue re-emerged in the discussions leading up to the negotiations on the ToN, and the revised Article 133 now specifically includes 'trade in services' and the 'commercial aspects of intellectual property'. Thus the scope of Article 133 – and hence of the Article 133 Committee – has been extended significantly.

In international trade negotiations, the EU is represented by the Commission, which operates on the basis of a negotiating mandate determined by the (External Relations) Council, on the basis of a Commission proposal. This proposal is discussed by the Article 133 Committee and the relevant specialist sub-committees it has created to assist it in its work. It makes recommendations to the Council, which agrees the Commission's mandate and authorizes the Article 133 Committee to engage in constant dialogue with the Commission in the course of the negotiations, during which modifications to the EU's position might be required. This constant consultation is designed to allow the member governments to retain control over the Commission in the context of external trade negotiations.

Composition

The Article 133 Committee meets at two levels. The full members, who are responsible for overall policy, are senior civil servants from the national ministries of trade, foreign affairs or economic and financial affairs, depending on how foreign trade policy is dealt with in each particular member state. Each full member of the Article 133 Committee is accompanied by a team of experts, consisting of a deputy, officials from the permrep in Brussels who follow trade issues on a day-to-day basis, and advisers from the relevant ministry or ministries in the capital.

Some delegations may also include one or more Geneva-based officials, who are involved continuously in WTO negotiations, which take place under the auspices of the UN in Geneva. General EU policy for these negotiations is agreed on in Brussels, while responsibility for their day-to-day conduct is left in the hands of officials in the permreps of the member states and the Commission's delegation to the UN in Geneva, who meet regularly to coordinate their positions as the negotiations progress.

The Commission is represented at the full members' meetings by the Director-General of DG Trade, who is accompanied by the relevant officials from that DG and from others, depending on the points on the agenda. The official secretary of the committee, who is a Council employee, is normally resident in Geneva, but travels to Brussels every month for the full members' meetings. The administrative backup for these meetings is provided by officials from DG E (External Relations) of the Council Secretariat, and also from the Legal Service.

The Article 133 Committee also meets at the level of deputies, who tend to deal with the nuts and bolts issues of foreign trade, rather than with overall policy. Most member states are represented by officials from their capital, though some send an official from the permrep in Brussels. The Commission is also represented at these meetings.

The number and scope of expert groups reporting to the Article 133 Committee may vary, depending on the negotiations in train. In 2004, the Article 133 Committee oversaw the work of five expert groups, covering textiles, services, steel, motor vehicles and mutual recognition. Once again, they are staffed by a mixture of officials from the permreps in Brussels and from capitals, depending on the preferences of individual member states.

Functions and working methods

The Article 133 Committee, according to the various treaties, has as its task 'to assist the Commission in the negotiation of agreements between the Community and one or more states or international organisations'. In each of its formations, the committee has a busy schedule. The full members normally meet one day a month (except for August, when little or no Community business is conducted), but they may meet between these scheduled meetings should the need arise. The deputies meet on a weekly basis between the full members' meetings, which they also attend, and during WTO rounds, one or more negotiating groups will normally meet weekly. The working parties meet when necessary.

The chief task of all levels of the Article 133 Committee is the monitoring of trade and tariff agreements with third countries or organizations, the decision-making process of which consists of three distinct phases:

- political decision, in which the Council authorizes the Commission to negotiate a particular agreement;
- negotiation by the Commission, in consultation with the Article 133 Committee; and
- conclusion of the agreement by the Council.

Throughout the second phase of the process, the Commission is required to keep the committee informed regularly of the state of play in the negotiations. The Article 133 Committee is in constant consultation with its specialized working parties on particular aspects of the agreement, and keeps the Council informed of how the negotiations are proceeding. It may also request a clarification of the Council's position on particular matters, which it then relays to the Commission. The EP is kept informed throughout the negotiations.

Since it is an advisory body, no formal voting takes place in the Article 133 Committee. However, since the opinions of its members are indicative of how their ministers would vote in Council, discussions in the committee are conducted with voting weights and thresholds very much in mind. Matters are discussed until such time as a clear consensus, an effective majority or a blocking minority, has been reached. The balance of power within the committee between the representatives of the Commission and the Council is potentially fragile. The Commission would be foolish to insist on going against the wishes of the Committee (which it is legally entitled to do), for the simple reason that its members reflect the wishes of the ministers who ultimately have the power to refuse to conclude and implement the agreement negotiated by the Commission with the third party. That being said, the Commission takes the lead in trade policy, and its delegation is composed of experts with long experience of international trade negotiations and agreements, whose views can consequently carry considerable weight in the event of a disagreement between the Council and the Commission in this area.

Above all, the Article 133 Committee is characterized by pragmatism. Created essentially to act as a watchdog for the member states in trade negotiations with third countries, it has become an important partner of the Commission in these exchanges. Working with rather than against the Commission, the committee articulates the member governments' attitudes to the Commission and indicates when the latter should refer back to the Council for new or modified negotiating directives. Its perceived usefulness may be gauged from the fact that, despite not being obliged to do so by the treaties, the Commission has agreed to the creation of similar committees to assist it in most other international negotiations.

Personal relations between the members of the committee are close, particularly among the deputies, who meet more regularly than do the full members. The members of both levels serve on the committee for an average of four to five years, giving rise to a club-like atmosphere. They are on first-name terms with one another and often hold bilateral meetings in each other's capitals between the official Brussels meetings. The practice has arisen over the years of having an informal lunch or dinner together during the regular meetings of the committee, where the more difficult or sensitive items on the agenda may be discussed in a more informal and convivial atmosphere, which frequently promotes agreement.

Relations between the Article 133 Committee and Coreper are less straightforward. The full members of the committee tend to be of a similar rank in their ministries to that of the PRs in the foreign ministries, a fact that could cause problems if it was felt that the ambassadors were throwing their weight around. This rarely happens, although Article 133 officials admit that they normally try to 'tie things up' at the level of their committee, and indeed in their national capitals, so that the involvement of Coreper will not be required.

The Special Committee on Agriculture (SCA)

Origins and development

The SCA occupies a special place in the middle ground of the Council hierarchy, being the second-oldest of the preparatory committees (dating back to May 1960), and the only one to have been created by means of a 'Decision of the representatives of the governments of the member states of the EEC meeting in Council'. The creation of the committee was dictated by administrative necessity, the agricultural policy having proved to be both substantial and highly technical, requiring time-consuming and detailed work for which Coreper had neither the expertise nor the time.

Composition

The SCA meets at one level only, that of senior officials from the ministries of agriculture of each of the member states, who lead national delegations composed of agricultural experts. Some of the SCA members are attached to the permreps in Brussels, but most are based in the capitals and travel to Brussels for the committee's meetings. The Deputy Director-General of the Commission's DG Agriculture normally attends the entire meeting, and is joined by various specialized Commission officials according to the agenda item being discussed. Officials from the Council Secretariat's Directorate General for Agriculture and Fisheries

(DG B) and the Council's Legal Service attend to take notes, to help in drafting compromises and to provide additional information where required. The SCA is chaired by the representative of the member state holding the Council presidency.

Functions and working methods

The committee meets very regularly, its timetable being driven by the monthly Agriculture and Fisheries (Agfish) Council, which the members of the SCA also attend as the chief advisers to their respective ministers. The SCA meets on a weekly basis to review the work of its twenty six specialized working parties and about eighty sub-groups (one for every product subject to a common market organization), and to discuss the items to be placed on the agenda of the next Agriculture Council. The SCA's meetings frequently take place over two days, and full interpretation is provided.

Because of the specialized nature of its work, the SCA reports directly to the Agfish Council on the issues it prepares, rather than indirectly through Coreper. However, the SCA's remit is narrower than that of the Agfish Council, since Coreper I has retained for itself some groups of agricultural dossiers – for example, proposals for the harmonization of legislation, the financial aspects of agricultural proposals, agricultural trade questions concerning third countries, and animal and plant health.

The SCA's primary function, then, is the preparation of the technical (as opposed to the financial or otherwise non-agricultural) aspects of the dossiers to be treated by the ministers in the Agfish Council. This use of the word 'technical' does not mean that these questions are in any sense non-political. Indeed, the importance of the agricultural sector in many member states and the significance for the EU budget of agricultural expenditure have given negotiations in this area high political salience, arguably greater than in any other sector. None the less, over the years it has broadly been accepted by Coreper that the SCA, although basically a subordinate body, should be granted a degree of operational autonomy because of the rather specialized nature of its work.

Relations between Coreper and the SCA appear to be fairly amicable, given that the scope of their respective activities in the agriculture field is now fairly well defined. Many of the members of the SCA have extensive experience in agriculture at both national and European levels, and most visibly carry weight at home on discussions within their area of competence. The SCA is the only other preparatory body apart from Coreper to be granted the right to agree 'A' items for adoption by the Council without discussion (Culley, 2004, p. 153), a clear indication of the confidence invested in the members of this 'special committee' by their ministers.

The working parties

Just as the foundations of a building are its real strength (and are all the more effective for being invisible), so the working parties, which form the base of the Council hierarchy, support the upper echelons of the edifice. Indeed, they are essential for its very existence as an effective decision-making body. With about fifteen or twenty groups meeting in Brussels every working day, bringing together officials from each of the member states as well as from the Commission and the Council Secretariat, the working parties form the backbone of the entire process of European integration, as it is within these groups that the basis for subsequent ministerial agreement is defined and, if necessary, refined.

Origins and development

It was never intended that Coreper should fulfil its preparatory functions *vis-à-vis* the Council unaided. The original internal rules of procedure of the Council, which were adopted in 1958 and applied to all levels of the Council hierarchy, provided that Coreper 'may set up working parties and instruct them to carry out such preparatory work or studies as it shall define'. No time was lost in doing so, and, as Figure 3.1 in Chapter 3 indicates, every area of EU policy is now covered by one or more working parties engaged in the initial detailed examination of dossiers that the ambassadors and their deputies have neither the time nor the expertise to undertake. The vast majority of the working parties are created by and report to Coreper (either the ambassadors or the deputies, depending on which grouping is ultimately responsible for the preparation of the dossier in question before it goes to Council). Other working parties operate under the aegis of one of the other senior preparatory committees that, either independently or via Coreper, reports to a specialist Council.

Until the 1990s, it was difficult to determine exactly how many Council working parties were in existence at any one time, resulting in wildly differing estimates. The official list now maintained and updated regularly by the Council Secretariat in accordance with Article 19(3) of the CRPs has facilitated the task enormously. In June 2005 it contained some 283 preparatory bodies, including committees, working parties and sub-groups. However, estimation is still required to ascertain how many are in fact active at any point in time, since working parties may be permanent, temporary or *ad hoc*, and can meet at various intervals, ranging from weekly to six-monthly; they may even meet on a single occasion and then be disbanded. This list is of crucial importance to an incoming presidency, since that member state is responsible for providing both a chair and national spokesperson for every working party scheduled to meet during its term in office, and a working party may only meet under the aegis of the Council if it is included on the list.

Whatever the ambiguity surrounding the precise number of working parties, a detailed record of the number of days spent at such meetings is maintained by the Council Secretariat (see Table 3.2). As the amount and complexity of the Council's work has increased over the years, a concurrent rise in the number of working parties and the total number of days spent on them has been apparent. Table 3.2 also illustrates clearly the relative amounts of time expended on work at the various levels of the Council hierarchy.

Composition

Every working day, hundreds of national officials converge on the Justus Lipsius building in Brussels to attend the fifteen or more meetings of Council working parties scheduled for that day. These officials may have travelled from their national capital for the meeting, or may be attached to the national permrep in Brussels. The choice of whom to send is entirely up to each member state, but efficiency (and economy) normally dictate that the busiest (in the sense of most frequently convened) working parties tend to be those composed of Brussels-based national officials. To qualify as a member of a Council working party, the national official must have expertise in the subject area, ideally a working knowledge of at least English and French, and an understanding of the EU's decision-making process and procedures. Meetings of the working parties are also attended by one or more officials from the relevant Commission DG, whose job it is to present and defend the proposal on the table. Officials from the Council Secretariat provide the necessary administrative and legal backup for the negotiations, as well as experience and expertise in the policy area.

The national delegations in the working parties are composed of government representatives, operating on the basis of instructions emanating from their respective national capitals. Depending on their seniority and expertise in the area, the individual members of the group will have been more or less active in the formulation of their instructions. The same factors will have some bearing on the margin of manoeuvre they may enjoy in departing from their negotiating mandate in order to facilitate agreement within the working party. While national identity remains the overriding factor governing the behaviour of the national representatives in the working parties, there is some evidence that the individual members nevertheless often come to identify with the group as a whole, developing a feeling of mutual responsibility for the outcome of the group's work (Beyers and Dierickx, 1996, 1998). This is particularly true for those groups and individuals meeting most regularly,

Table 3.2 Days spent at meetings in the Council hierarchy, 1997–2004

Year	European Council		Council of Ministers		Coreper 1		Coreper 2		Working parties	
	Meetings	Days spent	Meetings	Days spent	Meetings	Days spent	Meetings	Days spent	Meetings	Days spent
1997	3	5	80	109.5	59	47.5	65	45	2705	2425.5
1998	2	4	92	116	57	53	59	49.5	3140	2735
1999	4	8	82	114	56	53.5	51	48	3350	2656
2000	4	10	87	117	75	60.5	55	38	3537	2679
2001	5	8	78+6	130.5	76	66	64	52.5	4216	3074
2002	4	8	76+1	108.5	87	79	69	57.5	4420	3322
2003	4+2	10	77	110.5	70	64	64	52.5	4333	3175.5
2004	4+1	8	75+1	109.5	61	57.5	67	52	3971	3037.5

Note: + indicates additional or extraordinary meetings of the European Council and Council.

Source: Data provided by the Council Secretariat.

or for many years. However, this sense of allegiance to the supranational level is viewed as being complementary and definitely secondary to their national identity (Egeberg, 1999).

Functions and working methods

The working relationship between Coreper and its working parties mirrors that between the committee and the Council, though at a lower, more technical level. Essentially, the task of the working parties is to reduce the number of problem areas to be dealt with by Coreper and subsequently by the Council. This means that the officials in the working parties concentrate on the most general as well as the most technical parts of each dossier, reaching agreement where possible, and leaving the more contentious and 'political' issues to be discussed and prepared by the members of Coreper. In so doing, they operate on the basis of the same norms that govern the work of Coreper, typified by the search for consensus, if necessary by means of compromise.

Working party agendas comprise two main types of item sent to them by Coreper. The first consists of new dossiers, coming before the working party for the first time, and requiring discussion of every point. The second consists of dossiers that have already been discussed at Coreper or even Council level after an initial discussion in the working party, and are now returning for further discussion on particular points that have not yet been the subject of agreement. Each point is discussed in turn, with the Commission presenting and defending its proposal, and the member state representatives highlighting problem areas and proposing amendments where necessary. Discussion continues until such time as the presidency judges either that a consensus in favour of a particular wording has been reached, or else that nothing further can be achieved at that time by continuing the discussion at that particular level. Any lack of agreement on specific points is indicated in the note on the meeting prepared by a Secretariat official for Coreper, as are reserves placed by delegates on offending words, phrases or even entire articles in the draft proposal. No voting takes place at working party level, although every delegate (particularly the president) operates with the relevant voting rules very much in mind.

The Secretariat's report of the working party's meeting forms the basis for discussions of that dossier in the subsequent Coreper meeting (or meetings), and the individual members of the working parties may attend these meetings as advisers to their respective Coreper members. Agreements reached at working party level (indicated in the first part of Coreper's agenda and known as Roman I points) are normally accepted as they stand, and discussion continues on those points where the working party has failed to achieve a consensus (Roman II points). Following discussion by the ambassadors or deputies (the responsible

Coreper configuration depends on the division of labour between them), the matter may be referred back to the working party for further discussion on precise points, or may be sent to the Council for approval or further discussion, depending on whether or not agreement proves possible at Coreper level. Thus Coreper and the working parties in effect prepare each other's work by providing the input that sets the parameters for the next phase of negotiations.

Clearly, the work of this lowest level of the Council hierarchy is vital for the eventual outcome of the decision-making process on the dossiers in question. Although some officials may previously have been involved in expert groups convened by the Commission when drafting its proposal, the discussion in the Council working party constitutes the first opportunity within the forum of the Council for representatives of the member states to examine and discuss a new Commission proposal in detail. The Council working party can frequently represent the only real opportunity for a member state to have its views taken into account and reflected in the final wording of the piece of legislation under discussion, since agreement reached at this level is rarely unpicked at the level of Coreper or the Council itself. A member state with a vital interest in the final shape of a particular piece of legislation must therefore ensure its representation by a well-briefed and active individual in the relevant Council working party.

Chapter 4

Bureaucrats Organize and Advise: the Council Secretariat

When it was first created in the 1950s, the Council Secretariat was designed to fulfil two main functions: conference organization and committee servicing (in other words, organizing meetings and producing minutes). But over the years, and more particularly since the 1980s, a considerable expansion in the tasks and responsibilities of the Secretariat in general, and of its administrative head in particular has taken place. Indeed, in a speech to officials in 1999, Pierre de Boissieu (at that time newly appointed as Deputy Secretary-General (DSG) of the Council) maintained that the Secretariat had made the transition from being merely necessary to becoming indispensable to the Council. Further enlargement of the Union is likely to have the effect of reinforcing rather than reversing this trend.

This chapter will start by tracing the origins and development of the Secretariat briefly, before looking in more detail at its structure, functions, working methods and relations with other European Union (EU) institutions and bodies. Finally, we shall evaluate the current position of the Secretariat, and speculate about its future role in an enlarged Union.

Origins and development

The size, shape and role of the Council Secretariat have changed dramatically over the years as a result of a number of factors, many of them external to the Secretariat itself (see Appendix 4). Of these external factors, the most significant have been:

- successive enlargements, involving recruitment (and sometimes secondment) of officials from the new member states and, in some instances, a reorganization of the structure of the Secretariat in order better to accommodate them;
- extensions to the scope of action of the Council, necessitating the creation of new administrative units within the Secretariat, sometimes with operational or executive functions;
- changes introduced in the decision-making procedures, requiring much more intensive contacts with the European Parliament (EP) than in the past (and the personnel to engage in them); and

- greater provision for majority voting, increasingly involving the Secretariat in consensus-building and the drafting of compromise texts in close cooperation with the presidency-in-office.

As is so often the case, the legal texts providing for and documenting the changes to the Council Secretariat tell only a very small part of the story. Indeed, a reliance on the legal texts alone would provide a most misleading picture. For example, a perusal of the treaties would suggest that the Council Secretariat was set up only in the 1990s, since the first treaty in which it was mentioned was the 1992 Maastricht Treaty on European Union (TEU). In fact, the Secretariat owes its existence to the Council's internal rules of procedure (CRPs), both in the case of the European Coal and Steel Community (ECSC) and the later European Economic Community (EEC) and European Atomic Energy Community (Euratom).

Article 17 of the EEC and Euratom's provisional rules of procedure of 1958 provided that:

> The Council shall be assisted by a Secretariat under the direction of a Secretary-General. The Secretary-General shall be appointed by the Council acting unanimously.

> The Council shall determine the organisation of the Secretariat.

The much more extensive article relating to the Secretariat in the most recent (2004) version of the CRPs (see Appendix 3) demonstrates the extent to which the official role and stature of the Secretariat in general, and its Secretary-General (SG) in particular, have increased over the years.

As mentioned above, the TEU was the first treaty to mention the Council Secretariat explicitly, adding it to the article that had previously been devoted solely to the Committee of Permanent Representatives (Coreper). By grouping the Secretariat and Coreper in the same article, the TEU indicated their dual responsibility for preparing the work of the Council in all its facets. The 1997 Treaty of Amsterdam (ToA) attributed an additional role to the SG – that of High Representative for the common foreign and security policy (HRCFSP) – and provided for the appointment of a DSG with responsibility for the day-to-day management of the Secretariat.

The 2001 Treaty of Nice (ToN) did away with the requirement for unanimity among the members of the Council when appointing the SG and the DSG, replacing it with a qualified majority. The paragraph relating to the Secretariat in the 2004 Constitutional Treaty (CT) does not mention the post of DSG, and specifies a voting procedure (simple majority) for decisions on the organization of the General Secretariat. Arguably, the enhanced profile of the Council in general and of the presidency in particular has propelled the Secretariat and its most senior officials into a more central role than had perhaps originally been intended for them. Indeed, in detailing the history of the Secretariat, the importance of personality should not be overlooked. It is quite legitimate to maintain that the Secretariat would not be the body it is today were it not for the vision, intellectual ability and ambition of such people as Niels Ersbøll (SG from 1980 until 1994), Jean-Claude Piris (the long-standing head of the Council Legal Service) and the current DSG, Pierre de Boissieu. Each of these men, in his own way, has contributed to the transformation of the Secretariat into the authoritative body it is today.

Evolution has now given way to rapid and, in some areas, fundamental change. Since the mid-1990s, the Secretariat has undergone a process of internal and external review, resulting in a number of fundamental structural and administrative reforms, and more are in the pipeline. The avowed aim is to streamline the Secretariat's organization and working methods, thereby enhancing its ability to meet the operational requirements of a significantly enlarged Council. These reforms will be discussed in the following sections of this chapter.

Structure of the Secretariat

The overall size of the Council Secretariat has increased steadily over the years as a result of the gradual expansion of the Council's areas of activity and successive enlargements (see Figure 4.1). Thus, the doubling in the size of the Secretariat between 1970 and 1975 can be explained by the accession of Denmark, Ireland and the United Kingdom (UK) in 1973, while the Secretariat's new responsibilities in the areas of the CFSP and justice and home affairs (JHA), as well as the accession of Austria, Finland and Sweden, account for the increase in its personnel between 1990 and 1995. The rather higher figure for 2005 is explained by the 2004 enlargement and the advent of military personnel following the establishment of the European security and defence policy (ESDP) in the late 1990s.

The structure of the Secretariat has changed more slowly, with new administrative units known as DGs (Directorates-General) being created when the Council's agenda has been extended to include a new issue area (see Appendix 4). A general tidying-up of the structure of the Secretariat has taken place in recent years, resulting in a reduced number of DGs, a regrouping of responsibilities for some of the existing DGs and new lines of command for some formerly more independent units. One example of the latter is the Press Office, which used to report directly to the SG, but is now housed within DG F, which is responsible for press, communications and protocol.

Figure 4.1   *Total staffing of the Council Secretariat, 1958–2005*

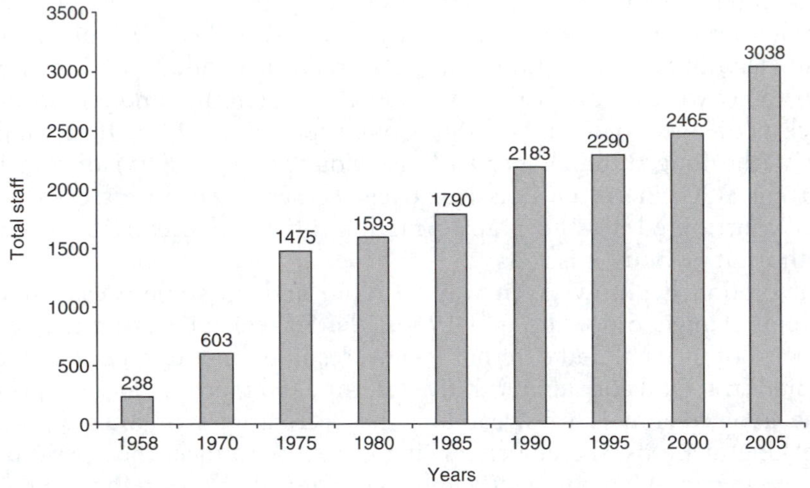

Source: Council Secretariat.

Of the eight current DGs (see Figure 4.2), two have horizontal responsibilities, while the other six are organized on a functional basis according to the Council configurations they serve. Flanked by a horizontal Legal Service, the DGs and a number of other specialized units (mentioned below) report to the SG and the DSG and their private offices. A short description of each of the different sections of the Secretariat will be followed by an analysis of their respective functions.

The Secretary-General (SG) and the Deputy Secretary-General (DSG)

The 1997 ToA laid down that the SG and the DSG of the Council would be 'appointed by the Council acting unanimously', a process in line with previous practice. Nominations for the posts are submitted by the member governments, and it is a mark of the perceived importance of these positions that the final decision has not only been taken but also actively discussed in recent years by the European Council. The appointment process can become highly political, particularly if there are a number of good candidates for the job, or if other high-profile positions are due to be filled at the same time. It is therefore not surprising that the 2001 ToN replaced the requirement of unanimity with that of qualified majority.

At first, there was no set period of tenure for the post of SG, but the incumbents tended to remain in the position for long periods of time – Javier Solana is only the fifth individual to occupy the post since 1952

Figure 4.2   *Organigram of the Council Secretariat, 2005*

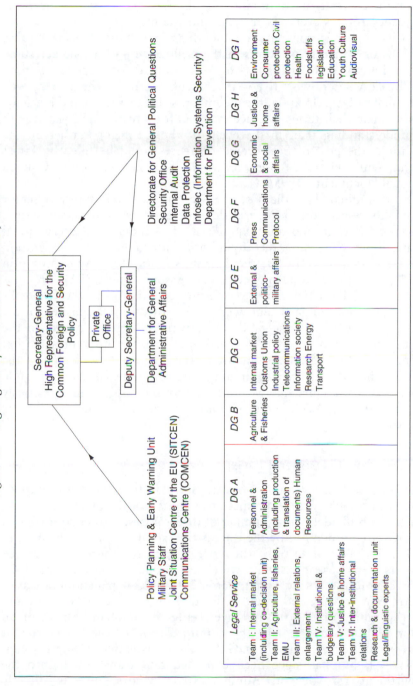

Note: There is no DG D, its areas of responsibility having been shared out among the other DGs in a reorganization of the Secretariat in 2000–2.

(see Appendix 4). These relatively long periods in office introduced an important element of continuity into the Council system, where the presidency rotates every six months and the membership of a sectoral Council can change from month to month as a result of cabinet reshuffles, elections or a myriad of events in the political life of a member state. Jürgen Trumpf was the first SG to be appointed for a specific period, and the ToA laid down a five-year renewable term for the post, as well as for that of DSG. In 2004, the incumbents, Javier Solana and Pierre de Boissieu, had their terms in office renewed for a further five years, with the understanding that, in the event of the CT being ratified in the meantime, the post of EU Foreign Minister would be filled by Javier Solana, while Pierre de Boissieu would become SG of the Council (Council Document 10995/04).

Those nominated for the post of SG in the past were typically senior and highly respected officials from the member states, normally with a diplomatic background and experience of one or more international organizations such as the the the Organisation for Economic Co-operation and Development (OECD), the North Atlantic Treaty Organisation (NATO), or the European Free Trade Association (EFTA). Previous experience of the Community system in general, and of the Council's working methods in particular, were other obvious prerequisites for the job, usually gained in the national ministry of foreign affairs in the capital and often also in the national permanent representation (permrep) in Brussels. The coupling of the post of SG with that of the HRCFSP in 1999 clearly required a rather different candidate profile. Javier Solana was eminently well qualified for the post, having previously served as SG of NATO, and being widely respected throughout Europe and beyond.

The Directorates-General (DGs)

As Figure 4.2 shows, the Council Secretariat is currently (2005) divided into eight main administrative units known as DGs, each of which is sub-divided into a number of directorates. Rather confusingly, the DGs are known not by their areas of responsibility, but by a letter (DG A, DG B, and so on). Still more perplexing, there is no DG D, since its areas of responsibility were shared out among the other DGs in a reorganization of the Secretariat in 2000–02. A small administrative reform unit was created in 2002, headed by a Director-General, and charged with drawing up and overseeing the implementation of an action plan for modernizing the administration of the Secretariat. It was initially known as the DG for Administrative Modernisation (DG MA), but has since been extended and transformed into the Department for General Administrative Affairs, and is directly attached to the DSG.

DGs A and F are horizontal departments, covering the work of the entire Council, while the other six are organized on a vertical and functional basis. In terms of numbers employed, the size of the DGs differs (see Table 4.1), the largest being DG A (personnel and administration), and the smallest DG I (environment). As the 'Secretariat's secretariat', DG A (whose responsibilities include the production and translation of the Council's documents), is bound to increase in size with enlargement and with the extension in scope of the Council's competences. Note that DG B (agriculture and fisheries) is unique among the DGs in having remained almost exactly the same size over the decade covered by Table 4.1.

Each DG is headed by a Director-General, who oversees the work of that DG's various directorates. The senior posts of Director-General are much sought-after, and in the past, when numbers allowed, were divided as evenly as possible among the member states. This practice has now been abandoned, with the result that new entrants cannot 'expect' to see one of their nationals gain such a position at entry. The main body of the Secretariat is staffed predominantly by permanent officials, who are recruited by open competition from among the nationals of the member states. They are augmented by a small number of temporary and auxiliary staff, who may be appointed to fill particular posts for a defined period. In addition, a certain number of national officials and military personnel (88 and 136, respectively, in early 2005) are seconded to the Council Secretariat to deal with CFSP, European security and defence policy (ESDP) and JHA matters, reflecting the need to bring in officials with relevant experience and specialist knowledge from member governments in these policy areas. Each member of staff is attributed an administrative grade, depending on the functions fulfilled, their seniority and relevant experience. This grading system was reformed in 2004 (see below under 'personnel policy').

Other units

The SG and the DSG share a small *cabinet* or private office, staffed with personal advisers, who work closely together. Since March 2004, they include a Coordinator for the Fight Against Terrorism (the so-called Counter-Terrorism Coodinator), Gijs de Vries. In addition, a small number of specialized units or departments are directly responsible to one or other (or both) of the Secretariat's heads (see Figure 4.2).

The relatively large numbers employed by the Legal Service (202 in 2005) bear witness not only to the fact that it covers all areas and levels of Council activity, but also to the legal and legislative nature of much of the Council's output and therefore the need for attention to legal detail. It is headed by a legal adviser at Director-General level, a post

Table 4.1   *Staffing of the Council Secretariat by Directorate-General, 1995 and 2005*

Directorate-General (DG)/ Service	1995	2005		
		Officials	National experts	Total
Cabinet	38	24	–	24
Audit Office	3	–	–	–
Services directly answerable to the SG/HR and the DSG	–	220	39	259
Legal Service	106	202	–	202
DG A (Personnel & Administration)	1756	1818	2	1820
DG B (Agriculture & Fisheries)	44	45	–	45
DG C (Internal market)	36	57	–	57
DG D (Research, Energy & Transport)	30	–	–	–
DG E (External relations)	124	185	31	216
DG F (see note below)	82	124	1	125
DG G (Economic and Social affairs)	18	42	–	42
DG H (Justice and Home affairs)	19	49	15	64
DG I (Environment)	15	32	–	32
DG J (Economic & Social cohesion)	19	–	–	–
Military Staff	–	16	136	152
Total	**2290**	**2814**	**224**	**3038**

Notes: The high figures for DG A are explained by the fact that this DG houses the directorate responsible for the production and translation of documents, a labour-intensive job.

The 2005 figure for the Audit Office is included in the group of services directly answerable to the Secretary-General/High Representative (SG/HR) and the Deputy Secretary-General (DSG) – see Figure 4.1.

Following a reorganization of the Secretariat beginning in 2000, the responsibilities of some DGs were altered:

- DG D was disbanded, and responsibility for research, energy and transport was transferred to DG C;
- DG J was disbanded, and responsibility for economic and social cohesion transferred to DG G;
- In 1995, DG F was responsible for relations with the European Parliament (EP) and institutional questions; in 2005, it was responsible for press, communications and protocol, while relations with the EP (essentially relating to the co-decision procedure) had been transferred to the Legal Service; and
- In 1995, DG G was responsible for economic and financial affairs only.

Source: Council Secretariat.

held since 1988 by Jean-Claude Piris. The Legal Service, whose members are recruited by means of a specialized competition, is divided into six teams with broad specializations (see Figure 4.2). They are assisted by a research and documentation unit and legal-linguistic experts known as jurist-linguists (see below).

Personnel policy

Until 2004, the recruitment, promotion and mobility of the Council Secretariat's officials were governed by an EU-wide personnel policy that had been variously criticised over the years for its slowness, undue emphasis on national quotas and strong unionization. The division of the Secretariat's employees into four main grades (A – administrators, including an L/A grouping of translators and jurist-linguists, B – assistant administrators, C – clerical staff; and D – support staff, such as drivers, porters, messengers and general maintenance workers), each with its own pay scale, mobility rules and promotion pattern, had given rise to much dissatisfaction, as had the occasional practice of 'parachuting' national officials into senior and much sought-after positions in the Secretariat's hierarchy. Despite these weaknesses, the Secretariat continued to attract highly qualified and motivated individuals, enabling it to provide a quality service for the Council and, by extension, for the EU as a whole.

In May 2004, a new statute came into effect, introducing reforms designed to deal with previous criticisms and to bring the EU's institutions into line with European-level legislation on working conditions. The main reforms affecting Council Secretariat officials were as follows:

- The replacement of the previous four grades (A–D) with two function groups: Administrators (ADs – previously Grades A and L/A) and Assistants (ASTs – previously Grades B and C), and the gradual replacement of Grade D officials by new 'contract agents'.
- The introduction of a new linear career structure and pay scale with a greater number of smaller steps, designed to offer clearer incentives for good performance and greater possibilities for increased mobility.
- The possibility for Assistants (ASTs) to transfer to the Administrator (AD) function by means of a certification or attestation procedure (rather than via competition, as was previously the case).
- A modification of the pension scheme and the system of allowances.
- The provision of more modern working conditions, such as the right to work part-time, job-sharing and improved family-related leave.

The Secretariat's employees are chosen through an EU-wide selection process. They are drawn almost exclusively from the EU member states, although a small number of non-EU nationals are also employed from time to time to perform specific tasks for which they may be uniquely qualified. Open competitions or *concours* are organized for the recruitment of administrative and executive officers, in which the candidates are tested on their general knowledge, linguistic ability, knowledge of EU affairs and expertise in their field. More specialized competitions are held when necessary in order to recruit lawyers, jurist-linguists and translators, or other specialized individuals. Openings for other posts, such as secretaries and clerical staff, are advertised in national newspapers.

A tacit system of national quotas is operated, with recruitment procedures ensuring a fair representation of all EU nationalities among the Secretariat's staff. The accession of new member states results in the recruitment of a certain number of nationals of those states, although they can no longer automatically expect access to the more senior posts in the Secretariat merely as a result of accession. The Council Secretariat was expected to expand eventually by about 680 as a result of the 2004 enlargement, although only a small number of new recruits were *in situ* on the date of accession (1 May 2004).

In general, the calibre of the Secretariat's officials is not in question, enjoying as they do a reputation for high levels of professionalism, neutrality and integrity. The formal recruitment procedure for the administrative officials is highly competitive (if woefully slow), with the result that those taken on are unquestionably intelligent, capable and highly motivated. Maintaining these high levels of motivation, however, can prove more difficult, since much of the work, particularly at the lower levels, is purely administrative, with long hours being spent at meetings, following and recording the discussions of experts in their particular areas of responsibility. Nevertheless, there are many opportunities for an active desk officer to have a real effect on outcomes: first, through the building-up of contacts with officials from the member states, the EP and the Commission; and second, by means of the provision of written notes to, and oral briefing of, the presidency. However, much depends on the approach of the individual and of their more senior colleagues.

New entrants are struck by two main features of the Secretariat's management. The first is a rather rigid hierarchical structure, which concentrates management responsibility at the most senior levels. Many recruits have come from jobs where they were responsible for managing teams, and regret their inability to use this previous experience in the Secretariat. Some changes may eventually occur as a result of the 2004 reforms, and others are under discussion in an ongoing action plan for administrative modernization. The second striking feature for newcomers is the extent of unionization within the Secretariat, with decisions on mobility and promotion being taken by powerful *comités paritaires*, composed of officials from DG A (responsible for personnel) and union officials drawn from the other DGs, in equal numbers. While such a system has obvious benefits in terms of transparency, it can also have the effect of delaying and diffusing responsibility for decision-making on mobility and promotions, a source of much frustration for all involved.

Functions of the Secretariat

Four principal functions of the main body of the Council Secretariat are laid down in Article 23 of the CRPs : first, organizing; second, coordinating; third, ensuring the coherence of the Council's work and implementation of its annual programme; and, fourth, assisting the presidency in seeking solutions. These rather vague guidelines may be interpreted as broadly or as narrowly as those in charge see fit, and indeed the functions of the Secretariat can (and do) differ over time, depending on the role envisaged for it by the member states, the presidency and senior officials in the Secretariat itself. Treaty reform, accession negotiations and new areas of Council activity can also entail additional functions for specific parts or levels of the Secretariat (see below). Other Secretariat functions mentioned in the Council's rules of procedure include monitoring the completion of the written procedure, drawing up the draft Council budget, administering the funds placed at the disposal of the latter and representing the presidency before EP committees. Before examining how the Secretariat's four principal functions are fulfilled, we should first examine the role played by the two most senior members of the Secretariat.

The Secretary-General (SG) and the Deputy Secretary-General (DSG)

According to Article 23.1 of the CRPs, the SG has overall responsibility for the Secretariat. However, this is a 'twin-hatted' role and it is the wearing of the second hat – that of HRCFSP – that takes up the majority of the incumbent's time. In fulfilling this latter function, the SG is required to 'assist' the Council and the presidency, but the undoubted ability and unequalled experience of Javier Solana mean that it sometimes appears as if the relationship has been reversed. Inevitably, the job demands a great deal of travel, and Javier Solana has not shirked this aspect of the position. Indeed, there have been times when he has been present in Brussels for only one day a month. Days spent in Brussels are taken up with meetings, either of EU-level bodies or with representatives of third countries or organizations.

Given the demands of the job of SG/HRCFSP, the appointment of a DSG to take responsibility for the running of the Secretariat itself made a great deal of sense. The day-to-day administration of the Secretariat covers everything from personnel policy to the Council's internal budget, from building programmes to inter-institutional relations, to substantive preparation and attendance of meetings at the highest level – the list goes on and on. Add to this preparations for enlargement, and the need to institute reforms in order to prepare the Secretariat to meet the needs of an enlarged Council, and it is clear that Pierre de Boissieu's agenda, too, has been well-filled since 1999.

The SG and the DSG share a private office or *cabinet*, which operates slightly apart from and independently of the rest of the Secretariat, a fact that can give rise to some tensions. The *cabinet* maintains close links with officials from each of the member states and therefore works best when it is composed of a good cross-section of nationalities and not dominated by any one of them. The overall task of the *cabinet* is to assist the SG and the DSG in fulfilling their duties. Specifically, they are involved in coordinating and overseeing the work of the entire Secretariat and liaising with the presidency in order to foster continuity and coherence across the work of the Council.

The Legal Service

The horizontal Legal Service has three main functions. First, it acts as the Council's solicitor, advising all levels of the Council hierarchy on the legality of their proposed actions. Second, it may be required to fulfil the role of barrister for the Council, by pleading for the latter in the event of the Council having to appear before the European Court of Justice (ECJ) or the Court of First Instance (CFI). Third, its jurist-linguists behave as both legal and linguistic advisers, since they are responsible for ensuring the legal compatibility of all texts placed before and adopted by the Council (see below, in the discussion on coherence.)

Every meeting that takes place within the Council system, from the highest profile session of the European Council to the most infrequently meeting working party, needs the expertise of the Council's Legal Service. The Council must fulfil its commitments in a legal manner, and any proposed amendments must be compatible with EU law and any other legislation that might apply. As a result, the delegation from the Council Secretariat normally includes at least one official from the Legal Service, who may be called upon to clarify the legal position regarding a proposed amendment or a proposed course of action. This is particularly true in those areas where the member states have a greater right of initiative – for example, in some aspects of JHA.

It is hardly surprising that the Legal Service has a special role to play in the context of intergovernmental conferences (IGCs) and conventions, since the outcome of their deliberations is normally a legally binding agreement, whether in the form of a treaty or a declaration to which member states subscribe. For this reason, the head of the Council's Legal Service *ex officio* becomes the independent legal adviser to an IGC, and a number of members of his staff assist the presidency in its IGC-related tasks (see Christiansen, 2002; Beach, 2004).

The Directorates-General (DGs)

The DGs constitute the main body of the Secretariat, and it is here, along with the Legal Service, that the functions of organization, coordination, coherence and assistance are fulfilled. The two horizontal DGs (DG A – Personnel, Administration and Human Resources, and DG F – Press, Communication and Protocol) are involved in the organization and coordination of the work of the Secretariat as a whole. Each of the other six DGs coordinates the work of one or more related Council configurations through all stages of the decision-making process within the Council and with the EP. In addition, the more senior officials may become involved, along with the Legal Service, in ensuring the coherence of the Council's work across the board, and assisting the presidency in seeking solutions in the course of negotiations.

Organization

Conference organization is what the Council Secretariat does most, and best. About 90 per cent of the Secretariat's staff perform managerial and organizational functions such as the convening of meetings, the preparation of meeting rooms and the production of the many documents required by those attending sessions of the ministerial and European Councils and their various preparatory bodies. Document production is the most labour-intensive and time-consuming of these tasks, since the Secretariat is responsible for producing, translating, photocopying, distributing and archiving large numbers of documents every year. (Almost 92,000 documents were distributed by the Secretariat in 2003, necessitating just under 92 million copies.) This task has been facilitated to some extent by the vastly increased use of personal computers and email, but still represents a considerable drain on the Secretariat's resources. In fulfilling this function, the Secretariat works closely with the presidency-in-office.

Coordination

Being a supranational, permanent body composed of specialized officials, the Council Secretariat is well placed to undertake both the vertical and the horizontal coordination of all aspects of the Council's work. This covers both the day-to-day work of the Council (preparing, following and implementing the decisions of scheduled meetings of the Council and its preparatory bodies), as well as those additional secretarial tasks with which it is endowed because of its function as the Council's secretariat. Of the latter, two will be mentioned here: undertaking the function of Secretariat for, first, IGCs and conventions; and, second, for accession negotiations.

Regarding the Secretariat's day-to-day work, about 10 per cent of its officials are involved in committee servicing, a task that has several facets and spans three distinct time periods. In advance of each meeting (working party, Coreper or Council), the officials from the relevant DGs assist the presidency in preparing a provisional agenda, and may also provide briefing notes and tactical advice for the person chairing the meeting. During meetings, officials from the Legal Service may be asked to provide procedural and legal advice, while officials from the DGs take notes on the discussion, and may assist in drafting amendments. Once the meetings are over, these same officials are responsible for preparing the reports (in the case of working party and Coreper meetings) or draft minutes of the (Council) meeting (to be agreed on when the group next meets), which form the basis for further discussions (Nicoll, 1993).

The importance of the Secretariat's rather mundane-sounding task of minute-taking at Council meetings should not be underestimated, for at least three reasons. First, the Secretariat's minutes constitute the only official record of most of the meetings that take place within the Council hierarchy, since the practice of making and storing tapes of meetings was discontinued early in the new millennium. National delegates may take their own notes of the Council meetings they attend, but intra- and inter-delegation discussions at the margins of the meeting mean that they may not be as complete as those of the Secretariat officials, who have no position to defend and can therefore concentrate on note-taking. The televising of parts of some Council sessions provides an additional record of what was, or was not, said during those discussions, but this does not apply to the lower (and in many respects more productive) levels of the Council hierarchy.

Second, the accuracy of the official minutes is vitally important for the definitive adoption of decisions. The Secretariat's reports must be extremely precise, particularly where definitions, dates and figures are involved, since even a small discrepancy between what was agreed and what is detailed in the minutes could have the effect of dismantling a painfully worked-out compromise. Third, as the official recorders of Council agreements, Secretariat note-takers have an additional responsibility because, in the event of the Council being taken to court, their minutes may be used in the ensuing legal proceedings.

The resources of the Council Secretariat in Brussels are put at the disposal of IGCs and conventions organized within the EU. The normal practice is that a small secretariat for the IGC or convention is established, normally headed by a senior Secretariat official (often from the Legal Service), to which executive officials from the Council Secretariat are seconded for the duration, with logistical support being provided by the permanent services of the Council Secretariat. The president of the 2002–3 Convention on the Future of Europe (CFE) took a slightly different route, by appointing a non-*fonctionnaire* (a retired British diplomat) to head its secretariat, which was composed of five seconded officials from the Council Secretariat (of various nationalities and backgrounds), in addition to officials from the Commission, the EP and national diplomatic services (see Deloche-Gaudez, 2004; Norman 2005, pp. 31–3).

The perceived role of a secretariat in an IGC or a convention is that of an administrative assistant, a body to provide the logistical underpinning ensuring that the decision-makers can fulfil their mandate. In reality, a secretariat can be a very influential actor in such forums, chiefly because of their complexity. IGCs and (even more so) conventions bring together large numbers of participants to discuss a range of issues, both technical and political. Information and expertise are key to this process, and the secretariat frequently has the monopoly in these areas. It occupies a strategic position at the hub of the process, may be involved in drafting the texts on which subsequent discussions (and decisions) are based, and may be viewed by other participants as a trusted adviser or mediator (see Beach, 2004; Deloche-Gaudez, 2004).

The negotiation and drafting of accession agreements constitutes a large task for the Secretariat as the administrative and legal assistant of the member states. Indeed, the drafting of the 2003 Accession Treaty to admit ten new member states has been described as 'the single biggest task ever undertaken by the General Secretariat' (Willocks, 2003, p. 111). An Enlargement Working Group, composed of senior diplomats from each of the fifteen member states and chaired by the presidency, met regularly to draw up the common positions that eventually became the Union's official position in the bilateral Accession Conferences with each of the candidate states. A small, specially created team of Secretariat officials attended all meetings of the Enlargement Working Group, drafted and produced the amended texts that formed the basis of the discussion for subsequent meetings, and was responsible for ensuring consistency between the various common positions being prepared in parallel. The conclusion of negotiations in December 2002 marked the start of another major task for the Secretariat – the drafting of the Accession Treaty.

A special Drafting Group of (the fifteen) member state representatives was created in parallel to the Enlargement Working Group, with the Council Secretariat once again providing administrative, logistic and legal support. A single treaty document was drawn up in English, translated into the twenty other official EU languages, put on to CD-ROMs and distributed to the various parties for agreement. The signing of the Accession Treaty in Athens in April 2003 marked the end of an important task for the Council Secretariat, which had been fulfilled successfully in addition to the Secretariat's other basic tasks.

Coherence

The work of the Council covers a wide range of policy areas, is presided over by a rotating group of national officials, and is conducted in up to twenty distinct languages simultaneously (see Box 4.1). Ensuring coherence is therefore of the utmost importance. It is not enough for the left hand to know what the right hand is doing: both must be grasping the same rope and pulling in a similar direction. Clearly, this requires close coordination in a number of arenas and at a number of levels:

- within each member state, at both intra-ministerial and inter-ministerial level (see Chapter 9); this need obviously becomes particularly acute when a member state holds the presidency of the Council;
- between the main EU institutions – that is, the Council, the Commission and the EP (see Chapters 7 and 8); and
- within the Council itself.

The main responsibility for ensuring the coherence of the Council's work falls to the Council Secretariat, as one of the few permanent fixtures of the Council hierarchy. Regular meetings and contacts between the SG, the DSG and the Directors-General are designed to pool information on the activities of the various Council configurations, and to avoid incompatible (or worse, contradictory) outcomes. While the SG and the DSG shoulder the ultimate burden, it is the Legal Service (and more specifically the jurist-linguists) who carry out the duty of ensuring the legal coherence of Council activity on a day-to-day basis.

The chief task of the Legal Service is to ensure that every binding text produced in the name of the Council is both legally correct and coherent in the language in which it has been drafted (increasingly, in English, though often by non-native speakers). The jurist-linguists are responsible for determining that, when translated, the agreed text says and means exactly the same thing in each of the EU's official languages. There are three main aspects to the jurist-linguist's job. First, and most basically, they are responsible for ensuring that the translated texts are true to the original and to each other. Second, they may be required to adjust some of the terminology contained in the text, since most documents are the subject of amendment by non-lawyers in the course of meetings at various levels of the Council hierarchy, and the resulting non-legal language may need to be tightened up. Finally, the basic text as a whole may require clarification in order to be readily comprehensible to those to whom it is addressed. The low public profile of the jurist-linguists belies the vital importance of their work. Careless drafting or inaccurate translation of technical documents could result in the adoption of inconsistent or incoherent legislation and in uneven implementation between member states, thereby reducing the credibility of the Council as a legislative body.

Assistance in seeking solutions

Council officials have long been involved unofficially in advising the presidency, a task that has arisen naturally out of the Secretariat's central and avowedly neutral involvement in the Council's decision-making process. Their official right to do so, however, has only recently (in 2002) been acknowledged, in the sense of being alluded to explicitly in the Council's internal rules of procedure (in Article 23.3). This provision makes it abundantly clear, however, that such assistance is subject to the 'responsibility and guidance of the Presidency'. In addition, the extent of Secretariat involvement in advice and mediation will depend on the outlook, ability and inclination of the SG and his/her staff, as well as the attitude of individual national delegations.

However, presidencies faced with increasing numbers of often very technical dossiers have come to rely more and more on the advice of a Secretariat with many years of accumulated experience in keeping dossiers moving and finding compromise solutions which find favour with at least a majority of players. Such advice may be tactical (for example, the order in which to treat issues in a meeting, or to call on delegations to speak on a particular point) or substantive (for example, a proposal for a draft compromise text or a legal precedent allowing a certain mode of behaviour). Where the Secretariat official in question enjoys the respect and confidence of both the presidency and the national delegations, he or she may even get involved in mediating in disputes between delegations. In some cases, the Secretariat may even be required to draft in the name of the presidency.

How much influence the Secretariat exercises is, of course, hard to pin down exactly. Evidence has to be gathered from actual participants, while keeping in mind that the latter may not be completely reliable or sufficiently neutral to give either a complete or a realistic account of what has occurred. Yet Council insiders and practitioners readily acknowledge that the Secretariat (or at least certain officials in it, and not always the most senior) can and do play a central role in negotiations within the Council hierarchy, and while representing the Council *vis-à-vis* other institutions.

Working methods

Three elements of the Secretariat's work and working methods will be examined here: the production of documents; the linguistic regime; and the issue of transparency.

Production of documents

When preparing documents for the Council and its preparatory bodies, Secretariat officials have access to document templates and a detailed guide for their production (issued for the first time in March 2003). These practical aids for officials are an acknowledgement of the fact that an effective Council is dependent on documents that aid rather than hinder the negotiating process. In the enlarged Union, the need for clear and concise documents is even more acute. The documents produced by a typical Secretariat desk-officer at the different stages of the Council's decision-making process are as follows:

- 'Note to working party members' after a meeting, attached to a redrafted text. For those articles on which agreement could not be reached, the positions of the national delegations are contained in footnotes.
- 'Note to Coreper from the working party', outlining the main dates in the process, the stage that has been reached and the positions of key member states. The text under negotiation is attached to the note.
- 'Note to the chair of Coreper from the Secretariat', a more tactical document, which may include speaking notes. It may propose how to deal with the issue in Coreper, and the reasons for the positions being taken by certain member states, as well as which positions may be negotiable.
- 'Note from Coreper to the Council', similar to that from the working party to Coreper, and attached to the redrafted text, at this stage translated into all EU languages.
- 'Note to the chair of the Council from the Secretariat', similar to that to the chair of Coreper.

The documents produced by the Secretariat are designed to equip the Council and its preparatory bodies with the necessary background information and tactical advice to fulfil their decision-making functions as quickly and efficiently as possible. To this end, the documents are required either to provide a snapshot of the current state of the dossier under discussion, or else to introduce a new element designed to move the negotiations forward. In an EU where team presidencies appear to be the inescapable future, the existence of a streamlined, supranational and expert administrative body capable of producing documents of a consistently high standard and designed to move the debate forward will be essential.

Linguistic regime

The question of language in the EU is a sensitive one, and increases in complexity with each successive enlargement. Even before the 2004 enlargement increased the number of the institutions' official and working languages from eleven to twenty (see Box 4.1), the EU had

Box 4.1 *Official and working languages in the European Union, 2005*

Two sets of rules govern languages in the EU.

The first applies to the various basic treaties, the treaties amending them (together known as the constituent treaties) and agreements between the member states. These texts are drawn up in each of the official languages of the member states, and are deemed to be authentic in each one. In the EU-15, there were twelve such languages. As of 1 May 2004, there were **twenty-one official languages of the European Union** (see below).

The second applies to the institutions of the EU, and covers acts of the institutions and working languages. During its accession negotiations, Ireland waived the right to Irish becoming an official language of the institutions of the Community, but succeeded in having this situation reversed (subject to certain restrictions – see Council document 9645/05) in June 2005. Consequently, in the EU-15, there were eleven such languages. As of 1 May 2004, there were **twenty official and working languages of the European institutions**, and as of June 2005, **twenty-one such languages** (although the rules relating to Irish are only due to come into effect in 2007).

These are the official rules relating to the linguistic regime in the EU. The reality is sometimes rather different. Ensuring a sufficient supply of suitably skilled translators and interpreters to deal with the EU's linguistic needs is a tall order, and often the system cannot cope. So, for example, a pragmatic decision was taken in 2004 to waive the right of Maltese speakers to have all EU legislation made available in their native tongue for a period of three years, while the necessary personnel were trained and recruited.

In order to distinguish them one from another, documents produced in the different languages are identified by means of a two-letter code (see below). This replaces the previous system of colour-coding, which was unsustainable post-enlargement.

+ Czech	CZ	Danish	DA
German	DE	Greek	EL
English	EN	Spanish	ES
+ Estonian	ET	Finnish	FI
French	FR	° Irish	GA
+ Hungarian	HU	Italian	IT
+ Lithuanian	LT	+ Latvian	LV
+ Maltese	MT	Dutch	NL
+ Polish	PL	Portuguese	PT
+ Slovak	SK	+ Slovenian	SL
Swedish	SV		

Notes: + New in May 2004; ° Until June 2005, an official language of the EU only; thereafter also an official and working language of the European institutions, subject to certain restrictions (see Council document 9645/05).

more working languages than any other major body or international organization in the world. This linguistic diversity may be viewed as both a hallmark and a major asset of the EU, contributing as it does to the principles of equality, democracy and transparency that underpin the entire enterprise. The laudable aim is that any EU citizen should be able to obtain information about the EU in general, and the ongoing work and output of its institutions in particular, in the official language(s) of their member state. Where the Council is concerned, this means the interested public having access to documents, public Council debates and agreed legislation in their native tongue, and national officials and ministers being provided with the necessary translation and interpretation services to facilitate their full involvement in the Council and its preparatory bodies.

But linguistic diversity in the Council comes at a price. Although one important aspect of this price is obviously financial (and actual figures are virtually impossible to come by), there are also other costs that cannot be entered on a balance sheet. Extra time must be factored into the negotiating and decision-making processes in order to allow for simultaneous interpretation during meetings, the translation of the documents under discussion into each of the working languages between certain meetings, and the translation and linguistic checking of the agreed legislation into each of the Union's official languages before it can finally be adopted, published and implemented. Specialists must be employed to undertake this work, and be provided with the necessary technological and administrative infrastructure to produce it. Less tangibly, the officials involved in EU decision-making must learn to cope with the complexity, the uncertainty and, at times, the sheer frustration of operating in a multilingual environment, where words and their meanings are of the utmost importance. In an enlarged Union, such costs can be expected to increase exponentially, and ways will have to be found to reduce them if efficiency is not to be adversely affected.

The notion of moving, where possible, to a reduced number of working languages within the Council has much to recommend it, but member states have been hesitant to stick their heads above the parapet and make a formal proposal to this effect. Instead, the tendency has been to avoid confrontation and to allow a system to emerge based on pragmatism. But the step-change engendered by the 2004 enlargement has resulted in tough questions about necessity, efficiency and payment being posed behind the scenes, however tentatively, and answers are emerging only very slowly and painfully with regard to interpretation and translation.

Interpretation

The Council does not employ its own simultaneous interpreters, but leases the services of interpreters based in the Commission's DG for

Interpretation (formerly the Joint Interpretation and Conference Service – JICS), supplemented by free-lancers. Up to eleven teams of interpreters are available for meetings within the Council hierarchy on any given working day, their composition depending on need and availability. Full interpretation (into and out of each of the (currently) twenty working languages) is provided for all meetings of the Council and the European Council, with each member of these bodies having the chance to express him/herself in their own language. Senior preparatory bodies such as Coreper and the Economic and Financial Committee (EFC) conduct their formal meetings in three languages only (English, French and German), and operate in English and French (increasingly English only) in informal gatherings, such as working lunches.

Further down the hierarchy, however, a certain degree of pragmatism has operated for some time, because of a lack of space, personnel and money, with the result that interpretation has been provided on a needs-related basis. Some working parties have been provided with full or partial interpretation (often by relay), others have used a restricted number of languages, and a small number, particularly if composed exclusively of Brussels-based officials, have operated without any interpretation at all. The decisions relating to the allocation of interpreters have also been based on availability, and the number and requirements of other groups meeting at the same time.

Following discussions at the level of the Antici Group (see Chapter 3) in 2003, a new approach to the provision of interpretation services in the enlarged EU was proposed, consisting of three main elements:

- a substantial reduction in the number of preparatory bodies entitled to meet with full interpretation (into and out of the twenty working languages);
- an increase in the number of preparatory bodies that would meet without any interpretation at all; and
- the introduction of an 'on request' system for other preparatory bodies, financed by an 'envelope' of 2 million euros per language included in the Council budget.

It was estimated that such a regime would cost some 55 million euros in 2004, rising to 61 million in 2005 (see Council document 10174/03).

In an ideal world, delegates from the new member states would have had access to simultaneous interpretation at all meetings within the Council hierarchy from 1 May 2004. However, finding sufficient numbers of interpreters with the requisite qualifications and experience proved very difficult, with the result that many positions will remain unfilled for some time. Priority has been given to providing simultaneous interpretation for meetings of the Council and the European Council, while the Council as a whole has agreed to a three-year derogation for the provision of interpretation into and out of Maltese.

Translation

DG A III of the Council Secretariat is responsible for the translation and production of the Council's working documents, and has consequently been the largest directorate in the Secretariat. Prior to the 2004 enlargement, the then eleven language divisions were composed of about fifty-two officials each, but the aim now is to limit the number of translators to twenty-five per language division. This will be achieved through a gradual reduction in the numbers in the pre-enlargement divisions and the recruitment of only twenty-five officials per new language division. In effect, the translation work for twenty-one languages will be achieved with pre-enlargement (or even lower) numbers of translation staff.

This ambitious aim can and will only be achieved in tandem with other decisions that have been taken regarding document production within the Council. It has been recommended that fewer, shorter and better-quality documents be produced, and that the instances where translation will be required will be reduced. To this latter end, it has been decided that, in future, greater use will be made of relay and two-way translation, and only so-called 'core documents' will be translated at specific points in the decision-making process. Examples of such documents (contained in a Council Secretariat guide for producing documents for the Council and its preparatory bodies) are:

- draft legislation at certain 'milestone' stages (Commission proposal, important stages where the proposal is being examined by the working party, and each time the dossier is referred to the Coreper and the Council, provided deadlines are respected);
- agendas for the Council;
- 'A' item notes and their addenda;
- Council minutes; and
- European Council Presidency conclusions.

One final point as regards translation: Article 14.2 of the Council's rules of procedure provides that any member of the Council is entitled to oppose discussion of a text if any proposed amendments are not drawn up in a specified official working language. Recourse to this provision can be employed as a delaying tactic, allowing the member state in question more time to consider an amendment. Such a tactic needs to be used with some caution, however, because of the pressure it puts on the Secretariat's translation service, and the dilution of goodwill it can engender among the other members of the negotiating group. In urgent circumstances, the group can always agree unanimously that amendments will be accepted only in a given number of languages.

Transparency

The democratic accountability of the Council has always been an issue of great concern to both proponents and detractors of the process of European integration in general, and of the Council in particular. Claims that the Council is an over-secretive body that operates far from the public gaze have proved hard to shake off, even after reforms designed to refute them were introduced from the early 1990s onwards. As the body responsible for drafting the official minutes of Council meetings, holding the records of voting behaviour and maintaining the official archives of the Council, the Secretariat holds the key to important information to which many observers would welcome greater and easier access.

The major responsibility for the implementation of these reforms has therefore fallen on the Council Secretariat, which has had to adapt its organization and working practices in order to meet the challenges of the Council's evolving transparency policy. Initial resistance, arising out of entrenched attitudes and long-standing practices of secrecy, have gradually given way to a more open approach, although the rules governing access to sensitive and military information continue to give rise regularly to heated debate. Following the adoption of a joint Regulation regarding public access to EP, Council and Commission documents in May 2001 (OJ L 145, 31.5.2001, p. 43), a code of good administrative behaviour for the Council Secretariat was adopted as a decision of the Secretary-General in June 2001 (OJ C 189, 5.7.2001, pp. 1–4). It acts as a guide to Secretariat staff in their professional relations with the public, and covers such issues as non-discrimination, courtesy and data protection.

There are four main strands to the Council's transparency policy today: public access to documents, public access to the decision-making process, information policy and the quality of drafting of Community legislation (see Box 4.2). Proponents of greater transparency can still find much to criticize, but real progress has been made in several areas.

Public access to documents

Technology has been the key to improved access to current and previous Council documents, not only for the public, but also for

Box 4.2   *The Council's transparency policy*

Aspects	Means

Public access to documents	• Direct:
	  • Official Journal (OJ – in paper and electronic form);
	  • Internet (Register of Documents on Council website (http://consilium.eu.int); and
	  • Archives (most documents over 30 years old);
	
	• Indirect:
	  • By application in writing to the Council Secretariat; access may be:
	  • granted in full;
	  • granted in part; or
	  • refused.

Public access to the decision-making process	• Publication (on Council website) of draft agendas of Council and preparatory meetings; • Open Council debates and deliberations (when acting as legislator); • Publication (on Council website) of votes and explanations of votes taken in Council meetings (when acting as legislator); • Publication of minutes of meetings and statements in minute
Information policy	• Press Office (Directorate-General (DG) F) relays information to the media; • Public Information Unit (DG F) deals with requests for access to documents; • Official Journal publishes official documents; • Internet site (www.consilium.eu.int) publishes official and working documents, news of Council activities, etc. (see Appendix 2); • Publications; • Visits by groups to Justus Lipsius; • Library (Brussels); and • Historical archives (Brussels and Florence).
Quality of drafting of Community legislation	• Inter-institutional agreement on common guidelines for the quality of drafting of Community legislation adopted by the European Parliament (EP), the Council and the Commission, December 1998 (OJ C73, 17.3.1999, p. 1); and • Joint Practical Guide drawn up by the Legal Services of the EP, the Council and the Commission, March 2000

interested individuals working in other EU institutions or at the margins of the decision-making process. An early criticism that the public's right of access to documents (granted in 1993) was hindered by not knowing what documents actually existed was rectified by the creation of a register of documents in January 1999, which is updated on a daily basis by the Council Secretariat. However, as many members of the public have discovered to their cost, tracking down a document in the register does not automatically mean that it is directly or completely available. If a document is classified *'limité'*, the member of the public who wishes to obtain a copy of it must address a request in writing to the Public Information Unit in the Council Secretariat, which decides whether or not to release the document (see below). If partial access to the document is granted, the recipient may find that certain parts of it have been deleted, or that, for example, the names of delegations have been blocked out, as well as any content that would make it possible to identify the origin of the position.

All the Council's legislative acts, as well as a broad range of information and communication documents, are published in the *Official Journal of the European Communities* (OJ), to which the public has free access, either in EU documentation centres in the member states, or via the Council's website (www.consilium.eu.int – see Appendix 2 for more details). Council documents dating from the 1970s or earlier are held in the historical archives in Brussels and Florence, and are a valuable resource for researchers.

Public access to the decision-making process

The existence and widespread use of the internet has greatly facilitated the rapid provision of information relating to the Council's decision-making process. Thus draft agendas of Council and senior preparatory meetings, information on votes and explanations of votes taken in Council meetings where the Council is acting as a legislator, and minutes of Council meetings, are all available on the Council's website. Such information, however, while helpful for tracking legislation through the various stages of the decision-making process, is frequently lacking in the nuance and political detail most sought-after by Council observers.

Much has been made of the opening-up of parts of Council meetings to the public, as provided for in Article 8 of the CRPs, and indeed the presence of television cameras in the Council chamber during ministerial discussions is a truly innovative step. The cheers quickly die down, however, with the realization that what is being transmitted is very general orientation debates, a small number of public policy debates, and the beginning and end stages of the decision-making process on acts subject to the co-decision procedure. The cameras are therefore not present for the more interesting cut and thrust of negotiation and bargaining, which continues away from the public gaze. Little surprise is expressed by insiders at the low level of public interest in what then amount to stage-managed events.

Information policy

The hub of the Council's information policy is DG F in the Council Secretariat, which was restructured in recent years in order to group together under one roof the press service (previously attached to the SG's private office), the communication service (responsible for relations with the public in general), and the protocol service.

The principal task of the Council's Press Service is to provide the media with up-to-date and authoritative information and documentation on all areas of Council activity. On a day-to-day basis, this means following and documenting the work of each of the Councils, updating a large part of the Council website and dealing with specific requests for information from the large corps of Brussels-based journalists covering EU affairs. The ten or so administrative grade officials who comprise the service concentrate on the work of one or more Councils, and there is a dedicated spokesperson for the SG/HRCFSP. Accredited journalists have access to the Council Press Centre in the Justus Lipsius complex, which is managed by the Press Office. It includes facilities for over a thousand journalists, a large auditorium where official press conferences take place, and numerous smaller rooms, which are made available to individual delegations to brief the media.

The members of the Press Service brief journalists before Coreper and Council meetings on their areas of specialization, and are on hand to provide additional information during and after such meetings. A press release is produced very rapidly after every Council meeting (usually the following day, but sometimes on the day itself), providing information about what was discussed and decided. Before, during and in the aftermath of European Council meetings in Brussels, the members of the Press Service work closely with officials from the presidency member state in communicating with the media, as well as ensuring that rooms and other necessary facilities are available for press conferences and briefings by and for non-presidency delegations and journalists. Press Service officials also write press releases and background notes for the media briefing provided by the presidency in advance of Council and European Council meetings.

The Public Information Unit (also known as the Transparency Unit) is the body within the Secretariat that deals with written requests from members of the public for access to documents not directly available from the Council's website. Officials in this unit, in collaboration with other Secretariat and national officials, decide whether or not to grant access to requested documents, and whether access should be full or partial. This service has been available since 1997, and the number of applications has increased dramatically since that date, as Table 4.2 shows. Initially, an increasing proportion of such applications was successful, but since the implementation of a decision (taken at the end of 2001) to allow only partial access to some documents, the proportion of documents released in full has fallen somewhat. Taken together, however, the proportion of documents released either wholly or partially has been consistently over 80 per cent since 1998.

DG F also oversees the production of various brochures and publications, some of which are destined for Council officials, while others are aimed at the general public. DG F is responsible too for the maintenance and constant updating of the Council website, the organization of group visits to the Justus Lipsius building in Brussels, and the management of the Council's library and archives.

Quality of drafting of Community legislation

Public access to documents is pointless if the documents themselves are written in language that is unintelligible to the ordinary citizen, a maxim that applies particularly to legislative texts, in which the rights and obligations of citizens are set out. A meaningful transparency policy must therefore include the notion of quality drafting to produce clear, accessible and intelligible documents. A 1993 Council Resolution on the quality of drafting (facetiously termed 'the Ten Commandments' by insiders) was supplemented in 1998 by an inter-institutional agreement (IIA) on common guidelines for the quality of drafting of Community legislation (OJ C 73 17.3.1999, p. 1). The Legal Services of the three institutions involved produced a Joint Practical Guide for officials in 2000, and the Secretariat has provided training and information technology tools to aid the process.

Relations with other institutions and bodies

As the permanent, Brussels-based administrative arm of the EU's principal decision-making body, the Council Secretariat has ongoing contacts

Table 4.2 Public access to Council documents, 1997–2004

	1997	1998	1999	2000	2001	2002	2003	2004
No. of applications	282	338	889	1,294	1,234	2,394	2,830	2,160
No. of documents reviewed	2,431	3,984	6,747	7,032	8,090	8,942	12,565	12,937
Percentage of documents								
• released wholly	78.3	82.4	83.7	83.9	88.2	76.1	76.2	81.9
• released wholly and partially*						88.8	87.3	85.3

Notes: * At the end of 2001, it was agreed that partial access to documents could also be granted (with certain parts deleted, or with the names of delegations and any content that would make it possible to identify them blocked out).

Academics account for over a quarter of all requests for Council documents (27.6 per cent in 2004), with civil society (the industrial/commercial sector, lobbies and non-governmental organizations) being the next biggest group (21.9 per cent in 2004) requesting access to Council documents.

Source: Data provided by the Council Secretariat.

with the other institutions and bodies with which the Council is obliged to interact and on which it depends in fulfilling its EU-related duties. We will limit ourselves here to a necessarily short description of its dealings with three of them: the EP; the Commission; and the member states (including the presidency).

The European Parliament (EP)

The vastly increased contacts between the Council and the EP necessitated by the co-decision procedure (see Chapter 8 for more details) are reflected in the relations between the two institutions' secretariats. Since the introduction of the cooperation procedure in 1987, and even more so with the launching of the co-decision procedure in 1993, the EP has occupied (and preoccupied) the Council Secretariat to a far greater degree than was previously the case. Initially, relations with the EP (a euphemism for co-decision and conciliation matters) were dealt with from DG F, which was at that time responsible for institutional questions. However, one of the many changes introduced under the de Boissieu regime post-1999 was the transfer of responsibility for co-decision (and conciliation) matters to the Legal Service, interpreted by some as an indication of a more conflictual approach on the part of the Council.

In the past, disputes have frequently soured the atmosphere between the two institutions. As the point where they interact most regularly, the secretariats have often been the instigators (and have also borne the brunt) of the bad relations. The enforced cooperation demanded by the co-decision procedure has given rise to a close, if not always warm, working relationship between the two secretariats, although much obviously depends on the individuals involved and their attitude to their work. Much depends, too, on the attitude of the presidency-in-office regarding Council–EP relations, in that a pro-EP member state will try to add real substance to relations between the two institutions, rather than just going through the motions (see Chapter 8).

The Commission

Relations between the Council Secretariat and the Commission tend to be more frequent and direct than those with the EP, because Commission officials sit opposite the presidency delegation (which includes Secretariat officials) every day in meetings at working party, Coreper and ministerial level. More frequent and more direct does not necessarily imply more harmonious, however. The different interests of the two bodies make some degree of friction inevitable, but outright conflict can usually be avoided through sufficiently intensive contacts at all levels. In the area of the budget – a notorious inter-institutional battleground – relations are probably best described as intensive rather than good, and conflicts are usually avoided precisely because of this intensity.

There is an underlying, though rarely overtly expressed, attitude – among some Council Secretariat officials at least – that the Commission services need to be 'kept in check' and 'treated with firmness'. Others, however, readily acknowledge that mutual cooperation is the best means of ensuring that the two institutions' respective mandates are fulfilled. A relationship based on trust between the officials in the Council Secretariat and the Commission is very important. A willingness and ability to speak candidly to one another about the issues under discussion can greatly assist the process of ironing out difficulties and producing compromise proposals capable of being accepted by all sides. Conversely, a lack of cooperation between the Council and Commission officials working on a difficult file can have grave consequences for the progress of the negotiations.

The member states and the presidency

The close relations between the member states and the Council Secretariat are conducted either through the Brussels-based permreps (see Chapter 9) or directly with the ministries in the various capitals. Contacts with the national permreps are facilitated by their proximity to and daily dealings with the Council Secretariat. Officials from the permreps spend large parts of each working day in the Justus Lipsius building attending meetings, and during breaks they may take the opportunity to speak directly to Secretariat officials, in their offices, in the corridors or in the restaurant. At other times they may contact the relevant desk officer in the Secretariat for an update on the progress of a dossier for which they are responsible, or in order to pass on information about the national position on a particular point. Similarly, officials from the national capitals may have direct dealings with Secretariat officials on their visits to Brussels for meetings, or may contact them by telephone or (increasingly) by email.

Obviously, relations are particularly close when a member state is in the chair, even for those member governments that try to run the presidency from their capital rather than from Brussels. The presidency may choose (frequently at its peril) to exclude the Secretariat from the substantive preparation of the issues to be discussed at forthcoming meetings, but is dependent on the technical and administrative support provided by the Secretariat officials. When the Council Secretariat is used extensively (both technically and substantively) by a presidency, morale among the officials is boosted, which can foster goodwill and enthusiasm. The result can be a beneficial effect on the presidency's end-of-term 'balance-sheet'. On the other hand, Secretariat officials can be scathing about what they consider to be a badly managed presidency, giving rise to a rather negative and even uncooperative attitude, which can spell difficulty – if not disaster – for the member state representatives in the chair.

The relationship that exists between the Secretariat and the presidency is obviously rather special, given the need for them to work closely together in organizing and coordinating the Council's work. Each official has his/her own immediate boss within the Secretariat, but must also work for presidency officials, who have no real (or only temporary) authority over them. Personal relations become of paramount importance in such circumstances, and factors such as nationality, linguistic ability and common interests can affect the available stock of goodwill to an important extent.

Evolution – past and future

Over the years, the Secretariat has developed from a logistics provider, record keeper and purveyor of legal counsel into a negotiation manager, counsellor to the Presidency, 'good offices' mediator, crisis management coordinator and political foreign and security policy secretariat. These roles will continue to evolve after enlargement.

So wrote the Council's Deputy Secretary-General in the introduction to a manual produced in 2003 as an aid for Council Secretariat officials producing documents for the Council and its preparatory bodies. It encapsulates neatly and concisely the transformation of the Council Secretariat from passive assistant to much more active collaborator. In the first few years of the new century, the future evolution of the Council Secretariat was dependent on three main events: implementation of the Nice Treaty; enlargement; and ratification and implementation of the CT.

By the time the Nice Treaty came into effect in 2003, the member states were already engaged in negotiations governing the next stage in the EU's development – the IGC convened to draw up a draft Constitutional Treaty (CT). For the Secretariat, as the body responsible for ensuring the legality of the Council's operation, the Nice Treaty could be viewed in one of two ways. The more optimistic regarded it as a stepping-stone, a necessary stage in the development of the EU, while the new CT was being discussed and drafted in the CFE, agreed upon in the IGC and, in due course, ratified by each of the member states before coming into force across the expanded EU. Another school of thought questioned the automaticity of this, and suggested (rightly, as it turned out) that ratification of the CT by all member states could not be assumed as a given. In such a scenario, the fall-back position would be that agreed under the Nice Treaty, thereby imbuing it with enhanced importance.

The Nice Treaty and the enlargement of the EU were inextricably linked, with the former having been negotiated in an attempt to ready the EU and its institutions for the latter. The Council Secretariat bore the immediate brunt of enlargement in a number of ways. The very fabric of its buildings had to be altered and extended in order to make room for the new members. It was obliged to recruit new specialists at the same time as paring down some of its services in the interests of efficiency. Both its input (in terms of information and tactical advice) and its output (in terms of documents) increased exponentially. In a more positive sense (at least from the point of view of Secretariat officials), the need for a specialized body to actively support increasingly complex negotiations could no longer be questioned.

The wording in the CT relating to the Council Secretariat was sparse (Article III.344 (2) provided that: 'The Council shall be assisted by a General Secretariat, under the responsibility of a Secretary-General appointed by the Council. The Council shall decide on the organisation of the General Secretariat by a simple majority.'), but the underlying message was clear. It was to be the Council of Ministers (and not the European Council) that would decide on the appointment of the Secretary-General and on the organization of the Secretariat itself. Such decisions would be taken on the basis of a simple majority, rather than the qualified majority and unanimity that had been required in the past. Clearly, the aim was to simplify the process and to avoid its politicization, a sensible approach in an enlarged Union.

Council officials were unsure about the impact on the Secretariat, were the CT to be implemented. There was some anxiety about the creation of the post of EU Foreign Minister, and the potential merging or overlapping of parts of the Commission and Council Secretariats that this would imply. Similarly, the appointment of a President of the European Council was expected to give rise to some form of bureaucratic infrastructure, however light. In any case, the Council Secretariat can expect to continue to play an active role in the Council's decision-making activities, providing the necessary organization, coordination, coherence and assistance that have become its essential stock-in-trade.

Chapter 5

Taking Turns at the Wheel: the Presidency

The heated discussions regarding the presidency of the Council and the European Council which took place in and around the 2002–3 Convention on the Future of Europe (CFE) and the subsequent intergovernmental conference (IGC) bore eloquent witness to the presidency's perceived importance for the European Union (EU) in general, and the member states in particular. Clearly, the presidency is now viewed as a vital part of the EU's institutional structure and a critical component of the institutional balance. This is a far cry from the early days of the European Communities (EC), when the presidency was viewed merely as a means of fulfilling an administrative chore (the chairing of meetings), to be shared equally among the member states. Gradually, however, as first the EC and then the EU widened and deepened, the presidency was ascribed a more extensive role, including mediation and representation, while the management of Council business became a more substantive task, and eventually a much more visible one.

Today, national preparations for the presidency begin several years in advance of the actual period in office, reaching a peak in the six months immediately preceding assumption of the role. This is a huge undertaking for all member states, but particularly for smaller ones, which may experience greater difficulty in providing the necessary resources. The presidency is now conservatively estimated to cost in the region of €60 million (Sie Dhian Ho and Van Keulen, 2004), and the presidency member state can expect to organize, chair and manage the work of over 4,000 meetings during the six months in question (see Table 3.2, in Chapter 3). Every action, reaction and remark of its politicians and officials is open to scrutiny by their colleagues in the Council and the other EU institutions, while the external representational role of the presidency means that the ministers and prime minister may have to operate in the glare of a global media spotlight, a position which some, at least, might find uncomfortable. The role is therefore assumed with a mixture of pride, trepidation and determination to succeed, and at the end of the term of office, the mantle is passed on with a mixture of relief and regret. Indeed, a British official, on the eve of the United Kingdom (UK) taking over the Council presidency, likened it to driving home from the pub, saying 'You do it when it's your turn, but that doesn't necessarily mean that you look forward to it.'

133

In this chapter, we shall explain how and why the Council presidency has come to assume such importance in the EU system, by examining its origins and development, its operating rules, its current functions, its perceived strengths and weaknesses and how it may evolve in the future. But first, a point of clarification. The presidency of the Council is frequently and erroneously referred to in various media as the presidency of the EU. Indeed, the latter term has become so commonplace that 'to argue for the more accurate usage now appears pedantic' (Neligan, 1999). In strictly legal terms, the President of the Council is the Foreign Minister of the state currently holding the Council presidency, and a list of all the holders of the office since 1958 is available on the Council's website. In line with the EU's single institutional framework, a single presidency (with a small number of exceptions) is held by the same member state in every sphere of activity of the EU – Community matters, the common foreign and security policy (CFSP) and justice and home affairs (JHA) – and at all levels, from working parties to the European Council.

Origins and development

The initial designation of the presidency was brief and, as far as one can tell, barely thought through. Someone had to chair meetings of, and to speak for, the Council. This was viewed as a chore to be shared among the member states, so the founding treaties assigned it to each of them in turn. In the early years of the EC, that was more or less that, until the 1970s, when the Council presidency gradually took on a more extensive role, as a result of a number of developments.

The tilting balance of power from the Commission to the Council began to make the management of Council business a more substantive task, though still rather invisible. This was much reinforced from 1974 onwards, as the Communities acquired new members and the heads of state or government began to meet more often under the aegis of the European Council. The latter's construction as something apart from the regular institutional framework of the EC created a vacuum which the presidency filled, taking on some of the functions performed by the Commission and the Council Secretariat under the more orthodox Community procedures. In parallel, in the 1970s, European political cooperation (EPC) evolved as an increasingly active forum for foreign policy consultations among the member states. A combination of formal constraints (not being within the treaty framework) and practical necessity (notably the need to coordinate the overseas missions of the member states) served to make the presidency substantially and visibly more important.

The marked increase in Community activity from the mid-1980s onwards had three particular consequences for the presidency. First, the sheer volume of work of the Council meant quite simply that it required more active management. Both the enhanced importance of the Secretary-General of the Council and the increased expectations of the presidency from this point onwards reflected a general preoccupation with improving the effectiveness of the Council. Second, the heightened public profile of the Community and its legislative impact made the work of the Community much more visible within the member states and to a wider range of groups and citizens. Each incoming presidency thus found itself the target of increased domestic expectations, and was also tempted to make more of a public spectacle during the presidency. Two visible and enduring consequences of this were the introduction of the presidency logo in the early 1990s, and the creation of presidency websites towards the end of the same decade. Third, the EC became the focus of increasing efforts by third countries to establish a special relationship with the EC, or to upgrade their existing relationship with it. Since most of these involved both issues within Community competence and issues for which the member states wished to claim responsibility, the representation of the EC side was frequently bicephalous, provided by both the Commission and the Council, the latter in the form of the presidency.

After the Maastricht IGC of 1991, in a period when the Commission became less highly esteemed by the member states, the discussion of further institutional reform generated a proliferation of proposals to upgrade the presidency. This debate also reflected the aspirations of those who favoured a stronger common foreign and security policy, which logically would require clearer and more authoritative collective representation. The debate rumbled on for more than a decade, and was finally and directly addressed in the CFE and the subsequent IGC that produced the 2004 Constitutional Treaty (CT). The CT contained some innovations regarding the presidency (see the final section of this chapter), which were put on hold following the negative French and Dutch referendums in May and June 2005 respectively.

A persistent tension in the discussion of both the record and the potential of the presidency is related to differences between the member states. Differences of 'weight' between the larger member states and the rest are widely thought (especially in the 'weighty' countries) to make a case for them to play a greater part in the management of business and the representation of agreed common policies. This is the breeding-ground for the so-called nightmare about the 'micro-states' and the supposed horrors of a Maltese presidency, even though the record of small state presidencies is rather impressive. A second difference is often observed between the more integrationist and the more nationalist presidencies, the former being widely regarded as more reliable in the chair. The pertinence of these alleged differences certainly makes it harder to make general judgements about the effectiveness of the presidency. It also constrains the discussion about reforms to the presidency, as long as the office rotates among each of the member states in turn.

Early studies of the presidency made much of the differences in performance of individual member states in the chair (Edwards and Wallace, 1977; O'Nuallain, 1985). Published evidence on successive presidencies – for example, that produced by TEPSA, the Trans-European Policy Studies Association(see their website at www.tepsa.be) and by Peter Ludlow (available from www.eurocomment.be) – suggests that performance varies, but for many different reasons. It is hard to draw general conclusions in that much depends on the context of a particular period and the content of the agenda in that period, just as personalities, especially of the senior politicians from the incumbent presidency, have an impact on the atmosphere of an individual presidency. For a recent comparative account, see Elgström (2003), and for an overall analysis, see Tallberg (2003 and 2004).

Two main points should be made here regarding assumptions about the respective abilities of larger and smaller member states in the chair. First, larger countries can call on more resources of personnel and expertise in dealing with the range and volume of Council business, obviously an advantage to them and, at the margins, to the rest of the EU. However, this matters less than it used to, because of the consolidation of the role of the Council Secretariat. But, second, there is otherwise little evidence to suggest that larger member states perform better than smaller ones. On the contrary, there is much evidence to support the observation that smaller governments do at least as well and often better, within the limits of their resources. In recent years, some of the most effective presidencies have been exercised by small member states (for example, Denmark in the second half of 2002, and Ireland in the first half of 2004), while the French presidency in the second half of 2000 was described by one seasoned commentator as 'an acrimonious shambles' (Norman, 2003; p. 140), and the Italian presidency in the second half of 2003 was widely criticized.

The operating rules

The basic operating rules of the presidency are set out in the treaties and, with more precision, in successive versions of the Council's internal rules of procedure (CRPs). As regards EPC and later the CFSP, the various documents defining their scope need to be examined in order to ascertain the presidency's responsibilities in the area of foreign policy.

System of rotation

The most basic operating rule of the presidency is the order in which it is undertaken (see Appendix 5, Table 5.1 and Box 5.1). This rule determines not only the order in which the member states exercise the presidency, but also their place at the negotiating table at all levels of

Table 5.1   The Council presidency: member states' periods in office, 1958–2006

Member state											
Belgium (België/Belgique)	1/58	1/61	1/64	1/67	1/70	1/73	2/77	1/82	1/87	2/93	2/01
Denmark (Danmark)						2/73	1/78	2/82	2/87	1/93	2/02
Germany (Deutschland)	2/58	2/61	2/64	2/67	2/70	1/74	2/78	1/83	1/88	2/94	1/99
Greece (Ellas)								2/83	2/88	1/94	1/03
Spain (España)									1/89	2/95	1/02
France	1/59	1/62	1/65	1/68	1/71	2/74	1/79	1/84	2/89	1/95	2/00
Ireland						1/75	2/79	2/84	1/90	2/96	1/04
Italy (Italia)	2/59	2/62	2/65	2/68	2/71	2/75	1/80	1/85	2/90	1/96	2/03
Luxembourg	1/60	1/63	1/66	1/69	1/72	1/76	2/80	2/85	1/91	2/97	1/05
The Netherlands (Nederland)	2/60	2/63	2/66	2/69	2/72	2/76	1/81	1/86	2/91	1/97	2/04
Austria (Österreich)										2/98	1/06
Portugal										1/92	1/00
Finland (Suomi)										2/99	2/06
Sweden (Sverige)											1/01
United Kingdom						1/77	2/81	2/86	2/92	1/98	2/05

Notes: 1 = January–June; 2 = July–December.
The member states are listed in alphabetical order according to the name of their country as spelt in their native language (the criterion upon which the first order of rotation was based).

Box 5.1   *Presidency rotation, 2007–20*

In December 2004, the Council agreed the following order of rotation for the Council presidency for the period 2007–20. The member states (including Bulgaria and Romania, who signed an Accession Treaty in April 2005, and were at that time scheduled to become full members on 1 January 2007) are divided into groups of three, intended to reflect a balance of geographical situation, economic weight and 'old' and 'new' members.

2007	Germany	January–June
2007	Portugal	July–December
2008	Slovenia	January–June
2008	France	July–December
2009	Czech Republic	January–June
2009	Sweden	July–December
2010	Spain	January–June
2010	Belgium	July–December
2011	Hungary	January–June
2011	Poland	July–December
2012	Denmark	January–June
2012	Cyprus	July–December
2013	Ireland	January–June
2013	Lithuania	July–December
2014	Greece	January–June
2014	Italy	July–December
2015	Latvia	January–June
2015	Luxembourg	July–December
2016	The Netherlands	January–June
2016	Slovakia	July–December
2017	Malta	January–June
2017	United Kingdom	July–December
2018	Estonia	January–June
2018	Bulgaria	July–December
2019	Austria	January–June
2019	Romania	July–December
2020	Finland	January–June

If the arrangements outlined in the Constitutional Treaty were to come into force, each member of a group would chair all configurations of the Council for six months in turn, with the exception of the Foreign Affairs Council (which would be chaired by the new Union Minister for Foreign Affairs) and the European Council (which would be chaired by a new full-time president). The presidency would be able to call on the material support of the other members of the trio to fulfil its presidential responsibilities.

the Council hierarchy (see Figure 2.1 in chapter 2). It may also determine the order in which they are called upon to speak and, where applicable, to vote at meetings.

Three distinct systems of rotation (alphabetical, alternating and balanced) have existed since the inception of the European Communities (see Appendix 5), with a fourth due to begin in 2007. Article 27 of the 1951 Treaty of Paris, establishing the European Coal and Steel Community (ECSC), stated that the office of president would be held in turn by each member of the Council for three months, following the alphabetical order of the member states (construed to mean in the official language of the member state in question). The Treaties of Rome (in Articles 146 and 116 for the European Economic Community (EEC) and the European Atomic Energy Community (Euratom) respectively) extended the term to six months, while the Merger Treaty of 1965 adopted the six-month period for all three Communities. With each enlargement of the EC and then the EU, the new member states have been slotted in among the pre-existing members, and have taken their turn 'at the wheel'.

Twice the entire system of rotation has been altered in response to enlargement. The Act of Accession for Spain and Portugal introduced a second 'split rotation', with a first 'normal' cycle (commencing in 1986), and a second, alternating, cycle (which got under way in 1993). The aim was to ensure that, with an even number of members, an individual member state would not always hold the presidency during the same half of the year. This was deemed only fair, since the rhythm of work is very different in the first and second halves of the year because of the summer break that occurs early in the second semester, effectively bunching legislative activity in the final four months of the term of office.

The system was altered again in 1995, at the time of the European Free Trade Association (EFTA) enlargement, driven by considerations relating to CFSP. The new 'balanced' rotation system, established in the Act of Accession for Austria, Finland and Sweden (as amended for the non-accession of Norway), sought to ensure that the *troika* (a coordinating mechanism, bringing together the current, preceding and succeeding presidencies) would always consist of at least one larger member state (The Netherlands being viewed as larger for these purposes), and ensuring that neutral member states were grouped with non-neutral ones.

For the duration of the period between the signature of their accession treaties and their actual accession as full members, new member states are entitled to send non-voting observers to meetings of the Council and its preparatory bodies, and places are made available for them at the negotiating table. In the case of the ten countries that signed accession agreements in April 2003, fixed places were allocated to them at the Council table, flanked on either side by pre-existing members who rotated around them according to the balanced order of presidency rotation.

Following their accession in May 2004, this seating arrangement was maintained, pending a new decision on the rotating order of the presidency. Agreement was reached in December 2004, to the effect that a new system will come into being on 1 January 2007 dividing the member states into groups of three, who will together have the responsibility of the presidency for a period of 18 months, and will chair meetings for six months each (see Box 5.1). When places had to be found for the Bulgarian and Romanian observers following the signature of their Accession Treaty in April 2005, it was decided that the seating arrangements should be modified to reflect the new order, with the four presidencies remaining under the balanced system slotting into their new places at the table at the end of their periods in office, rather than, as is the normal practice, moving to the left of the presidency.

Rules regarding the tasks of the presidency

The presidency was initially and chiefly devised in order to ensure that each member state took a turn at chairing meetings of the Council. Over time, many other tasks have been ascribed to, or taken on by, the representatives of the member state in the chair. They have been defined broadly in successive treaties, and periodically clarified in the CRPs, while the rules relating specifically to EPC were laid down in successive reports agreed periodically by member governments. Each of these documents added to the sum of the presidency's tasks, usually following established practice rather than prescribing new practice, and thereby doing little to encourage new ways of handling business.

Thus the number of tasks attributed to or taken on by the presidency has mushroomed over the years, and even the mundane-sounding task of chairing meetings has taken on significant proportions. The duties facing an incoming presidency today are substantial (see Box 5.2 on pages 142–3), but adequate and timely preparation coupled with the considerable resources and support of the Council Secretariat can do much to prevent them becoming overwhelming. To this end, the Council Secretariat produces a presidency handbook for national officials, an invaluable guide to what should be done, and how, during their six months in the chair.

The main functions of the Council presidency

Insiders' accounts of the way in which the Council presidency operates are rare. That provided by Guy de Bassompierre (1988) was excellent, and broadly his observations still hold good. In particular, he conveyed vivid images of individual practitioners doing their best to facilitate the workings of the Council and of EPC. His volume should be read alongside the various contributions to the volume edited by Colm O'Nuallain (1985), and in particular their insights into the approaches of different member governments to their turn in the chair. Emil Kirchner's volume (1992) covers the presidencies of the late 1980s. EPC is explained by Philippe de Schoutheete (1986, 1988) and Simon Nuttall (1992, 2000). More recently and specifically, the role of the presidency has been chronicled in relation to IGCs (McDonagh, 1998) and European Councils (see, for example, Ludlow, 2002, 2004).

We have largely retained here the categorization of the presidency's main responsibilities that was first set out in Wallace and Edwards (1976) and Edwards and Wallace (1977) – that is, business manager, manager of foreign policy, promoter of initiatives, package-broker, liaison point, and collective representative. Each role has grown over the years and generated more systematic practice, propelled partly by the competition between member states to outshine each other and, in particular, by the considerable 'success' of governments from the smaller member states in demonstrating that the underlying parity, reflected so far in the presidency rotation, is well justified.

Business manager

The role of the presidency in managing the business of the Council is its baseline task. A presidency cannot be judged successful unless the basic technical tasks of management have been conducted efficiently. Credit for smooth and purposeful management is judged here in terms of peer group evaluation, rather than by more public plaudits, another result of the relative secrecy surrounding the inner workings of the Council. A presidency that handles the business efficiently can make a real difference to the progress of discussion, even though many other factors influence what is, and what cannot be, agreed. However, it should also be noted that an inefficient presidency could severely impede discussion, and hamper agreement on issues where the substantive problems may be small, to say nothing of occasions when they may be more contentious.

Increasingly, this management role has come to depend on active partnership between the presidency and the Council Secretariat. In the 1970s, it was a choice for individual governments how much to align their presidency objectives and tactics with the Secretariat, some believing that they could be relatively self-reliant. That choice has now more or less disappeared (although some larger member states still appear to exhibit reluctance to accept it on occasion). This greater reliance on the Secretariat reflects the increased volume of business to be transacted, and the longer intervals between presidencies (see Table 5.1), which make it harder for individual governments to accumulate on-the-job experience, and more pertinent to draw on the continuous experience of

Box 5.2   *What does the presidency do?*

Preparation (up to 3 years in advance)

Substantive:
(in cooperation with surrounding presidencies, the Commission and the EP)

- Drafts (jointly with five other member states) a multi-annual strategic programme, establishing the priorities for three years of Council activity;
- Drafts (jointly with the other member state due to hold the presidency in the same calendar year) an annual operational programme, refining the Council's priorities; and
- Establishes a presidency work programme, including indicative agendas for all scheduled Council meetings.

Logistical/technical:
(in cooperation with the Council Secretariat, the Commission and the EP)

- Draws up a timetable of formal and informal Council meetings (seven months before the start of its term in office);
- Draws up a schedule for other meetings in the Council hierarchy, including Association and Cooperation Councils;
- Draws up a schedule of public policy debates to be held during its term in office; and
- Agrees dates for conciliation meetings with the EP.

Personnel:

- Decides on chairs of committees and working parties;
- Transfers individuals to presidency posts in good time;
- Recruits personnel (if necessary); and
- Provides training for key personnel.

Coordination:

- Coordinates closely with the preceding presidency to ensure a smooth handover;
- Establishes or reinforces the system of domestic coordination (inter-ministerial, intra-ministerial, and with the Brussels-based permanent representation); and
- Establishes coordination systems with Secretariat officials from the Council, the Commission and the EP.

Other:

- Decides on the presidency logo, and creates the presidency website;
- Makes arrangements for meetings scheduled to take place in the member state.

In harness (6 months)

Regarding the Council:

- Convenes meetings on its own initiative or if requested by other member state(s);
- Prepares provisional agendas for (and chairs) meetings throughout the Council hierarchy (some exceptions);
- Oversees movement of dossiers within the Council hierarchy (in cooperation with the Council Secretariat and the Commission);

→

→

- Engages in negotiation with colleagues between meetings at all levels to ensure the progress of dossiers under discussion;
- Is expected to provide compromise suggestions in the event of stalemate;
- Opens voting in Council meetings on its own initiative or if required to do so by a majority of Council members;
- Signs texts of acts adopted by the Council, alone or jointly with the EP;
- Signs minutes of Council meetings; and
- Hosts and chairs informal Council meetings (usually in the member state).

Regarding the European Council:

- Prepares and chairs one or more meetings of the European Council;
- May convene an extraordinary meeting if it is deemed necessary; and
- Presents Presidency Conclusions to the media.

Regarding the European Parliament:

- Presents the presidency work programme to the EP at the start of its term in office;
- Reports to the EP on the outcome of the European Councils;
- Presidency ministers attend part-sessions of EP to answer questions, make statements or take part in debates on behalf of the Council;
- Presidency ministers may attend meetings of relevant EP committees;
- Chairs Conciliation Committee (jointly with EP);
- Acts as spokesperson for the Council in the Conciliation Committee;
- Presents a report to the EP on progress achieved at the end of the presidency;
- Takes part in formal and informal trialogue meetings (at political and official level) on budgetary matters, horizontal issues and in co-decision procedures.

Regarding the Commission:

- Meets the Commission President and Commissioners when drawing up the presidency work programme;
- Coordinates with the Commission college and officials throughout the presidency re dossiers under discussion;
- Takes part in trialogue meetings (at political and official level) on budgetary matters, horizontal issues and co-decision procedures.

Regarding CFSP/ESDP:

- Represents the EU and implements CFSP decisions in close cooperation with the High Representative.

Regarding external relations:

- May act as spokesperson for the Council in the administration of mixed international agreements (concluded jointly by the Community and the member states);
- May express the common position of the member states on a particular issue, and may be instrumental in defining it;
- Organizes coordination meetings for the representatives of EU member states in third countries or international organizations.

the Secretariat. Indeed, the partnership has at times become so close that the Secretariat has been seen by some as a presidency secretariat – although Secretariat officials would be quick to refute this view, as mentioned in Chapter 4.

A recurrent criticism of the system of the rotating presidency has been the risk it incurs of having new priorities imposed on the EU every six months at the whim of succeeding presidencies. A number of practical arrangements, agreed at the Seville European Council in June 2002, and implemented that same year, were aimed precisely at reducing this risk. Chief among these was the strategic programme covering three years that is now drawn up jointly by the six presidencies concerned, in consultation with the Commission, and submitted to the General Affairs and External Affairs Council (GAERC, previously the General Affairs Council – GAC) for adoption by the European Council. The first such programme, covering the years 2004–6, was submitted in 2003 by the incoming presidencies for the three-year period in question (Ireland, The Netherlands, Luxembourg, the UK, Austria and Finland).

From this multi-annual strategic programme, the two member states taking on the presidency in the same calendar year jointly submit a draft annual operational programme to the GAERC in the December prior to taking up office. Finally, each incoming presidency is required to establish a work programme, including indicative provisional agendas for all the Council meetings they have scheduled for their six-month term in office. Each of these documents is available on the Council website (www.consilium.eu.int – see Appendix 2). The resulting coherence and predictability is expected to assist successive presidencies in the management of Council business.

What constitutes effective management? This may be understood on two levels. At the macro level, it involves keeping matters moving up and down between the different levels of the Council hierarchy. The CRPs make it clear, however (in Annex IV), that this movement should not be merely for movement's sake. Files should move upwards between levels of the Council hierarchy only 'when there is reasonable prospect of progress or clarification of positions being achieved at that level' and downward movement should only occur 'when necessary, and in any event only with the remit to tackle precise, well-defined problems'.

Here, the individual presidency (even individuals from the presidency) can make a real difference to what happens. As mentioned in Chapter 4, the Council Secretariat provides the presidency with rather well-developed briefing documents, generally summarizing the known positions of each delegation and providing indications as to where any room for movement of positions may lie. This gives the presidency delegation an excellent working tool during its six-month stint. In order to be effective, the presidency also needs to have people in the chair, both ministers and officials, who understand the subjects and the state of debate on each of them, and who can judge with some skill or flair which dossiers are within range of agreement, given a nudge (even a shove) here or there. Here again, the input of the Secretariat can be invaluable, but it also requires the chair not to be too partisan or nationalist – or not overtly so.

At the micro level, individual meetings, if they are to produce the required results (that is, agreement on the issues under discussion), must be managed effectively. Here again (in Article 20 and Annex IV), the CRPs put the onus on the presidency, enabling it to determine numbers of delegates in the meeting room, the duration of discussions and individual interventions, and generally keeping the discussions focused, substantive and fruitful. Naturally, this requires the cooperation of the other delegations, which are exhorted to make the president's job easier in a number of ways: where possible, giving advance indication of the positions they are likely to take at a given meeting, nominating a single spokesperson to present a common position, keeping their interventions brief, substantive and to the point and, rather than expressing disagreement with a particular proposal, making concrete drafting proposals for its amendment.

Much of the work of the presidency falls most overtly on national foreign ministries (or other central coordinators), the national permanent representation in Brussels, the GAERC and the Committee of Permanent Representatives (Coreper), each of which is discussed in previous or subsequent chapters. These are the filtering points which offer scope for constructive coordination, an objective that the presidency has been repeatedly encouraged to pursue seriously. Tension persists between efforts to coordinate, for reasons of common sense and coherence, and the pull of specialized and segmented discussion, as we saw in earlier chapters. The ability of an individual presidency to moderate the tension depends greatly on how that government itself handles policy coordination at home, a subject to which we shall return in Chapter 9.

Manager of foreign policy

More intensive consultation on foreign policy from the 1970s onwards produced new and greater demands on the presidency. Initially, the indistinct informality of European political cooperation (EPC) left a potentially vast burden to fall on the presidency and the 'host' diplomatic service. EPC meetings were held in presidency capitals, the planning and logistics having to be provided locally, with the result that the presidency also had to fulfil the tasks of the Council Secretariat. Gradually, much of the work and many of the meetings shifted to Brussels, but it was not until the Single European Act (SEA) came into force in 1987 that a collective EPC secretariat was established. It became common *inter alia* from 1977 onwards for officials from prospective presidencies to be seconded to the current presidency, or later to the new secretariat, for familiarization experience and to aid continuity, a real problem without the collective memory provided elsewhere by the Commission or the Council Secretariat.

This vulnerability of the presidency was also influenced by domestic factors within foreign ministries, and between foreign and other ministries, that often made it hard to ensure coherence between EC and EPC business. None the less, as far as the strictly foreign policy matters were concerned, a series of collective improvisations were introduced to give EPC a firmer base. These included the *'coutumier'*, started by the Belgian presidency of 1977, a kind of handbook of procedural practice and precedent to guide successive presidencies, and the *'recueil'*, introduced by the British presidency of 1977, a collection of EPC statements (de Schoutheete, 1988, p. 77; Nuttall, 1992, pp. 147, 174).

The new EPC Secretariat, established in 1987, took over these tasks, which were later fulfilled by the Council's General Secretariat when the EPC Secretariat was subsumed into it in the early 1990s. We can thus observe an adaptive and pragmatic development of the presidency to deal with EPC. Specifically, this involved the testing of an alternative model to that of the EC in other fields, unavoidable given the reluctance of the member states to attribute more responsibility to a collective institution. It also reflected differences in the work being processed through EPC.

The 'new' second pillar established by the Maastricht Treaty on European Union (TEU) was not so new, in the sense that it built on the established experience of EPC. Considerable efforts had been made by successive presidencies to provide EPC with more efficient working tools, subject to the limits on the whole process. The step-change from EPC to CFSP, while retaining the intergovernmental framework, thus constituted a challenge to adapt these tools to the heightened expectations. The responses have varied in quality and impact. Some of the routines have simply been carried on rather than new ones being established. For example, coordination by the presidency of the member states in overseas posts in order to align positions has continued, in a process of accumulating habits and experience rather than aiming to provide the EU with an integrated system of reporting and analysis.

Coordination and discussion between relevant experts from national foreign ministries has also become routine and largely automatic, but this by no means provides the systematic information and planning base that an integrated foreign policy would demand. While individual presidencies can make a difference at the margins, the limitations rather reflect the historic reluctance of member governments to accept the case for a collective diplomatic machine. The Constitutional Treaty provided for a European External Action Service (EEAS), but it was unclear how this body would operate in practice.

None the less, the question as to whether a stronger presidency could provide the elements of such a machine hovers over the debate. Those who are reluctant to see the Commission contribute more to CFSP are quick to insist that the presidency has been strengthened and could be further enhanced. Yet the 1992 TEU succeeded only in formalizing the *troika*, whereby the preceding, incumbent and successor presidencies were required to share the tasks of representing the Union, and of implementing common actions. (After the appointment of the High Representative for the CFSP, the *troika* was made up of that post-holder, the current presidency and the External Relations Commissioner, with the succeeding presidency remaining closely involved.)

There is value in sharing out tasks, not least because of the heavy load of external business. The *troika* formula facilitates smoother hand-overs between presidencies, and the worries of some that smaller governments might not have the resources, human or physical, for single-handed presidencies, may thereby be assuaged. Yet the fact of needing help exposes the weakness of the presidency formula. Individual presidencies have lost responsibility for providing the secretariat function, now transferred to the Council Secretariat, and with it has been lost some of the old pressure on each presidency to display its diplomatic and persuasive skills.

The limits encountered by the presidency in the second pillar are bound up with a wider debate about the development of the CFSP as a whole. While an enterprising presidency may be able to stretch the limits a little, the presidency in itself cannot compensate for disagreement among the member states about either the substance or the shadowy collective personality of the EU. In these circumstances it is perhaps not surprising that 'ad hocery' should interpose: the Contact Group on Bosnia (involving only Germany, France and the UK from the EU) is one example, and the 'Quint' (a restricted forum for dialogue with Turkey) is another, both decoupled from the presidency and both a source of concern to excluded EU members.

Promoter of initiatives

As the presidency's responsibilities grew, it became commonplace to argue that this allowed not only for management but also for manipulation of the Council agenda. An incumbent president, the argument went, would have, and would take, opportunities to promote particular initiatives, an image that national politicians were often keen to encourage, and which their national press often fostered. Why did the idea catch on?

First, the tilt in the balance from the Commission to the Council furnished the members of the Council with temptations and occasions to try to structure the agenda, particularly during periods of weaker Commission leadership. Such temptations and occasions were all the more available to the member state in the chair at the time. Second, it is assumed in the Council, as often elsewhere, that whoever is in the chair can in fact use the power of a louder voice to influence the outcomes of debate and that, at least at ministerial level, the temptation is likely to be irresistible. However, there is little reason to suppose that officials will in this sense be more self-denying in the chair.

Third, the steadily increasing role of the European Council over the past thirty years, the attendant publicity it has engendered, and the status of its participants, generally encourage expectations of initiatives. Since the presidency is so visible as the chair of the European Council, initiatives at a particular session almost inevitably become associated with that country. Fourth, the presidency is the one clear, albeit occasional, opportunity for a member government to imprint a particular style on the Council, to impose a particular topic on colleagues, or to ride an individual minister's particular hobbyhorse.

For all these reasons, each incoming presidency prepares a six-month programme and generally sets out a number of targets it hopes to reach during its turn in the chair. In the past, regular agenda items were interspersed with some new ideas, with the clever presidencies trying to judge policies that suited their interests and were rising to a point of agreement in any case, thus claiming a double credit for their resolution. The 'State of the Union' presidency programme was discussed in advance with the Commission, presented to the European Parliament (EP) for debate and reviewed in a statement by the outgoing presidency to the EP at the end of its term of office. Since the introduction of strategic and operational programmes that have to be agreed jointly with other member states, there is greater constraint on individual presidencies regarding the content of their presidency programmes. Early experience of the strategic programme for 2004–6 and the annual operational programmes it has spawned appear to be positive in terms of continuity and coherence.

It should be pointed out, however, that the real opportunity to promote initiatives or to deliver to domestic expectations was always fairly heavily constrained. The Council is an institution of diffuse consensus, not easy to manipulate or to lead by the nose, and deeply resistant to the explicit peddling of sharp national interests. Thus leading from the centre is frequently a more successful strategy than attempting to do so from the front. Any initiative has to work with the grain of a large group of strong-minded national representatives. The segmentation of the Council is another inhibition that makes it difficult to carry through initiatives involving several Councils, such as major agricultural reform or a strategy towards eastern enlargement. No presidency can cater for the vicissitudes of events, whether these take the form of a sudden currency crisis, a major international crisis or an unexpected domestic one. Many presidencies have come into office with conscientiously well-prepared agendas, only to find that the six months disappear in a haze of meetings on quite unexpected topics. The Bosnian crisis of the mid-1990s, for example, displaced the other aims of several presidencies.

It follows that more modest or more focused objectives may be more rewarding and more prudent. Quite often, the presidency provides an opportunity to make procedural innovations by example, as several presidencies found over the years in EPC (de Schoutheete, 1988). But we should note that the presidency falls well short of being a tool of collective leadership, at least on its record to date.

Package-broker

Part of the skill of the chair in any committee system lies in its ability to draw out agreement from debate and from disputed positions. Necessarily, therefore, the Council presidency is under pressure to look for agreement and to manage business in such a way as to foster consensus. The CRPs go into some detail, in Article 20 and Annex IV, regarding the ways in which the presidency can facilitate discussions within the Council. This task is always compounded by the fact that the presidency (whatever the member state) suffers from a structural bias in favour of its own government's position. Indeed, this is accentuated because, during a presidency, it is the senior person in a national delegation that moves into the chair, leaving the deputy, sitting around the corner of the table, to speak for the member state of the presidency.

It was for this reason that so much hope was invested in the Commission as a mediator, on the grounds that it was detached from the particularist interests of governments. Indeed the Commission retains the ambition to act as a broker, both in the way it devises proposals and in its contribution to the closing stages of Council nego-tiations. None the less, the Commission's ability to broker effectively is variable, for both contingent and structural reasons. In any case, it sometimes needs an individual with a clear political mandate to steer through a difficult compromise, with accompanying face-savers for delegations under pressure. Thus the scope for the presidency compromise has always been a feature of the Council. Sometimes compromises have been achieved in partnership with the Commission, but on other occasions they have been achieved in antithesis to the Commission, with the Council deliberately taking the crux of the issue out of the hands of the Commission.

The role of the presidency compromise retains its importance today. One particular instrument of the compromise is the 'presidency confessional', a device through which the presidency abandons plenary sessions for bilateral discussions with individual delegations. The objectives are threefold: first, to encourage individual delegations to be more open and more direct about the 'bottom lines' of their negotiating positions; second, to put pressure more fiercely on individual delegations to make concessions; and, third, sometimes, to offer 'unofficial' inducements to cooperation. Views differ on the merits of the confessional: it can lead to much time being spent by ministers and officials waiting for everyone to troop through the office of the presidency; it can produce ragged compromises that save the day, but mortgage the future; and some people in the Commission regard it as a clear incursion into the Commission's brokering role.

Alternatively, the presidency may call on the offices of an *ad hoc* group of like-minded colleagues to engage simultaneously in parallel discussions with individual (or small groups of) member states to broker an agreement. Known as the 'Friends of the presidency', such groups can play an important role in expediting negotiations and bringing divergent positions closer. A recent good example was the group the Dutch prime minister gathered around himself at the Brussels summit in December 2004 to deal with the issue of Turkey's candidacy as a member of the EU (see Ludlow, 2005).

One final point on compromises concerns the neutrality or bias of the chair. It is often argued that governments from the smaller member states have an advantage as package-brokers, in that they have fewer pressing interests and stronger incentives to be consensual. There is some justification for this view, a good recent example being the successful brokering of an agreement on the CT in June 2003 under the Irish presidency. On the other hand, many practitioners wince at the memories of some other small-state presidencies, with historical examples involving Greece frequently being cited. The counterpart is often true, namely that larger member states tend to be cluttered with important interests to defend on almost every topic, a fact which may impede their ability to broker agreement with their partners. None the less, it sometimes takes a presidency with the most difficult interests to accommodate to broker a sustainable compromise.

Traditionally, package brokerage has entailed the building of compromises around texts to which all member states can agree, frequently with variations built into articles of the resulting text that reflect (often opaquely) the details of the concessions that have been given and taken. Though this consensual habit remains, many issues are, of course, put to the vote – or rather, are implicitly managed as if a vote might be called. It falls to the presidency to structure discussions around the opportunities for votes as well as threats for the calling of votes. While some governments are happier than others about using votes (and reflect this preference from the chair), all presidencies have to exercise prudence and judgement in calling for votes. In doing so, they are wise to take into account those who are silent in discussion. Under unanimity rules, any participant can block by using their veto, but abstentions in effect count as agreement. A smart president must therefore determine whether to flush out the silent blocker or to leave a likely abstainer undisturbed. Where votes are likely to be taken, the positions of those who remain silent must be identified and addressed.

Liaison point

The presidency acts as a main, but not exclusive, point of contact for the Council with the Commission and the EP. Since the main features of these inter-institutional relationships are discussed in Chapters 7 and 8, respectively, we shall limit ourselves here to a few general remarks.

All committed, responsible presidencies work closely with the relevant services and senior officials in the Commission in preparing for their six-month period in office, and in checking progress as the months go by. Staff from the relevant national permanent representation, from the Council Secretariat, and from Commission DGs and *cabinets*, exchange papers and briefs on forthcoming business. Many of the key contacts take place within the segments of specialized policy arenas. Some of the Commission services plan their work programmes in the hope of benefiting from a sympathetic presidency to give their proposals a fair wind and to nudge deliberations to a conclusion in the Council. Indeed, close partnership may suit the Commission very well on occasion, and there is probably scope for the Commission to make more of these opportunities than it already does. Such opportunities are easier to establish under the first pillar (where the Commission has the power of text) than under the second and third pillars, where the Commission's voice is often muted. In these circumstances much depends, first, on how much a particular presidency looks for opportunities to bring the Commission into the discussion; and second, on how subtle and effective the Commission is in making its voice heard by the weight of its arguments.

The quantum increase in the EP's role in the legislative process has made it one of the most important interfaces with the Council. Consequently, the EP is an important preoccupation of the presidency for issues under the various relevant procedures. To handle this smoothly is no mean task, given the extraordinary proliferation of procedures and the accumulating volume of disputed questions on which Council and EP positions have to be reconciled.

Collective representative

The role of the presidency as spokesman for the EU and for its members has grown exponentially since the 1970s. While the bulk of the work of representation is connected to the CFSP, it is important to recall that there are many areas of EU activity that are subject to mixed competence. These require someone to speak for the EU abroad in both bilateral and multilateral gatherings, to act as the reception point for incoming delegations from third countries, and to ensure coordination between missions based in third countries.

In earlier years, turf battles between the Commission and the Council presidency regarding external representation were common, with the Commission determined to stake its claim to speak for the Community/EU's interest and some Council presidencies at pains to keep the Commission in the outer room. Such disputes have become much less common and have given way to more practical cooperation and common-sense solutions. It is broadly accepted that issues that touch on Community competence, and that fall at least partly within what is now the first pillar, require both a Commission input and a contribution from the Council presidency in the external representation of European policies and positions.

Though governments from third countries are often still frustrated by not being quite sure who their interlocutors are, certain practices are being established that accommodate the ambiguities of the EU's international personality. Thus, as a matter of common sense, western summits of the G8 are, where possible, held during the presidency of an EU member state that is also a G8 member (as was the case under the British presidency in the second half of 2005). Regular transatlantic meetings routinely involve both Commission and Council presidencies, while political leaders from important partners visit the Commission as well as the capitals of the member states.

One explanation for this more practical approach lies in the sheer press of external business. Since the early 1990s, the EU has been inundated with 'external relations' to develop: the European Economic Area (EEA) and subsequent EFTA enlargement; a more active transatlantic relationship; efforts to strengthen contacts with Japan and other Asian countries; the proliferation of new forms of association and partnership (including EU membership) with central and eastern Europe and the former Soviet Union; and attempts to extend dialogue with Turkey and the whole Mediterranean basin. (Box 5.3 indicates the extent of the meetings arising from such commitments in

Box 5.3   *Council meetings with external partners, 2004*

	Joint Councils*	Summits and Ministerial Meetings	*Troika* or joint presidency+
January	EU–Uzbekistan		
February	EU–Moldova		
March		EU–Canada	EU–Ukraine (JHA)
April	EU–EEA EU–Russia EU–ACP (Togo)	EU–Africa	EU–South Africa
May	EU–Ukraine EU–ACP	EU–Latin America and Caribbean EU–Nigeria EU–GCC EU–Ecowas EU–Med Foreign Affairs	EU–Mexico EU–Cariforum EU–Chile
June	EU–Romania	EU–USA	
July	EU–ACP (Guinea) EU–Kyrgyz EU–Kazakhstan	EU–Ukraine	EU–Yemen
September	EU–Macedonia EU–Azerbaijan EU–Armenia EU–Georgia		
October	EU–Switzerland signature		Asia–Europe
November		EU–Med Foreign Affairs EU–Russia EU–Western Balkan Forum EU–India	EU–Ecowas
December	EU–EEA Council EU–Bulgaria	EU–China	EU–Nepal African–Europe dialogue

Notes:
* Joint Councils held routinely for Cooperation, Partnership and Association Agreements.
+ Meetings held either with the Council Presidency *troika*, or with bicephalous Council and Commission procedures.
ACP – African, Caribbean and Pacific states
Cariforum – Grouping of the Caribbean ACP states
Ecowas – Economic Community of West African States
EEA – European Economic Area
GCC – Gulf Cooperation Council
JHA – Justice and Home Affairs
Med – Mediterranean
USA – United States of America

Source: Council website (www.consoilium.eu.int).

2004 alone. It is accepted that all these relationships touch EC competences as well as the activities of the second, and even third, pillars. The
logic of involving both the Commission and the Council presidency is
not the issue; rather, it is a question of the level of intensity, attention
and resources that can be deployed collectively.

Strengths and weaknesses of the presidency

The arguments for and against the rotating six-monthly presidency
have been well aired in recent years, both within the Council during and
since the 1990s in the context of internal discussions on Council reform,
and more recently in the CFE and the subsequent IGC. (A selection of pros
and cons is reproduced in Box 5.4.) Worries about the effect of large-
scale enlargement on an already criticized office have been articulated
and refuted, and in the process significant differences in opinion have
emerged between the larger and smaller member states, at times spilling
over into outright conflict. As we have seen earlier in this chapter, some
changes have been made, most notably in the wake of agreements
reached at the Seville European Council in June 2002, aimed at reducing
volatility and increasing continuity and coherence between presidencies.
Other, more far-reaching, reforms were included in the Constitutional
Treaty, although many questions remain about their viability.

It is one thing to assess the presidency as one of several vehicles for
managing the work of the Council; it is quite another to envisage this
particular vehicle playing the primary role of collective leadership
(Metcalfe, 1998). The basic assumption underlying recent discussions
about the presidency has been that, in general, it can, and generally does,
make an invaluable contribution to keeping the Council show on the
road. It provides essential services to support the Council's collective
tasks; it acts as a useful interface with other EU institutions and with the
world outside the EU; and it is a focus for concentrating periodic strategic
and public attention on the EU within each member state in turn.
However, in order to fulfil this valuable role, the presidency depends on
complementarity between itself and other parts of the system – that is, on
a division of labour with the other components of the odd and diffuse
process of reaching collective decisions that characterizes the Council.

As we have seen, in this complex division of labour, the various tasks
of the presidency have become increasingly specific, partly under the
sheer pressure of work and partly as individual governments have
generated innovations in their efforts to perform well. The presidency's
tasks are clearly different from those of the Council Secretariat, though
woven into an interdependent partnership, and together they underpin
the Council's various interactions with the Commission and the EP, as
well as *vis-à-vis* third countries. The result has been to make the
presidency rather robust as a prop of the system.

Box 5.4   *Some strengths and weaknesses of the single rotating presidency*

Strengths	Weaknesses
• Reinforces notion of **equality** – each member state, regardless of size, takes its turn at the helm	• **Volatility** – changes at the helm result in new priorities
• **Coherence and efficiency** – resulting from a single presidency at all levels of the Council hierarchy	• **Discontinuity** – frequent changes in personnel unsettling for external partners
• **Education** (1) – brings EU closer to **citizens** of presidency member state, teaches them how it works	• **Long inter-presidency gap** (1) – **poor institutional memory** among national officials and politicians
• **Education** (2) – forces presidency **government** periodically to pay more attention to EU-wide rather than merely national policy concerns	• **Long inter-presidency gap** (2) – **lack of** feeling of **responsibility or commitment** on part of individual member states
• **Opportunity** (1) – to **showcase** presidency member state territory, culture and products	• **Variable quality** – some member states or individuals better/worse at the job; unsettling for colleagues and institutional partners; may have short-term negative effect on Council's work
• **Opportunity** (2) – for presidency member state to display (and if necessary improve) its **EU credentials**	• **Time-consuming** – consultation of and negotiation with 24+ partners requires considerable input of time
• **Socialization** – invaluable learning process for new, smaller and sceptical member states	• **Expensive** – costs to presidency member state can be significant
	• **Paucity of resources** – smaller member states may not have sufficient internal or external resources to carry out all presidency functions and duties adequately

Indeed, it could be argued that the presidency under the first pillar has become so institutionalized and so hedged in by operating constraints that it can withstand quite striking variations in performance by individual governments in the office. It can even withstand the extraordinary pressures of a major election in the country that provides the chair, the most recent example being France in 1995. (We should note, however, that not everyone is so sanguine about combining an EU presidency and a national election. The Germans opted to switch places with the Finns in the order of presidency rotation because a *Bundestag* election was scheduled to take place in September 2006, during what should have been their turn in the chair. In the event, the election was called early and took place in September 2005, during the British presidency.)

This is not to say that the rotation makes no effective difference. It is clear that particular presidencies can win justified plaudits for their constructive contribution in the chair, as the Irish did in the first half of 2004. But it seems equally clear that a weak presidency is also prevented by the system from causing too much damage, however irritated the insiders may be when they suffer, as they do, from ineffectual or bumbling presidencies.

Thus the presidency helps to make the Council tick over more smoothly and more quickly, but the Council is not completely dependent on the hazards of performance by particular presidencies. Indeed, a presidency handbook produced by the Council Secretariat makes it clear that the presidency is always in the hands of the Council, in that a simple majority of Council members may challenge any procedural decision by the presidency, and that any statement by or letter from the presidency expressing the Council's position must meet with the Council's agreement.

In sharp contrast, the performance of the presidency in those other areas of EU activity where institutional responsibilities are not clearly defined and where the Commission plays a minor role has given rise to recurrent criticisms. In the development of EPC and in the construction of the two new pillars, the presidency has been the target of quite different expectations, both as the provider of practical working tools and as a potential source of collective leadership and collective representation. Individual governments do make extraordinary efforts to perform the impossible. Some are determined to try to vindicate the case for intergovernmental methods and to show off their talents, expertise and experience. Others seek to fill the gap as well as they can and with professional flair, while continuing to argue for an alternative approach.

In looking back over what is now a rather long period of experience of the presidency outside the main Community structures, we can observe considerable variations. During the 1970s, as EPC developed from loose exploratory cooperation into a more systematic coordination of positions, the presidency rose in relevance and utility. It was a focal point for all the member states, and constituted an invaluable learning process for new and smaller member states in expanding their horizons with regard to foreign policy. It is tempting to credit the presidency with having made a large contribution to the confidence-building and increased collective purposive attitude that were later to permit the upgrading of EPC into the CFSP. However, the strength of this inference is questionable. The presidency has no doubt played an important part in this development, but it seems to us that a number of other factors played an equally important part in consolidating EPC, although often less visibly. The transition to the CFSP put the whole process to the test and events found it wanting.

The subject of the third pillar (JHA) evolved more slowly than EPC or the CFSP in its early years, reflecting the difference between diplomats and practitioners of 'home affairs'. Diplomats were able to import into EPC (and later into the CFSP) experience and working methods from other arenas of international policy coordination that were prompted by external pressures familiar from other contexts. In contrast, the third pillar could draw on only the limited and constrained experience of hesitant cooperation among the Twelve; the problem was to persuade EU colleagues to share work with each other before a collective view could be expressed to third countries.

Initially, the main presidency effort went into the intended new conventions for external frontiers and Europol, both of which were tricky for reasons of substance, and because of the reservations of some member states on core issues. Otherwise business was focused on opening up areas of still very tentative cooperation that permitted little scope for presidency activism. Slight variations between presidencies have been evident. Some have tried to use their time in the chair to place more emphasis on issues of particular interest to their member state, while others have chosen to put little effort into measures they do not support wholeheartedly. Yet even this ability is constrained by multi-annual action plans as well as by deadlines imposed by the Treaty of Amsterdam (ToA), the Tampere summit programme and a number of subsequent decisions, all of which inject an element of continuity into the rhythm of work in this area.

Proposals for reform

Any discussion touching on reforms to the presidency begs three bigger questions: first, how far the member governments really want to develop a common foreign and security policy, as opposed to policy coordination and periodic joint actions; second, how to develop the relationship between the Council and the Commission, since so much of the debate about the presidency is about responsibility for tasks under the second and third pillars that, on EC matters, would fall to the Commission; and third, how to accommodate the different weights, interests and ambitions of both large and small member states.

Inherent weaknesses in the system of rotating presidencies have come to light over the years, and some of the most persistent have been addressed in successive treaties and versions of the CRPs. Thus the ToA provided for the appointment of a High Representative for the CFSP, and the 2004 version of the CRPs contains detailed provisions on the programming of Council activities and the presidency's role in the conduct of Council meetings, drawn from the Seville Conclusions of

June 2002 and a Code of Conduct agreed in March 2003. Each of these decisions and provisions is designed to use the presidency to increase continuity within the Council.

Yet problems persist, with the result that reform of the presidency has been a recurrent subject for some time. It acquired a new urgency in the 1990s, for two main reasons. The first was the prospect of an enlargement which, at a stroke and if the current rotation system were to be retained, would extend the interval between an individual member state's presidencies by five years. With a twelve-and-a-half-year gap between its periods in the chair, the educational effects of the presidency on a member state's officials would run the risk of being lost.

The second reason was a very public display of what had always been an underlying but rarely publicly articulated cleavage between the larger and smaller member states. In the past, great care had always been taken to ensure that the interests of the smaller states were visibly 'taken care of' when such issues as the weighting of votes in the Council or the distribution of senior positions in the European administration were being discussed. But the prospect of an enlargement that would see the number of small and medium-sized members increase considerably had the effect of focusing the minds of the representatives of the larger member states on issues of relative weight and influence.

The outcome was a succession of bad-tempered debates on many aspects of Council reform, including the presidency, marked by suspicion and mistrust on both sides. The most notable among these were the European Councils in Biarritz and Nice in 2000, and in Seville in 2002. Worse, it was widely felt that the problems were exacerbated rather than attenuated by a biased (French) presidency in 2000 that, far from remaining neutral, used its position in the chair to promote the interests of the larger member states (Tallberg, 2004; Milton and Keller Noëllet, 2005). Consequently, the question of the reform of the presidency became a sticking point for many delegations, making it difficult to predict which formula would eventually be chosen for the future.

The various basic options under discussion were hardly novel, having drifted in and out of favour over the years, but in some cases original nuances were added. They comprised the following suggestions.

A longer term of office

This was an idea that was first floated in the early 1970s as an antidote to the discontinuity implicit in the six-monthly rotation. It has always been vulnerable to two criticisms: first, that it might be fine with an 'effective' presidency, but would be added purgatory with an 'ineffectual' or biased presidency; and second, that it would weaken the socialization function of the presidency for individual member states by increasing the length of time between their periods in office. This latter argument has diminished in cogency with each successive enlargement, as the cycle of rotation has lengthened.

An elected presidency

Another idea that was rather long in the tooth, this resurfaced in the context of the CFE in 2003, based on the notion that a gifted individual with an elected mandate of some kind would make all the difference. However, an individual could only do so much, and could only chair some meetings, leaving the question of how other presidency tasks would be accomplished, and what the overall effect on the institutional balance of the EU would be. A variant, more related to the management than the representational role, proposed that more Council committees could elect their own chairs, a system that appears to work very well for the Economic and Financial Committee (EFC) and the EU Military Committee (EUMC), among others.

A team presidency

This idea gained currency as an alternative to increasingly insistent proposals from the larger member states for an elected president of the Council. The increased burden of the presidency is clearly demanding, making the case for a sharing of tasks compelling. The idea, therefore, that a small number of member states might share responsibility for the presidency for a given period was viewed by some as a sensible solution to several problems at once. Others were not convinced, however, pointing out that, as in the current arrangements, the only constant members of the team for many purposes would be officials from the Commission and the Council Secretariat.

Concurrent cycles

Different presidencies for different areas of EU work were proposed in response, but concern was expressed about the problems of coordination that such a system would engender.

A 'directorate' or directoire

A quasi-permanent grouping of figures from key member states was also proposed as a measure of stability and continuity for the office of the presidency. The clear implication that some member governments would exercise more responsibility and enjoy more explicit power than others was not lost on those who considered themselves likely to be counted among 'the others'. The unsurprising result was that it was greeted with less than universal enthusiasm.

Appointing a Mr (or Ms) CFSP

This idea, finally achieved with the appointment of Javier Solana in 1999, drew its inspiration from three sources: the North Atlantic Treaty Organisation (NATO) and Western European Union (WEU) posts of Secretary-General; the occasional (though not to date all that happy) practice of the European Council appointing an individual to pursue a particular task, as in the former Yugoslavia; and the readiness of the French to suggest experienced candidates for such a post.

An enhanced partnership of the Council presidency and the Commission

Strengthening the role of the Commission is the obvious alternative in the case of the second (and, by extension, the third) pillars.

The 2002–3 CFE and the subsequent IGC gave rise to much vigorous debate regarding the pros and cons of the above options. With so many proposed reforms in contention, and no single solution commanding general assent, it was perhaps not surprising that different solutions were proposed for different purposes. The Constitutional Treaty therefore provided that the various parts of the Council hierarchy would be presided over in the following way:

- *The European Council* would have a president elected by qualified majority for a period of two-and-a-half years, renewable once.
- *The Foreign Affairs Council* would be presided over by the European Union Minister for Foreign Affairs, who would be appointed by qualified majority by the European Council, with the agreement of the President of the Commission. The EU Foreign Minister would also be a Vice-President of the Commission.
- *The other Council formations* would be presided over by predetermined groups of three member states for a period of eighteen months (team presidencies). Each member state would chair all Council configurations (with the exception of the Foreign Affairs Council) for a period of six months, and would be assisted in its presidential duties by the two other members of the team.
- *The Euro Group* would have a president elected by a majority of the Euro Group member states for a period of two-and-a-half years (already the case at the time of writing, since the election of the Luxembourg prime minister, Jean-Claude Juncker, to the post in 2004).
- *Coreper* would be chaired by the representative of the state chairing the General Affairs Council.
- *The Political and Security Committee (COPS)* would be presided over by a representative of the EU Foreign Minister.

- *Working parties and other preparatory bodies* would be chaired by a representative of the member state chairing the Council formation to which they reported, unless the Council decided otherwise.

If the provisions of the CT are not officially implemented in the near future (the inevitable consequence of its rejection by France and the Netherlands in 2005), the current situation as regards the chairing of meetings at different levels of the Council hierarchy will prevail. However, the germ of the idea of team presidencies has been down, and the new rotation system agreed for the period 2007–20 may prove to be fertile soil for its cultivation.

Part II

With Whom?

Chapter 6

Overlapping Competences: the Council and the European Council

Despite the apparent similarity in their names, the Council of the European Union and the European Council are two distinct bodies. As we have seen, the Council is composed of government ministers from each of the member states and now meets in nine different configurations about seventy-five times a year to discuss and decide on issues largely subject to the so-called 'Community method'. The European Council, on the other hand, is an altogether more exclusive body, which brings together the heads of state or government of each of the member states and the president of the Commission about four times a year in a much more obviously intergovernmental setting. Yet there is a large degree of overlap in their areas of competence and activity, and they can rightly claim to prepare and progress each other's work. This duality lies at the core of the Council–European Council relationship, which is the subject of this chapter.

The European Council was created as an intergovernmental initiative in order to answer a specific perceived need in the 1970s. It was subsequently allowed to evolve over the next two decades with a minimum of codification in order to preserve its unique nature and distinctive contribution to the process of European integration (Bulmer, 1985; Bulmer and Wessels, 1987; Werts, 1992). As a result, the European Council has developed into a locus of power second to none in the European Union's (EU's) institutional system today. It drives the process forward, the dates of its meetings 'mark[ing] the rhythm of the Union's various activities in the way religious feast days marked the rhythm of daily life in medieval Christendom' (de Schoutheete, 2006). Weaknesses have come to light over the years, but it was only in the late 1990s, in the context of discussions about reforming the Council as a whole in order to prepare it for enlargement, that serious attention was first paid to suggestions for reforming the European Council itself. Some non-treaty-based changes were implemented following decisions taken at the Seville European Council in June 2002, while others (including treaty-based changes) were dependent on the ratification and implementation of the Constitutional Treaty (CT).

165

This chapter is organized around four main questions, the answers to which will illuminate the current (and future) relationship between the Council and the European Council. First, can the two bodies be viewed as different parts of the same hierarchy, or is the European Council sufficiently dissimilar to the Council to justify its perceived separate status and position? An overview of the European Council's origins and development should go some way towards answering this question. Second, to the extent that the areas of competence of the ministerial and European Councils overlap, what are the criteria that determine the level at which an issue will be treated, and how does this affect relations between them? The functions and forms of the European Council are enumerated in response to this query. Third, what form does interaction between the European Council and the lower levels of the Council hierarchy take? A description of the preparation of European Council meetings, the proceedings themselves and their follow-up will illustrate the role played by bodies such as the Committee of Permanent Representatives (Coreper), the presidency and the Council Secretariat. Finally, what reforms of the European Council are in the pipeline, and how will they impact on Council–European Council relations in an enlarged EU?

Origins and development

Acquiring a legal basis and role

The Treaties of Paris and Rome did not attribute an institutional role to the heads of state or government of the member states. However, such was the latter's interest in, and desire not to be excluded from, this ground-breaking venture that they met informally and occasionally from 1961 onwards, to discuss developments in their member states and in the European Communities (EC). The perceived utility of these 'fireside chats' may be discerned from the decision, taken in Paris in December 1974, to hold regular summit meetings 'to ensure progress and overall consistency' in the activities of the Communities and in the work on political cooperation'. Dublin played host to the first regular European Council meeting in March 1975, since when the European Council has been convened over ninety times, on average between three and four times a year.

The *communiqué* issued at the end of the informal Paris summit of 1974, which officially set up the European Council, declared that the heads of government (*sic*) had decided to meet 'three times a year *and, whenever necessary, in the Council of the Communities* and in the context of political cooperation' (emphasis added). The clear implication was that the European Council would normally meet outside the Council framework but could, should the need arise, meet formally and act as the Council at a more senior level. Only in the latter cases would its activities be subject to the rules of procedure governing the Council.

A decade later, the European Council acquired a legal basis for the first time by means of Article 2 of the Single European Act (SEA), which focused on its composition and organization rather than its powers, while the 1992 Maastricht Treaty (Treaty on European Union – TEU) established the European Council as a formal institution of the EU, but not of the EC (Article D). It also set about clarifying the functions of the European Council, while repeating the organizational provisions laid down in the SEA. The 1997 Treaty of Amsterdam (ToA) continued the process of defining the powers of the European Council (for example in Article J.3 in the area of foreign and security policy, and in Artiicle 109q relating to employment), while the 2001 Treaty of Nice (ToN) laid down rules governing the venue of its meetings (in Declaration 22 annexed to the final act).

The current situation is that the European Council is not included in the list of EU institutions enumerated in Article 5 TEU, but is mentioned separately in Article 4. The CT, agreed in 2004 but rejected by France and the Netherlands in 2005, would have reversed this situation, making the European Council a fully-fledged institution along with the European Parliament (EP), the Council of Ministers (*sic*), the European Commission and the Court of Justice of the European Union (ECJ) (Article I-19). In addition, and most importantly for the future institutional balance of the EU, the CT provided for an elected, permanent president of the European Council (see final section).

Composition

The European Council has many club-like attributes, the most obvious one being its restrictive membership policy. In order to qualify as a full member, candidates must be the head of state or government of an EU member state or the President of the Commission. Two things should be noted here. First, the designation 'heads of state or government' was chosen to allow for the French and later the Finnish situations, where the president is both the head of state and the chief executive. Under conditions of *cohabitation* in France, both the French president and the French prime minister have on occasion attended European Council sessions together. Second, the Commission is represented as of right in the European Council, while merely being invited to attend ministerial Council meetings. The club-like atmosphere is heightened by the fact that, since they also meet regularly in other multilateral non-EU forums, most of the members of the European Council are on first-name terms with one another, and discussions are normally frank and sometimes bruising.

European Council meetings are clubby affairs too. Access to the room where the members meet is highly restricted. The heads of state or government may be accompanied only by their foreign or finance ministers, and the Commission President only by one other member of the Commission, depending on the issues being discussed. The only other individuals in the room are the Council Secretary-General and High Representative for the Common Foreign and Security Policy (SG/HRCFSP), the Deputy Secretary-General (DSG) of the Council, the SG of the Commission, a very small number of senior presidency and Council Secretariat officials, a 15-minute rotating relay of note-takers from the Council Secretariat, and technical staff. Of the above, only the SG and the DSG of the Council have seats at the main table, all the others being seated in a row behind the table. Separate dinners are arranged on the first evening for the heads of state or government and the president of the Commission on the one hand, and the foreign ministers and a senior member of the Commission on the other.

The European Council is presided over by the head of state or government whose member state currently holds the six-month presidency of the Council. This arrangement is designed to ensure coherence and efficiency between the Council and the European Council during a presidency, but is dependent on good internal coordination on the part of the presidency member state. Unlike the case in the ministerial Council, the president also represents his or her member state (there is no separate national delegation for the presidency member state), resulting sometimes in a rather overtly partisan chair. The subject of the presidency of the European Council was much discussed during the 2002–3 Conference on the Future of Europe (CFE) and the subsequent intergovernmental council (IGC), a discussion to which we shall return in the final section of this chapter.

European Councils are stage-managed events, from the security-conscious arrival of the major participants to the last simultaneously interpreted answer at the final official press conference. While intimacy and informality are the goals inside the meeting room, the scenes outside are frequently the exact opposite. Each head of state or government is accompanied to the meeting venue (though not to the meeting itself) by a large national delegation. The size of these delegations has been 'limited' since 2002, to a maximum of twenty per member state, plus twenty for the Commission, although this figure does not include technical and security staff. The summit in its entirety is covered by literally thousands of journalists – the Seville European Council of June 2002 attracted 4,000 accredited journalists from 766 different media representing 62 different countries (Stark, 2002).

Three other categories of participant play a role in the margins of the European Council:

- Since the late 1980s, the President of the EP has been invited to 'address' the members of the European Council at the beginning of their meetings, but not to remain for the main discussion. It is the EP President's task to inform the heads of state or government and the Commission President formally of the Parliament's views on the issues they are due to discuss.
- During accession negotiations, the political leaders of the candidate countries are normally given the opportunity to discuss relevant issues with the EU's heads of state or government on the second day of European Council meetings, sometimes over lunch. The value of such meetings is generally agreed to be symbolic rather than substantive. Sometimes, however, issues of real substance may be on the table, as was the case with the negotiation of the conditions for the opening of accession negotiations with Turkey at the Brussels European Council of December 2004 (see Ludlow, 2004).
- Time permitting and agenda allowing, the head of state or government of a third country may also be invited to meet and address the European Council. This may occur over lunch, as was the case with Prime Minister Allawi of Iraq in November 2004.

Number and location of meetings

The number of times the European Council has been convened on an annual basis has fluctuated over the years, and has now settled down to a basic tally of four – one at the end of each six-month presidency (in June and December), a spring meeting now normally devoted to economic and social questions (the so-called Lisbon process, after the first such meeting was convened in Lisbon in March 2000), and a fourth meeting in the autumn. Informal and extraordinary meetings (see below) are not excluded, but the already full agendas of the key players necessitate good reasons for the convening of such meetings.

Scheduled meetings normally take place over two days (although the now infamous Nice European Council in December 2000 spanned five), while extraordinary sessions normally last for one day or even part of a day. Until 2001, scheduled European Council meetings were normally held in the capital or one of the main cities of the presidency member state. The high point of each successive presidency, they were viewed as an opportunity not only to produce results, but also to acquaint (or re-acquaint) the members of this august body with the relevant location, and to provide a showcase for national products, such as food, drink or gifts for the delegates. At the Nice European Council of December 2000, it was decided that at least one scheduled European Council meeting would be held every year in Brussels until such time as the number of member states reached eighteen, after which date all summit meetings would be held there, which has been the case since 2004 (see Appendix 6). A wing of the Residence Palace building adjacent to the Justus Lipsius building in Brussels is being adapted to accommodate the European Council, with work scheduled to be completed around 2010. In the meantime, the heads of state or government will continue to meet amid tight security in the Justus Lipsius building.

The answer to our first question – whether the ministerial and European Councils can be viewed as being different parts of the same hierarchy – is clearly 'No'. In terms of its legal basis, its composition, and the physical arrangements for its meetings, the European Council is clearly sufficiently dissimilar to the Council to justify its perceived separate status and position. This distinctiveness is further underlined by an examination of the European Council's functions and working methods.

Functions and forms

The original *raison d'être* for the European Council was to engage the most senior political leaders of the member states and of the Commission in an informal process of reflection and discussion that would result in strategic direction for the European Communities as a whole. Operating as it did without a clear legal basis for the first decade of its formal existence, and thereafter in the absence of a clearly defined role or explicitly delimited functions, the European Council has felt free to deal with whatever issue it likes in whatever way it likes. As a result, the heads of state or government have been, and continue to be, involved directly in all the important issues on the EU's agenda. Official texts therefore quickly prove inadequate to describe the current functions of the European Council, which may be grouped under six main headings (de Schoutheete and Wallace, 2002).

Providing strategic guidelines and political impetus

This was the European Council's original and most important function. It fulfils it better than any other organ, for the simple reason that its members are the only ones with sufficient power to ensure that concrete actions follow what might otherwise be viewed as worthy rhetoric. All important new EU initiatives either originate in the European Council or receive from it its seal of approval, a process ensuring that they will see the light of day. Thus decisions to admit new members, to launch new policy initiatives (for example, economic and monetary union or the fight against terrorism), or to reform the treaties, can all be traced back to one or more meetings of the European Council.

Shaping foreign policy

The second major function of the European Council is the shaping of a collective foreign policy, a task it has undertaken since its inception.

It is no coincidence that the only other ministers who have attended European Council meetings from the outset are the national ministers of foreign affairs. External relations always figure prominently on the European Council's agenda, and in the conclusions and declarations that emerge from their meetings.

Decision-making on Community matters

Occupying as it does a position at the apex of the Council, the European Council has become an additional forum for Community decision-making. This has occurred in two ways. First, when ministers meeting in sectoral Councils have found themselves unable or unwilling to decide on difficult issues, they have developed the habit of passing these dossiers upwards, in effect using the European Council as a court of final appeal. Thus the heads of state or government have been called upon as the final arbiters for such controversial issues as taxation or, more prosaically, the colour of the European passport. The issues discussed and the decisions taken at their meetings are not always of such strategic or perceived importance, however, and it has been suggested that the European Council would do better to leave day-to-day decision-making to the relevant ministers (Solana, 2002).

Second, the heads of state or government have themselves taken an active interest in certain dossiers, ensuring that decisions on such major issues as financial packages, economic and monetary union (EMU) or the creation of the internal market are taken by the European Council. In addition, the European Council has acquired specific decision-making powers of its own in the field of EMU (de Schoutheete, 2006).

Extra-treaty decision-making

Over the years, it has fallen to the members of the European Council to decide on issues of domestic importance to the member states, such as the seat of the EU's institutions and agencies, and such senior appointments within the institutions as the High Representative for the Common Foreign and Security Policy (HRCFSP), the President of the Commission, or the Deputy Secretary-General of the Council. These decisions have been taken on the basis of consensus, which has frequently required a package deal in order to gain acceptance from all involved. The ToN provided that major appointments would in the future be taken by the Council acting by qualified majority, but if the aim was to avoid the involvement of the heads of state or government in such decisions, the attempt has already failed – in June 2004, the heads of state or government met in the 2595th meeting of the Council to designate the president of the Commission and to reappoint Javier Solana and Pierre de Boissieu as SG and DSG of the Council, respectively (Council Document 10995/04).

Amending the treaties

Treaty revision has been an ongoing fact of EU life for the best part of two decades, and the role played by the European Council in this process has grown exponentially. While its input into the revision processes that culminated in the SEA in 1986 and the TEU in 1992 was minimal, it has become more directly and minutely involved in more recent instances of treaty revision. Rules on transparency and access to documents enable those interested to detect the direct input of the Amsterdam European Council into what was to become the Treaty of Amsterdam (de Schoutheete, 2002, p. 41). The input of heads of state and government on detailed issues is, however, not always helpful; Coreper spent several weeks trying to sort out what their heads of state and government had agreed in Council votes in the final frantic hours of the Nice European Council in December 2000.

Engaging in open coordination (the Lisbon process)

This is the newest responsibility of the European Council, dating back to March 2000. A special spring meeting of the European Council is held each year to discuss socioeconomic issues, involving the heads of state or government in a process of soft coordination, designed to pool information at the highest level on different national experiences and experiments. The results of this process have so far been somewhat disappointing, and both the Kok Report of November 2004 and a mid-term review in March 2005 highlighted the need for a relaunch and improved implementation of the Lisbon Strategy.

In fulfilling these various functions, the European Council meets in a number of different forms:

- *Scheduled formal meetings*, as already described, are held four times a year, normally taking place over two days, and producing presidency conclusions and declarations.
- *Scheduled informal meetings* are intended to facilitate an exchange of views on specific issues, such as a current IGC or international situation. They are usually shorter than the formal meetings, may not include the foreign ministers, and do not normally produce official conclusions. The British decided to organize an informal summit to discuss the future of Europe during their presidency in the second half of 2005.
- *Emergency or extraordinary meetings* are convened at very short notice, normally in response to a particular event, to allow the European Council to discuss the event's implications and to make a joint statement. This was the case after the fall of the Berlin Wall in 1989, in the aftermath of the terrorist attacks in the USA on 11 September 2001 and, less successfully, in response to the situation in Iraq in February 2003.

The members of the European Council meet in two other forms, frequently directly before or after the meeting of the formal European Council itself, which makes it difficult for outsiders to distinguish between them:

- A *Conference of Europe* has, since March 1998, brought together periodically the heads of state and government of the EU member states, the candidate countries and Switzerland to discuss issues of mutual interest and concern. At a meeting of such a Conference in Nice on 7 December 2001, which immediately preceded the European Council, the decision was taken to expand its membership to include 'countries covered by the stabilisation and association process and the European Free Trade Association (EFTA) countries'.
- The members of the European Council also meet as the most senior level of *intergovernmental conferences* (IGCs), where issues of treaty reform are negotiated and decided.

At Nice, in December 2001, a morning meeting of the Conference of Europe was followed in the afternoon and the subsequent day by the European Council proper, after which the heads of state and government met in the form of an IGC. The agendas may have differentiated between the various meetings, but IGC issues were discussed at and in the margins of all three, making it difficult for outside observers to distinguish between them.

From the foregoing, it is clear that the European Council now occupies a position at the apex of the EU's institutional system, overseeing the work of each of the three pillars, and the specialized sectoral Councils that operate within them. It monitors their work, sets framework principles to guide their future deliberations, takes or clears major political decisions, and frequently engages in troubleshooting, which can involve the political leaders in extremely detailed discussions.

What determines whether or not a particular dossier will find its way on to the agenda of the European Council? Much depends on the nature and controversiality of the issue in question, as well as on the personalities involved. The Council is not obliged to refer any matters to the European Council, but some issues are more likely to be dealt with by the heads of state or government than others. This is particularly true for issues relating to political integration, including treaty reform and enlargement of the EU. The European Council is less likely to deal with very technical matters, such as steel or fisheries, unless the dossier in question has a strong political impact or is of major domestic interest to a number of member states, and the ministers in Council decide that an input from their political chiefs would be either beneficial or politic (or both).

In any event, all major decisions now go through the European Council in some shape or form, whether merely for clearance or for more detailed discussion. This fact is frequently used to bolster the argument that the Council's legal and political authority has declined, and that it has lost power to the European Council. It is indeed true that, in those policy areas where the European Council takes an active interest, the relevant sectoral Council can in effect, and at one extreme, be reduced to a subordinate body. The ministers can find themselves responsible for preparing the discussions of the heads of state or government, and carrying out their instructions or acting according to the guidelines they lay down. Other Councils may find themselves responsible for day-to-day decision-making in their relevant policy areas, applying to the European Council for political guidance on those occasions when they cannot reach agreement at their own level.

The input of the European Council takes the form of a political decision, which only has legal force once it has been adopted by the Council according to the relevant legislative procedures. To this extent, the two levels are interdependent: without the preparatory and executive functions of the Council, the European Council would be unable to operate, and in the absence of the political impetus and guiding principles laid down by the European Council, the Council could become bogged down.

Yet it would be erroneous to think that the various Councils have each been affected in the same way, or to the same extent, by the creation and operation of the European Council. It is both necessary and useful to distinguish between the General Affairs and External Relations Council (GAERC) on the one hand, and the remaining sectoral Councils on the other.

The foreign ministers who make up the GAERC constitute an important link between the ministerial and European Councils. They enjoy a great measure of authority and responsibility in the preparatory phase of the European Council, not only because of their competence to deal with both Community affairs and CFSP issues, but also, and more significantly, because they in fact participate in the meetings of the European Council itself, as assistants to their respective heads of state or government. As such, they help to shape the agenda of these meetings, engage in the discussions that ensue, and are chiefly responsible for ensuring that the stated policy wishes of their political leaders are subsequently fulfilled.

However, the central coordinating and strategic role of the original General Affairs Council (GAC) had been weakened by the existence of the European Council. The GAC had frequently found itself reduced to the role of a clearing-house for issues moving between the sectoral Councils and the European Council. This may be in part because the members of other sectoral Councils prefer not to have the foreign ministers (who are frequently members of another political party in those countries with coalition governments) solving their problems for them. This is particularly true of those ministers dealing with economic and financial affairs (Ecofin) and agriculture, who have preferred to involve the European Council directly in their detailed conflicts over budgetary rebates and milk quotas.

As regards the other sectoral Councils, it can be argued that the very existence of the European Council has given rise to a constant upward pressure in decision-making and the resulting danger of overloading the top of the hierarchy. There is also the possibility that issues can become unnecessarily politicized; where once the ministers might have tried to work out a compromise at Council level, or sent the matter back down to Coreper, or even the relevant working party, for more technical discussion, the existence of the higher, more political, level as a court of appeal can sometimes prove irresistible.

An overlap in the areas of competence of the ministerial and European Councils means that the two levels must interact on a large number of dossiers, each providing the input appropriate to their position. The various sectoral Councils normally act independently of the European Council, in that most of the dossiers they deal with are not discussed actively at the level of the political heads. Rather, the deliberations of the sectoral ministers are informed by general guidelines discussed and jointly agreed by the heads of state or government.

Preparation, proceedings and follow-up

Clearly, the relationship between the ministerial Councils and the European Council is one of interdependence, but what of relations between the latter and the other components of the Council hierarchy? They will be discussed here in relation to the preparation of the European Council's meetings, the proceedings of the meetings themselves and the follow-up to their conclusions.

Preparation

According to rules laid down in Seville in December 2001 (see Appendix 7), European Council meetings are prepared by the GAERC, meeting in its General Affairs configuration. In practice, however, this responsibility is shared on the one hand with the Council's various preparatory bodies as regards substance, and on the other with the presidency, assisted by the Council Secretariat, as regards political and strategic input.

Who decides what will be discussed when the heads of state or government meet? In keeping with the principles of informality and light institutionalization that underpinned the European Council from its inception, the standard line was always that no official agenda existed in advance of meetings. In practice, however, the presidency invariably communicated a list of items for discussion to the other members of the European Council in the weeks or days preceding the meeting, and additional items could be (and usually were) added at the beginning of the meeting itself. That this was not necessarily the most efficient way to proceed was acknowledged at the Seville European Council in December 2001, since when the following procedure has applied:

- An annotated draft agenda (see Box 6.1) is proposed by the presidency, discussed in detail by Coreper and agreed by the GAERC at least four weeks before the European Council meeting. It distinguishes between:

Box 6.1   *Sample European Council draft annotated agenda*

Produced by the Dutch presidency on 19 November 2004 in preparation for the Brussels European Council of 16–17 December 2004

  The Presidency intends to limit the agenda to the following items:

 I.   Enlargement
 II.   Terrorism
 III. Financial Framework 2007–2013: principles and guidelines
 IV.   Area of freedom, security and justice: the EU Drugs Strategy 2005–2012
 V.   External affairs
 VI.   Other issues

The meeting will be preceded by an *exposé* by the President of the European Parliament, Mr Josep Borrell, followed by an exchange of views.

I.   ENLARGEMENT

The European Council is expected to take decisions on outstanding enlargement questions, in particular on:

- conclusion of negotiations with Bulgaria and Romania; and
- opening of negotiations with Croatia and Turkey.

II.   THE FIGHT AGAINST TERRORISM

The European Council is expected, in line with conclusions reached at its meeting in June 2004, to review progress made in the fight against terrorism. In this context it will discuss the report by the SG/HR on the implementation and revision of the Action Plan/Roadmap on combating terrorism and take note of other relevant reports and proposals on related subjects, *inter alia*:

- integrating an intelligence capacity in the General Secretariat of the Council;
- integrating the fight against terrorism into external policy;

→

- items to be approved or endorsed without debate;
- items for discussion with a view to defining general political guidelines;
- items for discussion with a view to adopting a decision (in the context of enlargement and in exceptional cases); and
- items for discussion, but not intended to be the subject of conclusions.

- With regard to the second and third items listed above, the presidency prepares a brief outline paper, setting out the main issues, the questions to be debated and the main options available.
- On the eve of the European Council, the GAERC holds a final preparatory session and adopts the definitive agenda .

- enhancing cooperation on civil protection; and
- enhancing protection of critical infrastructure.

III.   PREPARATION OF THE FINANCIAL FRAMEWORK 2007–2013

The European Council is expected to welcome a Presidency report on progress achieved since June 2004. In line with its June conclusions, the European Council is expected to decide on principles and guidelines as part of the process leading to agreement on the new Financial Framework and related issues, including own resources.

IV.   AREA OF FREEDOM, SECURITY AND JUSTICE: THE EU DRUGS STRATEGY 2005–2012

The European Council is expected to take note of the adoption by the Council of a new EU Drugs Strategy for the period 2005–2012, and endorse its approach and main lines of action. It is unlikely to invite the Commission to present proposals in 2005 to implement the strategy.

V.   EXTERNAL AFFAIRS

The European Council is expected to discuss the Middle East Peace Process, Iran, Iraq, Sudan, Afghanistan, and the strategic partnership for the Mediterranean and the Middle East.
The European Council is also expected to:

- take note of the procedure for preparatory work leading to the establishment of the External Action Service; and
- take note of the Presidency report on ESDP.

VI.   OTHER ISSUES

The European Council is expected to take note of the outcome of a series of debates during the semester on commonly shared values.
The European Council might take note of the state of play relating to the process of ratification of the Constitutional Treaty.

A meeting of the European Council is the president's show. As the host and chair, the responsibility for the outcome of the meeting falls squarely on his or her shoulders. Just as organizing a 'good presidency' has become a point of pride among the member states, so the hosting of a 'successful European Council' can enhance, restore or harm the reputation and European credentials of an individual as well as that of their member state. Indeed, it is probably true to say that, fairly or unfairly, the success or otherwise of European Council meetings has become one of the most important criteria by which presidencies are now judged.

In preparing a meeting of the European Council, therefore, the presidency team is anxious to ensure that as many potential difficulties as possible are ironed out before the heads of state or government meet as a group. This is achieved in three main ways:

- through detailed and sustained efforts at all levels of the Council hierarchy, in close cooperation with the Council Secretariat, in an attempt to reach agreement on details, and to find a form of words acceptable to all participants;
- by means of bilateral meetings with some or all of the other members of the European Council in the weeks immediately preceding the summit, in order to sound out their views and concerns on the issues to be discussed. In the past, this entailed a 'tour of the capitals' undertaken by the president of the European Council, an increasingly time-consuming practice in an enlarged EU. More recently, the other heads of state and government have come to see the president in his or her own capital.
- by agreeing in advance as many as possible of the draft conclusions to be endorsed by the heads of state or government during the final working session of their meeting. The draft conclusions may be penned by the presidency, working alone or in close cooperation with the Council Secretariat and the Commission. They are reviewed in detail by Coreper II in the weeks preceding the summit, and finally by the General Affairs Council.

Clearly, the substantive preparation of European Council meetings is undertaken at various levels of the Council hierarchy. Sometimes the heads of state or government may request a special preparatory committee composed of their personal representatives and chaired by the representative of the presidency member state to prepare a detailed report for them on a particularly sensitive or detailed matter. One such example is the Bastarreche Group that reported on reform of the Council to the Seville European Council of June 2002. Alternatively, the committee may be chaired by an individual appointed by the Commission, with the members being chosen for their expertise in the area in question. A recent example is the Kok Group, whose report reviewing the Lisbon Strategy was presented to the European Council in Brussels in November 2004.

For the most part, however, the matters discussed in the European Council are those on which ministers meeting in Council have been unable or unwilling to decide. Consequently, the initial preparation of the substance of the issue will normally have been undertaken by the relevant Council's preparatory groups (see Chapter 3). In this respect, Coreper occupies a strategic position, being responsible not only for reviewing the work of the vast majority of the Council's specialized working parties, but also for preparing the meeting of the GAERC that precedes and prepares the meeting of the European Council. It is also at the level of Coreper that detailed consideration of the draft conclusions is carried out well in advance of the European Council itself. In this sense, it can be argued that Corepeir II now fulfils the role previously undertaken by the heads of state or government themselves in their final summit working session.

At the same time as they fulfil their Coreper-related functions, the individual members of the committee are closely involved in the preparation of their respective national positions on the issues on the agenda. Because of their intimate knowledge of the dossiers in question, and their up-to-date information on the other national positions, they may be called upon to advise their political leaders on the strategy to adopt at the meeting in order to gain a national objective, although the influence of the individual permanent representatives differs between member states.

The input of the Political and Security Committee (COPS – see Chapter 3) into meetings of the European Council is significant, given the presence of its immediate masters, the foreign ministers, at the meeting itself. The Committee normally agrees on the CFSP and ESDP (European security and defence policy) agenda items – which can subsequently be modified by the foreign ministers – two days before the European Council. It meets on the first day of the summit to discuss and draft the CFSP declarations to be included in the final conclusions. The individual members of the committee are senior figures in their national delegations, and trusted advisers to their foreign and prime ministers. To them, in conjunction with the foreign ministers, falls the responsibility, after the summit, of ensuring that any necessary actions flowing from the CFSP-related conclusions of the meeting are undertaken.

Spanning and working closely with each presidency, the Council Secretariat has been involved in the preparation and running of the ninety or so meetings of the European Council that have taken place since 1974. The wealth of experience that it enjoys as a consequence is made freely available to each incoming presidency. However, the actual role allotted to it in the preparation of meetings of the European Council will depend on several factors, among them the size and experience of the member state in office, as well as the personality of the relevant head of state or government.

In helping to prepare a meeting of the European Council, the Council Secretariat's input may be logistical, substantive or even political. Secretariat officials advise and assist national officials on the administrative support required for the meeting, and are frequently able to help in organising the often complicated logistics involved. Their intimate knowledge of the dossiers on the agenda, which they will normally have followed on their passage through the Council hierarchy, is made available to the chair in the form of a 'Note to the President', which may also contain tactical negotiating advice on the strategy to adopt in order to reach the outcome desired by the presidency.

Proceedings

In these security-conscious times, it is hardly surprising that access to the site of the European Council is very strictly regulated. Those authorized to attend – whether as members of a delegation, as accredited journalists or as technical assistants – are assigned coloured badges, allowing them access to specified areas only, often far removed from the meeting room itself (de Schoutheete, 2006). The heads of state or government are separated from their officials and advisers for long periods of time, a clear source of worry to some! As valued advisers, the members of Coreper are present at the site of the European Council meeting (although not allowed to enter the meeting room), and Coreper as a body may be required to meet in order to work out the details of an issue being discussed in more general terms by their political masters.

The European Council normally meets over a period of two days. For the heads of state or government, it consists primarily of plenary working sessions (some of which may be attended by the foreign ministers or the ministers for economic and financial affairs, depending on the items on the agenda) punctuated by working lunches and dinners. Full interpretation is provided during the working sessions (the heads of state or government are not expected to be adept polyglots as well as eminent politicians!), and the individual members of the European Council may be accompanied by whispering translators during the scheduled meals. A meeting with the President of the EP normally precedes the first working session, and meetings with the political leaders of candidate or third countries may also be scheduled at various points. In addition, the margins of European Council meetings have proved to be useful opportunities for bilateral meetings between the political leaders of member states or of transnational political parties.

In the course of the working sessions and over lunch or dinner, the heads of state or government discuss each of the issues on the agenda in turn. The working sessions may be suspended in order to allow the presidency to speak to the heads of state or government individually (a system known as 'confessionals', also utilized in Council meetings), or sometimes in small groups, in an attempt to reach agreement on a particularly contentious matter. During such breaks, the other members of the European Council may take the opportunity to confer with their respective delegations, and to brief them on the current state of discussions.

In addition to such direct, if unscheduled, reports, summary briefings on the outcome and substance of the discussions on each item are provided for the waiting delegations at regular intervals in the course of the working sessions. Much care is taken to safeguard the confidentiality of the discussions at the time of such briefings, but a sufficiently determined, well-informed and interested observer can piece together a pretty complete picture from information gleaned from several national or institutional sources at a later date.

Where necessary, the pre-prepared draft conclusions are adapted to take into account the discussions that have taken place during the working sessions, and of any subsequent agreements reached. They are then translated into each of the EU's working languages and presented to the heads of state or government for agreement at their final working session. Decisions are normally taken by consensus, although some major appointments, such as that of the Commission President, only require a qualified majority. The official end of the European Council is signalled by means of a presidency press conference, where the conclusions are presented by the president to the waiting media.

Clearly, the presidency in general and the president in particular, are the driving force behind every European Council, for better or worse. They largely determine the items to be included on the agenda, try to coordinate the preparatory work in order to ensure the best possible chance of gaining agreement, and are responsible throughout the meeting for keeping their colleagues on track. Council Secretariat officials can and do assist greatly in the fulfilment of these tasks, through their unique mixture of expertise and experience. Indeed, their detailed grasp of seemingly arcane decision-making mechanisms and legalistic niceties makes them invaluable assistants to the individual in the chair, who, in addition to everything else, is responsible for ensuring that decisions are taken according to the rules currently in force.

Follow-up

The working sessions of European Council meetings are recorded, but the only person with access to the recordings after the event is the SG of the Council, who may be requested to verify a specific point in the discussion (de Schoutheete, 2006). The only tangible and publicly available outcome of meetings of the European Council, therefore, is the document known as the Conclusions of the Presidency, which enumerates the agreements reached between the protagonists at their meeting. For this reason, it is examined minutely by interested parties for signs of success, failure or disagreement. For the presidency, the European Council conclusions represent a vital part of the balance sheet that is drawn up at the end of each six-month period, and by which the member state in the chair is judged by its colleagues. Since key meetings of the European Council normally take place towards the end of a presidency, the member state in question generally hands on the direct responsibility for overseeing the follow-up of these meetings to its successor.

The presidency conclusions may take a number of different forms:

- political declarations on matters of external or internal policy;
- requests to the Commission to draft a report or a proposal on a specific matter;
- political guidelines for national representatives who have reached an impasse when discussing something at Council or a lower level in the hierarchy; or
- instructions to the Council to implement internal reforms.

At its first meeting after the European Council meeting, Coreper reviews the presidency conclusions. At this point, each ambassador may, on behalf of his or her member government, add comments to the conclusions, which are normally accepted without further debate. These comments indicate the interpretation attached by the member state in question to particular points in the *communiqué*.

The follow-up to the conclusions adopted by a European Council is undertaken by the GAERC, assisted by Coreper for first pillar issues, by COPS for second pillar (CFSP and ESDP) issues, and by the Article 36 Committee (CATS – see Chapter 3) for third pillar (justice and home affairs – JHA) issues. In each case, this follow-up work is overseen by the presidency-in-office, assisted by the Council Secretariat. The latter is responsible for ensuring that, where necessary, the issues discussed at the European Council are placed on the agendas of the relevant subsequent meetings of the Council. Sometimes the European Council requests that a progress report be provided for a forthcoming meeting of the heads of state or government, and it is the responsibility of the GAERC, again assisted by the presidency and the Council Secretariat, to ensure that this deadline is respected.

Although the input of the Council's working parties into the European Council is indirect, these lower levels of the Council hierarchy can be affected directly by the outcome of meetings of the heads of state or government. Individual working parties may find themselves discussing matters on which the relevant ministerial Council was unable to decide, but on which the European Council provided political guidance, opening the way for further discussion at the level of officials. In this way, the task of the working parties can be facilitated by the political leaders of the member states.

Reforming the European Council

The Solana Report on reform of the Council, submitted to the Barcelona European Council of March 2002, was very critical of this highest level of the Council hierarchy. Instead of fulfilling its original purpose – that of providing the Union with the necessary impetus for its development and defining general political guidelines – the European Council, claimed the report, all too often engaged in 'laborious low-level drafting work', 'report-approval' or 'inappropriate exercises in self-congratulation' (see Ludlow, 2002; pp. 269–73). Changes were clearly required in order to put 'the Union's supreme political authority' back on track.

The Seville European Council of June 2002 approved a number of rules for organizing the proceedings of the European Council, which were contained in an annex to the Presidency Conclusions of that meeting (included as Appendix 7 in this volume). These rules were a response to the problems identified by Solana, and subsequent suggestions put forward by the Spanish presidency following the Bastarreche Group's consultations with representatives of each of the other member states. The rules covered three main areas – the preparation, conduct and conclusions of meetings of the European Council – and have been discussed in detail in the relevant sections of this chapter. Here, we shall limit ourselves to a discussion of their likely impact on relations between the ministerial and European Councils.

Preparation

The very explicit attribution for responsibility for the preparatory function to the GAERC may be seen as an attempt to reinstate this formation of the Council to the central coordinating position that it originally occupied. Other formations of the Council are now required to route their reports to the European Council through the GAERC, which should normally be the final preparatory body to meet before a summit meeting. For the spring European Council which, since 2000, now normally concentrates on socioeconomic policy, a Key Issues Paper is drawn up by Ecofin as a preparatory document, but passes through the GAERC on its way to the European Council.

As the body chiefly responsible for preparing the work of the GAERC, the central role of Coreper II (the ambassadors) in the EU process has been reinforced through the implementation of the Seville reforms. This follows a period of slippage, during which Coreper suffered from the dual effects of a weak General Affairs Council and a rise in the profile of other senior preparatory bodies, such as COPS and the Economic and Financial Committee (see Chapter 3).

Conduct

The exclusion of the foreign ministers from the first session of the European Council which, according to the guidelines laid down in Seville, takes place on the eve of the full-day session, may be viewed as an attempt to return to the 'fire-side chats' that were the aim of the original summits. Similarly, the restriction of each delegation to two seats in the main meeting room is an attempt to reintroduce the intimacy required for frank discussions between national leaders. The implication is that either the Foreign Minister or the Finance Minister (but not both) will be able to take a seat beside their respective president or prime minister.

Much of the work of the European Council is now pre-programmed and largely agreed in advance of the session itself, an unsurprising development in an enlarged EU. That being said, real political discussions can and do still occur, although probably now more frequently at the lunch or dinner table than at the plenary negotiating table.

Conclusions of meetings

As the final preparatory body of the European Council and a participant in the meeting itself, the GAERC can influence the content of the conclusions to a large degree. It may accept agreements reached lower down the Council hierarchy, or discuss and agree something itself that will be adopted without discussion by the heads of state or government and will figure in the final conclusions. On more politically sensitive issues, or those where the heads of state or government are anxious to be seen to have had a direct input themselves, the members of the GAERC may reach an agreement in principle which their political masters will discuss and adopt. On deeply divisive issues, the foreign ministers may limit themselves to indicating existing cleavages, and leave the resolution of these issues entirely to their political masters and mistresses. Once agreement has been reached at European Council level, it is the responsibility of the GAERC to ensure that the necessary implementing measures are undertaken.

More broadly, the issue now on the table is whether, or how, the European Council should develop in the overall institutional system of the Union. It is clear that, in recent years, a number of key decisions have been taken only because the European Council was involved strategically. Often these decisions have led to important new policy tasks being entrusted to the Union; EMU is a clear and compelling example of this. Simultaneously and paradoxically, the European Council has often been bogged down with matters of detail that should surely have been amenable to decision at a less elevated level (for example, the number of Council votes to be allocated to each member state in an enlarged Union).

Meanwhile, the competition for primacy between the Commission and the Council on the one hand, and between the Commission and the European Council on the other, has led to a lively debate as to how to improve the strategic direction of the Union, and how to develop political leadership. In discussions about reform of the presidency that took place from the late 1990s onwards, it was suggested (chiefly by representatives of the larger member states) that the European Council would benefit from the appointment of a long-term president, who would ensure continuity in the work of this body. The smaller member states were less convinced, believing that their interests would be best served by a rotating presidency and a more powerful Commission President with a clear political mandate. Some senior officials in the Council Secretariat tended to agree, arguing that discontinuity only ensued when the system did not work, and pointing to various instances of seamless movement between presidencies. In the event, disagreement was so deep-seated that it was decided not to discuss the issue at the Copenhagen European Council in December 2002, as had previously been envisaged.

The discussion could not be postponed indefinitely, however, and it eventually got underway in the 2002–3 CFE and the subsequent IGC. The resulting Constitutional Treaty, currently in abeyance following negative referendums in France and the Netherlands, came down on the side of the president of the European Council. In providing for an elected president with a mandate of two and a half years, renewable once, the signatories of the CT indicated their preference for a strong, permanent head of the European Council, despite deep reservations voiced in heated debates during the Convention (de Schoutheete, 2006). The Commission in understandably wary of such a development, as are the representatives of the smaller member states, who feel that their interests as well as that of the EU as a whole, may not be best served thereby. It remains to be seen whether or not they will be proved right.

Chapter 7

Competition and Cooperation: the Council and the Commission

The political debate about the development of European institutions is permeated by images of competition between institutions, of struggles for turf and of 'either/or' definitions of institutional roles: either the Commission or the Council is predominant; either the member states or 'Brussels' call the shots; either national parliaments or the European Parliament (EP) provide accountability; either the whole construction is intergovernmental or it is 'centralized' (recurrent British politicians' parlance for supranational). So perhaps our discussion of the evolving relationship between the Council and the Commission should take competition as its theme and aim to bring to bear a judgement on the results of that competition.

However, in a European Union (EU) with many different operating modes, such an approach would be overly simplistic. We therefore take a more modulated approach in looking for both partnership and competition between these two institutions, in defining the division of labour between them, and in seeking to explore the dynamics of their relationship. In the early history of the European Communities (EC), the founders intended to make the Commission and the Council the two most important institutions, recognizing that whether or not the whole experiment would work would depend on how the two institutions worked together. Thus it was that one of the present authors could be given the metaphor of the 'Council–Commission tandem' as her first academic instruction on decision-making in the EC in autumn 1967 by Emile Noël, then Secretary-General (SG) of the Commission.

The incentives to cooperate

Why this early notion of synergy? Some of it stemmed from more or less benevolent elitism and paternalism. There was an assumption that the Council and the Commission (in the early days known as the High Authority) would be run by professional, expert and non-partisan public officials, even though the former would speak to, and for, member state constituencies, while the latter would speak for the overall Community constituency. But both would work closely in developing

186

common rules and joint policies. This happened in the early years, or at least it happened to a certain extent, and initially neither the Council nor the Commission had to pay too much attention to the other institutions or to wider political opinion. The institutional story of the EC was dominated by the Council and the Commission, as is reflected in the early literature on European political integration. The core themes focus on the Commission as 'proposer', the Council as 'disposer' and the consequential mediation through a distinctive 'Community method' of bargaining.

Most analysts of European integration accepted that the original process was one of power-sharing, and thus in some sense quintessentially cooperative in nature. For the realists and neo-realists, of course, this was (and remains) conditional and heavily constrained cooperation, while for the neo-functionalists and their intellectual successors, cooperation and its distinctive features became the core of the process. This was reflected in Wolfgang Wessels' notion of 'cooperative federalism' (Wessels, 1992) and Philippe Schmitter's inventive 'neo-latinisms' of *condominio*, *consocio* and so on (Schmitter, 1992).

The balance tilts towards the Council

This institutional dyarchy began to change in the 1960s, for several reasons. First, the Council developed as an institution in ways unimagined by the early founders. The heavy institutionalization we have described in earlier chapters gave the Council a depth and breadth as an institution that turned it into a quite different kind of interlocutor for the Commission. The development of the Committee of Permanent Representatives (Coreper) and all the other specialized Council committees meant that the Commission found itself interacting, not just with the visiting representatives of the member states, but with a kind of permanent expression of the Council, albeit with different visages.

The Council Secretariat developed too, taking on some functions of managing the agenda, coordinating business and defining legal parameters that, in other circumstances, might have been fulfilled by the Commission. The Council presidency began to emerge, in part at least, as a collective face for the EC as a whole, a role that the Commission would very much have liked to capture. We recall here that one of the causes of the 1965 crisis had been the attempt by Walter Hallstein to give the Commission President some of the representational attributes of a head of state (von der Groeben, 1982; Loth *et al.*, 1995). The national permanent representations (permreps) that extended around Coreper gave the individual member states a continuous presence and a depth of expertise in Brussels, a factor that caused much suspicion and resentment in the Commission, as the commentary of the mid-1960s reveals.

Meanwhile the European Court of Justice (ECJ) began to emerge from the shadows as a very important institution indeed and, although in many ways an ally of the Commission, a rather more complex institutional configuration than some had expected.

The other major factor of change was the general 'politicization' of Community bargaining. For a mixture of reasons, some to do with issues, some to do with process, and others to do with individual politicians, the whole business of building Community policies and legislation came to depend on a much sharper exchange of political positions, preferences and benefits than could sit easily with the notion of benevolent technocracy and covert elitism. Most of this politicization was played out in and around gatherings in the Council, to which the Commission contributed, but which it could not dominate.

This is not to deny that the Commission is political in character or behaviour, but rather to state that it has only a half-life politically. Commissioners are often (indeed increasingly) politicians by background or ambition, and the defining of policy initiatives is rarely performed well by political eunuchs. But the Commission was allowed no independent political base, no explicit partisan or programmatic foundation and no clear political standing. These were all broadly accepted attributes of individual member governments that endowed the Council, as 'their' institution, with an incorrigibly political and competitive character. Consequently, part of the interaction between the Commission and the Council was an interplay between the technical and the political or, perhaps better, between knowledge and judgement. The Commission had to know what policy ideas were plausible and feasible, but the Council had to judge which of these ideas could be made 'yesable' (see Chapter 11) and delivered on the ground.

But, as is well recognized in political science, institutions acquire their own interests in the political process, and these interests sit alongside the political goals and ambitions of individuals and groups. Thus the Commission itself developed its own political goals as an institution, and it has been led by individuals who, in differing ways at different periods, have pursued their own political agendas. Consequently, the Commission has become a political actor with concerns to increase its leverage and influence on decisions and to mobilize its own, sometimes alternative, political constituencies (Edwards and Spence, 1997). The periods in office as Commission President of Walter Hallstein and Jacques Delors, in particular, provoked discussion precisely about such political ambitions. The subsequent choices for the post of three successive former prime ministers and former members of the European Council seemed to confirm this trend. The presence of the Commission as an actor within the Council invites it to project an alternative political agenda. Moreover, as the Commission acquired its own vested interests in the development and maintenance of 'its' policies, in some ways it necessarily became more partisan in the negotiation and projection of policy.

The counterpoint to this lay in the reaction of some member governments and some national political leaders. Some commentators, both contemporary political scientists and historians able to weigh evidence and events over time, have argued that the very resilience of nation state structures and 'interests of state' kept the core politics of European integration locked in dealings among the participating governments (Hoffman, 1966; Milward, 2000). Thus the Council could not but be the predominant institution in terms of exercising power, with the Commission necessarily operating in some ways in its shadow. Some governments at some periods in EC history have been very explicit about this being their aim. The Gaullist-inspired Fouchet plans of the early 1960s sought to strengthen the intergovernmental character of the EC, even suggesting a watered-down version of the Council and clearly intending a subordination of the Commission (Dinan, 1999). The dramatic collision of French policy with Commission ambitions in 1965 took as its centrepiece the relative roles and powers of the Council and the Commission (Newhouse, 1968). One thread in the discussion of European foreign policy consultations has always concerned the relative roles and political weight of these two institutions. This has recurred more recently in the development of discussions on judicial and home affairs.

The elements of competition

So much is easy to state. It is rather harder for any but a cold-blooded realist to disentangle the key factors that explain the tensions between the Council and the Commission. One factor clearly does relate to the sovereignty, or assumed sovereignty, of governments. Here we note the evidence for differences of response among member states. Thus governments from some countries, notably France, the UK and Denmark, have more often been willing to assert explicitly their preference for Council predominance and their irritation at Commission ambitions. But others have, apparently sincerely, argued the opposite, namely for respect of the Commission's existing powers and for the extension of these. This, typically, has been the expressed view of the Italian and Benelux governments. While some may question the sincerity of this view and suggest that it is an easy position to take when others are likely to prevent its attainment, the consistency of the position is remarkable. There may be substantive explanations, in that rewards may be reaped from providing institutional support for the Commission within and against the Council.

Another factor has been related to partisanship and policy preferences. Member governments that find a comfortable congruence between their own goals and those proposed by the Commission are likely to support the Commission generally, and to give weight to its interventions within the Council. One explanation for the varying attitudes of both General de Gaulle and Mrs Thatcher towards the Commission is related to how good the policy fit was for them on specific issues where the Commission intervened. Part of the explanation for the softening of French policy towards the Commission under Giscard d'Estaing, and eventually under François Mitterrand, was precisely that Commission proposals helped them within *un débat franco-français*. This was reflected in turn in their greater willingness to support the Commission within the Council, and to talk up some of its ideas.

A third factor, and one that was to trouble Ernst Haas, was the impact of political personality and individual political leadership (Haas, 1975). There have been some spectacular conflicts played out through the Council between individual national politicians and the Commission, most famously between General de Gaulle and Walter Hallstein in the 1960s (Loth *et al.*, 1995) and between Margaret Thatcher and Jacques Delors some two decades later (Grant, 1994; Ross, 1995). In any political process, some space needs to be left for powerful personalities, although the prudent analyst should not exaggerate their importance. What is perhaps surprising is that personality factors have not played a greater part in the interplay between the Council and the Commission. On the one hand, the experience of the two Delors Commissions (1985–9 and 1989–95, the final two years being an extension of his term in office) seemed to signal a new trend. On the other hand, the periods in office of Jacques Santer and Romano Prodi seemed – despite both having previously been prime ministers – to mark a waning of political influence by the Commission and its lower standing *vis-à-vis* the Council.

These, then, are all elements of the background to the Council–Commission relationship. The trend has probably been towards more frequent competition, although the period around the formulation of the 1992 programme and the drafting of the Single European Act (SEA) in the mid-1980s was broadly cooperative. More recently, conflict and lack of mutual confidence have been more prevalent, reflected in the greater willingness of increasing numbers of Council members to volunteer more vehement criticism of the Commission as an institution. Indeed, it could be argued that the Commission has been undergoing a period of secular decline *vis-à-vis* the Council, constituting a tandem with differently-sized, rather than balanced, wheels. This having been said, some care should be taken in drawing conclusions. One pertinent hypothesis to be borne in mind is that the EU as a whole 'works better' in periods of Council–Commission cooperation. So we need to examine the modes of collaboration more closely, as well as to bear in mind the outcomes of such synergy.

Implicit and explicit models of governance

In their stimulating essay on the Council–Commission relationship, Dietrich Rometsch and Wolfgang Wessels (1994) set out four variants of the model of governance that underpins the relationship between the two institutions:

- a *technocracy* model, with a Commission of 'wise persons' winning the debate with a Council of compromisers;
- a *federal executive* model, with the Commission emerging as the 'government' and the Council as the 'second chamber';
- a *secretariat* model, in which the Commission provides expert and administrative support for the Council as the key decision-maker; and
- a *promotional brokerage* model, reflecting the dual legitimacy built into the EU system, in which the Commission develops and promotes collective policies, but is always obliged to persuade the Council to accept them.

Rometsch and Wessels (1994, pp. 208–10) clearly preferred the last of these models. They argued that it accorded well with the empirical record of the EU and, indeed, that it had been reinforced by constitutional and political developments over the years. It reflected the push–pull character of the relationship and stressed the interdependence and complementarity of the two institutions.

Broadly, we share their approach, but with an important nuance. We follow the presumption that the core institutional relationships in the EU are not stable, but subject to flux (Wallace, 2005), and that the continuing competition between the two institutions has two important consequences. One is that their relationship differs between policy arenas and, explicitly under the 1992 Treaty on European Union (TEU), between the three pillars. The second is the incomplete character of the EU system, which enables alternative models of governance to coexist and to jockey for position and prominence. Voices continue to be heard calling for the embedding of alternative models, usually including the federal executive model (albeit in muted tones) and the secretariat model (although explicitly from only a minority of member governments).

This debate might have been resolved in the discussions leading to the adoption of the Constitutional Treaty (CT) by the European Council in June 2004, but unfortunately the new text preserved the elements of ambiguity that have marked the history of the EU. Some added weight was given to the Council and the European Council, while some of the steps that might have enabled the Commission to become a more explicitly political executive were put on hold, despite the impact of enlargement as a possible trigger for reform.

An erratic tandem

The tandem metaphor springs from the fact that, at every stage of the EU's policy-formulation and decision-making processes, not only is interaction between the Council and the Commission necessary, but the two need to be pedalling in the same direction for movement to be sustained. If either brakes hard, movement is virtually impossible. There is a kind of division of labour between the two institutions, but there is also an interweaving and an overlapping of functions. This complex complementarity operates in different ways at each stage of the decision-making process. Further on in this chapter, we distinguish between six such stages:

- agenda-setting;
- 'pre-negotiation' of proposals;
- gathering feedback;
- negotiation;
- implementation of decisions; and
- representing agreed policy to third parties.

One of the sharpest reminders of the tandem as a metaphor is that electorates in EU countries are often confused as to which of the two institutions is determining or delivering the European policies that affect them. A second, and equally powerful, reminder is the under-standable concern of third-country governments to know which of the two institutions 'speaks for the Union'. The often accurate reply of 'it depends' is not of much use or comfort to either group. This confusing dualism thus raises real issues of legitimacy, authority and responsibility, while allowing much scope for buck-passing, scapegoating and hidden agendas. This tension persists in the institutional design of the EU.

The Commission within the Council

The Commission normally sits in the Council and is fully engaged in its activities, sometimes even being dubbed (now) the '26th member state'. It speaks, proposes and defends its positions, and is a full participant in negotiations within all areas where there is clear Community competence, as under the so-called first pillar. The only formal power it lacks is the vote, although this is not necessarily crucial, since decisions 'emerge' and consensus remains more typical than roll-call voting (see Chapters 10 and 11). The Commission's assent to a proposal is an institutional commitment to defend its outcome, and it is entitled to withdraw its proposal from Council consideration at any stage before the ministers have reached final agreement on the text. It can only be overruled by unanimity among the voting members of the Council, a rule that has been observed remarkably strictly, and rarely invoked.

But the Council does not operate so directly within the Commission. On the contrary, the Commission has been stubbornly independent and jealous of its status. Commissioners are not appointed to be the representatives of governments, and on the whole do not act as if they were, although some are seen to favour the positions of their countries. The Council can instruct the Commission to prepare a text, but cannot command its contents. The Commission is neither technically nor practically accountable to the Council, nor can it be collectively or individually censured by the Council. In principle, therefore, the Commission can distance itself more easily from the Council on policy positions than vice versa.

In practice, the extent to which the Commission adopts sharply distinctive positions in the Council depends on its judgement of how best to maximize its influence tactically or strategically. Often, it should be stressed, the principal contribution of the Commission to a policy debate lies in defending the reasoned concerns of one or more member states whose interests risk being overridden by other member states. The Commission has to choose when and whether to be tough or accommodating *vis-à-vis* the Council. It is much harder for the Council as a body to take a collective position towards the Commission since, on any single issue and at any given time, the Commission will have supporters as well as opponents in the Council chamber. Indeed, beleaguered member governments in the Council often find that the Commission is their best friend among those at the table, and often trust the Commission more than they trust other member states.

Proposals are floated periodically to alter this basic feature by clearly subordinating the Commission to the Council. Some authors argued in the early 1990s that the Commission should be more of a secretariat and less of an embryonic executive, thereby proposing a fundamental restructuring of power between these two institutions (Gonzalez Sanchez, 1994; Vibert, 1994). A softer version of the same notion, and for some the thin end of the wedge, is the idea of removing the Commission's sole right of initiative for EC business in the first pillar, a right that has much to do with its leverage in the Council. Moreover, the fierce emphasis placed by many governments on the need to keep 'their' Commissioners was a key point of conflict in discussions in and around the 2003–4 intergovernmental conference (IGC). The obvious consequent risk is the emergence of a college of national representatives rather than independent individuals, a development that would surely further alter the 'balance' between the Council and the Commission.

In contrast to the situation that pertains in the first (Community) pillar, the role ascribed to the Commission within the two new pillars created by the TEU was much less clear and its functions much more conditional, even though it was assumed that the Commission would usually be present as a participant in the relevant Council sessions. For second (common foreign and security policy – CFSP) and third (justice and home affairs – JHA) pillar issues, the Commission was not given the sole right of initiative, ownership of the texts under discussion or responsibility for implementing decisions. The early experience of this more intergovernmental method was disappointng (Council of the European Union, 1995; European Commission, 1995), but events and the commitments of the Treaty of Amsterdam (ToA) served to inject both more focus and more urgency over subsequent years.

The JHA case has been the clearer of the two. A huge increase in activity and the development of both common measures and converging interests has meant that the Commission has acquired some of its classical functions in steering policy discussions and framing collective decisions. This has occurred notwithstanding the fact that, in the parts of this domain where national sensitivities and idiosyncracies remain strong, the Council has greater charge of the subject matter and the Council Secretariat provides some of the underpinnings that the Commission might otherwise have provided. But the relative roles and weight of the two institutions are evolving in this domain.

The cases of the CFSP and the related European security and defence policy (ESDP) are harder to characterize. On the one hand, the pressures for more closely aligned and common approaches, even policies, have grown in response to events, and have led to a much more direct involvement in the debate of the defence policy community. On the other hand, national stances and capabilities remain very diverse, and there are continuing inhibitions against the direct attribution of responsibilities to the Commission. In this context, the CT tried to square the circle through its proposed introduction of a 'foreign minister' for the Union. This individual would be both a member (indeed a vice-president) of the Commission, and the president of the Foreign Affairs Council, an innovative experiment in merged institutional roles.

Member governments in dialogue with the Commission

The Council does not normally act in a unitary way *vis-à-vis* the Commission. Much of the dialogue and interaction between them is bilateral, with the Commission engaging in discussions with individual member governments, either at its behest or at theirs. The Commission may attempt to exploit the opportunities offered by multilateral negotiation in and around the Council, sometimes even allying itself with one part of an individual government against another. At all levels of Council discussion, representatives of the member governments try to influence the behaviour of the Commission within the Council, just as Commissioners and their officials seek to influence the behaviour of individual member governments within the Council. Member states seek, on an individual rather than a collective basis, to operate within the Commission through the 'comitology' procedures, and via the private office of the Commissioner of their country.

'Comitology' is a misleading term for a fairly normal tool of the policy-maker and the policy-implementer, namely the convening of groups through which the Commission discusses policy ideas with relevant 'clients' in advance of their introduction or, subsequently, the progress of policy implementation (see Box 7.1). In the case of the EU, the member governments clearly count as 'relevant clients'. Those committees that have formal powers, most of which relate to implementation, prescribe formal procedures for taking decisions, usually a version of the Council's qualified majority decision rules. Other committees, often more informal, are convened by the Commission to take soundings from national officials in advance of presenting formal legislative proposals. In both kinds of committee, individual member states seek to influence Commission thinking and practice.

The private offices or *cabinets* of all Commissioners are also in continuous contact with member governments, especially on issues currently the subject of negotiation in the Council. Not surprisingly, during their term in Brussels, most Commissioners retain close links with individuals and institutions in their own countries, and are the object of lobbying by these. Some actively seek to build close links in other member states; for example, Jacques Delors was not alone in giving high priority to developing and maintaining contacts in Germany.

Until the late 1990s, when the members of a *cabinet* almost always shared the same nationality as their Commissioner, the private offices were widely and unashamedly regarded as the agents of their member states. Responding to the negative aspects of this situation, new rules were implemented under the Prodi presidency, requiring each Commissioner to appoint a head or deputy head of *cabinet* from a member state other than their own, and to ensure that a range of nationalities was represented among the six officials comprising the office. It is tempting to infer that the nationalities of Commissioners and the members of their *cabinets* leave an imprint on their links with individual member states. Of course, there is an ease of communication that may relate to nationality, language, party labels or shared public-service loyalties, but this should not be exaggerated. Other factors relating to substantive policy positions may be just as important, and in any case the links are functional in identifying relevant needs and problems that will come into play in the Council discussions, of which the Commission needs to be aware.

Box 7.1   *The Commission, the Council and comitology*

What is comitology?
'Comitology' or 'committee procedure' is the term for a system of committees that assist the Commission in the exercise of its powers when implementing adopted legislation.

Where can information on comitology be found?
The rules governing the types, scope, powers and rules of procedure of the comitology committees can be found in:
*   Article 202 TEC (which lays down the Council's right to confer implementing powers on the Commission);
*   Council Decision 1999/468/EC, repealing Council Decision 87/373/EEC (which describes the various procedures); and
*   Official Journal 2001/C 38/03 (containing the standard rules of procedure for comitology committees drawn up by the Commission).
The Commission publishes an annual report on the comitology committees, available on its website (http://europa.eu.int/comm, in the section devoted to the General Secretariat). The 2003 report was published in March 2005.

How do the committees work?
*   Comitology committees are created by means of a basic legislative act adopted by the Council, or the Council and the European Parliament (EP), that confers implementing powers on the Commission.
*   Each committee adopts its own rules of procedure, based on a standard model adopted by the Commission in January 2001 (see above).
*   The committees are composed of representatives of each of the member states and chaired by an official from the Commission.
*   They meet several times a year, usually in Brussels in the Commission's buildings. In 2003, there were 1,024 meetings of comitology committees, delivering 2,981 opinions, and the Commission adopted 2,768 implementing measures.
*   The Commission submits a draft implementing measure to one of these committees for its opinion.
*   The committee's opinion may be binding or non-binding on the Commission, but the final decision rests with the Commission or the Council, depending on the type of procedure being followed (see below).
*   The EP is informed of the proceedings of the committees on a regular basis, and is entitled to scrutinize those proposed implementing measures that are based on legislation adopted pursuant to the co-decision procedure.
*   The Commission publishes summary records and voting results of each comitology meeting (available on the Commission's website).
*   Despite rules permitting voting, virtually all the committees' decisions are reached by consensus (Dehousse, 2003). In 2003, no issues were referred to the Council.
*   Comitology has given rise to inter-institutional disputes in the past, because of the varying degrees of autonomy and control the different procedures confer on the Council, the Commission and the EP. A more positive view of comitology is put forward by Ballmann *et al.* (2002).

What are the different types of procedure and committee?

- *Advisory procedure*: Advisory Committees are created whenever they are considered the most appropriate. No rules are laid down regarding voting, and the Commission is not bound by their opinions.
- *Management procedure*: Management Committees are typically used to implement the common agricultural and fisheries policies, and other programmes with substantial budgets. They may use qualified majority voting (QMV) and the Commission is bound by their opinions. In the event of a negative opinion from the Committee, the Commission must delay the implementation of the relevant measure for up to three months and submit its proposal to the Council, which can modify it by QMV. If the Committee fails to issue an opinion, this is interpreted as a positive opinion, and the Commission may implement its proposed measure.
- *Regulatory procedure*: Regulatory Committees deal with measures of general scope; for example, protection of health or safety of humans, animals or plants. This procedure circumscribes the Commission's powers more than any other. Regulatory Committees may vote by QMV and their opinions are binding on the Commission. In the event of a negative opinion from the Committee, the Commission is obliged to consult and submit its proposal to the Council and to inform the EP. The Council may adopt, amend or reject the proposal. In the latter case, the so-called 'Safety Net Procedure' comes into play, under which the Commission may submit a new, a modified, or the same proposal, to seek the agreement of the member states. If the Committee fails to issue an opinion, this is interpreted as a negative opinion, and the Commission may not implement its proposed measure.
- *Safeguard procedure*: This procedure applies in cases where the basic instrument confers on the Commission the power to decide on safeguard clauses. The Commission may be required to consult the member states before adopting a decision. Any member state may refer the Commission's decision to the Council, which may overrule the Commission by QMV or may (again by QMV) confirm, amend or revoke the Commission's decision.

Some committees operate under several procedures.

How many comitology committees are there?

In 2003, there were 256 comitology committees, distributed according to procedure, as follows:

- Advisory Committees   31
- Management Committees   74
- Regulatory Committees   100
- Safeguard Committees   2
- Committees operating under several procedures   49

What changes are in the pipeline?

In December 2002, the Commission submitted a proposal for a revised regulatory procedure, designed to place the EP on an equal footing with the Council in supervising the Commission's exercise of implementing powers in areas subject to the co-decision procedure. In early 2005, an amended proposal issued by the Commission in April 2004 was still under examination in the Council.

None the less, there is some evidence in recent years of nationality considerations playing an important part in the positions taken by some individual Commissioners, and of the vigorous concern of some to keep open their opportunities to return to national politics. Evidence of the latter was obvious all too frequently in the final months of the Prodi Commission, when some of its members engaged in a rather unseemly scramble for domestic careers, and abandoned their Commission posts before their terms in office had expired.

The Council presidency, the Council Secretariat and the Commission

Two of the most important intersections of the Commission and the Council are with the Council Secretariat and the Council presidency, as we saw in Chapters 4 and 5. The Commission works closely with both bodies in preparing decisions, identifying areas of potential compromise as well as blockages to decision, and projecting the results of decision afterwards. In negotiations with third countries, mandates are pursued more or less jointly. In the newer areas of work, including the development of the two new pillars of the TEU, the partnership tends to be more exploratory, with a less settled division of labour between them. Each of these functions is elaborated a little further below.

So far we have referred to the Commission as if it were a monolith, which it is not. None the less, it is a unitary actor in two important respects. First, it is composed as a college – that is to say, the Commissioners themselves are subject to operating rules of collective decision. Policy positions have to be endorsed by the Commission as a whole and thereafter, in principle at least, followed by all Commissioners. There are real and sometimes fierce debates at the weekly Commission meetings over the content and tactics of collective positions. Decisions are taken on the basis of a simple majority, although formal votes are extremely rare, numbering barely more than a handful a year. Of course, occasionally those out-voted may still try to alter Commission policy, or to persuade particular member states to adopt and sustain the relevant argument, if and when the matter is discussed in the Council. Differentiated positions may persist and become public, but Commissioners none the less generally recognize the principle of collegiality, and especially so in relations with the Council.

Second, the Commission does have some collective interests as an institution that, on some issues, induce a cohesive position that overrides substantive differences within the Commission. Over the past decade, however, the Commission seems to have become a less collegial and more fragmented institution. It has more rarely than hitherto taken a collective view about itself, or about collective strategic goals. Hence it is less easy than perhaps it once was to generalize about the collective stance or influence of the Commission *vis-à-vis* the Council. This makes our judgements on the influence of the Commission on and in the Council rather more dependent on individual Commissioners, their services and specific policy domains or issues.

At the operational level, some services of the Commission are engaged specifically in interaction with the Council, and with managing the relationship with the Council Secretariat and presidency. The General Secretariat of the Commission has units dedicated to managing this relationship, responsible for fielding items at Coreper I and II and at Council sessions, in cooperation with the Directorates-General (DGs). The Commission Secretary-General himself is always present at Commission meetings and usually present in the more important Council and European Council sessions. However, we should note that these more strategic contacts relate mainly to points that will arrive on the ministerial table as 'B' points (Part II points at Coreper level – see Chapters 2 and 3). The items that are resolved by Council working parties are dealt with in a more functional and segmented way by the direct involvement of staff from the specialized services. This reinforces the lines of segmentation within the Council.

Another important interface is the Legal Service of the Commission. This advises the Commission, monitors the work of the ECJ and has what may best be described as 'fraternal' (in other words, frequently competitive) relations with the Council's Legal Service. While these two high-status groups of lawyers often take different views on the interpretation of Community law, they also rise readily to the challenge of trying to win the argument.

Of necessity, officials from several Commission DGs have to liaise constantly with officials from the Council Secretariat and the Council presidency on issues such as external negotiating mandates, representation *vis-à-vis* third countries or other international bodies, and negotiations with candidates for accession. Prior to the arrival of Romano Prodi as Commission President in late 1999, this meant especially DG I (external economic relations), DG IA (external political relations), DG VIII (development) and the periodic Task Force on enlargement. In the Commission reorganisation of 2000, these services were regrouped as DG RELEX (that is, external relations), DG Trade, DG Development, and DG Enlargement. These diffuse arrangements have facilitated strong function-based links between the relevant parts of the Commission and particular groupings of ministers in the Council, but have not been conducive to improving the coherence and coordination of policy.

The relationship developed by the Commission with the Council Secretariat has varied over time. In the early years of the EC, the Commission was somewhat suspicious of the Council Secretariat, being fearful of its own displacement. That stance softened into a cooperative rather than a competitive relationship, as those who worked within the Commission came to assume that, on the whole, the Council Secretariat was ill-equipped to take on policy-making as opposed to administrative and secretarial functions. Similarly, the Commission began to approach new Council presidencies looking for allies, and recognizing that this would normally be a six-month period when the relevant member government was under pressure to be more *communautaire* than usual. Indeed, each presidency offered one or more Commissioners or Commission services the opportunity to push a favoured dossier forward. This did not prevent periodic friction, when, for example, either a Council presidency as a whole or some of its leading ministers and officials attempted to sideline or subordinate the Commission.

Since the mid-1990s, however, things have changed. The growth of activity under the second and third pillars has built in a more explicit form of competition between the Council Secretariat and the Commission, to the extent that the former has started, for some purposes, to be overtly and specifically an arm of the decision-makers in the Council. Moreover, recent moves to reform the rotating Council presidency, as documented in the Constitutional Treaty, may create strategic opportunities for the Council presidency and the Council Secretariat to gain influence *vis-à-vis* the Commission in the framing and preparation of policy proposals.

Different phases of the relationship

Agenda-setting

In one sense, the Commission sets the agenda of the Council under the first pillar by using its right of initiative to trigger draft proposals. Its own annual work programme, presented at the beginning of each year, indicates the issues on which it hopes to develop proposals. In practice, things are more complicated and more fluid. Technically, as we saw in Chapters 3 and 5, the Council presidency sets the agenda of individual Council meetings, in cooperation with the Council Secretariat and in discussion with the Antici and Mertens Groups. Here, Commission influence is informal rather than formal. External events force items on to the agenda, thus demanding action by both the Commission and the Council.

The Council itself may (and frequently does) determine the Commission's agenda, as well as its own, by calling for reports or proposals, for example on the implications of enlargement, on the 'pre-accession strategy' for the Europe Associates, or on issues of competitiveness, notably in recent years with regard to much of the Lisbon Strategy adopted in 2000. Individual Council presidencies have 'bright ideas', hobbyhorses and preferences that they seek to push on to the agenda and for which they seek Commission support, although this practice is now less marked since the introduction of multi-annual strategic programmes of Council activity. None the less, timing and prioritizing are often crucial, since potential business generally exceeds the negotiating time available. Thus Commission–Council links are a necessary prerequisite for the definition and ordering of the Council's agenda. Here, the staff work of the Council Secretariat is a consistent element, while the differing habits of individual member governments condition the way each Council presidency approaches this task, as we saw in Chapter 5.

Pre-negotiation of proposals

It should be stressed that agenda-setting is not a purely formal or mechanical task. It involves making choices over the relative salience of individual dossiers, judgements as to their relative merits, efforts to get proposals into a shape in which they can be negotiated, and an assessment of their acceptability by the Council. Thus a form of 'pre-negotiation' takes place between the Commission and the Council, as the agenda is set and its contours defined. Much of this occurs as Commission proposals are being drafted. Often, the national officials, who will subsequently sit in Council working parties, are engaged in efforts to influence the drafts; sometimes they are consulted explicitly and sometimes they lobby the Commission themselves. This blurring of the lines between the two institutions is all the more pronounced when the Commission presents the Council with a 'Communication' rather than a fully drafted legislative proposal. In such cases, the Commission is accepting that it needs to test the water in the Council first.

Gathering feedback

In a period in which the legitimacy, relevance, acceptability and responsiveness of the EU are generally under greater scrutiny, it is pertinent to ask how these issues affect the relationship between the Council and the Commission. Both have been under pressure to be more 'transparent'; both are under pressure to pay more attention to subsidiarity; both are the targets of lobbyists, consultants and conventional interest groups; and both are addressed by political parties that seek to influence their respective agendas and negotiations.

Two factors distinguish the profiles and behaviour of the Council from those of the Commission: focus and responsibility. The members of the Council look at most issues with an intense but narrow focus on their relevance, their cost–benefit ratio and their potential impact on the individual member state, or the governing party or parties. They look at the concerns of other member states primarily to assess the negotiability and sustainability of particular outcomes, and have incomplete knowledge of the particular topic as it manifests itself across the EU. This makes each member government authoritative, but only up to a point, since its information base is generally incomplete. By contrast, the Commission is supposed to take a broad focus, and to make up for what it might lack in its central focus by the range of its peripheral vision. The Commission is expected to be conversant with every issue as it affects each of the now twenty-five member states, as well as with the aggregate implications. As the target of so many lobbies and so much special pleading, it often has considerable, if diffuse, expertise.

The other point of difference is related to effective political responsibility. Each member of the Council judges policy in terms of likely citizen or electoral acceptability at home, often with the short-term pressures of the electoral cycle uppermost in his or her mind. The Commission is free from such direct pressures and can take a more detached and longer-term view. The corollary is a degree of irresponsibility or remoteness from the ground on which policy has to be delivered. These different perspectives make for some potential complementarity, but also for possible friction.

Negotiation

The Commission has two distinct and not always easily reconciled purposes within the Council. Sometimes it acts as a protagonist and at other times as a mediator. The Commission is the protagonist when it operates as the deviser and 'owner' of the texts on the table in the Council chamber. It therefore has a distinct position to articulate and to defend. If the relevant negotiators from the Commission believe that their case is a good one, or that it must be retained for long enough to define the terms of any potential settlement, they may hold rather inflexibly and for a long time to their 'ideal' or 'maximalist' objectives. Council members therefore have to attune themselves to stubbornness from the Commission. Indeed, even on very complex and contentious issues, the Commission may hold to a very determined and distinct set of propositions.

Perhaps the clearest examples of this are the so-called Delors 1 (1988), Delors 2 (1992) and Agenda 2000 packages on budgetary and cohesion issues. All these produced agreed Council decisions that, to a remarkable degree, coincided with the original Commission proposals (Laffan and Shackleton, 2000). The same has been true of enlargement, both in admitting Austria, Finland and Sweden, and in the more recent case of the ten members who acceded in 2004. Even though the Commission had a less clearly defined responsibility in this area, since accession is negotiated with a Conference of representatives of the member states rather than with the Council, on both occasions it did much of the detailed negotiation for the member states, keeping a sharp eye on its own sense of what would be collectively beneficial (Avery, 1995; Granell, 1995; Sedelmeier 2000).

However, the Commission also sees itself as a mediator and as the architect of compromise between conflicting positions in the Council. Indeed, part of the Commission's 'street credibility' and proven ability to win confidence from its interlocutors in the Council has been dependent precisely on its capacity to stitch agreements together. Thus the Commission's negotiators need to be very alert to the nuances of individual positions in the Council, to find the means and the moment to introduce possible compromises and, if necessary, to soften its own starting position and modify its text. Here, the Commission is confronted with both tactical and strategic judgements. It should be noted that the Commission never (deliberately, at least) introduces proposals that are contrary to the interests of all twenty-five member states, but it can and often does seek to defend the concerns of individual member states, benefiting from the frequent willingness of individual governments to accept the good offices of the Commission.

None the less, the Commission is not the only potential source of mediation in the EU system. Sometimes the Council Secretariat succeeds in sketching a basis for negotiated agreement, and the Council presidency frequently attempts to act as a source of compromise. The increasing recourse to 'presidency compromises' and the use of presidency 'confessionals' during Council sessions are an important development (see Chapter 5), although they are viewed by some as being overly tactical and *ad hoc*. Proponents of the latter view would argue that the Commission, on the other hand, tries more to broker packages that will have a longer-term resilience.

Implementation of decisions

Building confidence in negotiations and securing sustainable agreement requires guarantees of shared commitments to outcomes. In the Community system, much of this hinges on the legal system, and thus on the justiciability of decisions through the ECJ and national courts. As regards the implementation of legislation and enforcement of Community rules and programmes, the Council is little involved as an institution, either in litigation with the Commission or in administration. The individual members are, however, intensely engaged in the implementation process and sometimes in litigation with the Commission, but with their primary focus being the implications of decisions for their particular circumstances.

The Commission, on the other hand, is directly involved as implementer and policing officer, dealing with individual member governments, as and when required, or with them all collectively in the various management and regulatory committees (Ballmann *et al.*, 2002; Docksey and Williams, 1994). The Commission is responsible for managing policy regimes, programmes and expenditure, working with and through agencies in the member states. Complicated committee procedures, using majority voting rules, give member governments the opportunity to challenge or to endorse Commission proposals, requiring sometimes positive and sometimes negative majorities for an objection to the Commission's proposal to be sustained (see Box 7.1). Where such a challenge is upheld, the issue can be taken on appeal to the Council, for one of its statutory or *ad hoc* committees to pronounce. In most policy areas, such challenges are unusual. The development of policy thus depends on procedural agreements between the Council and the Commission, as well as on the Council's confidence in the quality of Commission management.

In some areas there is dispute over what are issues of principle and of implementation. Article 202 (EC) permits the Council to delegate powers of implementation to the Commission. Recurrently, the Commission argues that the Council under-uses Article 202, and that the reluctance to do so leaves too much detailed and updating legislation in the hands of the Council. However, in the recent period of decreased trust in the Commission, it has been difficult to sustain a convincing case for more extensive delegation to the Commission.

None the less, the option to do so should be borne in mind as a factor relevant to the efficiency of the Council. Also, there are some borderline areas where both the Commission and the Council may legislate, since the Commission also enjoys some scope to make subordinate legislation and, under the competition rules (Articles 81-89 (TEC)), even to enact primary legislation.

One further point should be made here. Occasionally, both the Commission and the Council may be subject to challenge for having together behaved in a way that was judged contestable or *ultra vires*. Perhaps the most famous instance was the 1980 isoglucose case, which arose after the Commission and the Council had, in complete agreement, produced a very speedy new regulation to tax the producers of isoglucose and thus subject them to trading conditions comparable to those of the producers of sugar beet. In a case brought by companies producing isoglucose, the ECJ found that the Council had behaved incorrectly in the way that it had calculated and structured the tax, although not in the principle it had followed. The case was interesting for the wider reason that the ECJ upheld the associated complaint from the EP that its opinion had not been duly taken into account when the Council decided the issue. What is noteworthy here is that the Commission and Council 'colluded', very quickly, to produce an alternative tax regime that met the ECJ's objections to their first effort.

Representing agreed policy to third parties

As we saw in Chapter 5, a structural tension permeates the external representation of EU policies, depending on whether policy competence has been attributed clearly to the EU level or is shared with the member states. This fluidity and complexity imposes a tricky division of labour between the Commission and the Council. Sometimes the Commission negotiates for the collectivity and is also the authorized representative, as is the case on many trade issues. At other times, the Commission negotiates but is not the sole representative, as pertains in the negotiation of association agreements. On other occasions, the Council presidency negotiates or represents, or more often represents (up to a point), while the member states negotiate. Often both are involved, since so many external discussions touch on both the Community's and the member states' responsibilities.

The result, as we suggested in Chapter 5, is a mix of competition and partnership. On a day-to-day basis, the Commission and the Council have to find operating procedures to handle external representation, which take into account institutional sensitivities and address the issues of substance in a sensible fashion. There is a push–pull effect between, on the one hand, efforts to project EU positions as effectively as possible and, on the other, internal manoeuvrings within the EU. In the better-established areas of Community work, a *modus vivendi* has been developed, although arguments do, and can be expected to, persist.

In newer areas of policy development within the EU, operating practices are harder to define and sustain. None the less, some of the argument about joint representation depends on the extent to which there is substantive agreement among member governments. When it is in fact the case that they have a clearly defined common view, the rest of the world will hear voices in unison or modulated harmonies. Voices out of tune reflect serious differences of substance, which may sometimes be blamed on the institutional ambiguities. Thus, while institutional and legal factors may be very much in evidence, they should always be read carefully for the lurking issues of substance.

The Constitutional Treaty envisaged a new European External Action Service (EEAS), intended to pull together and to make much more effective the EU's and the member states' collective instruments for representing their shared interests, and for providing collective information to the Council and the Commission. But it will be some time before a judgement can be reached on the potential impact of such a body against the legacy of more fragmented arrangements.

The history of the EC, and subsequently the EU, has thus been shaped by this core relationship between the Commission and the Council. Periods of synergy and synthesis have been interspersed with periods of tension and antithesis. Thus the period 1985–90 was broadly one of productive synergy, while the succeeding years have been marked more often by debilitating tensions. None the less, this later period has also included episodes of productive synergy, as for example in taking forward successive phases of enlargement. The content of the CT reflects a kind of structural ambivalence on the part of its drafters about the possible future relationship between the Council and the Commission, and its detailed text includes elements of ambiguity that can only be tested by practice. Whether or not its proposals are implemented, the CT is an indication of a familiar reluctance to settle – and indeed persistent discord about – the core relationship between these two central institutions. None the less, we believe that the EU system as a whole works much better in periods of productive partnership between the Council and the Commission.

It is striking, however, that the Council as a collective entity has paid so little attention to the case for improving the efficiency and effectiveness of the Commission. Council debates over the Commission as such have tended to revolve around three main issues: the appointment of Commissioners and senior Commission officials; Commission staff cases regarding appointments and promotions, taken on appeal to the Council; and efforts to control the Commission through the various comitology procedures.

The Council has repeatedly taken two 'negative' stances *vis-à-vis* the Commission. It has continually resisted increasing the staff complements of the Commission services, even in the face of huge new tasks, such as the effort to assist reforms in central and eastern Europe. It has also given little encouragement to those who have sought to reform the internal structures and management of the Commission. Even after the debilitating episodes that led to the resignation of the Santer Commission in 1999, the Council's response was half-hearted, and it gave little active support to Vice-President Kinnock, the Commissioner changed with reforming and modernizing the Commission. It could be argued that this demonstrates clearly the Council's collective determination to keep the Commission in its place. Indeed, for some member governments, this has been a deliberate policy. Yet much of the evidence suggests that this detachment from the issue of the effectiveness of the Commission rests on unconsidered and, in our view, counterproductive neglect.

Chapter 8

An Evolving Partnership: the Council and the European Parliament

The basic relationship between the Council and the European Parliament (EP) revolves around both the formal and informal legislative and budgetary roles of each institution. It stems initially from formal treaty provisions and then, importantly, from the implementation and interpretation of the latter by both parties. It therefore follows that key changes in this relationship have flowed largely from treaty reforms, the resulting altered inter-institutional circumstances, and the formal and informal arrangements made by both institutions to adapt to them.

Relations between the two bodies are founded on a basic and mutual antagonism, which may be viewed as no more than the natural tension or rivalry that exists between all executives and legislatures (although neither conforms fully to the country model of such bodies). In this case, however, a large part of the rivalry has arisen from the EP's unremitting and largely successful campaign to wrest increasing amounts of legislative and budgetary power from the reluctant grasp of the Council. There have been profound implications for their relationship, which has ranged from openly confrontational to closely cooperative.

For most of its life, the EP was viewed and treated by most members of the Council as the weaker of the two institutions, a result of the limited powers initially attributed to the EP by the founding treaties and then the very gradual, piecemeal way in which they were increased. Today, the situation is very different. The EP has developed into a real force to be reckoned with in the European Union's (EU's) legislative and budgetary processes, and one of the leading proponents of greater democratic legitimacy in the process of European integration. The Council has been persuaded, however reluctantly, to share increasing amounts of its legislative power with the EP, for two main reasons: first, the cumulative effect of successive treaty reforms, each of which has increased the EP's formal powers; and second, because of evidence of greater discipline and responsibility on the part of members of the EP (MEPs) in exerting the additional power granted to them. In learning to treat the EP as an equal partner in a growing number of policy fields, the Council has had to adapt to the EP's new role and growing power.

Fresh dynamics have been injected into their historically troubled relationship, giving rise to a new legislative culture in which mutual respect is still tempered to a degree by mutual suspicion.

The central focus of this chapter will be the impact on the Council and its members of the EP's changing formal powers, and the new inter-institutional dynamics they have engendered. These will be addressed by considering three main questions: first, how have the relationship and attitudes of the two institutions been affected as the EP's formal decision-making powers have increased? Second, what are the nature of the contacts between the EP and the various parts of the Council hierarchy? And, third, to what extent can the EP be described as influencing the Council? In a final section, we explore the question of the future, and the stability or otherwise of the still developing Council–EP tandem.

Relationship and attitudes

The Council–EP relationship is subject to a number of complicated procedures, each of which governs particular areas of internal and external policy, and implies different powers for each institution (see Boxes 1.4 and 1.5 in Chapter 1). In some areas, such as the negotiation of external trade agreements with third countries, the EP is little more than an observer in a process dominated by the Commission and the Council. In other areas, however, the EP and the Council are equal partners. Thus, under the budgetary procedure, the EP acts as joint authority with the Council, and has the power to reject unilaterally the annual budget, while in the large number of areas now covered by the co-decision procedure, decisions can only be reached with the agreement of both the Council and the EP acting together. Given the implications for the Council–EP relationship, this chapter will focus mainly on the latter two procedures.

Relevant changes in the EP's powers

In speaking about the EP's powers, it is important to distinguish between its budgetary powers and its legislative powers. In terms of budgetary powers, the EP scored an early success as a result of the introduction, in 1970, of the system of 'own resources' in place of national contributions to the Community budget. It was decided that the EP and the Council should both be involved in decisions about how such Community funds should be spent, and the budgetary and financial treaties of 1970 and 1975 had the effect of making the EP the 'joint budgetary authority' with the Council. However, the powers of the two institutions under the complex budgetary procedure were asymmetrical – the EP was granted no powers concerning the revenue side of the budget, and its ability to affect so-called 'compulsory expenditure' (essentially spending on the common agricultural policy – CAP), which for many years accounted for some 75 per cent of the overall budget) was limited. On the plus side, the EP had the power to reject the budget as a whole, a mighty weapon against the Council, which it wisely used sparingly.

Finding this asymmetry unacceptable, the EP attempted to maximize its budgetary powers and to use them to affect decisions on substantive policy areas. As a direct result of this strategy, the following decade was one of bitter inter-institutional rivalry, in which the budget became the central, defining and very divisive element of the EP–Council relationship. An annual, and frequently very public, battle was waged, in which both sides sought to assert their respective rights. Ultimately, however, the instability inherent in this situation became untenable, with the result that an inter-institutional agreement (IIA) on budgetary discipline and the improvement of the budgetary procedure was adopted by the Council, the Commission and the EP in 1988. Known as the Delors I package, this IIA incorporated a multi-annual financial perspective, setting expenditure limits for the period 1988–92. Further agreements were signed in 1992 (the Delors II package) and in 1999 (Agenda 2000), each covering a seven-year period (see Laffan, 2000, pp. 725–43). An agreement for the period 2007–13, due to be signed in 2006, ran into difficulties in 2005, amid bitter recriminations from net contributors and net recipients.

Generally speaking, however, the practice of agreeing financial perspectives has transformed the Council–EP relationship in the budgetary field, making it 'more predictable, consensual and rule-bound' (Laffan, 2000, p. 733). Annual conflicts, in which budgetary negotiations are viewed as zero-sum games, and 'winner' and 'loser' tags reinforce inter-institutional rivalry, are thankfully a thing of the past – although sour memories were stirred up in the run-up to, and the aftermath of, the June 2005 summit, where budgetary matters were discussed. Much of the EU's expenditure is now subject to multi-annual programmes, and budgetary disputes over limits of expenditure, though they still happen, occur at much more infrequent intervals and within a context of agreed rules of budgetary discipline. Consequently, the budgetary procedure may now be viewed as an exercise in 'joint management' (Shackleton 2002, p. 108). As such, it may lack the drama of earlier times, but it serves to imbue the EU system in general, and the Council–EP relationship in particular (at least in the budgetary field) with greater stability.

In contrast to its accumulation of budgetary powers, the EP's progress in increasing its more general legislative powers was much slower. Although granted advisory and supervisory powers under the Treaties of Rome, the then Common Assembly played a very limited role in the legislative process, and was (rightly, in legal terms) viewed by the Council as being a purely consultative body. Even after its direct election in 1979 and the introduction of the cooperation and assent procedures under the Single European Act (SEA) of 1986, the Council continued to view and to treat the EP as a somewhat less than equal partner. It was only with the introduction of the co-decision procedure under the Maastricht Treaty (TEU) of 1992, its simplification under the 1997 Treaty of Amsterdam (ToA) and the extensions of its scope under the ToA and the 2001 Treaty of Nice (ToN) that the EP could rightly claim to have come of age as a legislative authority. (However, it should be noted that only about a fifth of all legislation adopted by the Council – albeit among the most important – is currently subject to the cooperation or co-decision procedures (Maurer, 2003a, p. 234), although the Constitutional Treaty (CT), if ratified, would establish the co-decision procedure as the 'ordinary legislative procedure'.)

The net effect of these changes is that it is no longer feasible or even politically correct to view the Council as operating independently of the EP. Rather, the Council is obliged to pay serious and regular attention to the work and opinions of the directly elected representatives of the peoples of the EU (as the MEPs repeatedly and correctly describe themselves) if it is to achieve its legislative and budgetary goals. This is a radical departure from the past, and has had profound implications for the way in which the Council behaves and conducts its business at all levels.

The effect on the Council

The Council, like a previously only child confronted with a new and unsought sibling, has experienced some difficulty in accepting the new relationship and learning to share its toys with the newcomer. The result has been frequent, mostly EP-led, disputes between the two institutions over various aspects of their legislative and budgetary rights and obligations. These disputes have normally been settled in one of three ways:

• by means of *documented agreements*, laying down the agreed means of proceeding in the future, which take the form of joint declarations, IIAs or treaty reforms;
• through *informal undocumented arrangements*, conventions or rules of the game governing the working practices and interactions of the two bodies, aimed at reducing the risk of similar disputes in the future; and
• (most rarely) via *rulings from the European Court of Justice* (ECJ) settling a dispute about which institution has acted outside its competences, or chosen an erroneous interpretation of agreed rules.

New procedures need to be run in, and the main protagonists need time to adapt to them. The cooperation and co-decision procedures were no exception, requiring as they did a novel approach on the part of the Council in its attitude *vis-à-vis* the EP. Wrinkles had to be ironed out, contesting interpretations of the rules adjudicated upon, and ways found to make the procedures work effectively. The process of adaptation has not always been easy, but the general consensus a decade after its introduction was that the co-decision procedure (which has replaced the cooperation procedure for all but four legal bases, all related to economic and monetary union (EMU – see Box 1.5 in Chapter 1) works, and works well, although there is still room for improvement (see Council document 13316/1/00 and European Parliament 2004).

The EP's increased powers, in particular its role in the co-decision procedure, have affected the Council in three main ways, each one leading to the next. The first and most obvious effect on the Council has been a substantial increase in its workload. Dossiers that could previously have been decided essentially by the Council acting alone must now be discussed in detail with the EP in several distinct stages, some of which are subject to strict time-limits, and most of which can only be adopted with the explicit agreement of the parliamentary body. Under the co-decision procedure alone, the number of legislative proposals to be dealt with every year has more than doubled, with a parallel rise in the number of meetings and contacts required at every level (Council Document 13316/1/00).

The burden of this increased workload is felt throughout the Council and its General Secretariat, but has fallen most heavily on three main groups of individuals:

- successive presidencies, who must steer the process while they are in the chair;
- the deputy permanent representatives meeting in Coreper I (the less senior level of the Committee of Permanent Representatives – see Chapter 3), who are responsible for most areas subject to the co-decision procedure (of the 346 dossiers concluded under the co-decision procedure between July 1999 and December 2003, for example, Coreper I dealt with 292, Coreper II with 46, and the Special Committee on Agriculture with 8); and
- the 'co-decision backbone' in the Council Secretariat (see below).

As a direct result of the introduction of the co-decision procedure, presidency officials and the members of Coreper I now spend a considerable amount of their time either attempting to avoid, or actually engaged in, the time-consuming formal conciliation process that concludes difficult co-decision procedures.

Early worries that the introduction of the co-decision procedure would result in a dramatic reduction in decision-making speed have failed to materialize. Indeed, there is some evidence to suggest that decisions are now reached more quickly under this procedure (see Box 2.5), although further comparative research and analysis remains to be done on the pre-Maastricht period. This increase in decision-making speed under co-decision is no doubt partly related to growing familiarity with the procedure and the strict time-limits which apply once the Council has adopted its common position.

Another possible contributory factor, and the second main effect on the Council of the EP's increased powers, is a fundamental change in the Council's focus and aims in the legislative process. In the early years following the introduction of the co-decision procedure, most of the Council's resources and attention were focused on the conciliation phase of the process, where lack of agreement could result in the proposed piece of legislation failing to materialize. Once the ToA introduced the possibility of reaching agreement after the first EP reading, and removed the Council's right to reintroduce its common position following failure to agree in the Conciliation Committee, the Council's attention shifted to the earlier stages of the process. Its strategy now is to reach agreement as swiftly as possible whenever possible, thereby reducing the number of issues that end up in conciliation. It has enjoyed some success in the pursuit of this aim: in comparing the Maastricht and Amsterdam periods, it is clear that, while the number of dossiers concluded at the conciliation stage each year has increased, they constitute a smaller proportion of the total number of co-decision procedures concluded annually (see Table 8.1).

This altered strategy on the part of the Council has only been possible because of the introduction of changes to its working methods and the organization of its Secretariat, the third main effect on the Council of the EP's increased powers. It was quickly realised that agreement at the stage of first or second reading in the EP could only be achieved if work was conducted in both institutions in parallel. This could only be achieved if underpinned by an intensive and ongoing exchange of information between the two parties (often via the Commission, which participates in the meetings of both bodies) and the virtually constant availability of the Council presidency for exploratory contacts and negotiations with the EP. The Council quickly set about ensuring that these conditions would apply.

The rotating presidency was given responsibility for:

- liaising with the EP to establish and, if necessary, to adapt parallel timetables and work schedules for the period of its term in office;
- monitoring the progress of on-going co-decision dossiers; and
- identifying opportunities for agreement.

Table 8.1 *Statistics relating to the co-decision procedure, 1993–2004*

	1993–1999 (Maastricht period)	1999–2004 (Amsterdam period)
Co-decision dossiers concluded		
• Total number	165	403
• Annual average	33	80.6
Dossiers concluded at first reading	–	115 (28.5%)
Dossiers concluded at second reading	99 (60%)	200 (49.6%)
Dossiers concluded at third reading (conciliation)	63 (38%)	86 (21.4%)
Failures – no agreement reached	3 (2%)	2 (0.5%)

Notes: The failed co-decision procedures were the following:
- In the Maastricht period:
  - Voice Telephony Directive, 1994
  - Biotechnology Directive, 1995
  - Transferable Securities Committee, 1998
- In the Amsterdam period:
  - Takeover Directive, 2001 (see Box 10.4 in Chapter 10)
  - Port Services Directive, 2003.

Source: Activity reports of the European Parliament's delegation to the Conciliation Committee, available on the EP's website http://www.europarl.eu.int

It is helped in the latter two tasks by a mushrooming of contacts between all levels of the Council and the EP at all stages of the co-decision procedure (see below). A special section with overall responsibility for co-decision, known as the '*dorsale*', or backbone, has been created in the Council Secretariat, composed of officials who follow co-decision dossiers as they move through the various stages of discussion and decision in the EP. A reorganization of the Secretariat, which began in 2000, saw responsibility for conciliation being shifted from DG F (previously charged with relations with the EP and institutional questions) to the Legal Service, an indication perhaps of the more legalistic approach of the Council to this area.

New dynamics

The changes in the relative powers of the Council and the EP, the resulting new working relationships between them, and consequent changes in the attitudes and behaviour of the two institutions towards one another have together had the effect of introducing new dynamics into their relationship (Garrett, 1995). The EP has been the chief beneficiary of the changes introduced to the budgetary and legislative procedures at various stages over the years, while the Council has suffered what it considers to be a corresponding loss in power, in the sense of having to share it with the EP. Yet it could be argued that the distinct constituencies represented by the two institutions – the member state governments in the case of the Council, and the peoples of Europe in the case of the EP – lend a greater legitimacy than before to any joint decisions reached.

The overall effect of the introduction of the cooperation and co-decision procedures (particularly the latter) has been to increase substantially the levels of interaction and interdependence between the two institutions. Above all, the Council is obliged not only to take the EP seriously, but to do so in a very visible fashion. One example of this is the greater effort now expended by the Council in explaining its rejection of proposed EP amendments and the reasons leading it to adopt its common positions. Whether or not it chooses to exercise it, the EP's right to say 'no' increases its bargaining position *vis-à-vis* the Council, and forces the latter to engage in serious negotiations with representatives of the EP, a fact that has implications for the degree of influence the EP can exert on the Council (see below).

Because they have to account much more publicly than before for their positions under the various procedures, both the Council and the EP are under pressure to develop convincing positions. Where majority votes are required, whether in the Council or the EP, questions of tactics may demand as much time and effort as the question of substance. A good deal of time has to be expended in ascertaining or second-guessing the other institution's viewpoint on proposals under consideration, hence the marked increase in contact between them at all levels. The members of the two institutions are also obliged to be increasingly sensitive to the currents of opinion shaping the position of their legislative partner, a novel experience for the Council in particular. The fact that less than 1 per cent (only five out of a total of 568) of concluded co-decision procedures have failed in the period from the beginning of November 1993 until the end of April 2004 bears striking testimony to the seriousness with which the two bodies now regard each other and engage in the process (see Table 8.1).

As regards public accountability for their actions, it can also happen that the EP and the Council are required to act together to defend the results of conciliation. This occurs when their joint decisions are challenged before the ECJ, as happened on three separate occasions in the period 1999–2004. Such cases may be brought by the Commission (as in the case of a regulation concerning the financial instrument for the environment), or by one or more member states (for example, Finland and Spain in the case of a directive on the organization of the working time of people carrying out mobile road transport activities, or France in the case of a directive on cosmetic products). The knowledge that their joint decisions can, and may be, challenged is an added impetus to both the Council and the EP to work closely together at all stages of the process to ensure the quality and legality of their legislation, and reinforces the level of parity between the two institutions.

Despite the more cooperative approach on the part of the two institutions ushered in by the cooperation and more particularly the co-decision procedures, the inherent antagonism between the Council and the EP can still spill over into disputes, running the gamut from disagreements between officials to full-scale court cases. Often these disputes take the form of legalistic squabbles over the interpretation of clauses in treaties, or of articles in pieces of technical legislation. They are difficult to describe without going into detail about the arcane minutiae of legislative procedures, the intricacies of the documents in question and legal rules. Issues of policy substance, of course, also give rise to disputes, as does the choice of the legal basis for proposed legislation (this determines which procedure will apply and the relative powers of the Council and the EP) and decisions about 'comitology'. The latter, as we saw in Chapter 7, entails the establishment of committees of national officials who, on behalf of the Council, oversee the delegated implementation powers exercised by the Commission. Unlike the Council, the EP is normally in favour of committees that provide the Commission with the most discretion (and thereby increase the latter's accountability to the Parliament).

The most public disputes between the EP and the Council have historically been over the budget, in the period before the introduction of the multi-annual financial perspectives. This was the first area where the Parliament gained significant legislative powers, and these were exploited with great gusto. In the 1970s and 1980s, the heyday of inter-institutional budgetary disputes, the Council had little or no direct contact with the EP and very limited means of communicating with it. The result was 'much shouting across the parade ground but very little close-up bargaining in smoke-filled rooms' (Corbett *et al.*, 2003, p. 363). The EP's frustration with this situation led it to use its ultimate weapon – outright rejection of the budget – on three occasions (in 1979, 1982 and 1984) during this period. Today, neither institution can complain of a lack of contact or of a dearth of opportunities for negotiation, and public disputes now signal the failure of established procedures of conciliation rather than attempts by the EP to draw attention to its perceived lack of power and influence in the budgetary procedure.

The new decision-making procedures established under the SEA and the TEU have given rise to their fair share of disputes, normally settled by means of IIAs. In testing the limits of the new procedures, the EP has sought to maximize its powers, frequently by means of following the letter rather than the spirit of the basic provisions. In so doing, it has not endeared itself to the Council, which has proved equally adept at exploiting procedural loopholes and foiling the EP's ambitions for greater leverage. More recently, the EP has attempted to establish a direct link between a requirement for qualified majority voting (QMV) in the Council and the use of the co-decision procedure. The member governments have been slow to come round to the EP's way of thinking, but the CT, providing as it does for co-decision as the 'ordinary legislative procedure' and for QMV as the normal voting procedure, seeks finally to establish this link.

The number and frequently very public nature of disputes between the Council and the EP should not be allowed to detract from the striking amount of cooperation that has also developed between them, particularly since the implementation of the provisions of the ToA. The statistics regarding the co-decision procedure in Table 8.1 bear eloquent testimony to this more cooperative and indeed conciliatory approach on the part of both institutions. The changes to its legislative powers have enabled the EP to become much more active and effective at intervening in the EU's legislative and scrutiny procedures, earning the infrequently articulated and often grudging respect of the Council. Proof of this is to be found in the acceptance, or indeed promotion, by the Council of additional informal processes that have the effect of extending the involvement of the EP in the legislative process.

One example of an initially informal process that has become a virtually standard fixture is the trialogue (sometimes referred to as a 'trilogue') – a tripartite gathering of representatives of the Council, the EP and the Commission. Originally introduced in the context of budgetary conciliation, it was subsequently adopted as part of the co-decision procedure, again in the context of conciliation. The trialogue is not mentioned as such in the treaties, which refer only to 'appropriate contacts' between the institutions. However, extensions in the scope of the co-decision procedure and the desire of both the Council and the EP to reach agreement as swiftly and early as possible, thereby avoiding conciliation, has resulted in a mushrooming of formal and informal trialogues at various levels and stages. In the period 1999–2004, the conciliation committee was convened forty-nine times, while trialogues took place on 193 occasions, a clear indication of a growing trend towards negotiating and reaching agreement on dossiers without the need for a discussion in the Conciliation Commitee.

Formal trialogues have more than proved their worth, but the EP is rather wary of the Council's enthusiasm for informal trialogues, preferring to engage in debate with the ministers via its more public committee meetings and plenary sessions. However, the EP cannot deny the utility of trialogues as a forum for a frank and open exchange of views and possible compromise solutions to joint problems. As a result, they have become an increasingly important part of the landscape of inter-institutional contacts in co-decision. In the enlarged EU, this situation is unlikely to change.

Contacts between the Council and the EP

The extent of the EP's contacts with the other EU institutions has increased in line with the development of its legislative powers. This is particularly true where the Council is concerned, or perhaps more correctly where members of the Council are concerned, since the two bodies never in fact meet face-to-face. Generally, the Council is represented by the presidency minister before the EP, sometimes accompanied by officials from the other member states (as in the Conciliation Committee). None the less, there is now a well-established range of both formal and informal contacts at various levels and at all stages of the processes in which the two institutions are involved, as Box 8.1 indicates.

Unlike the Commission, which in effect operates as a 26th delegation in the Council (see Chapter 7), representatives of the EP do not attend Council meetings. Consequently, they are dependent on information from those directly involved in order to ascertain what exactly happens when decisions are being taken and the EP's amendments are on the table. Recent measures designed to increase the transparency of Council proceedings (such as the transmission of parts of some meetings, the publication of votes, and increased access to documents) fall far short of what many MEPs consider acceptable or desirable. They have fallen back on their many and varied contacts and dealings at all levels of the Council hierarchy, as well as those with the Commission and the individual member states, to amass evidence on the attitudes and voting behaviour of Council members. Some of these contacts and dealings are more formal and direct than others, but all contribute to the flow of information and opinion between the two bodies that is vital for the efficient functioning of the legislative process.

Direct access to the European Council (see Chapter 5) was denied to the Parliament until 1988, when the EP President was first invited to address the opening session of the meeting, to give the EP's point of view on current EU affairs and the issues on the agenda for discussion by the heads of state and government. This practice has now become institutionalized and is valued by the EP President for the access it affords to the political leaders of all the member states simultaneously. Perhaps surprisingly, the EP is not anxious to have its president become a full member of the European Council. It argues that, by keeping its distance, it gains the independence to comment critically on the European Council, if need be. The fact that the EP President leaves the meeting after the opening session also means that he/she has the distinction of being the first person to speak to the large number of assembled

---

Box 8.1   *Council–European Parliament contacts*

Contacts occur at various levels:

At the level of the presidents:

- Since 1988, the EP President has been invited to address the heads of state or government meeting in the European Council, to present the EP's views on the issues on the agenda.
- The Presidents of the EP, the Council and the Commission meet on a monthly basis, usually in Strasbourg on the Wednesday of EP plenary sessions, to explore solutions in current areas of disagreement; these meetings are called 'trialogues' and are prepared by the Neunreither Group (see below).
- The President of the European Council reports to the EP on the outcome of European Council meetings.
- The EP President meets the new Council President before or at the beginning of his or her term in office.

At the level of the ministers and MEPs:

- The EP President and the chairs of the political groups meet regularly with ministers and prime ministers, especially those of their own political family, often before Council and particularly before European Council meetings.
- The chairs of the EP committees have close contact with the minister or ministers chairing the relevant configurations of the Council, often meeting just before Council meetings.
- Presidency ministers may attend plenary sessions or meetings of the relevant EP committee, to answer questions on their area of responsibility.

At the level of national officials and MEPs:

- The members of Coreper II meet MEPs during conciliation committee meetings.
- National officials and MEPs meet one another when representing governments and the EP in IGCs and Conventions.
- Each permanent representation has at least one official with particular responsibility for monitoring the work of the EP; they meet in the General Affairs Group and attend the EP's plenary sessions as observers.

At the level of Secretariat officials:

- There is regular contact between Council and EP Secretariat officials regarding the day-to-day negotiation of dossiers.
- The Neunreither Group (an inter-institutional working party of officials from the Council, the EP and the Commission) meets monthly to monitor the progress of issues currently under negotiation, and to search for solutions in areas of difficulty.
- There is close coordination of timetables, particularly with regard to co-decision dossiers, conciliation procedures and so on.

press about the issues being discussed at the European Council, and may thus get good coverage for the EP's views. The utility of attendance depends to a certain extent on the attitude of the president-in-office in the European Council and the issues the EP President decides to highlight.

Apart from the European Council, the EP deals only rarely with the representatives of all the member states, since most of its relations with the Council take place through the medium of the presidency (see Chapter 6). Thus, either the prime minister or the foreign minister of the presidency member state reports to the following EP plenary session on the outcome of the European Council. Presidency ministers address the EP at the beginning and end of their six months in office, and appear at least once before the relevant parliamentary committees. They report after all important Council meetings and take part in the Question Time slot scheduled in each EP plenary session, during which MEPs have the right to request and receive oral replies to their questions from the Council in the person of the president-in-office. The rather ritualistic nature of these encounters should not detract from the fact that they are the most obvious manifestations of accountability on the part of the Council before the EP.

Coreper as a body tends to keep its distance from the EP, since the treaties provide that the official interlocutor is the Council, but the individual members of Coreper may represent their respective ministers in dealings with the Parliament. Such is the case with the composition of Conciliation Committees under the co-decision procedure, where the president of the Council is normally the only minister present, a fact that rankles with MEPs. Officials from each of the national permanent representations (permreps) follow the work of the EP closely and keep their ambassadors and the deputy permanent representatives informed of the progress of reports and dossiers.

The furious pace and range of issues to be decided between their two institutions means that relations between the Council and EP secretariats are intense, if not always warm, although this may depend on the personalities involved. Officials from the various Directorates-General (DGs) in the Council Secretariat following particular dossiers in the Council hierarchy are in direct and often daily contact with their opposite numbers in the EP when dossiers are 'live', documenting agreements on proposed amendments and, in some cases, searching for and helping to draft compromise solutions.

Relations between the EP and the individual member states are conducted through the national permreps in Brussels (see Chapter 9 for more details). One or more of the officials on the staff of each representation is responsible for following the EP's activities in general, while the officials from the presidency member state are the focus of day-to-day enquiries from the MEPs. Some permreps make a point of keeping their national MEPs informed of activity and current thinking in the Council on existing and forthcoming dossiers. Information thus passes between the two institutions on an informal basis, although representatives of individual member states may experience differing tugs of loyalty, depending on their own or their country's attitude towards the present and future role of the EP.

In the past, some member states, such as Germany, The Netherlands, Denmark and Italy, have been more supportive of the EP's demands for a greater role than others, and the EP has depended on the representatives of these countries to argue its case within the Council. This support can be expressed in a number of ways. Ministers can speak up for the Parliament when constitutional changes are being discussed, both inside and outside the Council; they can support amendments proposed by the EP on pieces of legislation that they must adopt in association with their Council colleagues; and they can find ways to inform the EP about potential rifts within the Council that can be exploited, particularly where decisions are required to be taken by majority voting.

The office of the presidency can also be used by a sympathetic member state to express its support for, and to further the cause of, the EP. Reporting to the Parliament on the outcome of important Council and European Council meetings can be given the aura of a real and prized debate rather than a ritual. Care can be taken to ensure that the spirit rather than merely the letter of the law regarding inter-institutional procedures is followed, and in some cases real innovations can be introduced. For example, it was the German presidency of 1988 that took the unusual step of inviting the EP President to address the members of the European Council at its opening session, which is now standard practice.

Clearly, a plethora of relations exists between all levels of the Council and the EP, a fact that appears to contradict the notion of a weak or antagonistic relationship between these two institutions. The importance of quality rather than quantity must therefore be considered. The EP seeks to exert influence on the Council wherever possible, from the level of prime minister down to national official. Making the Council listen to the point of view of the EP is the first step; the next, and infinitely more difficult, step is to make the member states act on the Parliament's advice.

Influencing the Council

The general notion of influence is notoriously difficult to pin down, involving as it does both subjective and objective interpretations, as well as the elements of quality and quantity. Trying to assess the degree of influence exerted by the EP over the Council is further complicated by the fact that the reasons why particular decisions are reached in the Council are many and varied, and not always clear even to those most directly involved. In exercising their legislative functions, the members of the Council are open to influence from many quarters, of which the EP is only one and not always the most important. With these qualifications in mind, let us examine the evidence for and against claims of EP influence over the Council, using the four headings mentioned above.

Subjective interpretations

The EP has always had a vested interest in asserting that it has a considerable impact on the Council, not only to demonstrate its utility to its electorate but also to strengthen its case for increased powers. It is not surprising, therefore, that most claims regarding the EP's influence on the Council come from the EP itself. Much of the evidence put forward to back up these claims is anecdotal, sometimes backed up by statistics purporting to demonstrate and quantify the extent of this influence (see below).

MEPs or officials from the EP Secretariat may maintain that a particular legislative outcome is a direct result of their, or their institution's, intervention and the Council's decision to follow where they have led. Given the competitive nature of the relationship between the two institutions, however, the Council is more likely than not to play down the degree to which it has been influenced by the EP in taking its decisions, and to attribute its actions to other motives or the input of other actors. Sometimes, however, the link between parliamentary pressure and the Council's subsequent actions is clear – past budgetary disputes are a good example.

Objective interpretations

Objectively, it is possible to identify four main areas where the EP clearly has a direct impact on the Council, the first being on *the content of Council decisions*. The EP can influence the final shape of Council legislative acts to varying degrees, depending on the procedure being used. In the budgetary procedure, through its veto over non-compulsory expenditure, the EP has gained an indirect say, within certain limits, over many areas of legislation. It decides on the amount to be allocated to these areas of expenditure and can thereby influence the purposes for which the money will be used.

The cooperation procedure enables the EP to enter into negotiations with the Council over the content of some of its legislative acts, now confined to just four legal bases, all in the area of EMU. The EP must, however, use the weapon of rejecting the result of the Council's first reading (the common position) with great care. There is always the risk of ending up with no legislation at all, if the Commission is not prepared to support the EP by withdrawing its proposal, and there is no unanimity in the Council to re-introduce the common position.

Parliamentary influence is often greatest in the informal inter-institutional bargaining that runs parallel to the formal stages of the cooperation procedure, the most important stage for the EP being that immediately prior to its second reading.

Under the co-decision procedure too, the EP is able to influence the content of Council decisions to a considerable extent, and not only those that result in conciliation. In cases where the Council is anxious to reach agreement early in the procedure, the EP may stand a good chance of having many of its amendments accepted and included in the final act. The small number of co-decision procedures that had failed following conciliation by the middle of 2004 (as noted earlier, only five out of a total of 568 concluded procedures over a decade) is evidence of mutual influence on the part of both the Council and the EP. In the short term, these failures have soured relations between the two bodies, but the lessons learned from them in the longer term (including the need for close and constant contact right up to and including the final stage of the process) should serve to improve the efficiency of the procedure as a whole.

The habit of relying on consensus within the Council also has a bearing on how much influence the Parliament can be expected to exert on the content of the final policy outcome. A determined search for consensus on the part of Council members weakens the position of the EP, depriving it of the possibility of exploiting divisions among the member states. On the other hand, differences of opinion among the member states can be exploited by the EP for its own ends, particularly where majority voting is the order of the day. In the final analysis, however, much depends on the desire of the Council in fact to produce a legislative outcome in the area concerned, and whether or not to produce it unanimously.

A second area where the Parliament has a direct impact on the Council is in *the ratification of Council decisions*. Under the budgetary, cooperation and co-decision procedures, the EP is involved throughout the decision-making process, and can to varying degrees determine the content of the final act. However, in the case of other procedures, where its role in the actual negotiation of the final act is less direct, the EP is not without influence. Under the assent procedure, for example, created by the SEA and extended by the TEU, it has the ability at least to delay and at most to veto Council decisions. On a more general level, the EP has the right to appeal to the ECJ against a decision of the Council.

The EP can also have an impact on the content of Council acts by either endorsing or undermining important Council decisions. The rapid accession of the five former East German *Länder* to the European Communities (EC) in 1990 was possible only because the EP was prepared to support the decision of the Council (Spence, 1991). On the other hand, the EP's objection to several of the European Council's nominees as members of the Barroso Commission in October 2004 resulted in the nomination of new candidates by two member governments, a mini re-allocation of portfolios and a delayed start to the new Commission's mandate, once it had been confirmed by a Council decision. In thus flexing its muscles, the new EP was not only acting well within its legal rights but also reminding the other institutions, if such a reminder were needed, that the EP is a powerful force to be reckoned with.

Third, the EP can exercise an implicit or explicit *right of initiative*, thereby affecting the content of the Council's agenda. Although the EP only achieved a limited explicit right of initiative under the TEU, the Commission has always been prepared in principle to accept any EP proposal to which it had no major objections and, where possible, to accept EP amendments to Commission proposals. In attempting to get an EP amendment accepted by the Council under the co-decision procedure, the EP must first produce a proposed amendment attractive enough to gain the support of a sufficient number of Council members. Intensive contacts between the two bodies and input from the Commission provides an early indication of which amendments are likely to fly and which to fall. At the same time, the EP must be confident of its ability to muster the large majority of MEPs required to adopt an amendment. Similarly, it must work hard to ensure that a sufficient majority of its members will vote in support of the agreements reached in conciliation, an outcome that cannot be taken for granted, as was all too obviously demonstrated in the cases of the Biotechnology Directive in 1995, the Takeover Directive in 2001 and the Port Services Directive in 2003.

Finally, the EP can have an impact on the Council by exercising its *powers of scrutiny*. MEPs have the right to address written and oral questions to the Council, although they are frequently less than satisfied with the answers they receive. The replies to written questions from MEPs to the Council are drafted by officials in the Council Secretariat and discussed in the General Affairs Group (GAG), composed of officials from each of the twenty-five permreps. Before the existence of the Council website and the large amounts of information readily available on it, MEPs' questions were one of the few means of extracting information publicly from the Council on precise issues. The appearance of presidency ministers and prime ministers before the EP plenary at the beginning and end of their term in office, and to report on the outcome of Council and European Council meetings during their six months in the chair, provides another series of opportunities for MEPs to question representatives of the Council directly. Similarly, the attendance of presidency ministers and officials at EP committee meetings represent yet more occasions for the MEPs to exercise their powers of scrutiny.

In exploiting to the full its potential to exert influence over the Council in general, and the content of legislative acts in particular, timing is all-important for the EP. A sympathetic presidency can be invaluable for ensuring that the EP's point of view is at least given a fair hearing. Certain initiatives can benefit from delay until such time as a rather less supportive member state has relinquished the office of president in favour of one that is deemed more likely to pay greater attention to the concerns of the EP. Similarly, it is better for the EP not to launch a major initiative at a time when the presidency is being handed over, or another issue is taking centre-stage.

Quantity of influence

The EP, for reasons mentioned above, is keen to present itself as an influential actor in the EU's legislative process. Providing evidence to back up these claims has not always been easy, but has been facilitated somewhat by two developments. First, new transparency rules mean that access to the key documents in the legislative procedures are more readily available to outsiders, who can independently track the development of the final act through its various negotiation stages and thereby attempt to identify its influential authors. Second, the cooperation and co-decision procedures have proved fertile ground for lovers of statistics, spawning a huge array of figures, comparative tables and bar charts.

Table 8.2 is an example of the statistics advanced by the EP and its supporters to demonstrate its purported influence in the legislative field. It shows the fate of 1,344 amendments adopted by the EP at second reading in the eighty-six conciliation procedures completed during the period 1999–2004, and compares them to the situation in the period 1994–9. The large number of amendments accepted as the result of a

Table 8.2   *Take-up of European Parliament amendments in conciliation,*
1994–2004

Fate of EP amendments	1994–1999	1999–2004
Accepted as proposed	27%	23%
Accepted following compromise	51%	60%
Withdrawn	22%	17%

Source: European Parliament, 2004, p. 14.

compromise between the Council and the EP is presented as proof of 'the importance and positive results of direct contacts between the co-legislators in reaching compromises acceptable to both sides in the conciliation procedure' (European Parliament 2004, p. 14).

Statistics in general, and those relating to amendments in particular, need to be examined and treated with care, for a number of reasons (Maurer, 2003a). First, they make no distinction between the relative importance of the various amendments, many of which may merely be drafting improvements, thereby affecting the textual rather than the substantive content of the final document. Second, they give no information about the extent to which rejected amendments are taken up in a modified form in new proposals. And third, they do not distinguish between what Earnshaw and Judge (1996, p. 102) term 'substantive' and 'propagandistic' amendments, the first having a realistic chance of being accepted, and the second being designed to draw attention to an issue without any expectation that it will be included in the final legislative act.

Quality of influence

If we accept that the EP can have an impact on the Council by influencing the content of their joint decisions, by endorsing or undermining other Council decisions, by employing its right of initiative to shape the Council's agenda, and by exercising its powers of scrutiny over the representatives of the Council, we are left with the question of the quality of such influence. Clearly, this is linked to the question of the calibre of the representatives of the EP, be they MEPs or officials, and the degree of responsibility they exhibit in fulfilling their formal powers. The gradual accumulation of powers by the EP has been accompanied by a toning-down of its behaviour and antagonistic attitude *vis-à-vis* the Council. Posturing and megaphone diplomacy on both sides have been replaced almost completely and almost always by a shared belief in the benefits of ongoing cooperation and negotiation.

The large numbers of proposed amendments put forward by the EP for consideration by the Council and the Commission need to be differentiated, since they can vary largely in significance. Some are likely to be of considerable political or substantive importance, having a real and lasting impact on the final legislative act and all those affected by it (for example, provisions relating to the environment). Others may be purely technical or administrative and therefore non-controversial, with little or no impact or any real importance.

Another quality-related question focuses on the negotiated outcomes of the legislative processes in which the Council and the EP are jointly engaged. It is legitimate to ask whether the final acts may be regarded as pieces of quality legislation, or whether indeed they represent least common denominator compromises, only agreed to because they are better than no legislation at all. The answers to this question will doubt-less vary depending on the respondent and on individual pieces of legis-lation, and are probably best sought in individual case-studies.

A stable tandem for the future?

The legitimacy of the EP as the co-legislative authority with the Council is now unquestioned, to the extent that no member government would dare to challenge it openly. This is not to say that some member govern-ments do not privately have reservations about the EP's current role and powers, particularly on those occasions when the EP acts in a way viewed as being detrimental to the interests of the member state in ques-tion. In the EU today, the Council–EP tandem is a fact of life; each insti-tution provides a wheel apiece, does its share of the pedalling and takes its turn at the front. But what of the future of this particular tandem? Is it likely to be stable, increasing its pace and power, or will it prove unstable, grinding to a halt because of disputes between the riders?

The argument in favour of future stability in the relationship is based on the substantially increased levels of interaction and interdependence between the two institutions that the co-decision procedure, in particular, has engendered. The treaty articles describing the legislative procedures constitute starting-points only, and are supplemented by joint declarations, IIAs and other formal documents that add detail to the basic procedures, making them more workable and efficient. These formal documents are in turn based on and surrounded by a profusion of other semi-formal, quasi-formal and informal procedures that have grown up around the co-decision procedure in particular (Farrell and Héritier, 2003). These informal contacts, as well as the continued successful management of the co-decision procedure, are expected to reinforce the relationship, cementing ties, promoting cooperation and aiding in the settlement of eventual disputes.

But future instability cannot be ruled out, given the nature of the institutions themselves. A new parliamentary body is elected every five years, normally implying a significant number (sometimes as high as 60 per cent) of new MEPs, who need time to become acquainted not only with the working methods of the EP itself, but also with the way in which it conducts its business with the Council. A hiatus or period of adaptation therefore has to be factored into the relationship every five years. The political colour of the EP may change, or the attitudes of a significant group within it may affect the overall opinion of the EP and the way in which it conducts its business. Thus the election of large numbers of anti-EU MEPs in 2004 was viewed with some dismay by the more integrationist members of the Council, who foresaw potentially difficult times ahead.

As a body, the EP is much more heterogeneous than the Council, and as a consequence it can experience real difficulties in mustering the necessary majorities required of it for taking decisions at committee or plenary level. The implications for the EP's relationship with the Council are clear. Members of the Council will be prepared to expend the large amounts of time required for pre-negotiation in co-decision and conciliation only if they can be reasonably confident that any agreement reached, whether inside or outside the Conciliation Committee, will subsequently be endorsed by the EP plenary. Another worrying factor for both the EP and the Council is the continuing downward trend in turnout figures for EP elections, and the effect this might have on the declared legitimacy of the EP.

The Council–EP relationship has shown signs of significant development, particularly in the course of the 1990s. However, there is a lingering suspicion that the Council has only agreed to share its legislative powers with the EP because public opinion and the force of circumstances have left it with no alternative, if it wishes to be viewed as a body committed to democratic legitimacy. None the less, the Council has made real progress, both in changing its working methods to accommodate the increased role and powers of the EP in the legislative process and in establishing working practices that aid the search for agreement between the two bodies in the co-decision procedure. The EP, for its part, is anxious to consolidate the degree of parity it has achieved so far, to enhance the efficiency of the process and to increase its transparency. In so doing, it will no doubt experience some degree of resistance on the part of the Council, but the effect on the operation of the tandem of such disagreements is likely to be minimal.

Chapter 9

Not Just Governments: the Council and the Member States

To most observers of the European Union (EU), the Council is the member states, in that it consists of representatives of the member governments articulating 'national interests'. It is true that the Council is the most unashamedly national of the EU's institutions, having been created and organized in such a way as to ensure a specifically national, as opposed to supranational, input into EU affairs. However, the Council should be viewed more correctly as being synonymous with the member governments, and indeed sometimes with only parts of them.

The Council is composed at all levels of twenty-five national components – the ministerial and official representatives of the national governments – through which national and Union interests are welded together. As we saw earlier, some 70 per cent of Council business is settled at the level of the working parties, composed of national officials, the majority of whom are based in the member capitals. However, the expansion of the range and extent of EU policies over the years has resulted in burgeoning contacts between non-governmental national individuals and groups on the one hand, and EU institutions on the other. This development has been viewed with some disquiet by the member governments, who are anxious to retain their role as chief interlocutors with the Council.

In this chapter, we focus on the way in which the member states and the Council affect and are affected by one another. Here, the term 'the member states' includes not only the member governments but also such other national actors as the national parliaments, interest groups and sub-national governments. In the same vein, the term 'the Council' is an abbreviated form describing the ministerial Council, its sub-structures and supporting bodies. Two main questions will be addressed in what follows. First, how have the member states been forced to organize and comport themselves in order to deal with the ways in which the Council is structured and functions? Second, what impact does the behaviour of the member states have on the Council and the way in which it operates? A first section describes the internal structures and mechanisms by means of which each of the member states arrives at their 'national position', which they subsequently communicate to the Council, and defend at all levels of the Council hirearchy. The impact of the Council on domestic policy-making and actors will then be assessed, followed by some thoughts on the ways in which domestic politics can and does affect the work of the Council.

Communicating with the Council

Information is vital to any negotiating process and, to this end, vast amounts of documentation and correspondence pass between the EU institutions and various bodies in each of the member states on a daily basis. Electronic mail, telephones, faxes, coded telegrams and diplomatic bags are all employed to keep the flow of information moving rapidly between the main actors, in a process where speed and up-to-date information are vital ingredients for playing a leading role.

Representatives of each member state attend meetings at all levels of the Council hierarchy, where their job is to articulate and defend the pre-defined 'national position' on each of the points on the agenda. This position may have to be redefined in the course of negotiations, in response to such factors as changing national or international circumstances, the impact of parallel negotiations in other policy areas, the shifting positions of other national negotiators, or proposed amendments from other institutional actors, such as the Commission or the European Parliament (EP).

For each member state, then, communicating with the Council involves two main aspects:

- defining and, in response to communications from the Council and other actors, often redefining the national position on every point under discussion in each of the Council's configurations; and
- transmitting this information to the Council.

Controlling these information flows is an obvious priority for the chief actors in the process, and to this end the member governments have taken steps to ensure that, to the greatest extent possible, the flow of communications between the Council and the member states follows a strict and highly regulated path. The benefits of a tightly controlled system are apparent to both sides, in that it contributes to the coherence and consistency of each government's approach to EU affairs, with positive effects on the negotiating process as a whole.

The Council's chief interlocutors in each of the member states are the various government departments and the Brussels-based permanent representations (permreps), while rather more indirect contacts are maintained with the national parliaments, national interest groups and sub-national governmental authorities. In this section, the communications between the Council and each of these bodies will be examined in turn, and the idiosyncrasies of particular member states highlighted.

Government departments

National representatives meeting in the Council hierarchy react to issues under discussion according to instructions agreed upon in or with their national capitals. The rigidity of these instructions may differ from one member state to another, or from issue to issue, but each negotiating brief constitutes a 'national position' to be articulated and defended by the relevant official or minister. This 'single viewpoint', however, does not come about naturally or necessarily easily. Member states are not monoliths; they are composed of different regions, classes, parties and groups, each with its own preoccupations and interests, and which each wishes to see accommodated in eventual Council decisions. As a result, agencies have been created in each member state to canvass views on particular issues and to reach agreement on a single approach that becomes the national negotiating position. The coordinators of national policy *vis-à-vis* the EU seek advice on Commission proposals from a wide range of ministries and governmental agencies; they also consult regional and local government agencies, and other relevant interest groups and special constituencies. Approaches to the inter- and intra-ministerial coordination of the national position vary from state to state, but a number of shared features, functions and impacts can be observed.

Intra-ministerial coordination

Today, virtually every national ministry is affected to some extent by the EU, and most have a unit responsible for the internal coordination of European business. Some, like the ministries of foreign affairs, economic affairs and agriculture, spend the greater (or a very large) proportion of their time, and have a large number of their personnel engaged, on EU business, because of the extent of EU involvement in these policy areas. Others may be required to commit fewer resources in terms of personnel and time, or may experience varying demands on these resources.

The distribution of nationally-based officials engaged directly on EU business at any given time depends on a number of factors. Where a member state has a particular stake in a specific policy area (for example, Spain in fisheries, Sweden in environmental affairs or France in agriculture), the government invests extra effort (usually evident in the form of additional personnel or time), in following dossiers in this area, preparing for EU-level meetings, liaising with officials and groups from other member states and drawing up possible compromise proposals, in the hope of playing a leading role at the European level. This is obviously particularly true during the period of preparation for and exercising the office of the presidency of the Council.

The distribution of personnel is also affected by the issues currently being discussed at EU level. Some, such as the budget and the setting of agricultural prices, recur annually, and require the input of specialized individuals over a concentrated period of the year. Others form part of a continuing policy, with alternate periods of intensive activity (for example, when a new proposal is being drawn up or final decisions are being made) and ones of relative calm (for example, while the policy is being implemented and reviewed). The extension of the scope of the EU to embrace policy areas previously the subject of informal, intergovernmental cooperation (such as justice and home affairs – JHA; or the common foreign and security policy – CFSP) normally produces an increase in personnel engaged in that area, as the need for national coordination also increases.

The coordination of a national position in a specific policy area or on a specific proposal starts within the responsible ministry, as the relevant officials use established channels of communication to contact appropriate interest groups and special constituencies. These groups frequently provide the officials with expert advice on the policy area, information on implementation and general feedback, and sometimes with special knowledge of other member states. In drawing up a national position, officials from the national ministries are also in regular contact with the relevant official(s) in the national permrep in Brussels (see below), who may be able to provide an advance indication of the chances of success of a given position with the other member states.

Depending on how the member government organizes its business, meetings of Council working parties, where issues are discussed between the representatives of each of the member states and of the Commission (see Chapter 3), may be attended by an official from the permrep, or the relevant official from the national ministry may travel to Brussels for the meeting. Either way, preparation for such meetings requires instructions, whether oral or written, as to the position to adopt on the various points on the agenda. The margin for manoeuvre allowed to these officials depends on the national approach, the rigidity of the national position and, possibly, the seniority and expertise of the official in the area. Participants are normally required to report on the outcome of the meeting, thereby aiding the maintenance of consistency and coherence in the national position.

It is thus clear that the formulation of a position at the level of the individual ministry is frequently the result of protracted and detailed discussion with specialized agencies and interest groups. It is just the first stage in the process of agreeing on a national position to be defended against those of other member states, the Commission and the EP.

Inter-ministerial coordination

The formulation of national positions for EU negotiations is normally the result of debate and frequently of compromise between several ministerial departments (Wallace, 1973; Bulmer, 1983). Each member government has a system of inter-ministerial coordination to combine the different sectoral approaches into a single global stance. Systematic inter-ministerial coordination also provides a measure of consistency and coherence in the national approach across all policy sectors, useful for both domestic and European purposes. Repeated inconsistencies in the national position suggest poor coordination and fuzzy lines of authority. National officials at the receiving end of inconsistency may find, at best, that they lack credibility among their European colleagues during negotiations and, at worst, may be forced into embarrassing climb-downs when their instructions are changed. Inter-ministerial coordination becomes of paramount importance when a member government holds the presidency and weakness in coordination affects not only the relevant member state, but the EU as a whole.

The various systems of inter-ministerial coordination differ both in their organization and in the efficiency of their results (see Kassim *et al.*, 2000; Wessels *et al.*, 2003 and Bulmer and Lequesne, 2005 for details). They are largely a result of historical, cultural, administrative and political differences between the member states, and new member states tend to go 'window-shopping' before setting up their own systems, in order to determine the approach that will suit them best. In most cases, the ministry of foreign affairs is intimately involved in the coordination of national policy *vis-à-vis* the EU, a result of the historical tendency to view EU affairs primarily as an aspect of external relations. Some member governments have divided the responsibility for overall coordination between the ministry of foreign affairs and another department (for example, the Finance Ministry in Germany, the Ministry of National Economy in Greece, and the Chancellor's Office in Austria). Yet others, such as the United Kingdom (UK) and France, have created special inter-ministerial administrative units to ensure coordination of the national position on EU policies. In all member states, inter-ministerial committees exist at official and political level to manage inter-departmental relations in respect of EU policy.

While each ministry is responsible for the coordination of policy within its own sphere of activity, rivalry between national ministries can some-times spill over into dispute and, if not rapidly resolved, can weaken the overall position of the member state in question. The issue of which ministry is to coordinate national policy in areas not previously subject to EU cooperation is frequently a source of debate. Tension between spending and non-spending ministries is a factor in the formulation of a national position for EU policies that involve an allocation of funds.

Each member government has a recognized arbiter in the event of a dispute between ministries, be it a specialized committee, the cabinet or the prime minister, although this may differ according to the issue at stake or its political saliency. Ministries with primary responsibility for a subject may draw on their EU contacts to bolster their positions within the national discussion. Having an official in the permrep in Brussels can thus serve to reinforce the weight of the relevant ministry in the national policy formulation process, when the national position on certain issues is being decided.

One striking aspect of EU integration throughout and since the 1990s has been the increasingly central role now played by the heads of state or government in EU affairs. They and their support staffs have become important links in the coordination chain, at least on certain salient issues (which may differ from one member state to another) and at certain times (for example, in advance of a European Council meeting or at the conclusion of an intergovernmental conference – IGC).

Senior officials from the national permreps in Brussels also make a crucial contribution to national coordination, although the way in which they do this can differ between member states. Their systematic and close association with the formulation of national positions can be an important asset in the setting of realistic negotiating goals. Some permanent representatives or their deputies are associated even to the extent of attending weekly coordination meetings in the capital. Officials from the permreps add oral or written clarifications and comments to Commission draft texts and reports on meetings in the Council hierarchy before passing them on to interested officials in the capitals.

The basic rule is that documentation is normally sent to the department or body responsible for inter-ministerial coordination, whose job it is to copy it to all interested parties. However, pressures of time and work, as well as the wonders of modern technology (e-mail in particular), mean that it is frequently more efficient for the officials from the permrep also to copy it 'for information' to the relevant ministries. Coded telegrams are used for the most sensitive information, but to a much lesser degree than is the case for bilateral embassies, and also less frequently than in the early days of the European Communities (EC).

Each official in the permrep is in regular contact with individuals in the relevant national ministries, sometimes several times a day. Routine questions tend to be settled at this working level, with the organs of inter-ministerial coordination being kept informed. The latter only meet to discuss politically sensitive issues, and to ensure overall coordination of the national position across all policy areas.

In some member states and during some specific periods, the permanent representative (PR) and other Brussels-based staff have an enhanced coordination role. This may be the case, for example, where responsibility for overall coordination in the capital is not very well defined or is the subject of controversy between competing units. Alternatively, it may occur when a member state holds the Council presidency, or (as is frequently the case in smaller member states) where personnel numbers are limited. Much coordination is done on a relatively informal and oral basis, frequently allowing a fairly wide margin of manoeuvre and quite a high degree of autonomy for the PRs and their staff in the various working party and Coreper (Committee of Permanent Representatives – see Chapter 3) meetings they attend.

The permanent representations (permreps)

Each member government, as of right and also of necessity, maintains a permrep in Brussels, while governments from aspiring member states and third countries have missions there (see Kassim *et al.*, 2001; and for earlier periods, Hayes-Renshaw *et al.*, 1989 and Tizzano, 1989). Given the relentless schedule of meetings throughout the Council hierarchy, the favoured location for the permreps is within walking distance of the Council's conference centre (in the Justus Lipsius building at the heart of the European quarter of the city), and most are to be found in that area. Less fortunate member governments, such as the Dutch and the Poles, have found offices a metro-ride away, and must put up with the consequent inconvenience when time is short or the hour is late. Each national delegation also has access to a small suite of offices in Justus Lipsius, which can be used as meeting rooms, for making telephone calls to the relevant capital for supplementary instructions during negotiations, for private discussions, and so on.

Given that they all exist to perform the same basic functions, it should come as no surprise that the twenty-five permreps conform to a single organizational model and operate in a broadly similar fashion. That being said, some dissimilarities are also apparent, and may be attributed to politico-cultural differences, geographical considerations, national values and policy priorities. The single feature common to all the national representations is that they are headed by a PR, invariably a career diplomat of ambassadorial rank. The PR represents his or her (the latter only applicable since 2000 with the appointment of the first female PR, an Irish woman) member government in Coreper II. Past EU experience is an advantage, and many PRs have previously served at a senior level in the representation, in their national civil service dealing with Community affairs, or in some forum of multilateral diplomacy (for example, as a member of the national delegation to the United Nations (UN)). This post is considered without exception to be one of the most senior and important appointments in each national diplomatic service. It is only rarely made on a partisan basis, and even then, those appointed are normally specialists in EU affairs.

Each permrep also contains a deputy permanent representative (DPR) who speaks and acts for his or her member state in Coreper I. This, too, is a senior and prestigious position, with more than half the incumbents in 2004 enjoying the rank of ambassador or minister plenipotentiary. The word 'deputy' in the title refers to the fact that the DPRs may stand in for their PR when required to do so, and are subject to the overall authority of the head of the permrep, but otherwise they operate with virtual autonomy in their areas of responsibility (see Chapter 3). There is less uniformity as regards the DPRs' ministries of origin, with much depending on national arrangements for the coordination of EU policy. As a general rule, however, they tend to be drawn from either the foreign or the economic ministries.

In recent years, each of the permreps has acquired a third senior figure, in the form of the national permanent representative to the Political and Security Committee (COPS – see Chapter 3). They are normally drawn from the national ministries of foreign affairs and most have the rank of ambassador.

The size of its permanent delegation in Brussels is an individual choice for each member government, and is subject to changes over time (see Table 9.1). The overall numbers reflect several factors, of which the following are the most important:

Table 9.1   *Staffing of the permanent representations, 1958–2004*

Member state	1958	1978	1986	1995	2004
Belgium	6	24	26	36	66
France	5	26	29	50	77
Germany	5	41	41	62	112
Italy	5	27	40	42	67
Luxembourg	1	2	6	14	46
The Netherlands	5	20	24	45	88
Denmark	–	26	31	38	47
Ireland	–	22	24	37	98
United Kingdom	–	37	45	50	76
Greece	–	–	48	66	84
Portugal	–	–	36	48	48
Spain	–	–	31	54	77
Austria	–	–	–	65	76
Finland	–	–	–	37	54
Sweden	–	–	–	52	61
Cyprus	–	–	–	–	31
Czech Republic	–	–	–	–	58
Estonia	–	–	–	–	41
Hungary	–	–	–	–	56
Latvia	–	–	–	–	36
Lithuania	–	–	–	–	35
Malta	–	–	–	–	31
Poland	–	–	–	–	56
Slovakia	–	–	–	–	43
Slovenia	–	–	–	–	34
Total	**27**	**225**	**381**	**696**	**1498**

Sources:
1958: Salmon (1971, p. 583–9).
1978 & 1986: Hayes-Renshaw and Wallace (1997, p. 223).
1995: Lewis (2002, p. 283).
2004: IDEA online available at www.europa.eu.int/idea (data collected in August 2004).

- the *size of the member state*. Thus, Malta's delegation was the smallest in 2004 and Germany's the largest (see Table 9.2);
- the *distance* separating the national capital from Brussels. Member states such as Greece, which are situated at a great distance from Brussels, prefer to keep a large number of officials on the spot for meetings;
- the *range of issues* in which the member state has an important interest. For example, Luxembourg has a fairly limited range of issues in which it is keenly interested, and frequently depends on its Benelux partners to represent it at certain meetings;
- the *intensity of negotiations*: when issues of particular importance to a member government are being negotiated intensively, it may be cheaper to station one or more officials in Brussels than for them to

Table 9.2   *Ranking of the member states by size of permanent representation and by population, 2004*

Member state	Ranking by size of permanent representation, 2004		Ranking by size of population, 2004 ('000s)	
Germany	1	112	1	82,532
Ireland	2	98	18	4,028
The Netherlands	3	88	7	16,258
Greece	4	84	8	11,041
France	5	77	2	61,685
Spain		77	5	42,345
United Kingdom	7	76	3	59,652
Austria		76	14	8,114
Italy	9	67	4	57,888
Belgium	10	66	10	10,396
Sweden	11	61	13	8,976
Czech Republic	12	58	11	10,212
Poland	13	56	6	38,191
Hungary		56	12	10,117
Finland	15	54	17	5,220
Portugal	16	48	9	10,475
Denmark	17	47	15	5,398
Luxembourg	18	46	24	452
Slovakia	19	43	16	5,380
Estonia	20	41	22	1,351
Latvia	21	36	20	2,319
Lithuania	22	35	19	3,446
Slovenia	23	34	21	1,996
Cyprus	24	31	23	730
Malta		31	25	400

Sources: IDEA online (www.europa.eu.int/idea) and rounded-up figures from Council Document 12712/04 of 8 October 2004 (see also Table 10.1 in Chapter 10.)

travel regularly, since social and personal contacts can also be important elements in the negotiating process; and

- the *presidency* of the Council: in the run-up to and during the presidency, governments tend to increase the size of the national representation in Brussels by anything up to 25 per cent, in order to help with all the extra work involved in preparing and guiding the Council machine for six months. The relatively elevated numbers in the Irish and Dutch permreps in 2004, as evidenced in Table 9.1, are a direct result of their presidential duties in that year.

Each permrep is staffed by a mixture of diplomats and technicians, the latter being officials from ministries other than that of foreign affairs. They represent their member governments in one or more working parties where the work of the Council is prepared, and support their ambassadors and deputies in Coreper. The proportion of officials based in the permreps and engaged in policy areas other than foreign affairs has increased in recent years (from about 60 per cent in 1995 to almost 65 per cent in 2004), a clear indication of the increasing scope of the EU and the more technical nature of its work. At the same time, the number (although not the overall proportion) of diplomats has increased, as a result of the increased importance of foreign and security policy matters at EU level.

A number of interesting points emerge from an analysis of the composition of the permreps in 2004 (on the basis of information posted on the IDEA website as of August 2004):

- Most government departments and other national authorities whose work is directly affected by the EU have stationed one or more of their officials in Brussels in order to follow policy developments at European level (see Table 9.3).
- The ministries of foreign affairs and of economic and/or financial affairs continue to dominate, in the sense of being represented in all permreps.
- The dense presence of officials from the national ministries of justice and home affairs is proof, if it were needed, of the importance attached to this relatively new EU policy area by the member states.
- National ministries of defence are increasing their presence in Brussels in order to follow developments in the area of the European security and defence policy (ESDP).
- Most member states appoint officials to deal specifically with legal and press issues, an indication of the importance attributed to these aspects of the work of the permreps.
- Over half of the permreps contain officials whose sole task is to follow the work of the EP across all policy areas. In other cases, this task is performed by the policy specialists themselves.
- Several permreps contain representatives of the regions (see below, regarding regional government offices), an indication of the growing

Table 9.3   *Ministries, other bodies and policy sectors represented in the permanent representations, 2004*

Name of ministry, body or policy sector	Number of permanent representations in which represented
Foreign Affairs	25
Economic Affairs; Finance	25
Agriculture; Fisheries	24
Justice; Home Affairs	24
Transport; Communications	24
Health; Social Affairs	21
Defence	20
Employment; Labour	20
Education; Research	20
Energy; Environment	19
Industry; Trade	17
Administration	17
Other	11
Legal Service	11
Press Office	11
Parliament	8
Regions	6
National Bank	6
Cultural Affairs	6
Regional policy; Development	5
Tax; Customs	2

Note: Information for this table was obtained in August 2004 from the IDEA online website (www.europa.eu.int/idea), which lists the members of each permanent representation, and is updated periodically. There is a certain lack of uniformity in the information, as some officials are listed according to the policy-area in which they work, while others are listed by ministry of origin. Nor is the division of labour between ministries the same across the board, with some officials being responsible for areas that cover two of the above listings.

acceptance, even in non-federal member states, of the role they play, and their legitimate interest, in national policy *vis-à-vis* the EU.

- The task of supporting and promoting the interests of national civil servants employed by or wishing to work for the EU institutions has been attributed very openly to some permreps. Thus there is a French official responsible for 'French presence in the European institutions', a Dutch 'coordinator for the appointment of senior EU posts', a Swede responsible for 'EU institutions recruitment' and a Czech official charged with 'secondment of national experts'.
- A small number of permreps include representatives of the national bank.
- Finally, the Austrian permrep is unique in including a number of officials representing major national economic interest groups, a

reflection of the central role of these groups in domestic policy-making in Austria. Other national permreps (such as the British one) announce a contact person for the business community.

The Janus-like members of the permreps serve two masters simultaneously: the Council (as members of Coreper or one of its working parties) and their own governments (as permanent delegates) (Hayes-Renshaw, 1990a; Lewis, 1998b). As representatives, they are expected to articulate their government's point of view at all levels, including informal and even social occasions. As informants, the PRs and their staff are expected to become 'the servant, the eye and the ear' (Houben, 1964, pp. 142, note 87) of the governments they serve, using their pivotal position (both in Brussels and in the EU's decision-making process) to sound out the attitudes and concerns of the Commission and other member states, and to transmit them back to the relevant authorities in their own member state. This information may be official (arising out of meetings of working parties, Coreper and so on), or may result from informal contacts with various interlocutors. Increased recourse to qualified majority voting (QMV) in the Council has made it even more necessary to influence the content of proposals at an early stage of the decision-making process, and has increased the importance of the working party and Coreper levels within the Council hierarchy.

The margin of manoeuvre allowed to members of the permreps differs between member states and among issue areas. Some work within a fairly loose framework, being allowed to negotiate flexibly and to decide on relatively important questions at all levels. Such an approach promotes speed and efficiency, in that fewer decisions have to be referred to more senior groups, which can then concentrate on issues causing fundamental problems. However, much is dependent on the capabilities of the negotiators, who must be confident of carrying their home team with them – after all, a speedy decision is worthless if the domestic constituency tries to backtrack on it at a later date. Hence, some member governments insist on more rigid guidelines and try to refer a large number of decisions upwards to ministerial level. When this practice is widespread, it clogs up the Council machinery, as the lower levels hesitate to take responsibility for decisions, even on technical issues. It is doubtful whether such an approach in fact ensures greater consistency and effectiveness in negotiation, as is often claimed. Much depends on the quality of coordination and communication between the various levels.

National parliaments

Relations between the national parliaments and the Council are indirect, to say the least. The Council collectively is not directly answerable to national parliaments, although the individual ministerial members of the Council are each accountable to their respective national parliamentary bodies. Most prime ministers and ministers report back to their respective national parliaments after meetings of the Council and European Council, and are expected to account for the decisions taken with their European partners in Brussels and Luxembourg. They are also answerable to their national electorates, both at election time and in the rare event of a European topic becoming an issue of confidence in the government.

The forerunner of the directly elected EP was a European Assembly composed of national parliamentarians nominated by their own parliaments. This system of dual mandates allowed a flow of information in both directions, as well as direct links between the two levels. However, the dual mandate was overtaken by the introduction of direct elections to the EP in 1979, since which time national parliaments have had a more indirect monitoring and scrutiny role. Until the coming into force of the Treaty on European Union (TEU) in 1993, most national parliaments were curiously reticent to demand the right to have a more direct impact on what happened at European level, probably because of a lack of the resources required to follow the work of the EU institutions in detail. In the post-Maastricht EU, however, national parliaments have demanded, if not always a greater say in, at least a greater amount of information about what is happening at the European level. Specifically, they want to be informed at an earlier stage and in a more complete way about the legislative proposals under discussion in the Council. Some national parliaments even managed to secure a commitment from their governments to introduce greater scrutiny as a quid pro quo for their agreement to ratify the TEU.

Each of the EU's twenty-five national parliaments now has some form or other of monitoring mechanism, which operate with varying degrees of effectiveness. They usually take the form of one or more specialized European committees, whose job it is to monitor proposed legislation coming out of Brussels and to examine the positions being adopted and defended by their ministers in the Council. Ministers are encouraged – in some cases required – to appear before these committees, where they exist, in order to keep the committee members informed directly about Council affairs, but the extent to which they do so differs from state to state.

The Danish system (imitated, in part at least, by the Swedes and the Finns) has always been the most rigorous, with the European Affairs Committee of the Danish parliament (the *Folketing*) meeting once a week to advise Danish ministers on the negotiating position to adopt in forthcoming Council meetings. At the end of 2004, the Danes altered their system of monitoring the EU legislative system, in order to allow the *Folketing*'s specialist standing committees to participate more actively in the scrutiny of EU affairs (*European Voice*, 17–23 March

2005), a procedure already favoured by the Finns. In some member states, such as the UK and Ireland, committees were created early on to monitor EU affairs *ex post facto* – that is, after the decision had been taken by the Council, with obvious, rather negative, implications for the purposes of scrutiny.

Other member states have come rather late to the game. The French and the Germans, for example, set up such committees only in the aftermath of Maastricht, and the Dutch government, under some pressure, undertook not to take any decisions under the third pillar (JHA) without prior referral to its national parliament. A number of national parliaments have introduced measures designed to ensure that they are informed of legislative proposals as soon as they are forwarded to the Council. Most recently, the Latvians have taken the unusual step of including two members of the Latvian Parliament in their permrep in Brussels, although it remains to be seen whether this will be a long-term arrangement. (It should be noted here that many national parliaments maintain offices in Brussels for the purposes of information-gathering and lobbying – 16 separate ones were mentioned on the EP's website in March 2005 – although they tend to be more focused on the EP than on the Council.)

Effective monitoring of European negotiations is much impeded by the degree of secrecy that surrounds the Council. While ministers may be happy to outline their objectives in advance of Council and European Council meetings, they are more reticent about explaining afterwards the compromises they have made (or been forced to make). Measures to improve transparency have been introduced, but it is hard to determine any substantive benefit yet for national parliamentary scrutiny. Another obvious problem is that much of the decision-making takes place in the Council's preparatory bodies. The difficulty for national parliaments and monitoring bodies is that the officials involved at these levels are accountable to the parliament only through their ministers, although some specialized parliamentary committees can take evidence from officials. However, this presupposes a degree of willingness on the part of national parliamentarians to get to grips with often rather technical issues that are not always apparent on the ground.

The pressure to report back to national parliaments before committing oneself to agreement at European level demonstrates the inherent tension between democracy and efficiency that pervades the Council system. Decision-making is slowed down if a delegation has to clear new instructions with its parliament whenever negotiations take an unexpected turn. This is more relevant where the decision in question needs to be taken quickly (for example, when a time limit applies), or where the vote of that country really counts (for example, if unanimity is required, or if there is a close vote in prospect, and a qualified majority or a blocking minority hangs in the balance). Thus greater accountability can have the effect of reducing margins of manoeuvre in EU bargaining, a feature common in federal systems.

Other national interlocutors

Over the years, a growing number of non-governmental national actors have been drawn into the European process. This development has led to disquiet among the member governments, who have worked hard to maintain their position as principal 'gatekeepers' for relations between the Council and the member states. They have to a great extent succeeded in this endeavour, not least because the Council is composed of representatives of the national governments. However, the member governments have been unable to prevent other national actors affecting, and being affected by, the work of the Council. The most important of these actors are national interest groups and sub-national governmental authorities.

National interest groups

These groups labour under many of the same difficulties as national parliaments, and most therefore choose to band together at European level in an attempt to influence the Council as a whole, while continuing to lobby at national level. Corporate lobbying has also become big business in Brussels, and most of the larger European, and indeed global, companies now maintain offices there of varying sizes. Smaller companies tend to operate through sectoral groups, while companies of all sizes belong to the European Union of Employers' Confederations (UNICE) via their national federation or confederation of industry. The perceived importance of the EU level of governance for interest groups may be gleaned from the fact that, at the beginning of the new millennium, about 2,600 of them maintained permanent offices in Brussels (van Schendelen 2003, p. 46), while many other smaller or less affluent groups chose to be represented through national federations or international confederations. Generally, small and medium-sized enterprises (SMEs) find Brussels-level lobbying difficult to achieve.

The degree of influence exerted by these groups is difficult to assess, but presumably they would not maintain a presence in Brussels if they did not feel it was worthwhile. Lobbying can be an extremely expensive business, and the cost of maintaining an office and even a small staff in Brussels is not negligible. Some lobby groups are there for information-gathering purposes alone, while others concentrate on networking, and attempting to ensure that their point of view is taken into account when decisions are being taken in the Council hierarchy. However, their main target is normally the Commission, rather than the Council.

The question for this study, then, is to what extent the lobbies can influence the Council. As the final decision-maker in most areas, it is the obvious but also the most difficult target, except for the most powerful interests. The Council meets behind closed doors, and does not allow for easy access, although the presidency is a useful point of entry for the simultaneous lobbying of all member states. Frequently, the most useful route for national interest groups is through individual governments, preferably through the medium of the official in the national permrep who is responsible for the dossier in question. These officials tend to be rather detached about lobbyists, viewing them as potential sources of useful and technical arguments, but taking their views on board only if they are in line with instructions already received from the capital. A nationally-based company will try to lobby its own government to accommodate its views, while an international corporation will lobby the various governments in whose territories it operates. Often, the national route to lobbying is the most effective, although the declining number of areas in which a national veto can be exercised means that lobbyists can no longer rely on 'their' government to veto a proposed decision. However, the high threshold set for a qualified majority means that coordinated lobbying at national level in order to achieve a blocking minority can be very effective.

Sub-national governmental authorities

The emergence of sub-national authorities as distinct interests and potentially direct interlocutors with the Council is more recent. It used to be presumed that the interests of sub-national levels of government, such as regional and local authorities, would be incorporated into the overall national position, or articulated through the EP, the Economic and Social Committee (ESC) or, more recently, the Committee of the Regions (CoR). Each of these bodies has, from time to time, championed regional causes in their relations with the Council, but never as their primary focus.

In federal systems such as those that exist in Austria, Belgium, Germany and Spain, regional points of view are systematically taken into account in national policy formation, and ministers from the regions may even act as national representatives in certain Councils. In the other member states, however, which operate under more centralized systems of government, regional interests have found it harder to have a voice.

Increasingly over the past decade, some regional authorities have come to the conclusion that their interests are sufficiently distinct to justify a separate presence in Brussels, in order to obtain information directly applicable to their region (in particular, relating to funding) and to bring the interests of their region directly to the attention of decision-makers in the Council, the Commission and the EP. In addition, these offices often act as information and tourist offices for the region in question. The more prosperous regions set about establishing regional economic promotion offices in the mid-1980s, with the German *Länder* being the quickest off the mark. These regional offices are sometimes attached to the national permrep, but more frequently are totally separate.

Other local and regional authorities have appointed Community liaison officers, very much focused on discovering what EU finance is available for such areas, and on helping local groups and businesses with their grant applications. Yet others have created *ad hoc* delegations to work on particular projects, bringing the needs and interests of the area to the attention of those responsible for deciding on the allocation of Community resources to regional areas. These direct links generally bypass national governments and, to an extent, weaken their influence at European level.

Idiosyncrasies of particular countries

Each member state has chosen a system of coordinating its national position and communicating it to the Council that, while conforming to a basic pattern, exhibits additional facets that reflect to some degree the state's cultural, administrative and political systems. In the case of some member states, these national idiosyncrasies are so pronounced that they have a very visible impact on the formulation of the national position and the stance adopted by the national representatives at EU level. It must be said, however, that the consequences of these national idiosyncrasies are not always positive, in terms of efficiency or the perception of colleagues.

Member states with federal systems of government have additional, formalized layers of coordination to deal with, particularly in those areas where the regional governments have acquired policy-making powers or are responsible for implementing EU legislation or programmes. The result is often elaborate systems, designed to ensure the high levels of internal coordination required to ensure consistency in the national position. In Germany, for example, vertical coordination between the *Bund* and the *Länder* must be ensured, and the latter must be fully included in the preparation of the national position in areas such as education (see Mittag and Wessels, 2003; Anderson, 2005). In Belgium, depending on the issue being discussed, regional representatives are involved to varying degrees in pre-negotiations on the national position, and Belgium is represented in the Council by federal or regional representatives or a combination of the two (Franck *et al.*, 2003). The result in both cases is fragmented policy-making and a certain diffuseness in national negotiating positions. For their partners in the Council, the consequence is reduced predictability and a perception that negotiations in advance with these member states are of little use.

The role of the French and Finnish presidents in their countries' foreign policy, and consequently in the formulation of their country's national position *vis-à-vis* the EU, sets them apart from the other member states. Indeed, it is their participation as of right in European Councils that has given rise to the rather unwieldy term 'heads of state or government' when describing the composition of this body. However, their previously pre-eminent role is under attack from several quarters today, not least the prime ministers and their private offices or *cabinets*, and particularly the national ministers of economic affairs and/or finance. Indeed, a new Finnish constitution, which came into force in 2000, documents the shared responsibility of the president and the prime minister with regard to Finland's EU policy, reinforcing the role of the head of government (see Tiilikainen, 2003).

Denmark's distinctiveness because of the control exerted over its national representatives in the Council by the European Affairs Committee in the Danish Parliament is now being contested. Both Sweden and Finland followed (but did not completely mirror) the Danish example when setting up their own systems of scrutiny (see Egeberg, 2005), and changes have been introduced to the Danish system itself, giving greater powers to the specialist standing committees. The European Affairs Committee remains powerful, however, composed as it is of seventeen members in proportion to the representation of each political party in the *Folketing*. Since this normally includes parties that are completely opposed to, or ambivalent about, Danish membership of the EU, the Committee's support is not necessarily easy to obtain. Before each meeting of a ministerial Council, the (frequently minority) Danish government has, in the past, been obliged to submit its proposed positions to this group, the aim being to gain the support of the Committee for the government's approach, in the form of a binding mandate to negotiate. In future, the specialized standing committees will play a greater role in determining the government's negotiating mandate.

The advantage of the Danish system, in principle, is that the national negotiators have a clear sense of what the wider national political opinion will tolerate on EU issues. The downside is that their margin of manoeuvre may be somewhat limited. In the event of speedy reactions being required to new compromise proposals introduced in the course of the negotiations, the Danish representative may have to place a 'parliamentary reserve' on his or her position, awaiting a favourable opinion from the national parliamentary committee. On the plus side, this rather rigid system enables Danish negotiators, by and large, to agree to measures at EU level in the knowledge that they are less likely to be contested or to be subject to backtracking when it comes to implementation at home. In the case of more contentious issues, however, Danish negotiators must always operate with one eye on the domestic situation, where hostility to the integration process is rife. Denmark's system of strong parliamentary control over its representatives at EU level can be very irritating for the other member governments, not only because of the impact it has on the Danish negotiating style, and consequently on the Council's decision-making process as a whole, but also because current concerns about the 'democratic deficit' mean that they find themselves increasingly under pressure to emulate it. However, it is questionable whether the Council system could cope with more than a few national monitoring systems of such severity.

No matter how they are organized, the outcome of each of the national systems of coordination is a set of instructions for national representatives in the Council hierarchy. Those member states with strong, centralized systems of coordination, such as France and the UK, tend to provide their representatives in Brussels with a detailed, usually written, negotiating brief containing instructions regarding how to react to the various issues on the agenda. The rigidity of these instructions depends on the issue in question, and whether there is a sensitive interest to be defended. Indeed, sometimes such instructions are seen merely as a means for the capital to prove that it has 'done its job' (Lewis, 2006). The French and British approaches to negotiation are among the most highly respected in Brussels. Both countries enjoy a reputation for rigorous preparation and defence of their national positions, combined with a marked capacity to irritate their colleagues with their dogmatism.

Other member governments exhibit greater flexibility, especially those from the smaller member states. The Dutch system of coordination is generally viewed as being the most supple and among the most effective, often allowing a speedy reaction to developments that occur in the course of meetings in Brussels. Luxembourg is probably the best example (at least before the 2004 enlargement) of a system of coordination being pragmatic rather than highly formalized (see Bossaert, 2003). Close contact between the small numbers involved ensures a rapid and flexible approach to the definition of the national position, obviating the need for an institutionalized system of inter-ministerial coordination. Luxembourg's representatives in the Council hierarchy are frequently perceived as having the greatest degree of autonomy of all participants.

Sufficient time has yet to elapse in order to speculate on the long-term efficiency and effectiveness (or otherwise) of the national coordination systems set up by the new member states to formulate and communicate their respective national positions at the European level (see Goetz, 2005). Of course, these governments have had experience of coordinating policy for the accession negotiations but, as previous new members have discovered, managing EU business on a daily basis across all issues is a very different task, and adaptation can take some time.

It is thus clear that the chosen system of coordination differs from one member state to another, and operates with varying degrees of efficiency. Some are viewed as being more effective than others, in the sense of resulting in a clear and consistent approach to EU negotiations, and lending a certain amount of predictability to the position of the member state in question. In a negotiating process where national positions are constantly being demanded and articulated across a broad range of policy areas, consistency and predictability are obviously a great help in determining the attitude of one's colleagues, both to new proposals and to suggested national negotiating stances. Such attributes are more likely to result from systems with a strong degree of coordination than those, such as Germany, that are perceived as lacking a truly collegial and coordinated position in the national capital. However, the participants in EU negotiations, be they member state representatives or officials from the EU institutions, are tolerant of the various systems, accepting their strengths and weaknesses as part of the rich tapestry that results from the voluntary cooperation of such diverse members.

The Council and domestic policy-making and actors

In the early 1970s, it was possible to argue that EC policies were so limited in number and scope as to leave domestic politics, and much of national policy-making, largely unaffected. European issues were dealt with exclusively by elites within the executive of each member state, with the result that these questions were mainly treated as a specific and separate bundle of issues rather than as a new dimension of existing national policies (Wallace, 1971, p. 538). The difference today is that many more national actors are now involved. The EU's policy agenda has drawn in an increasing number of ministers and officials across the entire range of domestic ministries; in parallel, each of their policy communities has been 'Europeanized' to a greater or lesser extent. As Table 9.3 on page 238 demonstrates, almost the entire range of domestic ministries sends officials to the national permrep in Brussels, and a wide array of people from the member states are engaged in the various consultative forums. The interesting questions that follow concern the effect of these developments on national politics and national policy-making.

The first and most obvious impact of the Council is the time that national actors must now devote to EU issues. The formulation of a national position on any particular issue often requires extensive consultations with domestic interests as well as intra-ministerial coordination. Occasionally, national actors find groups and organizations from other member states wishing to address them as useful purveyors of additional information. Ministers and officials based in the capital must travel to and from Brussels for Council and working party meetings. Between meetings, it may be necessary to contact colleagues from other member states in order to canvass opinions on, or to gain support for, a national initiative. Such demands on the time of national officials are even greater in the period when their member state holds the presidency of the Council.

Second, the enlarged number of national actors involved across the range of EU policies makes for a different kind of coordination at the national level. Coherence and consistency of the national position are harder to achieve. Also, increasingly, direct contacts are being forged between line ministries and their opposite numbers in other member states and inside the EU institutions, about which foreign ministries are only partially informed.

A third effect on national actors results from the fact that Council negotiations involve multilateral cooperation. Ministers and officials from the national ministries of foreign affairs, used to dealing regularly with their counterparts in other countries, may have long shared a culture of bilateral and multilateral consultation and coordination. The adjustment is greater and more difficult for others for whom this enforced contact may be very new and, depending on their outlook and the issue area in question, perhaps even unwelcome. Questions of national sovereignty or the predominance of national policy may be foremost in the minds of some officials or ministers from the national ministries of justice, education or social affairs, especially under pressure to replace what may have been very informal cooperation with the trappings of EU rules, institutionalized contacts and expectations of results. Indeed, many of the early criticisms of the working of the third pillar of the TEU (covering JHA issues) were precisely on this point. This increased multilateralism is a symptom of a kind of merging of domestic and foreign policies. Areas of policy that were previously viewed as being purely domestic have now gained a European dimension, with the result that few national officials can see themselves as dealing exclusively with domestic or foreign policies.

Fourth, direct and recurrent participation in the Council has an impact of socialization on national ministers and officials. Attitudes and behaviour do change and, to a significant extent, produce a cohort of participants who are neither wholly intergovernmental nor wholly supranational in their outlook and approach. The permreps in Brussels play a particular role here as training-grounds for national officials, not just in the Council's working methods and for forging links with their opposite numbers from other member states, but also for devising professional responses to this *demi-monde* between the national and the Community processes.

Newcomers are encouraged to acclimatize as quickly as possible to the ethos that permeates the Council system. They have to learn, through specialized training programmes and experience on the ground, that European decision-making is characterized by complex procedures, specialist jargon and long-established voting practices. Formal and informal rules of the game must be followed, the latter often being even more important than the former. They have to acquire broader perspectives and become more aware of the needs, interests and motives of those representing other member states. Only then can they gain a more realistic view of what is and what is not 'acceptable' at European level, what lines of argument in defence of a national position will be likely to attract support from other European-level actors, and where possible alliances can be forged. These are onerous demands to make on newcomers, who tend to be disadvantaged players of the game at first, although some master the learning curve more quickly than others.

Among the national officials involved most regularly and most deeply in the Council system, a marked *esprit de corps* has been noted, characterized by common concerns and shared commitments. It used to be the case that this spirit was most widespread among officials residing in Brussels, but increasingly officials based in the capitals are forging transnational links with like-minded officials in other member states. Such links, and the genuine friendships that sometimes grow out of them, can be instrumental in solving problems that might otherwise hold up the entire decision-making process.

Finally, the idiosyncratic nature of the Council itself has affected national policy-making in a number of ways. The impact of the following four aspects has been the most easily discernible.

- National policy processes are most affected during the presidency of the Council, when national actors find themselves at the centre of the Council system. This can be an uncomfortable experience for some, since it may require a focus on unfamiliar issues, or may demand the defence of an EU position at variance with the national one. On the other hand, smaller member states acquire unaccustomed status and opportunities for promoting their own favoured causes.
- The Council's timetable of decision-making does not always allow much time for domestic consultation. A 'good' government may thus be frustrated in its efforts to consult widely in the process of formulating its national position, making it harder to develop fall-back positions, or to minimize problems regarding subsequent implementation.
- The secrecy of the Council makes it difficult for domestic policy-makers not directly involved to know and to monitor what is going on. Members of national parliaments and domestic interest groups are dependent on reports from their ministers and the informed media. Some national actors have information advantages over others, but the members of the Council thereby retain a certain flexibility. Issues of accountability, access to information and negotiating manoeuvrability collide with one other and are not easily reconciled.
- Changes in the Council's voting procedures away from unanimity towards a greater opportunity for the use of QMV have altered the way in which member governments formulate national negotiating positions. No longer able to rely on the expedient of the veto,

national policy-makers must take into account the possibility of 'their' representative being outvoted in the Council, but none the less bound by the decision of the majority. This changes the pressures within national politics with regard to the remedies to be sought to protect a distinct national preference or a specific domestic group.

Domestic politics and the work of the Council

Just as the Council affects national policy-making and actors, so domestic politics have an impact on the Council and its work. This impact is governed by three important factors: the general policy stances of the participants; the pace and rhythm of domestic politics; and the degree of sensitivity of the issues.

Policy stances

The overall policy stances of member governments, of sizeable constituencies within the member states, or of individuals representing that member state at EU level, all have a direct and significant effect on the Council. These stances may relate to general issues (such as core goals of integration) or to very specific questions of substance (for example, support for (or opposition to) particular EU-level policies).

The attitude of the member government towards membership of the EU as such can have a significant impact on the efficiency of the Council. Where a member government holds a clear-cut and widely shared position on membership, its representatives at all levels of the Council hierarchy can operate with greater confidence, sure of widespread domestic support for their position. This enables them to take initiatives where necessary, and to respond quickly, clearly and consistently to new proposals, compromises or ideas. The resulting predictability of the national position simplifies the discussion in the Council, in that the support or opposition of that government can be factored into any calculations that need to be made in order to ensure that a decision is reached.

Clearly, opposition to proposed EU measures sustained by important politicians, prominent interest groups or sizeable parts of the population or media in any member state poses problems for the Council as a whole. In practice, representatives of a member state in which the very issue of membership of the Union is the subject of heated debate may find their position weakened among their European colleagues. They are obliged to pay even more attention than usual to the minute details of every decision being taken, and constantly to second-guess the domestic reaction to what is being discussed. As a result, issues may have to be decided at a higher level in the Council hierarchy than would otherwise be the case, because of the unwillingness on the part of officials at the level of working parties to endorse issues within their area of technical expertise. Problems of non-ratification or non-compliance can result where the government or national parliament is found to be out of synch with the domestic constituency, as was the case with the first Irish referendum on the Treaty of Nice (ToN) in June 2001. National representatives who are perceived as not commandning the majority opinion within their own member state obviously suffer in terms of credibility among their EU colleagues.

The opposition of one or a small number of member states to a particular policy or a specific decision affects the work of the Council in a number of ways. The Council may be prevented from reaching any agreement at all, as was the case for many years on the issue of the seat of the EU's institutions, because of French opposition to the idea of moving the European Parliament to Brussels. Some policy issues remain intractable because of political conflicts between member states, or between one of them and a third country, an obvious example being the political dispute between Cyprus and Turkey. Much time and effort may be required to negotiate new formulas, as in the case of the British budget rebate (finally settled at the Fontainebleau European Council in June 1984, but appearing to re-emerge at the Brussels summit in June 2005), or the situation may call for institutional or organizational innovations (as witness the arrangements agreed at the Maastricht European Council of December 1991 regarding the British opt-out on the social chapter).

The ever-present tension that exists between those who favour a more intergovernmental EU and those who would prefer to emphasize its supranational qualities also affects the work of the Council. These preferences, despite normally being unspoken and even in many cases largely subconscious, none the less have an impact on the Council's work. They give rise to differences of opinion over proposed legal bases for draft legislative acts, which determine not only which decision-making procedure will apply (and, consequently, the extent to which the EP will be involved in the final decision), but also the method of voting inside the Council and the responsibilities of the Commission (for example, with regard to implementing committees, the so-called 'comitology' issue – see Chapter 7).

What determines the attitudes and consequent behaviour of national representatives when they operate in the Council? The first factor stems from differences among the political systems from which the national representatives derive, which may prepare them to a greater or lesser extent for working within the Council. Compared with their colleagues who are used to one-party government, the representatives of governments with experience and knowledge of working with explicit coalitions have a starting advantage in preparing to deal with the high degree of compromise required in the Council. On the other hand, those who come from centralized systems (for example, France and the UK), where the coordination of the national position is more authoritative and less time-consuming than it is, say, in federal systems, may reap the benefits in terms of rapid reactions and a greater degree of self-confidence. National representatives whose hands are tied by their domestic parliaments, as in the case of Denmark, may lack a margin of manoeuvre in negotiations in the Council, but know quite decisively the limits of their national positions.

A second factor is the strength or weakness of the government that the national ministers or officials represent in the Council. Representatives of a newly elected government with a brand new mandate have the chance to establish medium-term objectives and a definite line to follow, thereby imbuing them with confidence in their dealings with their EU colleagues. A long period in office, on the other hand, can be a mixed blessing for a government and its representatives in the Council. Where confidence in the government and its European policy is still high, its representatives will continue to function efficiently. Conversely, the policy fatigue all too often associated with a long tenure can result in a government appearing to lose its way, and issuing less clear and consistent instructions to its representatives, with a consequent loss of effectiveness on their part.

Finally, the profile of the member state can affect the degree of confidence with which its representatives operate within the Council hierarchy. Clearly, representatives of new member states take time to learn the ropes, while the more experienced are normally much more at ease with Council procedures. The relative size of a member state is less important than one might expect in determining the influence and resulting confidence of national representatives in the Council. It would be naïve to suggest that some member states do not carry more weight than others in the Council, but it is not always the same ones that carry the most weight. Much depends on the issues being discussed, the voting procedure being used and whether the measures involved have major financial implications. Hence the Luxembourg representative may have a key role to play in negotiations on financial services, the vote of the Irish representative may be vital in achieving a qualified majority, and the support of Germany may be critical in gaining agreement for a new initiative requiring additional funds.

Pace and rhythm

The pace and rhythm of domestic politics affects the work of the Council in a number of ways. The first and most obvious way is the presidency, during which the political spotlight falls directly on the member state in question, and domestic issues gain added weight. The presidency was not designed to be the vehicle for promoting issues of domestic importance, but every presidency member state tries, with the complicity of its colleagues from the other member states, to emphasise one or two issues of specific national interest, whether by launching a new initiative, trying to move an issue along, or bringing it to a conclusion (see Chapter 5).

Second, domestic politics has a direct impact on the Council through national elections, referendums and party political crises, which can have an unsettling effect on the work of the Council, particularly on the politically more high-profile issues. Elections, whether scheduled or precipitated, give rise to uncertainty. Campaigning and cross-party discussions may have significant implications for the country's overall policy towards the EU, and many issues may have to be put on hold until such time as the incoming government's policy *vis-à-vis* the EU and particular policies is clarified. A recent additional phenomenon of national elections has been the rise in regional parties and their consequent demands for greater representation at European level. Where such demands are accommodated, the member states in question have to put in place and adapt to new forms of consultation and representation.

Where a national election occurs in the presidency member state, there may be problems not only for the member state itself, but also for the Council as a whole. If the election results in a change of personnel, the introduction of a new president in mid-term may affect the smooth running of the Council. The Danes managed to survive a domestic election during their 1993 presidency, but others appear to be less sanguine about their ability to do so – witness the German decision to change places with the Finns in the presidency rota in order to avoid a domestic election due to take place during their scheduled time in the Council chair (the second half of 2006 – ironically, the election took place early, in September 2005).

More dramatically, referendums can have a direct impact on the work of the Council. Discussions in the Council and the European Council may be hugely affected, many issues put on hold, and strenuous efforts made to encourage the 'right' result. In the period preceding the French referendum on the Constitutional Treaty (CT) in May 2005, discussions regarding the Commission's proposed services directive and changes to the state aid regime were regarded as virtually 'off-limits' for fear of provoking unpopular headlines in France during the campaign (*European Voice*, 14–20 April 2005). Close or negative results in several recent referendums (including those in France and the Netherlands on the CT in early 2005 have demonstrated to all the members of the Council, if indeed they needed to be reminded of the fact, that public support for their work cannot be taken for granted. The Council, in spite of its secretive working practices, operates 'in a goldfish bowl'.

Domestic crises, such as natural disasters, political scandals or economic difficulties, can also affect individual members of the Council and have an impact on the latter's work. The member state in question may find that its voice is muted and that it exercises less influence than usual at European level, as the energies of its ministerial representatives are devoted to dealing with the domestic crisis. But it is revealing how far other governmental representatives are prepared to go in order not to punish their colleagues for their individual local difficulties. At the back of every minister's and official's mind is the thought that they might be the next one requiring the special treatment.

Sensitivity of the issues

A third factor governing the impact of domestic politics on the Council and its work relates to the degree of sensitivity of the issues involved. Every member state has on its policy agenda one or more issues deemed to be politically sensitive or controversial in the domestic arena. Such issues vary from one member state to another, and may even change within a particular member state over time as domestic circumstances alter, or the government changes, bringing with it a radical change in policy. At the level of the Council, therefore, an issue that constitutes a mere technical problem for some member states may be perceived as being highly politically charged for others, and may consequently be approached and treated by them in an entirely different way.

Obviously, the greater the number of member states arguing that an issue is politically sensitive in the domestic arena, the greater the possibility of seeing this reflected in the final decision taken by the Council. In any case, the majority must be convinced at an early stage of the need to treat the issue as a special case. This then involves the opposing minority in a process of intensive lobbying at all stages and levels of the legislative process, in an effort to gain support from other member states, the Commission, the EP and, where necessary, the ESC and the CoR.

Issues generally viewed as being politically sensitive tend to be subject to much more rigorous examination and public debate at EU level than the more straightforward technical ones. The consultation process at national level may be more thorough and more extensive, with the result that national positions can be rather rigid. This can have the effect of delaying a resolution of the issue, and usually means that the Council spends more time discussing it than would normally be the case. The additional time and effort demanded from all levels of the Council hierarchy, as well as of its legislative partners, makes for inefficient decision-making, frequently giving rise to a certain resentment on the part of the majority.

Clearly, much depends on the perceived importance of controversial issues for the Union as a whole, the price sought by the opposing minority and the willingness of the majority to search for and agree on a solution. The rigidity of a government's position will also have a bearing on the final outcome. As long as it is not too deeply entrenched in terms of details, and enough room for manoeuvre is left to the national representatives in the Council hierarchy, a compromise solution can usually be found. In all cases, much work can be done away from the glare of publicity at the level of the working parties and of Coreper, where compromise proposals can be aired and examined, and details thrashed out. This allows the final solution to be 'worked out' by the ministers meeting in Council or, in the case of highly controversial issues, by the European Council.

To sum up, relations between the Council and the member states are complex and multi-layered. National parliaments, political parties, interest groups and citizens are included, to a greater or lesser degree, in the formulation of the national position to be articulated in the Council, yet are largely excluded from direct contact with this body, which is conducted by and through the member governments. The member states consist of much more than the member governments, but it is the latter who speak for them in the Council, with each member state choosing its own (often distinctive) way of ensuring that all the relevant voices are heard at some stage in the process of defining 'the national position'.

Part III

How?

Chapter 10

Less Often than Expected: Voting in the Council

This chapter examines the evolution of voting rules in the Council and the ways in which these have operated in practice, both formally and as defined by informal understandings and conventions. As we saw in Chapter 2, the Council has three main formal voting rules: unanimity; qualified majority voting (QMV); and simple majority. Over the years these have been the subject of discussion and at times fierce argument, particularly with regard to which rule should be applied to which kinds of decision, and more specifically how to define QMV.

These arguments notwithstanding, explicit voting takes place on a minority of the issues that go to ministers in Council for resolution. According to our calculations, only about 14 per cent of decisions taken are explicitly contested at ministerial level, and of these approximately half are on agriculture or fisheries. This is partly because so many issues are in practice resolved at a prior stage in the Council, and partly because there has been a recurrent preference for operating on the basis of consensus. Implicitly, of course, voting rules influence decision outcomes, either by shaping the contours of those proposals that are agreed, or by preventing proposals from going forward for further discussion.

In commenting on the patterns we can observe, we draw on such systematic data as have become available since contested voting behaviour was made public in the 1990s, as well as on supplementary calculations of our own. (The details are set out in Appendix 8.) We also use case-study and interview evidence for previous periods, and to identify cases of implicit voting.

Voting rules

Broadly, unanimity rules are retained for four areas:

- 'constitutional' issues (such as treaty reform);
- choices of principle about new policy competences;
- areas accepted by the member states as particularly sensitive (such as the common foreign and security policy (CFSP) and the related

European security and defence policy (ESDP), police and judicial cooperation in criminal matters, and revenue-raising for the European Union (EU) budget, or taxation); and
- systemic agreements with third countries.

In many of these areas a unanimous decision by the Council also requires endorsement from either the EP or national parliaments, and sometimes both. In addition, by and large those issues that go to the European Council for resolution tend to be resolved either by explicit unanimity or by brokering a consensus. Thus, for example, the multi-annual packages to agree the 'financial perspectives', which always include a decision on how much EU revenue needs to be raised, result from unanimity-based decisions. An overview was set out in Box 1.5 in Chapter 1.

This array of decision rules is unusual in traditional international organizations, which rely mainly on unanimity, with one vote per member state. In contrast, the various EC and EU treaties import into their decision rules a majoritarian rule more familiar from national democratic politics, conveying an ambition to be a polity-in-the-making. The early acceptance of the principle of majority voting had two other historical explanations that retain some pertinence. First, it reassured the participating countries that a difficult country, especially a large one, could be outvoted and bound by a majority vote. In the early days of the EC, the possibility of thus holding Germany in check was not a trivial concern. Second, the retention of the unanimity rule for some purposes conveyed a reassuring sense of parity among the member states in certain respects – nominally, for some purposes, Luxembourg could walk as tall as France or Germany. Thus the range of decision rules was designed to build political confidence in what was at the outset a small and relatively intimate grouping of only six countries.

Weighted or qualified majority voting is often the prescribed rule in the treaties, and its scope has expanded steadily with each treaty reform. Under QMV, each member state is attributed a set number of votes, designed to reflect both the equality of states as members of the Union and, in a very general sense, their difference in terms of population. As we shall see, the Treaty of Nice (ToN) and the Constitutional Treaty (CT) made some important changes to the rules. Generally, QMV applies to operating decisions and those that follow up an agreement of principle, and has become the decision-making rule for implementing many of the most important EU policies. Simple majority voting has been the default rule, a fact that explains the occasional oddity of simple majority voting in the European Council.

The CT would instead make QMV the default rule. This would leave simple majority voting to apply only in the case of specific pieces of legislation in which this has been established, notably the regulation on anti-dumping and some procedural matters. This evolution is set out in Box 2.4 in Chapter 2. In recent years, around 70 per cent of the decisions reached in the Council have been on a legal base subject to QMV, about 30 per cent subject to unanimity, and a very few subject to simple majority (see Figure 10.1).

The voting rules are often linked to procedures for interaction with the EP on budgetary and most legislative issues (see Chapter 8), and are echoed in the 'comitology' procedures operated by the Commission to manage specific areas of EC policy (see Chapter 7). Thus those regulatory and management committees that have a formal role in confirming decisions proposed by the Commission have historically largely used the same arrangements as those of the Council for weighted votes and for establishing majority thresholds. Some of these committees need a positive qualified majority to uphold a Commission proposal, while in others Commission proposals stand unless overturned by a qualified majority of member states. Details are set out in individual legislative decisions.

Table 10.1 shows the weighting of votes for different member states under the different treaties, and the formal threshold for majority votes to be reached or – the tone sounds different – for blocking minorities to obstruct agreement. The threshold for constituting a qualified majority consists both of numbers of votes cast and, for some purposes, the number of members casting their vote and, since the ToN, an explicit population criterion. The intention has been to build in a safety net to prevent particular countries, groups (or kinds) of countries exercising undue power, however that is defined. Broadly, three kinds of consideration have historically been in play:

- a concern that the larger members, especially the Franco-German couple, might play too large a role;
- the issue of the massed weight of a large number of smaller member states; and
- the fear of repeated collisions between coalitions of richer and poorer members, or northern and southern, or founders and late-joiners, or maximalists and minimalists, or inner and outer circles.

What does the weighting reflect and how were the weights determined? The original agreement was devised for only six countries, with at each extreme Germany and Luxembourg. Germany – at the time only West Germany – was a country that had recently exercised overweening political and military power; at the very least it had to be put on a par with France and Italy, which conveniently had similar population sizes. Luxembourg symbolized the opportunity for even a very small country to have international legitimacy as an independent state. Thus the wider

262

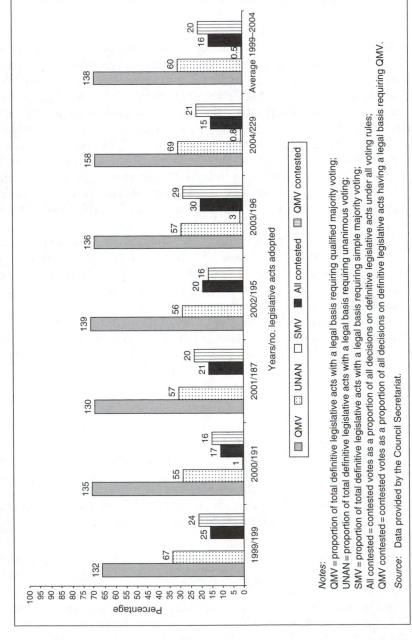

Figure 10.1   Contested and uncontested votes under different voting rules, 1999–2004

Notes:
QMV = proportion of total definitive legislative acts with a legal basis requiring qualified majority voting;
UNAN = proportion of total definitive legislative acts with a legal basis requiring unanimous voting;
SMV = proportion of total definitive legislative acts with a legal basis requiring simple majority voting;
All contested = contested votes as a proportion of all decisions on definitive legislative acts under all voting rules;
QMV contested = contested votes as a proportion of all decisions on definitive legislative acts having a legal basis requiring QMV.

Source: Data provided by the Council Secretariat.

settlement after the Second World War permeated the arrangement. The allocation of votes to countries did not follow an exact arithmetic formula, but was based on ranges between larger, medium-sized and smaller countries.

Table 10.1 also relates weighted votes in the Council to population sizes at different periods, both before and after German unification, and taking into account the recent enlargement. One footnote on history – under the 1951 Treaty of Paris that created the European Coal and Steel Community (ECSC), voting weights were related to shares of production of coal and steel, while under the 1957 Treaties of Rome creating the European Economic Community (EEC) and the European Atomic Energy Community (Euratom), expenditure from certain funds was determined by a voting rule weighted according to member states' budget contributions, a formula similar to that used by the International Monetary Fund (IMF). These correlations were rarely debated for many years, except at each point of enlargement, when new members had to be ascribed weights and the threshold for majorities adapted. These were extrapolated from the original deal among the Six, which had required roughly two-thirds of weighted votes for a majority. This rose gradually with each enlargement, but for over forty years the pattern of weighting was generally accepted.

Inhibitions on voting and the Luxembourg compromise

The Treaty of Rome (EEC) had stated that QMV would be introduced progressively into decision-making in the Council. In the early 1960s there were already some signs of discontent about this, notably in the French-led (but unsuccessful) Fouchet Plans for political cooperation 'intergovernmentally' outside the treaty structures. In 1965 a row erupted between the French government and the Commission over the funding of the common agricultural policy (CAP) and associated issues. This led the French to withdraw their ministers from the Council, provoking the 'empty chair crisis' (Newhouse, 1967), on the grounds that their core concerns were in danger of being overridden.

A settlement to the row was found in January 1966 in the form of the (in) famous 'Luxembourg compromise', which appeared to the French to preserve the right of individual member states to prevent any agreement by QMV that prejudiced 'very important interests'. The text, reprinted in Box 10.1, deserves careful reading. It did not constitute an unequivocal right of veto or enjoy clear legal status; it was only an entry in a footnote to the minutes of a Council session. Moreover it was not subject to uniform interpretations across the member states and remained deeply unpopular with the Commission.

Table 10.1 Voting weights, population and majority thresholds

	European Coal and Steel Community (ECSC)		European Economic Community (EEC) & Euratom	European Social Fund (ESF)	European Community (EC) – European Union (EU)			
	6 MS	15 MS	6 MS	6 MS	1973> 9 MS	1981> 10 MS	1986> 12 MS	1995> 15 MS
Belgium	1	1	2	8	5	5	5	5
France	1	1	4	32	10	10	10	10
Germany	1	1	4	32	10	10	10	10
Italy	1	1	4	20	10	10	10	10
Luxembourg	1	1	1	1	2	2	2	2
Netherlands	1	1	2	7	5	5	5	5
Denmark		1			3	3	3	3
Ireland		1			3	3	3	3
UK		1			10	10	10	10
Greece		1				5	5	5
Portugal		1					5	5
Spain		1					8	8
Austria		1						4
Finland		1						3
Sweden		1						4
Cyprus								
Czech Rep.								
Estonia								
Hungary								
Latvia								
Lithuania								
Malta								
Poland								
Slovakia								
Slovenia								
Bulgaria								
Romania								
Qualified majority	Inc 1 MS with 1/6 pr	Inc 2 MS with 1/9 pr	12/17	67/90	41/58	45/63	54/76	62/87
Super-qualified majority	Inc 2 MS With 1/6 pr	Inc 3 MS with 1/9 pr	4/6 MS	—	6/9 MS	7/10 MS	8/12 MS	10/15 MS

	European Union (EU) 2004>				Population ('000s) ** Total EU-25 458,602
	25 MS		27 MS		
	01/05/04–31/10/04	Nice 01/11/04>	Nice 01/01/2007*	Constitutional Treaty	EU-27 488,867
Belgium	5	12	12	1	10,396
France	10	29	29	1	61,685
Germany	10	29	29	1	82,532
Italy	10	29	29	1	57,888
Luxembourg	2	3	3	1	452
Netherlands	5	13	13	1	16,258
Denmark	3	7	7	1	5,398
Ireland	3	7	7	1	4,028
UK	10	29	29	1	59,652
Greece	5	12	12	1	11,041
Portugal	5	12	12	1	10,475
Spain	8	27	27	1	42,345
Austria	4	10	10	1	8,114
Finland	3	7	7	1	5,220
Sweden	4	10	10	1	8,976
Cyprus	2	3	3	1	730
Czech Rep.	5	12	12	1	10,212
Estonia	3	4	4	1	1,351
Hungary	5	12	12	1	10,117
Latvia	3	4	4	1	2,319
Lithuania	3	7	7	1	3,446
Malta	2	3	3	1	400
Poland	8	27	27	1	38,191
Slovakia	3	7	7	1	5,380
Slovenia	3	4	4	1	1,996
Bulgaria			10	1	7,965
Romania			14	1	22,300
Qualified majority	88/124	232/321 with 13 MS 62% pop	255/345 with 14 MS 62% pop	At least 15 MS 55% MS 65% pop	
Super-Qualified majority	—	—	—	—	

Notes: Czech Rep. = Czech Republic; MS = member state; pr = share of production of coal and steel; UK = United Kingdom
* Proposed but not (at time of writing) definite date for the accession of Bulgaria and Romania
** EU-25 figures are for 2004; figures for Bulgaria and Romania are from 2002 (see sources)

Sources: The (rounded-up) population data for EU-25 were obtained from a Council Decision amending the Council's Rules of Procedure (Council document 12712/04 of 8 October 2004, available from the register on the Council website (www.consilium.eu.int). This Decision established the total population of each member state for the period 1/11/2004 to 31/12/2005, and is subject to annual revision. The population data for Bulgaria and Romania were obtained from the World Bank's World Development Indicators 2002.

Box 10.1   *The Luxembourg compromise*

The following is the abridged text of what became known as 'the Luxembourg compromise', as agreed at the Council meeting of 18 January 1966, published in the *Bulletin of the European Economic Community (Bull. EEC) 3/66* and reported in the press release for the session:

I.   *Where, in the case of decisions which may be taken by majority vote on a proposal of the Commission, very important interests of one or more partners are at stake, the Members of the Council will endeavour, within a reasonable time, to reach solutions that can be adopted by all the Members of the Council while respecting their mutual interests and those of the Community, in accordance with Article 2 of the Treaty.*

II. *With regard to the preceding paragraph, the French delegation considers that, where very important interests are at stake, the discussion must be continued until unanimous agreement is reached.*

III. *The six delegations note that there is a divergence of views on what should be done in the event of a failure to reach complete agreement.*[1]

IV. *The six delegations nevertheless consider that this divergence does not prevent the Community's work being resumed in accordance with the normal procedure.*

V.   *The members of the Council propose to adopt the decisions below on the basis of common agreement by unanimity:*

   • *the financial regulation for agriculture;*
   • *extensions to the market organization for fruit and vegetables;*
   • *the regulation on the sugar market;*
   • *the regulation on the market for oils and fats;*
   • *the fixing of common prices for: beef and veal, rice, sugar, olive oil, oil seeds, and milk.*

In addition, it was recognised that all the questions concerning the Kennedy Round should be considered as 'very important'.[2]

We lack an authoritative and complete account of instances in which the Luxembourg compromise has been invoked in the Council by one or other member government on an issue argued to be 'very important'. The examples collated here show rare instances of largely unsuccessful attempts to invoke it. All are on agricultural or fisheries issues, and only two were 'successful':

• *May 1982*   The Belgian presidency called a vote on agricultural price-fixing. The British government invoked the Luxembourg compromise, arguing that the budgetary consequences were too costly. The Danes and Greeks upheld the British claim that this was a 'very important interest'. The French had been expected to follow suit, but overnight consultations with Paris produced the instruction from President Mitterrand that the

→

→

French delegation should agree to a vote by qualified majority voting (QMV), and hence the British invocation was blocked. The French government subsequently insisted that this did not mean its abandonment of the Luxembourg compromise.

- *December 1982* The Danish government sought unsuccessfully to invoke the Luxembourg compromise in order to resist part of the revised basic regulation on the common fisheries regime.
- *June 1983* The Danish government unsuccessfully invoked the Luxembourg compromise in an attempt to resist the arrangements for herring quotas.
- *June 1983* At the Stuttgart European Council which agreed the Genscher–Colombo Plan for a Solemn Declaration on European Union, declarations were recorded by Denmark, France, Greece, Ireland and the UK, reaffirming in various ways their attachment to the Luxembourg compromise. On the same occasion, Belgium, Germany, Italy, Luxembourg and The Netherlands recorded their preference for using QMV wherever this was the treaty rule.
- *June 1985* The German government successfully invoked the Luxembourg compromise to block a proposal aimed at reducing common agricultural policy (CAP) prices for cereals and colza. In the event, the Commission found another way of addressing the problem.
- *December 1986* After a 'lively' discussion, the Council's internal rules of procedure (CRPs) were amended in order to enable the Council presidency to call a vote if asked to do so by the Commission or a member government on the grounds that there was a QMV in favour of a proposal. The Danes added that any such instance should be signalled two weeks in advance of a Council session.
- *During 1988* The Greek government invoked the Luxembourg compromise in order to resist the implications of the devaluation of the 'green' drachma as part of the agricultural price-fixing, with support from Denmark, France, Ireland and the UK. Subsequently, the Greek government invoked it a second time to contest the Commission's interpretation of the attempted resolution of the problem, but this time without support from other governments.

These examples notwithstanding, there have been numerous cases where a government in a clear minority of one has succeeded in winning an accommodation of a specific and troublesome distinct concern, where it has been able to persuade others that there was a substantive or political case for its singular position.

[1] This is the translation published in *Bull. EEC* 3/66, but a more accurate version of the French original would be: '*should conciliation not end in a complete agreement.*'
[2] It should be noted that this last point is in the French text but was not included in the English version in *Bull. EEC* 3/66.

Sources: de Ruyt (1989); Teasdale (1993), and interview material.

There has been quite a debate about what this compromise amounted to substantively (see Palayret *et al.*, 2006). Over the latter part of the 1960s and 1970s, it is certainly the case that explicit voting hardly ever occurred on issues that were technically subject to QMV. On the other hand, it turned out rarely to be invoked in an explicit way. Moreover, it was assumed to be a legitimate and usable operating norm by some member states more than by others, especially (though with differing intensities) France, Greece, Denmark, Spain, Ireland and the United Kingdom (UK). Some insiders even described these states as the 'Luxembourg compromise club'. Box 10.1 shows that its formal invocation has indeed been exceptional, as we can see from the rare cases involving the UK, Germany, Greece, Denmark and Spain, which interestingly tend to cluster around arguments over the CAP. Even in these cases, its mention was in footnotes to declarations in the Council minutes, mainly to get negotiators off the hook.

None the less, the shadow of the Luxembourg compromise probably induced delegates in the Council not to push colleagues to the brink, when it was judged that their isolation stemmed from a very real and very intractable domestic inhibition. Also member governments have been reluctant to face the consequences of deliberate illegality by a government that might refuse to implement a decision that it had tried and failed to veto. Thus the Luxembourg compromise was one of the conditioning factors that helped to embed habits of consensus-building rather than majoritarian voting. The issue for a long time was whether, and if so, when, QMV could or should be made operational, and not the details of how QMV would work or what the relative power was of any individual member state under the original formula for weighting votes. De Ruyt (1989, p. 116) reports 'between six and ten' decisions by QMV in 1966–74, and 'around 35' between 1974 and 1979.

The shift to majority voting

Votes did, however, start to be taken more often from some point in the late 1970s, and with increasing frequency in the early 1980s. De Ruyt (1989, p. 116) reports 'more than 90' between 1980 and 1984, while de Bassompierre (1988, pp. 25–9) argues that the turning point came in 1982. A critical example (see Box 10.1) was the QMV vote called adroitly by the Belgian presidency in 1982 on the CAP price package. Voting seems to have been particularly frequent on annual budgetary appropriations, the detailed application of CAP rules and technical trade issues, where QMV was a clear option, in sharp contrast to Article 100 (EEC) on internal market legislation where the then treaty rule was unanimity.

Willingness to vote and, perhaps more importantly, to accept being outvoted, was confirmed in those committee procedures of the

Commission where an outvoted minority could appeal against the decision for a Council discussion, but this hardly ever happened. The Commission made efforts to extend this practice to the implementation and 'technical adaptation' of internal market rules before 1985. In 1986, for example, before the ratification of the Single European Act (SEA), some ninety-three decisions are reported as having been taken in the Council by QMV, and subsequently ninety-six in 1987, seventy-eight in 1988, and sixty-one in 1989 (Wessels, 1991, pp. 146–7). The 1986 cases are reported as: agriculture and fisheries (61), trade (18), budget (3), and other (11). There are, however, no public records of voting in this period, nor any clear accounts of which were explicitly-called votes and which were implicit votes at the level of officials. Indeed, in the same account, Wessels notes that many of these so-called votes were implicit in the sense that the presidency asserted an agreement without being contradicted. Thus, in 1989, of the sixty-one apparent votes, twenty-six passed as 'A' points and seventeen were implicit, leaving only eighteen to depend on positive confirmation.

The Luxembourg compromise still hung over the Council, but in a more nuanced way than has been widely assumed (Nicoll, 1984). The culture that developed in the Council was one where not only explicit vetoes were frowned on, but also where efforts were made to accommodate the concerns of member states having serious and substantive problems with a particular proposal. Where the treaty base was unanimity, member governments did not need to give solid reasons for withholding agreement. Where the treaty base was QMV, on the other hand, governments were under much greater pressure to justify their disagreement with proposals explicitly, and hence also the presidency had more leverage.

By the early 1980s, therefore, voting had become more common, the Luxembourg compromise had become increasingly a last resort, and there was a sense of frustration about what sometimes seemed to be arbitrary blockages of decisions by individual governments. Added to this were the experiences of the first (1973: Denmark, Ireland and the UK) and second (1981: Greece) enlargements, and the prospect of the third (1986: Portugal and Spain). The UK, Denmark and Greece had each in different ways been ready to sit tight on isolated national positions in the Council, enough to frustrate their colleagues and to increase the acceptability of QMV, especially, as it turned out, for the French. It was feared that an additional two 'inexperienced' new members might compound this. By the mid-1980s one could observe increased tolerance of the practice of voting, more frequent indications that voting weights at least implicitly affected decision outcomes, and a more widespread willingness to alter the treaties to make the possibility of recourse to QMV more common.

The issue of whether recourse to the veto on QMV issues could stand as a legitimate option was, however, not discussed in the pre-SEA intergovernmental conference (IGC), because of the perceived difficulty in formalizing the means whereby a member state could convince the others that an issue was really of vital national interest (de Ruyt, 1989). In the preparatory discussion of the Dooge Committee (Dooge, 1985), the three governmental representatives from Denmark, Greece and the UK had made it clear (as what came to be called 'footnote countries') that they would not accept a formal revocation of the Luxembourg compromise. It was therefore deemed preferable to let this reinterpretation be implicit, with the result that some member governments were able to argue to their domestic publics that nothing had changed, but practice was allowed to evolve. These changes, as we shall see, also began to make a significant difference to the way in which committees of officials prepared ministerial decisions.

The SEA significantly extended QMV to the 'approximation of laws' for the internal market (Article 100), and enlarged its potential use in other policy areas, especially the environment and the implementation of research and development (R&D) programmes. In addition, the SEA relaxed attitudes more generally on voting, so that it became more frequent and more readily accepted in many areas already amenable to QMV. We do not, however, have records that plot this evolution systematically, although one insider has reported that, of the 260 or so measures adopted for the 1992 programme, some 220 were agreed in practice by consensus rather than by explicit voting. In subsequent treaty revisions, as we have seen, there were modest extensions of the application of the QMV rule, although always with an intense discussion and always with reassertions by one or other member government of the need to retain the unanimity rule in what they regarded as sensitive areas and for new decisions of principle.

By the early 1990s, recourse to voting had increased, the Luxembourg compromise was rarely used (Teasdale, 1993), and therefore reliance on the veto was much less assured for any 'dissident' member state. Attention therefore switched to relative voting power, and to the numbers required to build majorities or blocking minorities, a discussion that started to go hand in hand with debates about 'variable geometry', and inner and outer circles of power. None the less, negotiators remained alert to any indication from one or other government in the Council that a particular issue was a 'very important' or 'vital' interest – Alain Juppé, then the French Foreign Minister, is said to have used such terms at least five times during the closing negotiations on the 1986–94 Uruguay Round of the General Agreement on Tariffs and Trade (GATT), making it quite clear that no vote could be called.

The prospect of enlargement and new policy developments

An animated debate then began on the issue of relative weights, for a number of reasons. At one end of the scale, it was clear that post-unification Germany was simply no longer the same size in terms of population or economic power as the other, 'larger' member states. Though the German government stated repeatedly that it had no wish to disturb voting weights in the Council, implicitly at least there was an obvious imbalance, and one that caused anxiety in other member states. (Representation in the European Parliament (EP) was another matter. In a succession of adaptations from December 1993 onwards, the population criterion was brought more explicitly into the assignment of EP seats to individual countries.)

A second factor was the emerging prospect of an enlargement that would add not just the odd new member here and there, but potentially many new countries simultaneously. A further complication arose from the fact that most of the states in question were smaller rather than larger, simply as a function of the new and changing political map of Europe. A membership application from Malta gave rise to sudden hysteria about 'micro-states', these being members with the right of veto and disproportionate weighted voting power. What had been accepted without demur for Luxembourg seemed to many unreasonable for Malta or Cyprus, let alone at some stage, Iceland or Liechtenstein. Unease grew that smaller countries could already, and would in the future, call too many of the shots.

The Treaty on European Union (TEU) agreed in Maastricht in 1992 did not, however, grapple directly with these issues. The very recent unification of Germany and the worries about its potential consequences for a time muzzled the debate. Instead, the TEU extended the use of QMV under the 'first pillar' – core Community business. The TEU extensions applied to some aspects of education, the development of trans-European networks (TENs), transport, consumer affairs, development aid, the implementation of European Regional Development Fund (ERDF) programmes (although not decisions of principle about its overall framework), and a wider swathe of environmental issues. The provisions for the CFSP and justice and home affairs (JHA) under the second and third pillars, respectively, of the TEU retained unanimity as the predominant decision rule, but with some scope for introducing QMV for follow-up decisions, and for the potential transfer of some issues to the first pillar.

The Ioannina compromise

As the accession of Austria, Finland, Norway and Sweden approached, an argument erupted concerning the thresholds for constituting a qualified majority or a 'blocking minority' (Table 10.1 on pages 264–5 shows the evolution of the latter). In advance of these accession negotiations, it had been agreed between the Council and the Commission that the institutions would not be subject to radical change. It had been widely assumed that this would also hold for the Council's voting rules, but in autumn 1993 the issue of relative voting power acquired a sharper tone, with regard to both principle and substance.

The British (then with a Conservative government) had specific policy concerns relating to the environment and social issues, where they believed themselves to be in a beleaguered and barely sustainable blocking position. The Spanish feared that the addition of more and richer small countries would disturb the balance of decision-making adversely, and be against their interests. There were hints from France, Germany and Italy of general worries about small states exercising too much leverage. It was already clear in December 1993, when the other institutional adaptations were agreed, that the QMV threshold would be a tricky issue, although no changes were made at that time to the weighting formula.

In the event, the British and Spanish governments found themselves alone in February 1994, with no support from Paris, Bonn or Rome. They argued for no change at all in the majority threshold, insisting that the threshold – and throughout it was articulated as concerning the scope for 'blocking minorities' – be retained at twenty-three votes, rather than the twenty-seven that had been proposed, in line with previous adjustments. The British came close to the paradoxical brink of vetoing the EFTA (European Free Trade Association) enlargement that they had long advocated. Other member states were puzzled by the logic, and hardened their support for twenty-seven votes.

A form of compromise was agreed at the Ioannina meeting of the foreign ministers in March 1994, widely thereafter referred to as the 'Ioannina compromise' (Council Decision 94/C 105/01, published in OJ C 105/1, 13 April 1994). The text, reprinted in Box 10.2, and resonant of the Luxembourg compromise, stated that the Council would continue for a time to seek a wider basis of agreement on issues where members representing twenty-three or more, but fewer than twenty-seven, votes (reduced to 'fewer than twenty-six' after the Norwegians voted against accession), indicated sustained opposition. The text is a Council Decision and therefore has a legal status (unlike the Luxembourg compromise). It does not amend the treaties, but its application is subject to compliance with the treaties (for example, with regard to specified deadlines for the Council to act), as well as with the Council's internal rules of procedure (CRPs), Article 11 of which specifies that at any moment a vote can be called by a simple majority of member states. For some, this was a necessary device to facilitate overall agreement; for others, it was a damaging deterioration in shared understanding about the rules of the game; and the British and Spanish presented it as a necessary safeguard. The Ioannina compromise cast its shadow a few times in 1995/6, but thereafter fell into disuse (see Box 10.2 on pages 274–5).

Enlargement as a continuing preoccupation

The Treaty of Amsterdam (ToA) was agreed in 1997 in the period immediately following the EFTA enlargement, and already in the shadow of the next enlargement to the east and the south. Three points stand out:

- no changes were made to the weighting formula for QMV, although this was becoming increasingly evident as an issue that would have to be addressed quite soon;
- the ToA made further extensions to the application of the QMV voting rule with regard to some aspects of employment, social and equal opportunities policies; implementing decisions for the CFSP, as long as at least ten member states signalled support; and similarly for aspects of JHA, much boosted by the inclusion of the Schengen treaties within the framework of the EU (although with opt-out provisions for Denmark, Ireland and the UK); and
- it sought to address the problem of 'dissident' or reluctant member states.

On this last point, the ToA introduced a provision (Article J.13, later Article 23 TEC – Treaty establishing the European Community) for 'constructive abstention' (in the case of the CFSP), enabling a member state to abstain on a reasoned basis from a unanimous decision and then 'not be obliged to apply the decision'. In the case of JHA, the ToA introduced a provision (Article K.12, later Article 40 TEC) for 'closer cooperation', as it also did for core Community fields (Article K.15–17, later Articles 43–45 TEC) (Stubb, 2002), so as to enable some decisions to be taken forward under certain conditions by only some member states which were 'at least a majority' of the total number.

In so doing, the ToA, for the first time, inserted language resonant of the Luxembourg compromise into treaty provisions. Thus the provisions for CFSP (Article 23.2) and JHA (Article 40.2) state that:

> If a member of the Council declares that, **for very important and stated reasons of national policy** [our emphasis], it intends to oppose the adoption of a decision to be taken by qualified majority [for CFSP matters; the relevant part of Article 40.2, relating to JHA, reads 'the granting of an authorisation by qualified majority'], a vote shall not be taken. The Council may, acting by qualified majority, request that the matter be referred to the European Council for decision by unanimity.

This provision came to be known as the 'emergency brake'.

Box 10.2   *The Ioannina compromise*

The following is the text of a Council Decision of 29 March 1994 concerning the taking of decisions by qualified majority by the Council, published in the *Official Journal* (OJ) C105/1 on 13 April 1994:

'If members of the Council representing a total of 23 to 26[1] votes indicate their intention to oppose the adoption by the Council of a Decision by qualified majority, the Council will do all in its power to reach, within a reasonable time and without prejudicing obligatory time limits laid down by the Treaties and by secondary law, such as in Articles 189b and 189c of the Treaty establishing the European Community, a satisfactory solution that could be adopted by at least 68[2] votes. During this period, and always respecting the Rules of Procedure of the Council, the President undertakes, with the assistance of the Commission, any initiative necessary to facilitate a wider basis of agreement in the Council. The Members of the Council lend him their assistance.'

The Ioannina compromise was adopted as a Council Decision on 29 March 1994 under pressure from the British and Spanish governments. They were seeking to maintain the ability to prevent agreement on sensitive issues, where there was a significant opposing minority large enough to have blocked a decision prior to enlargement (admitting Austria, Finland and Sweden in 1995), but fewer than required under the revised qualified majority voting (QMV) threshold. The decision accepted that a group of member states commanding at least 23 votes, but fewer than 27 (reduced to 26 after the negative Norwegian referendum) could invoke 'Ioannina' so as to require discussion to be continued until an acceptable compromise could be reached.

Several instances of its potential invocation arose in 1995 and 1996. These included:

* *Greek transport aid for fruit and vegetables* (20–21 February 1995): the United Kingdom (UK), Denmark and Germany were in a minority (23 votes), but the UK chose not to invoke Ioannina;

These provisions had barely had a chance to be tested before treaty reform came back on to the agenda. As in the case of the EFTA enlargement, there was concern about the scope for blocking minorities, sharpened by fear of small and inexperienced member governments blocking progress. The nervousness was based more on theoretical possibilities than on empirical evidence; as we shall see, the record does not show any firm or repeated alignments of small countries versus large countries. Nor does the record from 1995 onwards suggest any systematic pattern of new member states in recurrent opposition to old member states.

The issues came to a head in the IGC that prepared what became the Treaty of Nice in 2000. This was a singularly bad-tempered affair, and

⟶

- *Mandate for EU–Swiss agreement on transport* (14 March 1995): the UK, Italy and Portugal were in a minority (25 votes); the UK sought to invoke Ioannina, but Portugal switched to support the mandate;
- *Council Regulation on Aid to Shipbuilding* (6–7 November 1995): the UK, Germany and Sweden were opposed (24 votes), but none invoked Ioannina; and
- *Draft Directive on Postal Services* (18 December 1996): two successive compromise proposals were put forward. The first was defeated under QMV, the second opposed by the UK, Denmark, Finland, The Netherlands and Sweden (25 votes). The UK invoked Ioannina, secured two concessions and then supported the measure.

The most interesting case concerned the 1995–6 agricultural price package. The presidency proposal in June was opposed initially by Portugal, Spain, Sweden and the UK, for different reasons (27 votes). Portugal then switched to support the proposal, leaving a minority of 22 votes, too few to block a political agreement. In October, when the legal texts were presented, Spain switched to support the proposal. In the meantime, however, Italy had decided to oppose it, because of an awkward domestic problem about an agri-monetary measure that improved the export price of French beef and affected the Italian beef market. This resulted in a minority of 24 votes, and the UK therefore invoked Ioannina. The Commission and Sweden agreed some further unrelated concessions on Nordic agriculture, and the agri-monetary regulation was made more restrictive, on the basis of which the Swedes switched to support the revised legal texts. This produced a clear qualified majority in favour of the agricultural price package, which was adopted with the UK abstaining. Ioannina was never invoked after that in the Agriculture Council.

[1] Following a referendum in Norway which prevented that country's accession to the European Union, this part of the text was adjusted to read 'a total of 23 to 25' by means of an amending Council Decision published in OJ C1/1 on 1 January 1995.
[2] Adjusted to '65' after the Norwegian referendum by means of the same amending Council Decision published in OJ C1/1 on 1 January 1995.

the Nice European Council was the longest ever, lasting from 7–11 December. The British and Spanish maintained their concerns about the risks of being out-voted on core interests. The population 'imbalance' between Germany and the other 'large' member states became harder to ignore. Governments from these countries, and especially the French, became set more explicitly on reducing what they saw as the 'disproportionate' weight of smaller member states under the existing voting rules, and especially that of 'immature' new democracies. The IGC explored a number of options (Best *et al.*, 2000, Best, 2001, 2004; Galloway, 2001; Moberg, 2002; Hosli and Machover, 2004), ranging from modest adaptations of weights on more or less political criteria, through a complex Swedish proposal for a strictly arithmetical formula (member states to have voting weights equal to double the square root of their population sizes), to various forms of 'double' or 'triple' majority (combinations of voting weights, number of assenting member states, and proportion of EU population represented).

The outcome, shown in Table 10.1 on pages 264–5, was a compromise, set out in Article 3 of the Protocol on the Enlargement of the European Union annexed to the ToN, to take effect from 1 November 2004. Voting weights were revised extensively with a widened range of bands, not arithmetically proportional and still giving the four big members identical weights. Belgium kept a disproportionate advantage compared to The Netherlands. Spain's proportionate weight increased, from which Poland benefited after (from a distance) resisting the French effort to give it a lower weight than Spain. Similarly, the other new members were allocated weights in the Council in line with those of incumbents. Two scenarios were agreed: one for the EU-25; and another for an EU-27 (that is, including Bulgaria and Romania), although somehow Turkey disappeared mysteriously from the calculations. In addition – and especially at the insistence of the larger member states – it was added that the new qualified majority in an EU-25 should include the assent of at least thirteen member states (fourteen for the EU-27), embracing at least 62 per cent of the EU population (and leaving undefined exactly how the relevant population would be established).

As regards the scope of QMV during the IGC, both the Finnish Council presidency and the Commission had set out some criteria for determining when it should be applied. In the end, QMV was pragmatically and only rather modestly extended. Some instances were in categories such as JHA or CFSP, already identified in the ToA for implementing decisions, often still hedged with the condition that the Council must agree unanimously before it can proceed. Others were in economic areas such as trade and intellectual property, or the structural and cohesion funds (only after the cycle of Agenda 2000), but in both cases hedged with conditions as to their applicability or timing. Some areas – for example, taxation and social security – remained tied to unanimity. An innovation was the decision to open up to QMV a number of institutional decisions, notably on appointments to key posts, such as the President of the Commission. The ToN removed the 'emergency brake' with regard to JHA, but not for CFSP.

The ToN did not, however, produce a stable agreement on all of these matters, and indeed it was immediately acknowledged that further reforms should be made. These became the subject of the 2002–3 Convention on the Future of Europe (CFE) and the subsequent IGC that produced the Constitutional Treaty, signed in Rome on 29 October 2004 (and rejected the following year by France and the Netherlands). On the question of voting rules, an overarching ambition was to remove the distinction between 'pillars', seeking instead to reclassify different kinds of legislative acts and decisions, and then to apply appropriate voting rules. Moreover, Article I-23.3 stated that 'The Council shall act by a qualified majority except where the Constitution provides otherwise', with specific clauses across the new consolidated document indicating where the unanimity rule would be retained. Simple majority voting was specified for a number of procedural decisions.

The IGC did not agree to major extensions of QMV, despite more ambitious proposals from the Convention, but rather continued the pattern of incremental extension. The CT would retain the emergency brake for CFSP, although it also invited more use of provisions for 'permanent structured cooperation' by less than the total number of member states. These agreements were reached after tough bargaining in the IGC, in which it became quite evident that a number of member states had reservations about radical extensions of QMV.

The toughest discussions, however, took place over how to redefine the rules for what should be the basis for constituting a majority. The Polish and Spanish governments were particularly adamant in their insistence on not weakening their voting weight relative to what had been agreed in the ToN, and indeed it was on this issue that, for a time, the IGC was suspended. Eventually, after, first, a change of government in Spain in March 2004; and second, a great deal of pressure on the Polish government from other member states, a new compromise was reached (Article I-25).

The compromise moved away from the old weighted votes formula and sought to substitute a new double majority system, whereby a qualified majority would have to include at least 55 per cent of the members of the Council, comprising at least fifteen member states representing at least 65 per cent of the population of the Union. A blocking minority would have to include at least four Council members. Where decisions did not stem from a proposal from the Commission or the new EU Foreign Minister, the qualified majority would have to include at least 72 per cent of the members of the Council, representing at least 65 per cent of the population. A version of this was also introduced in Article III-312 for the newly-labelled category of decisions on the common security and defence policy (CSDP).

Voting in practice

Here we concentrate on evidence of voting practice and its evolution since the 1950s. We provide both a synthetic overview and a more detailed picture for recent years (1998–2004), drawing on new data on recent practice, though we still lack details on previous periods and have no systematic evidence on proposals not put up for decision because it was probable that they would fail to find a majority. Since 1999, the Council itself, under its transparency arrangements, has published monthly summaries of Council Acts on its website (http://www.consilium.eu.int), showing decisions taken and noting some information about negative votes and abstentions. In addition, it has published press releases since 1997 on each session of the Council, with similar information. Our data build on and supplement these records with additional details drawn from reports of individual Council sessions, as well as some interview material.

An overview

The simple picture (in our view far too simplistic) is that, until the SEA, decisions in the Council were generally either formally subject to the unanimity rule or subject to the implicit acceptance of the right to veto, but that thereafter QMV became the predominant rule and common practice, at least for the internal market and most of its legislative programme. However, this apparently well-defined transition from unanimity to the active use of QMV is not borne out by the evidence.

On the details of practice, it is certainly true that participants did not admit to voting very much before the mid-1980s. Records were kept within the Council, but were absolutely not publicly accessible, nor were they even widely distributed to member governments. None the less, delegates from member states knew very well that votes could be and sometimes were taken, and they also knew on which issues votes were technically possible and thus might be solicited. Well-briefed national delegates were given guidance on the circumstances in which they could agree to the use of voting (since agreement on the procedure preceded substantive votes) and thus when they might want to uphold what they took to be their (or another member state's) rights under the Luxembourg compromise.

There has been heavy reliance on consensus-building on many topics for functional reasons. As we have seen, some 30 per cent of decisions are taken formally on the basis of unanimity and some 75 to 80 per cent of those decisions technically subject to QMV are not contested explicitly at ministerial level in the Council. In a system that requires agreed decisions to be implemented in domestic law, consensus encourages compliance, and an outvoted government might evade this. The progressive strengthening of Community law began to provide an alternative pressure for compliance. What is hard to judge under a system of implicit consensus is how often member governments, when isolated on an issue, chose not to block decisions, or where the 'shadow of the vote' (Golub, 1999) settled the outcomes.

Over time, however, it became harder to invoke the Luxembourg compromise, and the reasons for doing so became less persuasive. Instead, governments concerned about retaining the opportunity to block proposals they did not like focused mainly on retaining the unanimity rule for those subjects. Now and again, however, on subjects already accepted under the QMV rule, one government or another has become nervous and insisted on including some form of protection against being overridden on a vote. Thus the Ioannina compromise of 1994 and the 'emergency brake' provisions of the ToA and ToN were introduced as forms of reassurance. Significantly, however, these have hardly been activated. On the other side of the debate, those member governments that claim to be supportive of more active majority voting and of the opportunity to override minorities have been instrumental in inserting into the treaties (especially the ToA and the ToN) provisions for 'enhanced cooperation' that in theory would make it easier to press ahead on specific issues. Significantly, these provisions have remained theoretical rather than operational.

The net result is that we observe – or at least have observed in the EU-15 – a pattern that works at the ministerial level mainly by consensus, with very few contested votes, and few efforts to circumvent the formal rules by activating the provisions or 'informal' conventions for dealing with awkward minorities. This pattern has proved itself to be remarkably robust over the years. While we have systematic data only for the period since the mid-1990s, these are consistent with case-study and interview evidence from the 1980s and earlier. Whether this pattern will continue in the EU-25 is, of course, another question. In addition, we lack systematic empirical data that would enable us to substantiate either the extent or the patterns of implicit voting in the various meetings at the level of officials, and it may be here that devices will have to be found to cope with the consequences of the arrival of ten new member states.

The hard evidence

The data on contested votes that has emerged since late 1993, when the first figures started to become available, show the proportions of decisions agreed under QMV on which negative votes or abstentions were declared, the pattern of contestation by member states and by issue areas, and which member states tended to vote with each other on which issues. The data come from several sources:

- some early information released informally;
- the data collected by Mattila and Lane (2001);
- data collected by Mattila (2004) (available at http://www.valt.helsinki.fi/staff/mmattila/contest/); and
- data collated for this volume (available online at http://www.palgrave.com/politics/hayes-renshaw), published in Hayes-Renshaw *et al.* (2006).

Appendix 8 reports the way in which our data set is constructed and the techniques that have been used for its analysis. More detailed analysis of these data will be published in due course. The data cover definitive legislation adopted, some 'political agreements' (that is, pre-final decisions) and 'common positions' for co-decision, as well as some operational decisions, such as those under the transparency provisions.

Table 10.2 reproduces the simple information first released in 1995. This showed several clear points. Some 25 per cent of those decisions

Table 10.2 Voting in the Council, 6 December 1993–31 December 1994 (on legislative decisions)

Sector	Contested votes	All decisions	B		Dk		Fr		Ger		Gr		Ire		It		L		N		P		Sp		UK		Negative votes	Abstentions
			N	A	N	A	N	A	N	A	N	A	N	A	N	A	N	A	N	A	N	A	N	A	N	A		
Agriculture	22	98	2		4		2		3	2		2			1		2		3	1	2				4	7	23	12
Fisheries	9	49									1		1						1	1				5	1	2	4	8
Internal Market	16	47			3		1	1	3	3					1	1	2		2	2	1		2		1	4	16	11
Environment	5	9			2				2						1				1						1	1	7	1
Transport	3	7				1										1				1							0	3
Social Affaires	2	3												1		1						1		1			0	4
Research	2	27							1											1							1	1
Education	1	4												1								1		1			0	3
Citizenship	1	2																				1					0	1
Consumer Protection	1	1					1		1																		2	0

Sector	Contested votes	All decisions	B	Dk	Fr	Ger	Gr	Ire	It	L	N	P	Sp	UK	Negative votes	Abstentions
			N A	N A	N A	N A	N A	N A	N A	N A	N A	N A	N A	N A		
Transparency	2	2		2			1				2				5	0
Others	0	12													0	0
Total	64	261	2 0	1 11	2 3	9 6	4 0	1 2	3 3	4 0	105	3 3	2 7	7 14	58	44

Notes: N = negative vote; A = abstention.

- Of the 64 contested votes:
  - 28 were contested by abstentions only (that is, no one voted against);
  - In 26 of the 28 cases, only one member state abstained (singletons).
- Of the remaining 36 contested votes:
  - 11 were opposed by only one member state;
  - 9 were contested by one opposer and one abstainer;
  - 9 were contested by two opposers;
  - Only 7 encountered resistance from three or more member states.

Key to member state abbreviations:

B – Belgium	Dk – Denmark	Fr – France	Ger – Germany	Gr – Greece	Ire – Ireland
It – Italy	L – Luxembourg	N – The Netherlands	P – Portugal	Sp – Spain	UK – United Kingdom

Source: Data released informally to the authors.

agreed under QMV had been contested. Of these, almost half were on agriculture and fisheries, with a further quarter on internal market issues, the remainder being spread thinly across other areas. On these votes, the numbers of 'nos' and abstentions by definition fall short of blocking minorities and are there for the record to show the absence of approval for a given decision. The most frequently contesting states were Denmark, Germany, The Netherlands and the UK. Mattila and Lane (2001, pp. 40–4) confirm that, in the period 1995–8, 25 per cent or fewer decisions were contested each year under the QMV rule, that contestation continued to be more common on agriculture, internal market and transport (they do not identify fisheries separately) than on other issues, and that Sweden and Italy had joined the group of states most likely to contest decisions.

We should, however, note that there were very particular reasons to do with agricultural policy and its financing that led the Swedish government to cast a series of negative votes in 1995. One factor was the eurosceptic Minister of Agriculture, and another was the awkward interface between the CAP and the recently reformed Swedish agricultural policy. The pattern changed subsequently. Mattila (2004, p. 38) extends the figures by country up to 2000, but not by issue area, and the same contesting member states are evident.

Table 10.3 shows the aggregate data on contested votes by member states in recent years. The picture remains very much in line with previous years. Thus some 'northern' countries, notably Germany, Denmark, The Netherlands and the UK, now joined by Italy, are more likely to abstain or to vote 'no', a set that includes both older and newer members, and both the more integrationist by tradition and the more critical.

Table 10.4 shows the picture by issue area and confirms the earlier picture of contested votes concentrated especially on agriculture, fisheries (where Spain becomes an active 'no'-sayer on some points), some of the internal market and public health issues, and then a scattering in other areas. It should be noted that, of the roll-call of explicit Council votes, 47 per cent are contested only by a single member state (so-called 'singletons'), a further 19 per cent by only two member governments; and 18 per cent by only three member governments, with the remaining 16 per cent being cases of contestation by more than three member states. Early evidence from votes taken in the year following the May 2004 enlargement shows a very similar pattern for the EU-25.

The data show very clearly that some member governments rarely choose to vote 'no' or to abstain on proposals that are known to command a clear majority. Thus, for example, Belgium, Finland, Ireland and Luxembourg rarely do so, and France and Spain rather less often than the other, larger, member states. This may reflect one of two phenomena: either these governments succeed repeatedly in getting

Table 10.3 Aggregate data on contested votes by member state, 1994–2004

Year	A N	A A	B N	B A	Dk N	Dk A	Fin N	Fin A	Fr N	Fr A	Ger N	Ger A	Gr N	Gr A	Ire N	Ire A	It N	It A	L N	L A	N N	N A	P N	P A	Sp N	Sp A	Sw N	Sw A	UK N	UK A	Total N	Total A
1994			2	0	11	1			2	3	9	6	4	0	1	2	3	3	4	0	10	5	3	3	2	7			7	14	58	44
1995	2	0	0	1	5	1	1	1	0	3	8	3	0	1	2	0	4	2	1	0	5	0	5	2	1	2	34	1	10	9	78	26
1996	2	1	5	1	2	0	1	0	3	1	14	4	2	0	2	0	6	1	0	2	2	2	1	2	4	0	4	0	7	0	55	14
1997	2	1	0	1	6	1	4	0	3	3	9	2	4	0	1	1	6	1	1	1	2	0	2	2	2	1	7	0	7	3	56	17
1998	3	0	4	3	7	1	0	0	3	2	11	7	2	2	2	0	8	5	0	2	12	1	2	4	1	7	3	0	2	0	60	34
1999	1	0	2	0	4	0	0	0	3	0	2	1	1	0	1	0	8	1	2	0	4	1	1	1	1	2	0	0	0	3	30	9
2000	2	0	1	5	3	2	1	1	1	0	4	0	3	0	0	0	1	2	0	0	2	1	0	0	0	0	2	0	2	1	22	12
2001	1	4	2	1	3	1	1	0	3	3	3	5	1	0	1	0	2	3	0	2	1	1	0	1	3	2	4	0	2	2	27	25
2002	1	0	0	1	2	3	2	2	0	6	2	3	2	0	0	0	2	0	1	1	5	1	1	3	1	1	6	4	1	4	26	29
2003	5	2	0	3	6	2	1	0	3	1	5	1	2	1	3	1	3	2	3	1	0	1	6	0	5	2	5	3	4	5	51	25
2004	4	4	5	5	2	5	5	0	3	4	1	1	1	0	0	3	2	3	2	0	4	2	2	0	2	0	3	2	1	3	37	32
Total	23	12	21	21	51	17	16	4	24	26	68	33	22	4	13	7	45	23	14	9	47	15	23	18	22	24	68	10	43	44	500	267

Notes: N = negative vote; A = abstention.

Key to member state abbreviations:

A – Austria   B – Belgium   Dk – Denmark   Fin – Finland   Fr – France
Ger – Germany   Gr – Greece   Ire – Ireland   It – Italy   L – Luxembourg
N – The Netherlands   P – Portugal   Sp – Spain   Sw – Sweden   UK – United Kingdom

Sources: 1994 data released informally to the authors; 1995 data from Mattrila and Lane (2001), supported by online database at http://www.valt.helsinki.fi/staff/mmattrila/julkaisu.htm; 1996–2004 data provided by the Council Secretariat.

Table 10.4   Aggregate data on contested votes by issue area, 1998–2004

Sector / Country	General Affairs		Finance Economy		Justice Economy		Employment		Social Policy		Health Consumer		Industry		Research		Internal Market		Transport		Telecoms		Energy		Agriculture		Fisheries		Environment		Culture Youth	
	N	A	N	A	N	A	N	A	N	A	N	A	N	A	N	A	N	A	N	A	N	A	N	A	N	A	N	A	N	A	N	A
A	1	0	1	0	0	0	0	0	0	0	2	1	0	0	1	0	1	1	2	3	0	0	0	1	8	2	0	0	0	3	0	0
B	0	0	0	0	0	0	0	0	0	0	0	4	0	0	0	0	6	4	4	3	0	0	0	0	2	4	2	3	0	0	0	0
Dk	1	0	0	1	0	1	1	0	1	0	4	1	2	0	0	0	0	0	0	2	0	0	0	1	17	5	1	0	1	0	0	0
Fin	0	0	0	0	0	0	0	0	0	0	0	0	2	0	0	0	0	1	1	0	0	0	0	0	3	2	0	0	0	1	0	0
Fr	0	0	1	0	0	0	0	0	0	0	1	1	0	1	0	0	2	3	0	1	0	0	0	1	6	0	3	3	1	3	0	0
Ger	0	0	2	0	0	0	0	0	0	0	3	5	0	0	0	2	3	1	1	2	1	0	0	2	12	7	5	1	1	1	1	1
Gr	1	1	1	0	0	0	0	0	0	0	0	0	0	0	0	0	1	1	1	0	0	0	0	0	4	2	2	3	0	1	0	0
Ire	0	0	2	0	0	0	0	0	0	0	0	0	0	0	0	0	1	1	1	0	0	0	0	0	1	0	3	0	1	0	0	0
It	1	0	1	0	0	0	0	0	0	1	1	4	0	0	1	0	6	3	0	0	1	0	0	0	11	5	3	3	2	4	0	0
L	0	0	1	1	0	0	0	0	0	0	3	1	2	0	0	0	0	0	4	0	1	0	0	0	3	2	0	1	0	0	0	0
N	0	0	1	0	0	0	0	0	0	0	0	0	0	0	0	0	5	2	0	0	0	0	0	0	12	3	2	0	1	0	2	0
P	0	0	0	0	0	0	0	0	0	0	1	1	0	0	1	1	2	0	0	0	0	2	0	0	6	5	1	1	2	0	0	0
Sp	1	0	1	0	0	1	0	0	0	0	0	0	2	0	0	0	2	3	1	0	0	0	0	0	5	9	2	3	0	1	0	0
Sw	0	0	0	0	0	0	0	0	0	0	2	0	0	0	0	0	1	0	0	1	0	0	0	1	14	7	4	1	2	0	0	0
UK	0	0	1	0	0	0	0	0	0	0	2	0	1	0	0	0	1	2	1	1	0	1	0	0	8	9	1	1	0	1	0	0
Total	5	1	12	2	0	1	1	0	1	1	17	18	9	1	3	3	31	21	16	13	3	3	0	6	112	62	29	20	11	15	3	1

Note: N = negative vote; A = Abstention.

Key to member state abbreviations:

A – Austria	B – Belgium	Dk – Denmark	Fr – France
Ger – Germany	Gr – Greece	Ire – Ireland	L – Luxembourg
N – The Netherlands	P – Portugal	Sp – Spain	UK – United Kingdom
Fin – Finland	It – Italy	Sw – Sweden	

Source: Compiled from Council press releases, 1998–2004.

their interests accommodated; or their political cultures lead them to prefer to appear at the final stage of decision on the side of the majority.

Our data set enables us to look at individual instances of voting and the issues at stake. Thus we learn that most contested votes are on detailed regulations (especially agriculture, where there are marketing arrangements and so on that have to be renewed annually) and directives (especially internal market, public health and food safety). The sources of contestation can be traced back to well-established differences of opinion among the member states. Sometimes these are on matters of social preferences, such as the authorization of bio-technology or genetically modified foods or plants (Patterson, 2000; Pollack and Shaffer, 2005); and contested decisions on tobacco controls are another example (Arregui, 2004). Others are on matters of policy principle, such as the costs of particular agricultural market decisions, where we can observe net payers into the budget taking a stand against particular items of, or increases to, expenditure.

Often, the contested votes are on more detailed points that relate to a distinct national constituency or a different national practice that is in conflict with the emerging EU provisions. The examples of contested voting on public health, bio-technology and food safety seem to fall into this category, being (perhaps not coincidentally) issues with vocal advocacy groups in some member states. One other explanation for contested voting is that some member governments may not feel able to commit other levels of government in their own countries – particularly, for example, where the relevant policy has to be implemented by regionally or federally devolved levels of government.

When contested voting takes place on issues where no prior EU rule exists, there is prima facie evidence to suggest that 'saying no' correlates with subsequent poor or delayed compliance by those same member states. One pertinent example here is the legislation on the patenting of bio-technology products, where a deeply controversial Directive was adopted, with Belgium and Italy abstaining and The Netherlands dissenting. The Directive was scheduled for implementation by the end of July 2000, but as of November 2004, it had still to come into force in eleven member states. In addition, the European Court of Justice (ECJ) had declared six member states (including Belgium) to be in breach of the law, with cases pending against a further three member states, including Italy and The Netherlands (*European Voice*, 10–17 November 2004). Further research is needed to correlate contestation in the Council with subsequent compliance records.

The data also shed light on Council votes on issues that are the subject of co-decision with the EP (see Chapter 8). In addition, there is a group of contested votes on the operation of the transparency provisions, where a recurrent grouping of Denmark, Finland, The Netherlands and Sweden votes against Council decisions to release information. The reason is that the Legal Service of the Council, typically supported by a majority of member states, holds that legal advice and opinions should not be released. The no-sayers register their protest to show that they favour a more generous release of information.

In looking at the patterns of contested voting, we note that some dogs do not appear to bark. In other words, there are issues that we know from case-study evidence to be deeply controversial, but which do not appear as being contested explicitly in the voting data. Two kinds of example stand out: trade issues; and budgetary issues. With regard to trade, there is a recurrent cleavage in the EU between the more liberal and the more protectionist member states. This plays into negotiations on big trade issues, such as the positions to be adopted in international trade negotiations, notably within the World Trade Organization (WTO). The tough debates on this mainly take place, not in full Council meetings, but in the Article 133 Committee (see Chapter 3), and (exceptionally) in ministerial sessions. Even then it seems to be the case that, once majorities for negotiating positions are established, those in a minority usually choose not to record negative votes or abstentions in the Council – and in any case, efforts are generally made to include in the package on the table elements that serve to bind in all of the member states.

The same seems to be true of 'micro' decisions on trade issues, such as contingent protection and, in particular, decisions about whether to impose definitive anti-dumping duties (as we recall, subject since the mid-1990s to simple majority voting). Here again there are lively arguments in the relevant Council working party, often resolved by implicit voting and in a context where which side is taken by each member government is sufficiently important for the procedural rule (under Council Regulation 461/2004, OJ L77/12, 13.3.2004) to have been adapted again on 8 March 2004 so as to require a 'positive' vote by a simple majority of member states, in the absence of which the Commission proposal stands.

The budgetary arena has somewhat different characteristics. Decisions on annual appropriations are framed by the multi-annual financial perspectives and are then expressed in an annual budgetary cycle (Laffan and Lindner, 2005; Lindner, 2005). Most of these details are handled in a rather routine way by the Council's Budget Committee, and are then passed to the Budget Council, a special configuration of Ecofin, which generally adopts its decisions by consensus and then interacts with the Commission and the EP in the annual cycle. We know from case studies and interview evidence that the Budget Committee regularly votes to resolve differences, but again, contested voting is not usually recorded in the ministerial sessions. Where operational budgetary concerns seem to generate explicitly contested votes the most is on apparently fairly technical agricultural issues that have budgetary consequences.

The situation with regard to multi-annual financial perspectives is different. These periodic packages always go to the European Council for resolution, and always contain some items formally subject to unanimity voting – for example, the setting of the revenue targets and ceilings – and the 'macro' allocations under most of the spending programmes. In practice, therefore, these packages are resolved by negotiations that continue until the consent of all member governments has been obtained.

In this context, we note that the picture presented by Kauppi and Widgrén (2004) is somewhat misleading in its attempt to correlate voting power in the Council with the pattern of receipts from, and contributions to, the EU budget. They argue that the out-turns from the macro budgetary packages are better correlated with the relative power of member states than with the relative economic needs and situations of member states. So far, so good. However, there are two flaws in the analysis, which relate to the details of EU budgetary bargains. First, the authors segregate bargaining about EU budget receipts from bargaining about contributions, thus missing the (increasingly) central importance of 'net contributions' as a factor in governments' positions. Second, they (wrongly) assume that bargains in the overall pattern of receipts are subject to QMV. On the contrary, this is a bargaining arena where the unanimity rule applies, and hence any member state can block by withholding consent. While it may well be the case that 'more powerful' member states can be more extractive in conditioning their assent, the 'less powerful' member states (in terms of the criteria used by Kauppi and Widgrén) can also extract rewards in return for consenting to the package.

Thus, while member governments have varying capacities to exercise power in these always tough and controversial negotiations, each member government has an opportunity to press for specific benefits, in the absence of which it can impede agreement. For a classic illustration of this with regard to the structural and cohesion funds under Agenda 2000, see Allen (2005). In this context, see also Box 10.2 on pages 274–5, which illustrates the pivotal role of Sweden in negotiations around a set of agri-monetary issues, on that occasion subject to QMV contested voting. Zimmer *et al.* (2005) address some of these issues, argue the importance of the clash between what they call the 'north' and the 'south', and anticipate that new member states are likely to join the 'southern' grouping, for reasons of subsidy dependence. However, we should note that the potential net budgetary burden on new member states might lead to a different alignment of positions. The contentious discussions on budgetary matters at the June 2005 European Council illustrate these points clearly.

There is an important recent new entrant into the records of contested voting, namely concerning the rules surrounding economic and monetary union (EMU) and the management of the euro. Box 10.3 summarizes the heated discussions in 2002/3 over the Stability and Growth Pact (SGP), set up to impose discipline on member states as regards the stability targets. Interestingly, a good many member governments were

---

Box 10.3   *Drama over the Stability and Growth Pact*

On 17 June 1997, the European Council agreed the Amsterdam Resolution on the Stability and Growth Pact (SGP), complemented by Regulations 1466/97 and 1467/97. The SGP was designed to commit member states, especially those adopting the single currency (the euro), to the agreed guidelines for maintaining fiscal stability.

Under the provisions of Article 104 of the consolidated Treaty on European Union (CTEU), the performance of the individual economies of the member states would be monitored by the Commission and the Council, and judgements would be made in the form of recommended actions, aimed in particular at correcting 'excessive government deficits'. The Council was entitled to make its recommendations public when it deemed that 'no effective action' had been taken by the member state in question (paragraph 8), and in the event of 'persistent' failure to implement its recommendations, the Council could set a specified timetable for reducing the deficit (paragraph 9). Further non-compliance could result in the imposition of sanctions (paragraph 11). The scrutinized member state could not vote on decisions taken under Articles 104(8) or 104(9), and only Euro Group members could vote on decisions under Article 104(9).

In 2001, it was already clear that decision-making in the Economic and Financial Affairs Council (Ecofin) on how to apply these rules would be difficult. On 12 February, in a discussion on the broad economic policy guidelines (BEPG), the other members of Ecofin controversially repri-manded Ireland for its budget surplus. In February 2002, the Commission, with the backing of several governments, called unsuccessfully for an early warning to be issued to Germany and Portugal regarding their excessive deficits.

Throughout 2002 and 2003, Ecofin scrutinized individual economies and examined government policies, notably against a backcloth of significant deviation by some from the agreed targets. In October 2002, the Euro Group agreed that all member states facing excessive deficits should reduce them in 2003. On 7 November 2002, Ecofin made a recommendation to Portugal about its excessive deficit, to be re-examined in tough terms on 7 March 2003, with the possibility of sanctions being invoked. In January 2003, Ecofin issued an early warning to France, and declared an excessive deficit in Germany, with a strong recommendation about the need for improvement. Scrutiny continued on the stability (and, for non-euro members, convergence) programmes of several other member states.

⟶

determined to vote publicly on one side of the argument or the other, in a highly politicized domain where the decisions clearly had to be taken at the level of ministers. This public positioning took on an extra dimension when the Council failed to find majorities in favour of disciplining

---

→

On 3 June 2003, Ecofin adopted a decision on the French deficit, but in terms that the Danes and the Dutch deemed insufficiently tough. They therefore voted against it, and the Dutch issued a fiercely critical declaration, arguing in effect that the French were being let off the hook, while Portugal and Germany had made far greater efforts to sort out their deficits. On 25 November 2003, at an Ecofin meeting (in restricted session), the Commission recommended decisions 'against' France and Germany under Articles 104(8) and 104(9) (CTEU). Both decisions were defeated, with the public record, unusually, showing which member states had voted unsuccessfully in favour of them, rather than recording dissenters. In the end, Ecofin abandoned the excessive deficit procedure, preferring to adopt 'soft recommendations' instead.

The details of the votes were as follows:

Re: France:

- *Recommended Decision, Article 104(8)* – the following member states voted in favour, but did not constitute a qualified majority: Austria, Belgium, Denmark, Finland, Greece, The Netherlands, Spain and Sweden.
- *Recommended Decision, Article 104(9)* – the following member states voted in favour, but did not constitute a qualified majority: Austria, Belgium, Finland, Greece, The Netherlands and Spain.
- *Soft recommendations* – the following member states voted in favour and constituted a qualified majority: Belgium, Germany, Greece, Ireland, Italy, Luxembourg and Portugal.

Re: Germany:

- *Recommended Decision, Article 104(8)* – the following member states voted in favour, but did not constitute a qualified majority: Austria, Belgium, Denmark, Finland, Greece, The Netherlands, Spain and Sweden.
- *Recommended Decision, Article 104(9)* – the following member states voted in favour, but did not constitute a qualified majority: Austria, Belgium, Finland, Greece, The Netherlands and Spain.
- *Soft recommendations* – the following member states voted in favour, and constituted a qualified majority: Belgium, France, Greece, Ireland, Italy, Luxembourg and Portugal.

The Commission subsequently took the Council to the European Court of Justice (ECJ) – Case C-27/04, with partial success, in that the ECJ reprimanded the Council for its behaviour.

Sources: Council press releases and minutes of individual Council sessions.

France and Germany, whereas smaller member state in this case especially Portugal, were much more vulnerable to tough conditionality and the threat of sanctions. The Council minutes for the Ecofin meeting of 25 November 2003 provide a rare record (to our knowledge, the *only* record) of explicit voting on failure to reach agreement.

One legitimate question that can be posed is whether there are identifiable coalitions of particular member states that tend to vote the same way on specific issues. Our analysis of our data set suggests that coalitions are of two kinds. On the one hand, there are recurrent groupings arising out of specific agricultural interests and shared societal preferences on issues such as genetically modified food and plants. On the other hand, the coinciding negative votes and abstentions tend, for the most part, to be rather more issue-specific than part of recurrent coalitions, and indeed simultaneous 'no'-voting or abstentions may be for entirely different reasons. Many negative votes seem to be country-specific, relating to a particular situation with regard to a particular legislative proposal that would have a specific impact on a local economic sector or regulatory practice. This is especially true on single market issues. This is consistent with an accumulation of qualitative case-study evidence on EU policy-making, a conclusion also reached by Zimmer *et al.* (2005). Box 10.4 traces one particular story over many years – namely, the Takeover Directive – where, in particular, the German government, despite being in a minority on several occasions, went to great lengths to resist the introduction of the EU legislation.

In particular, there is no systematic evidence of big or small member states, or of old or new members, voting together. On the contrary, one important feature of recorded dissent seems rather to be linked to domestic political cultures and perhaps to the need to defend positions in national parliaments, in so far as (with the exception of Italy under the Berlusconi period of government) the member states concerned include most of those with more systematic procedures of national parliamentary scrutiny. If we had more detailed evidence about position-taking at earlier stages in the Council, we could look for correlations with the use of 'parliamentary scrutiny reserves' by particular national delegations. Another possible correlation might be with the expression of subsidiarity concerns on particular issues.

Contrary to the supposition of Mattila (2004), we find no evidence of traditional left/right cleavages in the patterns of explicit voting. However, the clustered patterns of contested voting on agriculture and single market issues do suggest at least two recurrent cleavages. One, as we noted earlier, is between net payers to, and net recipients from, the budget, which coincides to some extent (although not in perfect alignment) with broad economic and fiscal policy stances. A second broad cleavage is between the more and the less free-market-minded member states on single market issues (as would probably also be clear if we had micro-level qualitative data on more of the external trade issues). The new evidence on EMU and the SGP is also broadly in line with these cleavages, in so far as it reflects a tension between the more and the less fiscally austere. In all cases, however, we should note some deviance from the patterns, since no member state is entirely consistent on these issues. Given the weight of these topics on the EU agenda, these patterns are not surprising, although we should be a little cautious before resting an analysis on only the final level of ministerial discussion for which the recorded contested votes are few in number.

Problems of inclusion and exclusion

This leads us to the broader issue of whether the voting rules recurrently disadvantage or isolate particular countries. A distinction should be borne in mind here between an erratic pattern of isolated countries, varying considerably according to issues, and a repeated pattern as regards individual countries, groups of countries or kinds of issues. EU governance depends on legitimation through the member states and their obedience to Community law. There is a real issue of how to legitimate individual decisions for a state whose government voted against them, perhaps to signal in advance the improbability of its compliance. The more frequently a member government is outvoted and visibly unhappy about it, the larger the problem becomes, at least for the member state concerned and arguably for the system as a whole.

Much depends on the degree of sympathy from other member governments and institutions for the beleaguered minority, and on how justified the minority position is considered to be. The situation has existed since the foundation of the EC, in both theory and practice, and a range of devices has developed over the years to correct such conflicts, with the Luxembourg compromise, the Ioannina compromise, or the 'emergency brake' acting very much as last resorts. Three particular practices have developed. The first, and perhaps the most obvious, is to put the onus on the Commission and the Council presidency to do their utmost to accommodate reasoned (and apparently reasonable) differences of position. Frequently, the accommodation is achieved through declarations in the Council minutes, and often attached to decisions taken, in the end, by consensus.

A second is to provide for a variety of formulations within the body of the relevant text for divergent interpretation or application of the relevant rules to particular member states. These may take the

Box 10.4   *A tortuous tale – negotiating the Takeover Directive*

In April 2004, a 14-year struggle to agree European Union (EU) legislation on take-over bids ended with the adoption of a joint directive of the European Parliament (EP) and of the Council (2004/25/EC). Initially designed to facilitate European mergers and acquisitions as part of the single market programme, the measure finally adopted may (in the eyes of Frits Bolkestein, the then responsible Competition Commissioner) make Europe more protectionist. A large share of the responsibility for this paradoxical outcome lies with the German government, acting in the interests of its domestic business community.

The proposed directive was intended to address the significant differences among member states' rules regarding takeover bids. In some, market forces were allowed to prevail, while in others a company attempting to acquire another encountered complex legal and institutional obstacles, particularly in Germany, where hostile (particularly foreign) takeovers were viewed as being undesirable.

Finding agreement proved elusive. The first Commission proposal, produced in January 1989, was criticized by many member states, which argued in favour of establishing only basic common principles, leaving the details to be worked out by the national authorities themselves. The United Kingdom (UK) in particular was very critical of the Commission's proposal, preferring its own traditional system of self-regulation. Towards the end of 1991, following consultations with officials from the member states, the Commission announced its intention to prepare another draft proposal.

The Commission's second proposal (this time for a framework directive) was forwarded to the Council and the EP on 8 February 1996, as the first step in the co-decision procedure to which this dossier was subject. It addressed the main criticisms of the first proposal, by containing general principles but few detailed provisions, and by enabling implementation not only by the enactment of national measures, but also (with the British in mind) by self-regulation. Within the EP, several large German corporations lobbied to such an extent that the EP's (German) *rapporteur* on the issue, Klaus-Heiner Lehne, was viewed by some as their spokesman (Skog, 2002: 308). At its first reading, in June 1997, the EP adopted Lehne's report and demanded 22 amendments to the proposed directive.

It took three years for the national officials to reach an agreement in principle on the Council's common position, which they did in the summer of 1999. When the common position went to the Council for agreement shortly afterwards, it was opposed by the Spanish minister, for reasons largely unrelated to takeover bids. A further year of negotiations was required in order to get the Spanish back on board, and the Council's common position was finally agreed unanimously on 19 June 2000.

In its opinion of 13 December 2000, which marked the end of its second reading, the EP proposed fifteen amendments to the Council's common position. The Council and the EP then found themselves at fundamental odds about the timing of shareholders' authorization to board members to engage in defensive measures in the event of a hostile takeover bid. As a result of this and a small number of other disagreements, the procedure then moved formally to the conciliation phase on 10 April 2001.

In the course of conciliation, the Council proved unwilling to compromise on defensive measures. The German business community, which shared the view of the EP on this issue, forced the German government to withdraw its support for the Council's common position (agreed unanimously without abstentions

→

in June 2000), earning Germany the opprobrium of the other fourteen member governments. At the second and final conciliation session on the matter, on 5 June 2001, an agreement on defensive measures was only reached after a split vote in the EP's delegation (eight in favour of the Commission's compromise amendment, and six against, including the *rapporteur*).

The joint text agreed in the conciliation committee had to be endorsed by a majority of MEPs in order to become law. After intensive lobbying of German MEPs by the German government, leading German companies and trade unions in advance of the vote in the EP's plenary session on 4 July 2001, they voted against the measure as a single national bloc, irrespective of EP party grouping. The result of the plenary vote was a tie – 273 votes in favour, 273 against and 22 abstentions. Parliament's rules of procedure hold that if there is a tied vote, the text is deemed to be rejected (see Table 8.1). German pressure was therefore largely responsible for the demise of the second proposal.

The fate of the Commission's third proposal for a takeover directive, tabled on 2 October 2002, could not have been more different, in that it took just 14 months for the Council and the EP to reach agreement at first reading on 22 December 2003, obviating the need for conciliation. However, the Commission's role in the affair was described as 'little short of disastrous', and Germany was accused of stripping the proposal of any force, and of persuading the UK to support it in this endeavour in return for German help in fighting Commission proposals on temporary workers' rights (*Financial Times*, 20 December 2003).

Once again, defensive measures proved to be a sticking-point between the member states, and with the Commission. Germany, supported by some Nordic countries, lobbied hard to have its interests taken into account on this matter. On 27 November 2003, while awaiting the result of the EP's first reading, the Competitiveness Council agreed on a general approach based on an Italian presidency compromise and agreed informally with the EP, proposing that the provisions of the articles on defensive measures be made optional. Since the Commission refused to agree to this compromise, the member states had to agree to it by unanimity, which they did, with Spain abstaining.

Intensive informal contacts between the Council, the EP and the Commission in the early stages of the co-decision procedure meant that the Council was able to accept all thirty amendments contained in the EP's opinion of 16 December 2003 following its first reading, which was adopted by 321 votes in favour, 219 against, and 9 abstentions. A unanimous political agreement was reached in the (Environment) Council on 22 December 2003, and the Directive was finally adopted by the Justice and Home Affairs (JHA) Council on 21 April 2004, and published in the Official Journal later that month (OJ L 142 30/04/2004, pp. 12–23).

After fourteen years of labour, the EU had (in the eyes of some observers) finally produced a mouse – a takeover directive which allowed companies to fend off hostile takeover bids without shareholder approval and enabled governments to apply different rules for takeover bids depending on the nationality of the would-be acquirer. Consequently, for better or for worse, some European companies remain close to impossible targets for hostile bidders, and a level playing-field has not been created. Although out-manoeuvred by the member states on this occasion, the Commission remained defiant. In a statement attached to the minutes of the JHA Council meeting where the directive was finally adopted (Council docu-ment 7945/ 04 ADD I, p. 12), it declared its intention 'to monitor the application of the directive and evolution of the situation in the Internal Market closely and come forward with further proposals where necessary'.

form of differentiated rules, exceptions, derogations, longer or shorter time delays or transitions (Ehlermann, 1984; Wallace and Wallace, 1995). This history of accommodating special problems helps to explain why explicit voting remains relatively infrequent in the Council.

A third option has become markedly more prevalent since the 1980s, namely the formulation of more generic special arrangements in the form of protocols and declarations attached to the treaties. Each of the EU treaties since the SEA has been accompanied by a mass of such devices, often to cater for highly idiosyncratic features of particular countries. Here, the borderline between the objective and the subjective has already been crossed, with the introduction of exceptions sought by particular and partisan governments, as distinct from points that could be argued more plausibly to be 'national interests'. Perhaps the most interesting example from the TEU was the insertion of the 'Irish abortion' clause, under the guise of the obscure Protocol 17, annexed to the TEU and to the Treaties establishing the European Communities (Cloos *et al.*, 1994, pp. 335–7).

Relative power

Behind many of the attempted analyses of voting behaviour and bargaining outcomes in the Council lie different ways of assessing the relative power of member states in the process. It is evident from the debates among practitioners that there are two rather different under-standings of relative power. On one side lie the observations of the 'insider practitioners' (culled usually from interview evidence) that voting rules and voting weights matter, but to only a limited extent. Alongside these lie substantive preoccupations on specific issues, the skills and persuasiveness of the negotiators, and the opportunities provided by specific situations for one government or another to exer-cise leverage on bargains.

On the other side lies the public debate among politicians, who engage in the treaty reform debates that examine options for changes to the voting rules, where stylized positions are often adopted, implying that relative power should be correlated in some way with formally assigned voting power. Enormous amounts of time and energy have been spent in successive IGCs arguing over proposed rule changes. (Interestingly, this was not the case in the IGC leading to the SEA and its 'breakthrough' on extending the QMV rule, which was despatched efficiently in just over three months!) Our data on contested voting and qualitative evidence from published case studies tend to give credence to the observations of the 'insider practitioners', rather than to the public political rhetoric.

In the scientific literature on the Council, we also find two very different lines of analysis, one broadly qualitative, the other broadly quantitative. Studies based on one or other form of qualitative analysis by and large argue that relative power depends on some combination of the rules and procedural setting with the substance of the issues being decided. As regards the latter, member governments exercise influence according to some combination of, on the one hand, their stake in the issue at hand (thus French voices count more on agriculture than British voices, just as, clearly, Spanish voices count much more than German voices on fisheries issues), and on the other, the persuasiveness of national positions *vis-à-vis* the proposals on the table. Thus practitioners cite many examples of instances in which a member government in a clear and isolated minority has succeeded in turning round an argument in the Council to its advantage. There is also a large literature on the relative impacts of member states as leaders or laggards, up-loaders or down-loaders in environmental negotiations (Jordan, 2002; Lenschow, 2005). Clearly, qualitative case-study material often does not lend itself to compelling generalizations. Quantitative analysis, on the other hand, does. Consequently, we have seen an explosion of literature on the Council that aims deliberately to develop rigorous models based on carefully calibrated quantitative analysis of potential explanations for voting behaviour, and especially relative power. We shall return to this in Chapter 11.

Conclusions

From the foregoing, we can draw several broad conclusions about the practice of voting in the Council. First, of course, rules matter, and the patterns of bargaining behaviour are different depending on the voting rule that applies to any given issue or set of issues. Thus far, the vigour of the arguments about changes to the rules is logically-based, whether in the context of periodic IGCs or in the context of efforts to introduce special conventions, more or less formalized, as in the case of Luxembourg and Ioannina. However, the rules matter less than it might appear, in so far as the predominant patterns of bargaining are aimed at either building consensus as far as possible about eventual decisions, or else at preventing measures from getting to the ministerial level of negotiation until and unless there is more or less a consensus.

Second, relative power matters, but not in a way that can easily be quantified as regards the empirical data. Too few of the agreed decisions are submitted to explicit and public voting for us to have a secure overview of the patterns of decision-influencing, and in the recorded instances of contested voting, the numbers are too small to support clear, overarching assertions. None the less, the data on contested voting by and large confirm the results of qualitative case studies and give them extra nuance. These data also show a fairly consistent pattern over the ten years that they record.

Third, the data show rather clearly that a very large proportion of decisions agreed are, crucially, framed and shaped well before the ministerial sessions. In these prior phases, implicit voting – or position-taking that could be supported if necessary by explicit vote-taking – almost certainly plays an important part, as qualitative studies have generally argued. But then two different phenomena can be observed at the ministerial level. On the one hand, we see decisions, which we know were controversial at an earlier stage, turn into widely endorsed outcomes; and on the other, formal expressions of opposition by explicit voting seem to be directed at least as often at domestic constituencies as at other members of the Council.

Where we have to depend on qualitative case studies is for accounts of what persuades individual governments to switch votes from one side to the other in the case of closely-fought decisions. The Takeover Directive is an apt example of this (see Box 10.4). Here, the evidence cannot be extracted from the statistical data, but only from careful investigation of cases that, by and large, indicate the considerable importance of bargaining to secure individualistic benefits, sometimes on very big issues (for example, in the historical discussions of the UK budget rebate), or by way of smaller side payments.

Fourth, there are some rather clear differences between issue areas. In some fields, such as agriculture, fisheries and the internal market, explicit voting at ministerial level is clearly more usual and more routinized, while in others it is hardly observable. In yet other fields – as, for example, in the case of trade policy, the impact of implicit voting is played out at the level of officials. Our lack of detailed data from earlier periods makes it a little difficult to draw hard and fast conclusions on this. None the less, it seems to be the case that routinized explicit voting at ministerial level or implicit voting at official level occurs more readily in those policy fields where there is a settled rhythm to EU decision-making; where the default position is that an existing agreement continues rather than that there is no agreement; where national positions are quite clear; and where habits of doing business together are fairly well established. In contrast, in fields that are rather newer for the EU, the effort to broker agreement may be considerable but, once reached, there is a reflex to state that there is a consensus even on issues that are subject to QMV. But, of course, in newer and more controversial issue areas, unanimity is still generally the decision rule.

Fifth, there are, of course, now and again sessions of the Council or European Council where there are very public disagreements, with explicitly segmented groups of member states rallied on opposite sides of the argument. Boxes 10.3 and 10.4 showed this for the Stability and Growth Pact and the Takeover Directive respectively. However, dramatic examples of this kind tend to be exceptions to the general rule.

Chapter 11

Compromise and Consensus: Negotiation and Bargaining in the Council

At the core of the work of the Council are processes of negotiation and bargaining across the levels and layers of ministerial and official exchanges. In this chapter, we explore these further and locate them in the analytical literature that seeks to explain their key features in the specific context of European integration as well as in a broader comparative context. The first section of the chapter provides some general observations on negotiation, mainly to give the reader with limited direct experience some points of reference about the character of negotiation as a generic process of developing binding agreements across state boundaries. The second section highlights notions of the European Union (EU) as a distinctive negotiating forum, in which the Council of Ministers plays a key role. The third section addresses the wider analytical literature.

The negotiating process

This section is based on a body of material on negotiation and negotiating techniques, much of which is practical and either practitioner-derived or practitioner-oriented. Much of it is also analytically agnostic in the sense that authors often do not – or at least not explicitly – locate their commentaries in one theoretical framework or another, but rather focus on ways of describing and sometimes also improving practice (see, for example, Gonzalez Sanchez, 1992). This literature is also often derived from, and feeds into, both simulations of negotiations, and training in negotiating techniques. In the case of the EU, there has been a growing interest in the use of role-play simulations as both educational and training tools. One or other of the authors of this volume has been involved in developing exercises for this purpose since 1975, when the first such exercise that we are aware of was developed in the UK (Clarke et al., 1971; Humphreys, 1996).

General features of negotiation

To engage in negotiation is to commit to structured dialogue with one or more interlocutors and to seeking agreement. Negotiation handbooks often refer to the interlocutors as 'adversaries', imply or assume that the interaction is necessarily competitive, and suggest that outcomes are to be assessed in terms of 'who wins' and 'who loses'. Some manuals use a different vocabulary, arguing that negotiation is about 'problems' as much as about 'actors', and indeed argue that the smart negotiator is one who can 'separate the problem from the person' (Zartman and Berman, 1982; Fisher *et al.*, 2003). The assumption is that concentration on the 'problem' encourages negotiators to focus on positions, and allows more scope for constructive, creative and cooperative approaches. This is a strongly prescriptive approach, though rooted in the utilitarian view that, if you have to negotiate, you may as well figure out a way of being as effective as possible.

Many analysts of negotiation, or trainers in negotiating techniques, argue that the guts of the process are much the same, whether you are buying or selling a second-hand car, dealing with an industrial pay dispute, or establishing an international environmental regime. Thus negotiations take place when each participant wants something that one or more of the others can grant, but the objective has to be reached by discussion, not coercion, and hence its attainment depends on an exchange of costs and benefits. Negotiations thus take place when actors with different goals, the advancement of which depends on a change in the behaviour of others, use a common framework to establish a joint outcome. There is a 'settlement' point when all, or by majority, most, participants agree that they can achieve more by cooperation than by defection.

There are several key words here. It is a process in which *actors* interact: actors with personalities, behaviour patterns, strategies and motivations. The actors have *goals* that they seek to attain; that is, identifiable concerns, needs, demands and interests. A *common framework* is required that will structure the process, whether that is loosely constructed or highly articulated. *Outcomes* matter, since the actors are results-oriented; they enter into the process in the hope of making tangible achievements. There is a choice between *cooperation* and *defection*: the actors may not be absolutely required to agree or to follow the majority. But there is a presumption that *settlement* is imaginable and acceptable. Defection or exit is more imaginable in some contexts than in others.

Negotiations take place for a variety of different purposes (Iklé, 1964). A specific conflict may have to be resolved, with negotiation as the means of limiting damage, assuaging friction, removing the subject of tension, or redefining the issues, so that an accommodation is possible. Resources may have to be allocated or reallocated, with the negotiation focused on distribution or redistribution. The participants may want to agree mutually binding rules to govern relations among them. They may seek to structure future collaboration, in terms of the mechanisms for joint work, or the substance of their interactions, or other shared concerns.

Negotiation as a term presumes that there is some form of balance or parity among the participants – that is, that they exercise roughly comparable power or influence. Here, we need to be clear as to our meaning. Of course, there are differences in power, or influencing ability, between participants in many, if not most, negotiations. Naturally, these differences in endowment affect the outcomes. But the decision to term the process 'negotiation' marks a willingness by the participants to behave for some purposes as if they were on a level playing field, and then let the attributes and skills of the players determine the outcome, subject to some refereeing rules. Participants have the capacity to obstruct each other, but also to grant concessions to each other. Each wants something that the other(s) can grant. The participants agree to negotiate because they believe that, by debate and by persuasion, they can improve on the *status quo ante*; that is, that the future can be made better than the past, or the present.

The whole notion of negotiation is thus about movement and changes of position; that is, a dynamic and fluid process. The questions that follow are, then, about the way movement is made, what factors facilitate movement, how the strategies and tactics of the participants are developed to permit or to obstruct movement, and what permits the results to be stabilized and agreements honoured in the observance.

Single versus recurrent negotiations

There is an important difference between 'one-off' negotiations and repeated or serial ones. In a single negotiation there is greater scope for dishonest or manipulative behaviour, since the participants do not have to meet again. However, where the links between participants are recurrent, and the impacts of their behaviour on each other persistent and significant, the incentives to behave constructively, and according to agreed codes of conduct, are much greater. In contexts where, by substance or by choice, the participants meet repeatedly, agreements on negotiating rules as well as on specific issues (that is, setting as well as substance) become important.

The decision to invest in the setting, and to develop distinct and durable rules of behaviour, thus conditions and reinforces the negotiating process by increasing the potential and the propensity for agreements to be reached. Rules need to include both codes of conduct for the negotiations themselves and enforcement mechanisms to deter reneging. It is an increasingly marked feature of the international system for such rules to be developed, so as to govern relationships among countries and to enable policy regimes to be sustained. Thus incentives to cooperate are improved, the risks of defection diminish and there is more chance that agreements will be cumulative – that is, enlarged in scope, intensity or longevity. Such negotiations are often termed 'integrative', because they encourage the emergence of stable and predictable relationships among the participants, solidify shared norms and intensify interdependence among the participants (Iklé, 1964).

Thus far, commentators are broadly in agreement. What is more controversial is the question of how far, or in what circumstances, norms and beliefs may have an impact on the definition of issues and the interpretation of both status and substance. Many analysts argue that status (or power) and substance are the key factors; they thus accept more readily very systematic characterizations of the 'rationality' of the actors, hence the appeal of rational choice models of negotiation. Others suggest that the less tangible, and perhaps implicit rather than explicit, factors of norms and beliefs may be pertinent to behaviour, at least in some contexts (Goldstein and Keohane, 1993). They may influence the definition of goals and calculation of advantage made by individual participants, and may differ from one participant to another.

Numbers, scope and layers

Three other factors affect the ways in which negotiations are conducted: the number of participants; the scope of issues embraced; and the layers of negotiation.

Numbers

We can draw a distinction between bilateral, restricted multilateral and extended multilateral forums (Ruggie, 1993). Bilateral negotiations, with only two main participants, are more straightforward to conduct and to describe than multilateral. Much of game theory finds its origins in efforts to explain bilateral, or 'two-person', games, where the variables and range of options can be set out fairly simply, and also where relative bargaining power and leverage seem easier to establish.

Restricted multilateral negotiations take place among a limited number of participants, where a degree of intimacy and mutual familiarity can be established, and where the terrain for cross-trading can be fairly easily identified. How many make a 'manageable' number for intimacy to be sustained is an important point of debate. The answer cannot be established in terms of crude numbers, since much depends on factors of interdependence, congruence of behaviour or characteristics among the participants, and overlapping definitions of goals. It is in such contexts that norms and beliefs probably play a particularly important part, and indeed may be a defining criterion for membership of the group.

Extended multilateralism applies when a large, and perhaps hardly confinable, membership chooses to adopt common regimes or to operate joint programmes. The United Nations (UN) and the World Trade Organization (WTO) are obvious examples. In this case, participation may rest on asymmetric relationships of dependence and interdependence, limited congruence and modest shared goals. Here, agreement is likely to be more fragile and more limited in scope and ambition.

Scope

Some forums are essentially single-issue and deal with a relatively straightforward agenda, irrespective of the number of participants. Here, everything depends on building agreement and sustaining a regime within the relevant issue arena. Other forums handle a clutch of more or less related issues, allowing for some issue linkage and for gains on one issue to offset losses on others.

Layers

Negotiating forums may engage a larger or a smaller number of layers of political decision, or plurality of players, beyond the formal representatives authorized to make commitments. Classical realist theory or intergovernmentalism assumes that, when the actors are states, they can be viewed as monoliths or quasi-monoliths, in the sense of being able to control the articulation of negotiating positions, to decide whether or not to settle, and thus to entertain the notion of either stalling or exit. Much of game theory rests on the engagement of unitary actors, or the plausibility of the judgement that, in the final analysis, actors combine their varied interests into a single hierarchy of rational preferences.

In contrast, the pluralist view argues that, in the international arena, transnational actors include not only governments but also others, such as firms or non-governmental organisations (NGOs), as well as a variety of actors within states. All of these may have an impact on the negotiating forum in advance of, during negotiations, and after agreements are reached; and hence governments do not necessarily adopt congruent or consistent preferences. Commentators range themselves between these two positions, reaching differing conclusions about the extent to which the layers interact and complicate the negotiating process. The recent literature on 'two-level games' aims to explain international negotiations from this perspective (Putnam, 1988; Evans *et al.*, 1993).

Compromise and consensus

Essential to the process of negotiation is the notion that there is a potential settlement point of agreement that would satisfy the preferences of the participants – by implication, some form of compromise. In this sense, compromise is virtuous, and especially in so far as it provides a 'best alternative to no agreement' (in the jargon BATNA) or is 'Pareto-optimal'; that is, the point at which no participant can achieve a better outcome than the one available.

Consensus is also vital in so far as it means an agreement by all participants to accept the resulting compromise (Buzan, 1981; Steinberg, 2002). Consensus may depend either on a rule of formal unanimity, under which specific assent has to be delivered by each participant to each outcome, or on a procedural consensus to follow a different decision rule, such as majority voting. In the latter case, consensus is built around the decision rule; it permits the enforcement of results to which some participants have not assented specifically. The maintenance of consensus around a majority rule is a tougher requirement than unanimity, but may be offset by the greater volume of results, in that compromises are expedited. But to use Roger Fisher's term, everything depends on making a proposition 'yesable' to as many participants as possible (Fisher *et al.*, 2003).

In a multilateral forum, coalition-building is a typical pattern, under both unanimity and majority decision rules. Coalitions simplify complex negotiations by reducing the range of alternative options, and by identifying the strength or weakness of particular groups of supporters or opponents of a proposed settlement. Coalitions may be recurrent or *ad hoc*, strategic or tactical, issue-specific or widely based, predictable or unpredictable. The longer-established a negotiating forum is, the more likely it is that coalitions will take on some repetitive characteristics and will in turn become an embedded feature of the forum.

Much then depends on how consistent the behaviour is of individual participants. In the construction of coalitions, some participants may become 'pivotal players' – that is, particularly and repeatedly necessary to construct a 'winning coalition' or 'minimum win-set'. Pivotal players are not necessarily those with the most obvious gross power in the negotiation. On the contrary, the literature on domestic governing coalitions repeatedly stresses the disproportionately high leverage that 'small' players may exercise, precisely because it is their otherwise marginal weight that tips the balance between a winning and a losing coalition (Browne and Franklin, 1973; Schofield and Laver, 1985).

One essential element in such a context is the scope for devising side-payments. These may not relate at all to the main issues in the negotiation, but provide, through some additional 'currency', the means to buy the support of participants who would otherwise be opposed to, or agnostic about, the main issues. It is typically argued that 'small' players will sell their support in return for side-payments, and thus that the 'larger' players need to carry suitable currency in their pockets in order to increase their leverage.

Notions of reciprocity are pertinent to the scope for and definition of compromise and the basis for exchanging costs and benefits (Axelrod and Keohane, 1985; Keohane, 1986). Reciprocity implies that the negotiators can extract comparable gains and share comparable costs. The more narrowly-drawn a negotiating forum, in terms of issues and participants, the more often reciprocity will be 'specific' – that is, precisely defined and calculable – and the more it will be subject to pressures from policy influencers for tight definitions of negotiating positions.

Where a negotiating forum is broadly based, in terms of issues and participants, the opportunity is greater for reciprocity to be 'diffuse' – that is, to embrace a wider range of elements as potential costs and benefits, and to incorporate less tangible factors and appeals to the welfare of wider constituencies as potential beneficiaries. Here, too, time considerations are pertinent. Specific reciprocity is often subject to a tight definition of the timescale over which benefits are to be extracted and costs levied. Diffuse reciprocity permits more generous assumptions of timescales for costs and benefits to emerge, for corollary agreements to be added, and for promises to pay later. Diffuse reciprocity also draws in factors to do with collective interests and collective obligations, thus sometimes including points about the relationships between participants, and the way in which these are structured and institutionalized. Thus the 'shadow of the future' (Keohane, 1986) and anticipated future gains, including matters of setting as well as substance, can be factored into the preferences of participants and so projected to relevant policy constituencies.

The European Union as a distinctive negotiating forum

Key features

We can now extrapolate from this general introduction those features of negotiation that characterize the EU as a forum. The EU is *par excellence* a recurrent forum in which, as we have seen in earlier chapters, there is a repeated rhythm of meetings, more intense in some policy sectors than others, but typically involving participants from across the member states. There have been repeated investments in efforts to consolidate the setting, its institutional rules and operating conventions, both by explicit treaty reform and by more informal adjustments of procedures. Within this highly regularized setting, the behaviour of the participants is conditioned by the way that the rules and procedures operate in practice. Various devices have been invented to tie future behaviour to previous agreements. The codification of the *acquis communautaire* illustrates this clearly, as a device for setting the parameters of precedent and the agreed boundaries of discussion.

As regards numbers, the EU is an example of restricted multilateralism. It has strong 'club rules' to define its membership. On each occasion at which enlargement of the membership has been under discussion, there has been a debate about the trade-off between an increase in numbers at the table and the feasibility of retaining the intimacy of the restricted membership. In the EU context it was also argued by Reinhard Rummel (1982) that much of the cement of multilateralism was provided by intimate and structured bilateral relations. His term for this is 'multiple bilateralism'. The recent enlargement may tip the EU over the boundary into extended multilateralism, and may also undermine the accompanying cement of supportive bilateralism. As we have suggested elsewhere in this volume, it is too early to have definitive evidence on this widely articulated concern.

The EU is a clear example of a multi-issue forum. It started with an initially limited policy scope, but has steadily developed to include a very wide range of policy domains. Its range is very much wider than most international regimes, and than other groupings for regional integration elsewhere in the world. Thus the member governments have to consider their EU negotiating objectives across a range of policy domains simultaneously, whether by testing the ground for balancing 'package deals' (within or across policy sectors), or by taming the domestic pressures to be maximalist on all subjects. Indeed, one of the features of EU negotiations is that member governments often accept 'satisficing' rather than 'optimizing' outcomes – that is, they make judgements about relative costs and benefits across a range of issues rather than absolute costs and benefits issue by issue. Reaching judgements of this kind is a primary purpose of the national coordination procedures in each member state.

The EU also operates through multiple layers of negotiation. Negotiations depend on satisfying a variety of national, sub-national and transnational players, and the negotiations apparently concentrated in the Council are susceptible to a large number of actual or would-be policy influencers. These multiple layers involve, on the one hand, pluralist processes within each member state, and, on the other, many processes through which influences are transferred from other member states or from transnational actors. Of course, these include the continuous exchange with and through the Commission, the European Parliament and other EU and EU-related bodies.

Table 11.1. summarizes these differences between the EU and other forms of international forum. It indicates that, on several dimensions, the EU is different in kind from other international negotiating forums. This might lead to the expectation that the decision mode in the EU

Table 11.1   *Types of negotiating forums, with examples*

Scope / Participants	Single issue	Multi-issue	Wide scope
Bilateral	Channel Tunnel	Poland/Ukraine	France/Germany
Restricted multilateral	European Space Agency	Nordic Council G7/8	European Union
Extended multilateral	World Trade Organization	Council of Europe	United Nations

Setting / Intensity	Weak rules	Limited rules	Strong rules
Occasional or time limited	Channel Tunnel		
Medium frequency	Poland/Ukraine Council of Europe G7/8	Nordic Council World Trade Organization	
Very frequent	UN	European Space Agency	European Union

might also be distinctive, not least given the considerable powers under the various EU treaties for taking decisions by qualified majority voting (QMV). Yet, as we saw in Chapter 10, in practice compromise and consensus-building characterize negotiations in the Council, even though only some 30 per cent of decisions are technically subject to a formal rule of unanimity. Rather than having regular recourse to the use of QMV on other issues, in practice a variety of techniques for developing consensus have evolved.

First-wave analyses

Much of the analytical literature about the EU hangs on the judgement as to whether a distinctive negotiating process has developed in and around the Council. Many of those involved in establishing the European Communities (EC) in the 1950s and 1960s believed that they were innovators, creating a new dynamic of negotiation among the participants that would be clearly different in character and results from other international organizations. This came to be called by many the 'Monnet method', a phrase that recurs in the vocabulary of practitioners in the EU institutions (Wallace, 1996). In response, a new literature developed in which the central bone of contention was precisely about whether indeed the EU was so distinctive in practice that it merited its own specific theoretical analysis (Rosamond, 2000).

Broadly three lines of interpretation emerged about the nature of the experiment. *Realists* took the view that nation-states would remain the key actors, with governments determining their negotiating preferences in the last resort on core issues of 'state interest' (Hoffman, 1966). Other interests and actors might intrude, but were likely to be influential only on 'low politics' issues. The *transactionalists* came from the bottom up; they argued that the primary requirement was to build a sense of 'community', based on a dense, extensive and sustained level of social, economic and political interchange between the participants (Deutsch *et al.*, 1957). Only then would a fruitful pattern of transnational negotiation be achieved, with their array of transactions defined with reference to that sense of shared community.

It was, however, the *neo-functionalists* who developed the argument that the Community method was special (Haas, [1958] 2004); Lindberg, 1963). They highlighted those features of the Community that would be conducive to agreements, and their preservation or extension. They argued that the key interactions were among specific political and economic elites, in and around the institutions of the EC, especially the Council and the Commission. In their view, Community negotiation was a dynamic and fluid process, in which participants' preferences were amenable to redefinition, according to a range of both political and economic factors, and could not be aligned neatly with predictable national positions, thus providing scope for coalitions to be struck across national boundaries. This notion of a distinctive 'Community method' has remained a recurrent element in the discussion of negotiating behaviour in the EU. It included an emphasis on a series of 'package deals', both within and between issue areas (Gerbet and Pépy, 1969), as well as the assertion that compromises could vary from those based on rather minimalist definitions of shared interests to those founded on expansive definitions of shared interests, some of which might be about anticipated future gains as well as immediate interest satisfaction (thus 'forward-linkage' and the notion that agreement on issue X today might 'spill over' into a willingness to discuss issue Y tomorrow). In this way, the participants would come to acquire an interest in the maintenance of the forum itself; they would be 'locked in' like enmeshed cogs (the idea of '*engrenage*'), and socialized by the intensity and rewards of their interaction. Over time, nationally based participants could develop loyalties to the transnational arena, in so far as it appeared to deliver worthwhile results.

The difficulty came with the extension of the neo-functionalist argument to assert that supranationalism would, or could, displace intergovernmentalism as the predominant mode. This argument encountered two particular objections. One was that the results of Community negotiation were very uneven. On some policy issues the Council agreed common rules and even extended them, while in other policy areas progress in the Council was negligible or nil. A second objection was that stubbornly defended and nationalist positions seemed to be able to derail the process rather easily, as the awkward intrusions of General de Gaulle and later Margaret Thatcher in particular seemed to demonstrate. The realists recaptured the apparently persuasive arguments, leaving the analytical ground to be dominated by intergovernmentalism, modest transnationalism and issue-specific studies (Webb, 1983).

Second-wave analyses in response to varied practice

Much of the early hard evidence on negotiation in the then European Communities came from the fields of agricultural and trade negotiations. Over time, however, it became possible to build up a more nuanced picture, which revealed considerable variation in the patterns of negotiating practice. Thus, in the 1980s, European-level policy-making spread into a wide spectrum of regulatory domains, notably with the agreement to create the single European market by 1992. In order to facilitate the achievement of the latter, the Single European Act (SEA) extended the use of QMV by the Council. In the same period, the Council found itself much more involved in (re)distributive bargaining over the raising of revenue and the development of spending programmes. In practice, unanimity was required for reaching agreement, and even where QMV was, in theory, the decision rule, it was hard to activate. These two arenas (regulation and redistribution) demonstrated quite distinctive negotiating patterns, the former more consensual and more resonant of the neofunctionalist paradigm, the latter more confrontational and more resonant of the realist paradigm.

New contributions to the analytical literature offered new kinds of explanation. Among the most cogent expositions of the difficulties of building agreement in the Council in the 1980s was the critique by Fritz Scharpf (1988, but first circulated in German in 1983) of the 'joint-decision trap', which he used to explain a paradox of European integration: 'frustration without disintegration and resilience without progress'. He stressed the *de facto* insistence on unanimity, drew parallels with *Bund/ Länder* negotiations inside West Germany, and sought much of his empirical evidence in the fate of the common agricultural policy (CAP). He contrasted 'problem solving' and 'bargaining' as being different modes of negotiation, asserting that it was the prevalent 'bargaining' mode that condemned the EC to frustration and frequent deadlock. The overwhelming reliance on unanimity, and therefore acceptance of multiple vetoes, impeded policy change and encouraged the status quo as the default option and, in the case of the CAP, thus preserved an inefficient policy. Vested interests could, and did, inhibit policy change and articulated opposition through their 'captured' governments. Politicization was chiefly revealed in threats of defection, most vocally by General de Gaulle and Mrs Thatcher, each of whom forced their accommodation by other partners. Constituencies of support for both CAP reform and for other policy initiatives could thus not be mobilized effectively through the bargaining process of the EC. Thus negotiation was more an exercise in individualist (occasionally confrontational) bargaining than in joint problem-solving which, in any case, would need to be underpinned by some strongly-held and clearly-shared common beliefs or norms (Richardson, 1982).

Scharpf provided a powerful assessment of the way certain kinds of negotiation proceeded in the Council. Many authors would agree that his analysis is frequently validated in negotiations on budgetary issues, notably both the big budgetary bargains and the overall allocations of expenditure under many major spending programmes (Allen, 2005; Laffan, 2000). This is hardly surprising, given the intense national positioning over budgetary contributions and receipts. None the less, even here we should note that the Council and the European Council have developed procedural routines for mitigating the national positioning on a more consensual basis in the annual budgetary cycle through the development of inter-institutional agreements (IIAs) with the Commission and the European Parliament (Laffan and Lindner, 2005). In addition, and as part of the explanation for this, the move since the mid-1980s to multi-annual financial perspecives has limited the more confrontational moments of hard bargaining to periodic intervals of sharp disputation. The meeting of the European Council in June 2005, which stalled on the twin issues of CAP reform and budgetary contributions and receipts, is a clear example of such disputation, and a vivid illustration of the 'joint decision-trap'.

The picture painted in earlier chapters of this book shows that negotiation modes have differed between sectors throughout the history of the EU, following the lines of vertical segmentation that permeate the structures of the Council. Sometimes, too, the boundary between different modes has become blurred. Thus accounts of EU trade negotiations reveal the Council operating somewhere between a bargaining mode and a problem-solving mode in developing collective positions, especially in the context of the GATT (General Agreement on Tariffs and Trade)/WTO (Meunier, 2000; Meunier and Nicolaidis, 1999; Smith, 2005; Woolcock, 2005) Significantly, the Council became particularly productive in developing regulatory legislation, leading Majone (1996) to argue that the EU institutional system was particularly well fitted for generating transnational regulation, in particular with recourse to ECJ (European Court of Justice) jurisprudence and the member states' willingness to delegate regulatory powers to the Commission as 'fiduciary' (Majone, 2000). In contrast, he argued, the EU lacked the accountability and legitimacy mechanisms needed for engaging in successful (re)distibutive bargaining.

Scharpf (1994a) put it a different way by stressing that the Council was more adept at developing mechanisms of 'negative' integration than at adopting measures of 'positive' integration. The former was more to do with removing some elements of contradictory national regulatory barriers, while the latter demanded a much higher threshold of agreement among the member states, on both principles and practice, to permit more interventionist measures. Leibfried (2005) makes a similar argument about the way in which social policy has developed, in particular through the adoption of decisions that subject the provision of social services in a broad sense to market mechanisms rather than by the development of active collective policies.

Other factors also help to explain why no single account of the process was entirely accurate. Contextual and contingent factors, both economic and political, clearly had important impacts on the climate of Council negotiations. During the 1970s, for example, EC negotiators had to contend with two major disturbances. The economic recession found the EC without either the pre-defined set of policy instruments or the shared policy paradigm on which to base EC-level problem-solving. The first enlargement in 1973 meant that the Council had to accommodate new, and as yet 'unsocialised', members within its codes of behaviour and operating conventions. The United Kingdom (UK), in particular, had a distinctly wobbly commitment to the setting, as well as a set of demands for substantive changes to current EC policies, and a domestic base marked by contestation on European issues (George, 1994; Wallace, 1997). Thus there were distinguishable new factors of friction and instability within the Council.

These examples highlight the relevance of common norms, values or beliefs in the Council as a prerequisite for building agreement, and for promoting not only positional bargaining but also a form of collective problem-solving – up to a point at least. The initial adoption of the CAP benefited from a shared policy paradigm about the welfare of farmers (Rieger, 2005). Since 1973 this paradigm has been contested and only partly modified by efforts at CAP reform. Similarly, the development of the single market was underpinned by a shared paradigm about market liberalization (Young, 2005). However, uneven progress with the single market has shown the limits to the shared paradigm – more present in the liberalization of goods and capital markets, less present for service provision or labour mobility. The eventual decision to go ahead with economic and monetary union (EMU) in the form agreed in the Treaty on European Union reflected a shared paradigm on a particular form of single currency regime, although it has not extended to the parallel negotiations on economic and fiscal policies (McNamara, 2005). Even in politically sensitive areas of 'high policy', such as the common foreign and security policy (CFSP), and justice and home affairs (JHA), elements of a shared set of norms and beliefs have become more evident in recent years, but again more at the meso levels of policy development and less at the macro levels.

Thus, in all these policy fields in various ways, we can see that, where a shared paradigm or epistemic community predominates, these help to shape the debates in the Council in the direction of collective decisions on the basis of convergent preferences and of adaptations to the procedures needed to develop policies. Where underlying paradigms and preferences remain divergent, on the other hand, negotiations have a more confrontational character. In addition, when looking at both ministerial and official levels of negotiation, many authors comment that patterns of socialization also play an important part in underpinning a sense of community and shared responsibility among negotiators (*Journal of European Public Policy*, 2000; Lewis, 2003, 2005; Tallberg, 2003, 2004; Elgström and Jönsson, 2005).

We can also observe stagnation and contestation in other policy sectors where there are differing national preferences, differing policy paradigms and weak socialization of the relevant policy-makers. The Lisbon economic reform agenda and the development of the European social model(s) are clear examples (Rhodes, 2005; Sapir *et al.*, 2004). The earlier policy agenda on economic and welfare issues benefited from a broad domestic policy consensus within many EC countries, linked to a kind of Christian Democrat/Social Democrat collusion at both national and European levels of governance (Lindberg, 1963). Interestingly, General de Gaulle and Mrs Thatcher stood on different political ground in important respects. This consensus eroded in the early 1970s, was replaced by different elements of consensus in the mid-1980s, and in the 1990s reached some policy areas but not others.

Domestic political factors

Several domestic political factors influence behaviour in the Council, not only in the obvious sense that different national preferences must be confronted, but also in the sense that differences in the processes and political cultures of individual member states influence their approaches to negotiations. In recent years there has been a welcome enriching of the comparative literature on this dimension (Kassim *et al.*, 2000, 2001; Wessels *et al.*, 2003; Bulmer and Lequesne, 2005). These contributions represent a valuable complement to studies of individual countries, as well as providing a counterpoint to the literature on 'Europeanization' that has been much more focused on the impact of the EU process on individual countries than on the impact of national processes on the EU (Wallace, 1999).

The first factor is that, in some areas, domestic politics intrudes particularly sharply on the preferences of individual member states. Every member state approaches issues with a sharp national specificity, although concerns may alter as governments-in-office change. However, some such concerns are recurrent: monetary policy for the British, agriculture for the French; environment for the Austrians; cohesion for the Portuguese; corporate taxation for the Irish; fisheries for the Spanish; and so on. Such issues become particularly troublesome at awkward points in the electoral cycles of individual member states, and even more so in those where the EU dimension is subject more generally to political contestation. Moreover, it is clear from the various negative referenda on EU treaty reforms over the years that specific policy concerns can also feed broader contestation. Thus in the Council we can see something of a pattern of 'serial exceptionalism', according to which individual governments signal that a given issue is indeed a 'very important interest' to be accommodated, and hence one on which they will not accept being outvoted (see the discussion in Chapter 10 on the Luxembourg and Ioannina compromises). So we should not understate the persistence of obstacles to integrative bargaining.

The second factor is that, in some countries in some periods, the EU as such is contested and hence domestic politics spills over pervasively into the negotiating stances of the government. This dimension of EU bargaining is covered widely in the media but less sytematically in the scholarly literature, much of which consists of country case studies rather than cross-country comparisons. On this, however, the research being conducted by the 'Opposing Europe' network of scholars has useful contributions to make, not least in also adding to our understanding of new as well as old member states (Taggart and Szczerbiak, 2006a, 2006b).

The third factor is that agreement by governments in the Council is subject to formal as well as informal constraints inside member states. Thus the issue of the role of national parliaments in sanctioning EU policies has come much more to the forefront in many member states. For decades – or at least since the 1973 enlargement – there have been some member states in which, as was explained in Chapter 9, governments are tied by their national parliaments to 'Danish' procedures – that is, national requirements to consult the national parliament in advance on Council negotiating positions – sometimes accompanied by threats of non-ratification of Council agreements. As regards the day-to-day work of the Council, 'parliamentary scrutiny reserves' are not uncommon, and indeed more national parliaments are looking to strengthen their ability to exercise such influence. This goes a stage further with developments such as the 2005 decision in France to require national referendums to endorse future new members of the Union. In addition, in some member states, notably those with federal or quasi-federal systems of governance, the consent of the national government to a proposition in the Council may be conditional on its acceptance by another tier of sub-national government. Here, too, there is scope for further analysis to connect domestic ratification processes more systematically with the stances of governments in the Council on a comparative basis, building on the work of scholars such as Börzel (2003).

This interface between domestic and international politics needs tools from the fields of both international relations and comparative politics. European scholars and practitioners can thus draw on Robert Putnam's (1988) vocabulary of 'two-level games' to explore the ways in which national representatives capitalize on EU negotiations to improve their domestic influence. Similarly, George Tsebelis's (1990) 'nested games' argument can be used to identify ways in which the resolution of political arguments within countries may lead to otherwise apparently 'irrational' negotiating strategies within the EU. Individual member countries have varying forms of embedded pluralism in their domestic polities, whether these are habits of coalition government, structured dialogue on public policy with the social partners, a significant presence of publicly-owned industry (albeit shrinking with privatization), or the involvement of public or semi-public agencies dealing with utilities, environmental controls, social adjudication and so on, depending on the contours of the welfare state. These various features feed into the ways in which governments handle Council negotiations. Often, as Donald Puchala observed in 1977, policy moves in Brussels are frozen until relevant policy changes have been made in at least some key member states. Sometimes a resource gained through a European programme can stimulate a policy change or political advantage at home. Often the EU arena provides useful alibis, excuses or scapegoats for national politicians. Thus there is an intimacy, directness and tangibility to the impact of domestic politics on European negotiation and vice versa.

The wider analytical literature

The fast-growing literature theorizing European integration includes valuable studies assessing institutional behaviour within the EU as a whole, as well as other studies focused on the Council. Pollack (2005a, 2005b) provides a valuable and up-to-date survey of these studies, particularly with regard to the analysis of policy-making processes within the EU. Much of this literature is relevant to our focus on negotiations in the Council, bearing in mind our repeated contention that the EU is characterized more generally by a variety of policy modes and practices (H. Wallace, 2005). Increasingly, this literature addresses both theoretical and methodological issues, as well as empirical analysis, and we can observe the development of more frequent attempts at quantitative as well as qualitative analysis. In addition, there is a richer literature available on EU negotiations in a broad sense, with useful overviews and empirical analyses in a special issue of the *Journal of European Public Policy* (2000); and Elgström and Jönsson (2005), as well as the emerging results of the 'Decision-Making in the European Union' project (on which, see below).

The strands of literature that are of particular relevance include those that emphasize:

- the strategic preferences and relative power of EU member governments or member states;
- the role of ideas, processes of persuasion and socialization, and operating norms;
- the relevance of particular institutional processes and techniques of mediation; and
- the evolution of EU negotiations as a means of resolving challenges of contemporary – for some, 'post-modern' – governance.

These are not mutually exclusive categories and many authors refer to more than one of the factors listed above.

Strategic preferences and power

For many scholars, the strategic preferences of governments are the determinants of their negotiating behaviour, a view that was already established in the writings of Moravcsik (notably 1991 and 1998) and Scharpf (notably 1997). This view has been further articulated in the growing literature that develops strategic voting models to analyse the Council as an institution. Moravcsik locates his approach in a liberal institutionalist paradigm that attaches crucial importance to the pluralist domestic processes through which such strategic preferences are formed in pursuit of domestically rooted goals. He further argues that the most important Council and European Council decisions are grand strategic bargains in which the more powerful member states exercise particularly strong influence on the outcomes, because they are able to exercise greater power in the bargaining phase. His case rests on his correlation between the defined preferences of these key players and the actual outcomes of Council and European Council negotiations, rather than on a detailed account of the intricacies of Council meetings. In his account, other member states have smaller power resources and are less well placed to achieve their strategic preferences.

Scharpf similarly puts the spotlight on the rational and strategic objectives of governments. He draws on game-theoretic approaches to identify the different kinds of games that governments may play, depending on the issues at stake and the options available for potential settlements. Thus, in some cases they may play more cooperative games, and in others more confrontational ones depending on contexts, issue areas and so on. In addition he is at pains to demonstrate that an analysis informed by game theory can be developed to understand negotiations in which there are many participants and many issues. From an empirical point of view, this approach remains hard to operationalize, since it requires both extensive data and sophisticated methodological tools.

Since the early 1990s, there has been a proliferation of studies that seek to develop rational choice models of EU decision-making, and especially of how the Council works (see, for example, Budden and Monroe, 1993). Much of this literature has concentrated on stylized model-building, using formal methodologies and, as far as possible, rigorous quantitative techniques. This literature comes not only from scholars of political science, but also those from economics and mathematical sociology. Bueno De Mesquita and Stokman (1994) gathered together one of the first collections of essays aimed at probing the use of formal models to analyse the Council. This branch of analysis took a more empirical turn in a range of articles that focused on presumed voting behaviour in the Council. The analysis was empirical more in the terms of economics than of political science, in that the authors concentrated mainly on positing possible empirical explanations of plausible patterns of voting and coalition-building. This literature provoked a lively debate over the most suitable power indices or spatial models on which to develop appropriate and plausible methodologies (Felsenthal and Machover, 1997). The founding of the journal *European Union Politics* in 2000 provided an opportunity to encourage the development of this field. It has also been a venue for wider scientific debates – see, for example, Albert (2003) and the responses of Felsenthal *et al.* (2003).

One by-product of this literature was the strong questioning of the assumption that it was the larger member states' preferences that determined the eventual outcomes. Authors stressed the importance of the coralling of 'minimum win-sets' in order to rally a majority, an assumption which presumed that relative voting weights were very important, that smaller member states could be highly 'pivotal' in constructing majorities, and that actual voting was practised. Indeed, a number of articles analysed the possible impacts of, first, the EFTA (European Free Trade Association) enlargement of the EU in the mid-1990s and, second, the more ambitious enlargement of the mid-2000s, which would bring a good many small member states into the EU (Hosli, 1994; Widgrén, 1994; König and Bräuninger, 2004).

The appearance of this literature coincided with practitioners' discussions about how the voting rules and relative voting weights of member states might need to be adapted to cope with enlargement. Indeed, several delegations went to the intergovernmental conference (IGC) that drafted the 2001 Treaty of Nice carrying spreadsheets that could model alternative scenarios. It should be emphasized that these studies were driven not by empirical data derived from the inner debates in the Council or evidence on actual voting behaviour, but rather by externally derived assumptions about plausible voting positions, such as relative wealth or poverty. Moreover, as we have argued elsewhere in this volume, no single set of factors will easily explain why votes are cast in one way or another when they are called. Hence, for example, Richard Baldwin (1994) in our view over-simplified the likely voting positions of the old EU members on issues relating to eastern enlargement by understating the political dimension. There is a wider issue here about how to establish ingredients of power that go beyond mathematical voting weights.

As data started to become available on actual records of voting in the Council (see Chapter 10), so the literature took another turn and became better grounded in evidence rather than stylized assumptions. Thereafter, studies were produced which brought together the systematic analytical techniques of formal modelling with the then available voting records. This led scholars into a debate about the plausible core explanations for the observed patterns of voting, and possible explanations for the bargaining that lay behind the votes. Thus, Mattila and Lane (2001), in a careful analysis, highlighted the persistence of 'unanimity' (in our language 'consensus') as a procedure, and argued that larger member states were more likely to be 'no-sayers' than were the smaller ones. Kauppi and Widgrén (2004) sought to correlate voting power with EU budgetary positions (although without acknowledging the reliance on unanimity in the Council for budgetary packages). A number of others also explored the budgetary power issue.

More recently, Mattila (2004) argued that voting patterns were influenced by both the traditional left-right cleavage and the 'independence versus integration' dimension. This debate did not take place on level ground. On the one hand, some hard data were indeed available, but on the other, the data were incomplete and the conclusions drawn rested on unproven assumptions about the practice of explicitly contested voting and neglected the extent to which consensus-building remained a strong behavioural pattern within the Council, even on issues technically open to the use of QMV. The availability of more extensive data now provides an opportunity to revisit the analysis. Heisenberg (2005) stresses the persistence of consensus as an informal procedure, and hence contests the utility of rationalist-institutionalist analyses. Her analysis, based on a slightly less complete data set than the one on which this volume draws, reaches very similar conclusions to those we reported in Chapter 10.

In the meantime, however, some of the scholars in the field had embarked on a major new collective research project to dig beneath the surface of EU Council negotiations. A large data set was compiled for the project on 'Decision-Making in the European Union' (DEU) by a network of European scholars. This has examined a body of sixty-six legislative proposals current in 1999/2000 through a series of some 150 structured interviews with key informants, and then coded the answers in such a way as to facilitate careful cross-case analysis. The results of this ambitious undertaking are reported in a special issue of *European Union Politics* (March 2004), Thomson *et al.* (2004), Thomson *et al.* (forthcoming), and a plethora of other articles. This project has the strong merit of having drawn together qualitative and quantitative methods of analysis in an effort to produce a more rounded picture of bargaining patterns and outcomes, and covering informal processes as well as formal ones. None the less, controversies as to how to interpret this and subsequently gathered data will no doubt continue. Thus Zimmer *et al.* (2005) contend that the DEU data confirm that the key cleavage is redistributive and north–south, while König and Proksch (2005) emphasize instead the importance of establishing policy preferences on specific issues in order to ascertain how exchanges of position facilitate agreements.

Ideas, persuasion, socialization and operating norms

With the constructivist turn in studies of the EU, we have seen an increasing emphasis in the literature on ideas, norms and beliefs both influencing how the EU works and what it is decided that the EU should do (*Journal of European Public Policy*, 2000; Christiansen *et al.*, 2001; Risse, 2004; Wiener and Diez, 2004). At various points in this volume, we have argued that these factors do indeed have an impact on issues of both procedure and substance. Constructivists argue vigorously that not only formal rules, but also informal norms, shape the identities and preferences of the actors involved. This approach seeks, of course, to challenge those who favour explanations of EU decision-making that view the actors involved as rational utility-maximizers. As Pollack (2005a, 2000b) argues, a good deal of progress has been made in the search for fruitful ways of drawing on constructive analysis that might complement rather than overturn rationalist explanations (Jupille *et al.*, 2003). None the less, much remains to be done by way of solid empirical testing and more closely argued studies. Moreover, it may well be the case that constructivist arguments will turn out to be more compelling as explanations of other phases in the EU policy and decision-making processes than those that take place deep inside the Council or the European Council. More studies are needed of the kind conducted by McNamara (1998) or Quaglia (2004), which aim to demonstrate that the accumulation of shared norms held by an epistemic community made the EMU project viable, and in a field typically regarded as a hard case of 'high politics' and contested bargaining.

By far the most systematic attempt to relate this literature and its approach to the EU Council is the work of Lewis (1998a; 2002; 2003), based on a thorough empirical investigation of Coreper (the Committee of Permanent Representatives to the European Union), using careful qualitative analysis. His work has two key features. One is the detailed account of the very important and continuing role of Coreper in building agreements to which ministers in the Council subsequently assent; while the other is his assessment of the processes of socialization at work among this rather special group of national officials whose full-time jobs in Brussels consist of oiling the machinery of the Council. He contends, rather convincingly, that these processes of socialization play a very important role in shaping attitudes and behaviour, and that this 'success' goes a good way to explaining the continuing bias at ministerial level in favour of consensual methods rather than confrontational ones. He reaches these conclusions while also accepting that these same officials retain characteristics deriving their roles as professional representatives of their governments.

Other studies have looked at other Council committees or working groups that bring together national officials from the member states to prepare the work of the Council (van Schendelen, 1996; Beyers and Dierickx, 1998; Trondal and Veggeland, 2003). These studies, often using quantitative as well as qualitative techniques, have reached somewhat different conclusions. They largely suggest that the weight of European socialization in the formation of the preferences of national officials is rather lower than the influence of their national professional orientations, although in some cases there may be a pull from a strong and shared functional or policy preference. Further work on other such cohorts of national officials would help in the mapping of these patterns more thoroughly.

Institutional processes and techniques

We have laid much stress in this volume on the importance of institutional processes and techniques, and their place in shaping the negotiation processes of the Council. Voting procedures are covered in detail in Chapter 10, and the analytical literature on these was indicated earlier in this chapter. As regards other techniques, much of the literature consists of thick description rather than more analytical or theoretical studies. In particular, we have only incomplete accounts of mediation techniques used within the Council. Thus, for example, it would be valuable to have an analytical assessment of the way that references are made to the *acquis communautaire* as a device for resolving problems or disagreements. It would also be helpful to have systematic analyses of the ways in which techniques of both specific and diffuse reciprocity are operationalized.

As regards the role of the presidency, recent contributions to the literature have begun to provide a more theoretically informed picture. Tallberg (2003) discusses the agenda-shaping powers of the presidency, drawing *inter alia* on theories of bargaining as well as on extensive qualitative research. Interestingly, while recognizing the limits to the influencing capacity of the presidency, he argues that the evidence shows both that presidencies have real opportunities to shape the Council agenda in various ways, and that this capacity may have increased as that of the Commission has declined in recent years – despite the speed of the six-monthly rotation. In a subsequent article, Tallberg (2004) analyses the brokerage or mediation role of the presidency. He argues that presidencies can make use of an array of formal and informal resources to steer the Council or European Council towards complex agreements and, under certain conditions, away from negotiation failures. His case studies of deeply contentious issues also show that even governments in the presidency with very strong direct interests at stake can sometimes broker widely-based compromise agreements, as in the case of the agreement on Agenda 2000 during the German presidency in 1999. Lewis (2005) valuably complements this analysis in arguing that the 'double-hatted' permanent representatives (having both national and European roles) play an important part in facilitating agreements through a form of 'supranational entrepreneurship'. These analyses challenge the conventional wisdom of those practitioners who have argued that the rotating Council presidency represents a source of procedural weakness in the Council.

Challenges of contemporary governance

Of course, a good deal of the literature on EU decision-making ranges much more broadly than our tight focus on negotiation and bargaining, and hence draws on quite different concepts and literature for their analyses. Thus authors such as Joerges and Neyer (1997) and others focus on deliberation as the heart of the process. Others, such as Peterson (1995) or Kohler-Koch and Eising (1999) emphasize the EU process as one of networked governance, and the EU as an arena through which national policy-makers are devising collective and networked processes to address the challenges of contemporary politics and policy-making. Generally speaking, studies of this kind do not separate out the intra-Council processes from the broader inter-institutional or multi-level exchanges in which the Council is embedded.

The current phase of EU development seems to have reached a moment of 'critical juncture' in which at least three 'disturbing' factors are present simultaneously: large-scale enlargement, with the arrival in 2004 of ten new member states to be socialized, and the possibility of a further two in 2007; contestation of the EU as such in a number of member states, as evidenced in the problems encountered in the ratification of the Constitutional Treaty in 2005; and missing shared paradigms on some key policy issues, notably economic, in a context of disappointing economic performance in some member states. It is to be expected that the combination of these factors will permeate the climate of Council negotiations, and will provide challenging material for current and future scholars of the process.

Chapter 12

Conclusions

This study has set out how the Council operates (Chapters 1–5); its interactions with other European Union (EU) institutions (Chapters 6–8); its engagement with the political processes of the member states (Chapter 9); when and how voting takes place (Chapter 10); and the character of Council negotiations (Chapter 11). In this final chapter, we draw some conclusions about the nature of the Council, its performance as an institution and the implications for European political integration. These are set in the context of change – a larger membership of the Union, evolving policy tasks, and differences in the institutional patterns. The Constitutional Treaty (CT), signed in Rome in October 2004 and, at the time of writing, in limbo following ratification problems, would make further changes to the rules governing the Council. Just as important, however, are informal developments of practice in determining the behaviour and impact of the Council.

The Council remains the fulcrum of the decision-making and legislative processes of the EU. This reflects the stubborn determination of member governments in the EU to maximize their involvement in framing the decisions and shaping the legislation that would have a bearing on their polities (Maurer, 2003b). Yet, to view the importance of the Council as the victory of intergovernmentalism over supranationalism, or to expect the Council to be able to 'run' the EU, is to misunderstand the institutional constellation of the EU. The Council shares and diffuses power between countries, between different kinds of interests and constituencies, and between national and EU levels of governance. The Council cannot act alone, but is dependent on intricate relationships with other EU institutions. Since the mid-1990s, however, these relationships have changed a good deal. The European Parliament (EP) has gained considerable power as co-legislator with the Council, the Commission has lost ground in what used to be the classic 'Council–Commission tandem', and the Council has gained a good deal more direct executive power in newer areas of EU collective policy-making. All these factors have made the Council both more interesting as an object of study and more diverse in its ways of operating.

The period since the mid-1990s has seen a massive change in the amount of information available about the Council. The combination of the new transparency rules and the Internet have provided access to detailed material on what the Council produces by way of output, how it operates, and who is involved in its activities. The specialist observer, at least, can now follow the work of the Council much more closely than before, and can build up a picture based on extensive empirical data. However, by no means everything is in the public domain. Parts of the Council's inner workings remain in the shadows, accessible only by interviews and not via the Internet. Practitioners in the Council have also continued to be adept at protecting access to what they do – by the tactical classification of documents, by reaching informal agreements rather than adopting formal acts, and by finding venues for negotiation other than official meeting rooms. Moreover, there is little evidence to suggest that the new transparency of the Council, driven mainly by nervousness at public complaints about its previous secrecy, has in practice improved the accountability of the Council or made it better understood by ordinary EU citizens.

However, the extent of material available now means that much greater care has to be taken in making general statements about how the Council works, since there is so much more evidence to hand and less excuse than hitherto for loose assertions. In Chapter 10, we have been able to illustrate this by collating an extensive set of data on explicitly contested voting in the Council on decisions that have been adopted. However, increased transparency does not provide comparable information, either on defeated proposals or on practices of informal and indicative voting used to test whether there is a qualified majority of support for a proposition or a potential blocking minority against it. For these occurrences, we continue to be reliant on case studies and qualitative interviews.

The evolving functions of the Council

Throughout this volume, we have insisted that the Council's functions are diverse, and indeed that they have become more diverse (Wallace, 2002). No simple analogies can be made with the workings of institutions in a national political system; there is no straightforward analogy to be found in terms of one or other federal model of government; and there is no clear separation of powers among the EU's institutions, or between the EU and national institutions. Instead, powers, functions and patterns of behaviour overlap and evolve: they differ between and within policy domains. The Council currently has four main functions:

- the *legislative* function: that is, developing Union legislation, usually prompted by the Commission, and generally iteratively with the Parliament as co-legislator;
- the *executive* function: that is, taking direct responsibility for exercising executive power on behalf of the Union in some key policy areas and on some key issues;
- the *steering* function: that is, the devising of big bargains that orient the future work of the Union: and
- the *forum* function: that is, providing an arena through which the member governments attempt to develop convergent national approaches to one or other policy challenge in fields where the Union does not have clear collective policy powers.

The Council as legislature

A big change since the mid-1990s has been the way in which the Council has had to learn to share legislative power with the EP (see Chapter 8). More and more areas of day-to-day legislation now depend on co-decisions between the Council and the EP, and the CT, if implemented, would make this even more often the normal procedure for adopting Union legislation. Innovative political and administrative routines have been developed in both institutions to make this new partnership, albeit one with adversarial features, work relatively smoothly. On the Council side, it is Coreper I (the Deputies' formation of the Committee of Permanent Representatives – see Chapter 3), together with the Council Secretariat staff, that has borne the main responsibility for engaging the Council in the processes of considering and refining amendments to draft legislation. They work closely with officials from the legislative coordination directorate of the EP Secretariat, and key chairs and *rapporteurs* from the relevant EP committees.

A debate continues among both practitioners and outside observers seeking to assess the relative influence of the Council and the EP in this iterative process. It is rather rare for dramatic, head-on confrontations to take place between the two institutions, but now and again a particular issue becomes the focus of strong disagreement – as, for example, the issue of whether the Union should adopt measures to provide data on passengers travelling to the United States (USA), which went to the European Court of Justice (ECJ) for adjudication in the autumn of 2004. Generally, the two arms of the legislative authority strive to find ways of reaching an accommodation. Involved practitioners, notably officials in Coreper I, stress that this has become a huge part of their work, since they deal with those areas of Council business with the most direct legislative content. They also emphasize just how testing it is to engage with the EP on co-decision, a process that puts them under greater pressure than the other areas of their work. It also subjects them to an exposure to scrutiny that is, by and large, not felt by Coreper II (the ambassadors – see Chapter 3), which works mainly on issues not subject to detailed and forensic exchanges with either European or national parliamentarians.

None the less, some commentators (such as Farrell and Héritier, 2003) have speculated that the prevalence of co-decision is prompting evasive action within the institutional nexus of the Union. There are indications that more extensive use may be being made of alternative routes to reaching agreement on collective action, not by the formal and, in principle, transparent mechanisms for legislative co-decision, but rather through 'delegation' to other committee-based or informal consensus-building procedures.

During the 2002–3 Convention on the Future of Europe (CFE), it was proposed, notably by one of the Convention's vice-presidents, Giuliano Amato, that a new 'legislative' formation of the Council should be created. It would meet routinely in public, would highlight the core legislative responsibilities of the Council, and would help to improve accountability in the EU system. The proposal was not adopted, with the result that, for the present, the only 'public' sessions of the regular Council configurations are one of two types: either general policy debates; or, in the context of the co-decision procedure, ministerial reactions to important legislative proposals from the Commission and the final 'B' item debates on issues before they are finally adopted as 'A' points (also in public, and sometimes with deliberations). Since practitioners readily admit that the real Council negotiations take place well away from these public forums, the issue of public scrutiny of the Council as a collective legislative body remains largely unresolved.

The Council as executive

The Council was always also an executive body, in the sense that it provided the key place for collective decisions to be reached on those policy issues not subject to clear Community competence, and not the subject of legislation in the form of regulations and directives. Since the 1990s, this executive function has also become a growing activity, as the EU has become so much more involved in developing common actions in new fields of increasingly collective or shared responsibility, notably in developing the non-monetary side of economic and monetary union (EMU), elements of the common foreign and security policy (CFSP) and the related European security and defence policy (ESDP), and the field of justice and home affairs (JHA).

As regards EMU, the picture is mixed. Ecofin (the Economic and Financial Affairs Council) has some legislative responsibilities, notably in fields such as financial services. However, it is also a kind of collective core executive responsible for developing policies to support EMU. Yet, in practice, this has turned out to be tricky. Since not all EU member states take part in the single currency regime of the euro, Ecofin has, for some purposes, been largely supplanted by the Euro Group, an as yet informal formation of ministers from the (currently) twelve countries who have adopted the euro as their national currency. Moreover, both Ecofin and the Euro Group lack clear powers to address the macroeconomic side of EMU, and there has been a running dispute over how far and on what terms the Stability and Growth Pact (SGP) can be made into an operational executive process for determining the Union's macroeconomic and fiscal policy stances. Some arrangements are in hand to strengthen the mandate of the Euro Group, now also with an elected president and deputy president, to provide more continuity and collective external representation, but as yet these changes are too recent for their real impact to be clear.

As regards foreign, security and defence policies, the picture is very different. In the period since the Secretary-General of the Council became the Union's High Representative, the executive and indeed operational functions of the Council have proliferated. The Union does indeed have elements of foreign policy capability. At the time of writing, the EU had seven 'special representatives' acting on behalf of the Union and reporting to the Council in addressing the problems of the former Yugoslavia, the South Caucasus, Afghanistan, the Palestinian conflict and Africa. The Council had also taken responsibility for managing several peace-keeping operations on behalf of the Union, including, in early 2005: Operation 'EUFOR–Althea (Bosnia and Herzegovina); EU Police Mission–EUPM (Bosnia and Herzegovina); EU Police Mission 'Proxima' (in the fomer Yugoslav Republic of Macedonia); and the EU Rule of Law Mission 'EUJUST–Themis' (Georgia). Even before the CT proposed the creation of an 'European external action service' (EEAS), the staff of the Council Secretariat was already carrying out many of the familiar functions of a diplomatic service in gathering information and developing the ingredients for shared policy interventions. Much of this work is also focused around the relentless press of meetings with external partners, both individually and in groups (see, for example, Box 5.3 in Chapter 5).

As regards JHA – here, too, there has been a spectacular growth in the executive role of the Council. In 2004 alone, the Council's website listed the 125 'texts adopted' over the year in this field, ranging from formal legislation to statements of position, but also significantly including many management decisions to implement Schengen and JHA policies. On the one hand, sufficient consensus had been reached for the 'communitarization' of some aspects of JHA within a form of shared Community-method decision-making between the Commission and the Council, including the possibility of using qualified majority voting (QMV) from January 2005. On the other hand, the fact that, on other topics, member states remained reluctant to accept clear Community competence by no means prevented them from accepting a collective frame of reference for taking policy development forward. The relevant services in the Council Secretariat had thus also acquired an operational orientation to their work, part of a wider phenomenon of the Secretariat moving beyond the management of the processes of deliberation to assuming quasi-operational functions (see Chapter 4).

The Council's steering function

The Council and the European Council play key roles in steering the Union, in setting guidelines for future developments, and in negotiating strategic bargains on issues of high policy. Since the 1990s, this role has gained in importance rather than diminished, in that there has been a particular concentration of strategic issues to be addressed regarding the future of the Union – the development of EMU, the periodic big budgetary bargains, the pursuit of new initiatives in foreign policy and JHA, the framing of enlargement policy, and iterative treaty reform. In particular, the Council and the European Council, reconstituted as an 'intergovernmental conference' (IGC – that is, as a gathering of the member governments to take strategic new decisions) have, in the ten years to 2005, managed three IGCs on treaty reform, leading to the Treaties of Amsterdam (ToA) and Nice (ToN) and to the CT (Beach, 2005).

The Council and the European Council have set the Union's policy on enlargement and, as an IGC, have negotiated accession – first, with the ten new member states which joined the Union in 2004, and then with Bulgaria and Romania, which signed Accession Treaties in April 2005. They continue to be involved in accession processes with already declared and accepted candidates (Croatia and Turkey), and there are other potential candidates in the wings. In addition, the considerable executive functions of the Council, identified above, have also brought the Council and the European Council into play more frequently as the most senior levels for strategic discussion on other issues, and for high-level meetings with external partners.

Behind these developments lies a more general trend (see Chapters 6 and 7). The European Council has taken on a greater importance in overseeing the development of Union policies (de Schoutheete and Wallace, 2002), and the European Commission has been through a period in which it has played less of a leadership role. How far this is a systemic trend as distinct from a contingent development is hard to judge. None the less, one key development in the discussions leading to the CT was the emphasis put upon reinforcing the capacity of the European Council. This led to the proposal to select a more 'permanent' president of that body, elected for two-and-a-half years.

This decision, subject to ratification of the CT, was propelled by a coalition of the larger member states, and based on the argument that the steering capacity of the European Council needed to be strengthened. Views vary enormously, both on the potential efficacy of this development and on its implications for the overall political architecture of the Union. Those who favour a strong role for the European Council tend to exaggerate their praise of its performance, while those who prefer a more classical Community method tend to play up its weaknesses, specifically the rather too *staccato* nature of its deliberations, and the fact that it is too disconnected from the routines of EU decision-making. Recent practice does not provide clear evidence for either case.

The Council as forum

The Council has always served as a forum for the discussion of issues that lay beyond agreed areas of competence and joint action. Thus dialogue in the Council has, over the years, been a mechanism for testing whether there was a consensus for enlarging the scope of collective endeavour. What started out as points of discussion over foreign policy, or later over justice and home affairs, prepared the ground for agreements to act together and, in some cases, to introduce specific treaty powers that would permit more extensive collaboration.

In recent years, however, a new element has come into play, namely the role of the Council as a forum for permanent dialogue in policy fields where there is very little prospect of collective powers being agreed. The clearest instance of this is the management of the Lisbon Strategy. Much of this is concerned with policy domains that remain clearly within the responsibility of member governments for domestic social, economic and fiscal policies. Yet, the clear connections of these domains to the performance of the overall European economy, with its very extensive interdependencies, have led to the Council itself now spending a great deal of its time comparing and contrasting national policy performances. Some of this discussion takes place in the often fraught Ecofin discussions about macroeconomic and fiscal policies. Other parts of the discussion on the Lisbon reform issues take place in the new Competitiveness Council and the 'spring' European Council. How this forum function will develop in the future is by no means clear. There are widely varying views among both practitioners and observers about the effectiveness of the Council in these kinds of areas in the absence of clear and agreed policy powers for the Union.

Images and reality: the core characteristics of the Council

The Council in the EU-12 developed several core characteristics that stayed remarkably consistent as the EU moved from twelve to fifteen members. Of course, a key question is how these characteristics have been, and will be, affected by the enlargement to twenty-five members, on which only a year of experience provides too little evidence to reach a clear judgement. These core characteristics include:

- the *institutional triangle*, through which the Council is locked into relationships with the Commission and the EP, albeit with variations between policy domains;
- the *sectoral organization* of the Council, as the persistent and deeply rooted way of organizing its work, albeit with reorganized configurations since 2002;
- a *bureaucratic method*, whereby national officials from member governments provide a multi-layered process of continuous negotiation;
- a *strongly consensual bias* in the approach to collective decision-making, with explicit contestation on adopted decisions being recorded on technical and practical issues rather than on highly politicized issues;
- *socialization and engrenage* as mechanisms for facilitating collaboration among governments in the Council, and between the Council and the other EU institutions; and
- *multiple rationales* as the bases for agreements, including interest-based calculations of potential costs and benefits, but also some shared values or paradigms, as well as the legacies of previous joint decisions.

The institutional triangle

The institutional configuration of the Union has altered, as the EP has become increasingly important in the Union's legislative processes. Thus, within the areas of clear Community competence (what used to be known as the 'first pillar'), there is a rather clear institutional triangle involving the Council, the Commission and the Parliament. Despite the persistent references by practitioners to the historic 'institutional balance', in practice there has been a significant rearrangement of powers and influence, in which the Commission has lost ground and become more dependent on how the Council and Parliament operate as the twin legislative bodies. Yet there are limits to the reach of this triangle. Within the arrangements for managing EMU, there is also an important fourth player – the European Central Bank (ECB).

In contrast, in the fields of foreign and security policies, and with regard to those parts of JHA that have not been communitarized, the Council is the central institutional player for the moment, given that, first, there is as yet less opportunity for the EP to constrain or to scrutinize the Council; second, that the Commission has not yet succeeded in establishing a clear role; and third, that the Council Secretariat has acquired some quasi-operational functions (Lavenex and Wallace,

2005; and W. Wallace, 2005). In these latter areas, there is an inherent inter-institutional tension rather than an institutional balance, which in turn limits the capacity of the Council to develop and sustain collective policies. None the less, the substantial increases in output from CFSP and JHA indicate that some ways have been found to navigate through the institutional ambiguities. The provisions of the CT would clarify some – but only some – of these tensions, since the drafters of the CT were not able to define a clear framework of institutional relationships outside the legislative arena.

Sectoral organization

Historically, the vertical segments of the Council, dealing with discrete sectors of policy, have been more productive than the mechanisms to determine overall policy or to coordinate between adjacent policy domains, thus allowing special interests much scope for pursuing their goals. Historically, the Council segments have also worked with the sectoral hierarchies for policy development in the Commission, and with the specialist committees in the EP. It remains to be seen how far the streamlining of Council configurations, introduced in 2002, will make a real difference to this historical pattern, in the first instance by altering practice within the Council, and secondly by altering the practices of its institutional interlocutors in the Commission and the Parliament (see Chapter 2). For the moment, it seems that only some of the new configurations have a clear identity and relative command of their fields of policy, and that these are, in practice, those that already had rather well-developed identities – notably the external relations formation of the General Affairs and External Relations Council (GAERC); Ecofin; the Environment Council; the JHA Council; and the Agriculture and Fisheries Council (although we should note that a good number of agricultural and fisheries issues in fact appear on the agendas of other configurations as 'A' points). The other new and specialist configurations (employment, social policy, health and consumer affairs – EPSCO; transport, telecommunications and energy – TTE; education, youth and culture – EYC; and internal market, industry and research – Competitiveness) do not yet seem to have found clear collective identities. Some recent efforts have been made to firm up the Competitiveness Council's identity, notably by ministers keen to press forward the Lisbon Strategy, but how well anchored this is remains a matter of discussion. In addition, we should note that the general affairs formation of the GAERC does not yet seem to have solved the coordination deficit in the Council.

A bureaucratic method

Those national representatives most involved in the Council are, as we saw in Chapters 3 and 9, not ministers, but national officials, whose views may or may not have been tempered by the political inputs of ministers, since national practices vary hugely. The Council consists of a hierarchy of committees in which the participants negotiate and bargain within and between different sectoral arenas at the levels of officials, ministers and prime ministers. Of course, issues move continually between levels. None the less, it remains the case that the majority of issues, including those with legislative impact, are in essence resolved by officials before being endorsed by ministers. On the one hand, this provides for a kind of functional efficiency, but on the other, it weakens political accountability through both national and European parliamentary channels, although the intensity of the co-decision procedure with the EP does increasingly subject relevant national officials to a new form of accountability. However, national practices remain hugely varied in terms of the extent to which the work of national officials in Council committees and working parties is scrutinized closely through national mechanisms.

A consensual bias

The Council is deeply consensual in its habits. Votes can be, and are, taken, but not all that often, and great efforts are made to accommodate the individual dissenter (see Chapters 10 and 11; also Heisenberg, 2005). Of course, arguments and fierce disagreements do occur in the Council, but the system operates so as to reduce the number of unresolved issues that go to ministerial level, and to concentrate the time of ministers on those issues where there is a plausible chance of agreement or where a practical deadline requires a decision to be reached. We note also that protracted marathon sessions (at least in the EU-15) have become less common than in earlier years, and that, in some Councils, retaining the interest of ministers and the presence at meetings of senior ministers has become something of a challenge. Our data in Chapter 10 show that explicit contestation of decisions that are formally adopted is concentrated in a few policy domains, notably agriculture, fisheries, internal market, and some health and safety issues. In both these and other areas, there is some indicative voting in meetings at official level on issues subject to a QMV legal base, but not in a form that we can pin down empirically and systematically. As the European Council has become even more institutionalized, it has developed some consensual routines of its own, as well as being the locus for trying to resolve big disagreements.

Socialization and engrenage

Embedded in informal practices, as well as rooted in formal procedures, there are forms of socialization and *engrenage* (as in the meshing-in of cog-wheels, denoting the process whereby national policy-makers become locked into the work of the EU), much on the lines long ago identified by the neo-functionalists (see Haas, [1958] (2004); Lindberg, 1963). Our study reveals that decision-makers in the Council, in spite of their national roots, become locked into the collective process, especially in areas of well-established and recurrent negotiation. This does not necessarily mean that the participants have transferred loyalties to the EU system, but it does mean that they acknowledge themselves in certain crucial ways as being part of a collective system of decision-making. There is now an identifiable cohort of decision-makers, albeit with primary affiliations to their member governments, who have specific common concerns and shared commitments to the collective arena.

The shared culture remains most evident in those bodies that meet most frequently – over the years, Coreper has been, and remains, the supreme illustration of this phenomenon. Whether or not this feature will remain so important in the enlarged EU (and perhaps soon to be enlarged further) remains at this stage necessarily a subject for speculation. Though these features fall well short of providing a strong form of executive power, they give the Council a collective identity, otherwise the Council would not have been able to generate the output that it has, and its members would not have established so firm a basis of mutual trust, both institutional and personal. Within this collective gathering, each individual government has a 'voice', its relative strength in part a reflection of the extent to which it, and its individual negotiators, retain the trust of its peers. These intangible factors are often more pertinent in the determination of outcomes than the formal weighting of member states' votes or the crude attribute of size. The three member states that joined the EU in 1995 seem to have been socialized relatively quickly into this process, and early evidence about the ten latest new members suggests that, to date, their participants in the Council and its committees have not disturbed the long established patterns of behaviour significantly.

Multiple rationales

Governments act in the Council on behalf of member states, using the vocabulary of 'national interests'. But many other factors come into play, symbols count as well as substance, and values and norms often make an identifiable difference to which outcomes emerge. The Council offers much scope for gamesmanship and skilled manipulation, as the participants seek advantage and press forward with their egotistical aims. Yet the sense of being partners in unavoidable collaboration makes mutual obligations necessary, and an atmosphere of collective trust an asset. The now extensive literature offering rational choice explanations of Council bargaining (discussed in Chapter 11), concentrates attention usefully on the way strategic preferences are devised and pursued, but takes too little notice of the informal, the idiosyncratic and the contingent, in which ideas as well as interests weigh in the reckoning (see Chapters 10 and 11). Both 'cosmopolitan' geopolitical concerns and the 'parochial' pull of local political territory sit alongside economic preoccupations in claiming attention and priority. We thus reject the notion that Council negotiations are exclusively interest-based. The games played are about the nature of cooperation, as well as about specific policy decisions, though the latter tend to be formulated much more explicitly and specifically than the former. Models of decision-making that neglect this wider context fail to characterize accurately the patterns of negotiation, over-emphasize a constricted set of interest-based preferences, and produce seriously distorted explanations of decision outcomes.

Of course, there is a continuous tension between the home affiliation and the pull of the collective forum, a tension that is much stronger for representatives from some member states than for others. The tension is least acute for those who have established, or benefited from, a high degree of congruence or complementarity between their 'home-based' policy preferences and those that form the basis of collective decision. This has been described (Jordan, 2002) as the difference between those who can 'upload' their practices into the EU process, and those who are repeatedly 'downloaders' of the practices of others. Not surprisingly, those who are most satisfied with the decisions of the Council are those who can make them 'fit' with their domestic contexts. However, congruence depends on symbols as well as on substance, and on the fit of ideas as well as the satisfaction of interests.

The development of the *acquis communautaire* (the whole range of principles, policies, laws, practices, obligations and objectives agreed within the EU) is very much the result of the embedding of member governments' preferences, which then becomes the collective property of the Council, as well as being pursued by the Commission and applied by the ECJ. The composition of the *acquis* is part ideas and part interests; it represents a form of collective patrimony. Interestingly, some insiders believe that the accession experience of the new member states, under which they have downloaded so many EU policy and legislative templates, may make them more ready supporters of future EU legislation than those old member states that fight to retain divergent and longer established domestic traditions.

The institutional performance of the Council

In our first edition, we commented that the Council was, in important respects, reaching the limits of performance as an effective organ of collective action. A combination of increasing membership (heterogeneity being as important as numbers), more controversial or difficult policy issues, and the charge of a legitimacy deficit, was bearing down on the Council, and was casting doubt on the performance of the European system of governance as a whole. This set of problems pervaded other European institutions and the way that both European and national institutions fed into the decision-making processes of the Council (Piris, 1994).

Almost a decade later, is the same judgement justified? In the intervening period, after all, the EU has been enlarged significantly, and a range of new policy initiatives has been put on the table. Some, notably EMU, have been implemented, and output in the areas of the CFSP and JHA has increased impressively. On the other hand, there are policy domains where achievements have been limited (many commentators would cite the Lisbon Strategy as an example), or where policy reforms have been stunted (agriculture and fisheries are both cases in point). The picture, therefore, is mixed, and not at all consistent across policy domains.

A system of governance by committee requires a high degree of procedural consensus to underpin substantive agreement and to sustain the decisions reached. The committee dynamic of the Council has, in the past, encouraged 'inclusive' behaviour – that is, efforts to pull as many members as possible into agreements, to promote coalitions and to accommodate individual members who are isolated. Much depends on prior preparatory work to pre-structure agreements, as Chapters 3 and 9 indicated, and reliable transmission systems are needed between the delegates of the member states and their domestic polities. Such conditions do not, however, facilitate the definition of clear strategic goals or radical policy change, and the price of accommodating the laggards and the reluctant is often paid in the appearance of ungainly compromise.

It is with these factors in mind that we comment on the institutional performance of the Council, based on three broad criteria:

- a judgement on how far Council activity has produced results (a kind of *productivity* evaluation);
- an overview of the correspondence between the policy tasks set before the Council and its substantive responses (a kind of *efficiency* audit); and
- a view of the extent to which the work of the Council is received as authoritative (a form of *legitimacy* test).

Productivity

The Council generates a considerable output in terms of both substantive and declaratory decisions, and often does so speedily (see Chapter 2). Within the fields of clear Community competence, its legislative output and its extensive record of negotiated agreements with third countries are comparable in volume to those of an established national government. The 1992 programme for the internal market provided the most precise test of the capacity of the Council to increase its legislative output. Its impressive response was helped, up to a point, by the more frequent evocation of the QMV rule – or, to be more precise, the overcoming of individual national vetoes by the knowledge that votes might be called. Insiders claim that 220 of the 260 or so relevant decisions were, in practice, agreed by consensus rather than on the basis of explicit voting. The volume of legislation diminished as the 1992 programme was set in place, and as European legislators drew back from 'hyperactivism' in the wake of the Maastricht Treaty ratification problems. In recent years, the legislative output of the Council (mostly in tandem with the EP) has stabilized at around 200 adopted pieces of legislation per year across policy domains (see Figure 2.2 in Chapter 2).

This slackening-off in the volume of output was as much a deliberate choice as a sign of declining capabilities to produce. In subsequent years, some member governments also argued, with some support from outside commentators (Majone, 2005), that the risk was of 'over-regulating' the internal market. Thus the British government, for example, argued that Council legislation should include 'sunset clauses' imposing a requirement to review rather than preserve *ad infinitum* specific items of market regulation. Indeed, in late 2004, there was a group of member governments arguing strongly against over-regulation of the internal market. According to this view, the quantity of legislation agreed is a misleading indicator of productivity. In other areas, Council business has maintained a steady rhythm, as we saw in Chapters 2 and 3. Newer entrants into the list include more consumer-related legislation on topics such as genetic modification and controls justified on the grounds of public health, although, as we noted in Chapter 10, these have often been contested in the Council.

The management of the Community budget provides another index of productivity. Annually, the three institutions that share budgetary responsibilities – the Council, the Commission and the Parliament – make expenditure appropriations through procedures based not only on treaty rules, but also on an inter-institutional agreement (IIA), and subject to periodic multi-annual financial perspectives on revenue and spending. This institutional process has proved remarkably 'robust' (Shackleton, 1990; Laffan and Shackleton, 1996, 2000; Laffan and Lindner, 2005). In contrast to earlier periods, the annual process now takes place remarkably smoothly, while the periodic financial perspectives are subject to tough and strategic bargaining in the Council and the European Council. The 2005 negotiations over the financial perspective for 2007–13 provided the first test of the ability of these two processes to stand up to the increased membership of the Union.

Interestingly, in the case of CFSP, output from the Council has increased and, in recent years, there has been a steady flow of declarations and coordinated positions, as well as occasional 'joint actions', despite the difficulties in developing EU policy *vis-à-vis* the Yugoslav wars, or the sharp arguments over the issue of intervention in Iraq. Indeed, the lists of agreements of one kind or another under CFSP reveal the emergence of a kind of routine and rhythm of productive activity. Policies towards Afghanistan, Russia and the Western Balkans, like that in the 1990s towards South Africa, are apt examples. Moreover, the EU has now agreed to take direct responsibility for a collective peace-keeping role in Bosnia, as well as several other 'operations', and is also in the process of setting up battle-groups capable of intervening in hot spots.

In this field, as indeed in the case of the external economic relations of the EU, achieving results does not lie only in the hands of EU decision-makers. Thus, for example, the absence of movement in the Doha Development Round of the World Trade Organization (WTO) was for reasons more external to the EU than internal. Moreover, many external policy decisions depend on achieving unanimity among all member states, and hence can be held hostage by individual member governments, which are under rather less pressure to justify their exceptionalism than is the case on issues formally subject to QMV. We should note that the EU is now also contracted in principle to a significant extension of external policy commitments, as, for example, under the 'neighbourhood policy' and 'action plans' for each of the countries concerned.

A decade ago, the third pillar of JHA was still very young and failed the productivity test, having generated little beyond vague declarations and resolutions. Early evidence revealed decision avoidance rather than decision-taking (Council of the European Union, 1995; European Commission, 1995; den Boer, 1996). However, a great deal has happened since then by way of substantive progress, both by softer methods in the Council (recommendations, peer review and so on), but also by the shifting of work to the first pillar as proposals for hard legislation. Indeed, on some estimates, the JHA field produces the greatest volume (some say as much as 40 per cent) of paper going through the Council machinery for discussion, helped by the reinforcement of staff in the Council Secretariat working in this field (see Table 4.1 in Chapter 4).

Another gauge of productivity is the time it takes for decisions to emerge – in other words, the time lag between the announcement of the Commission's proposal and the final decision being adopted. Although it is easy to castigate the cases of delay and prevarication, it is also clear that there is a kind of decisional conveyor belt in the Council. Routine business is processed relatively speedily, while slowness in reaching decisions generally reflects the difficulty or sensitivity generated by the substance of the issues being addressed, or the impact of electoral cycles in the member states. It has also become more common for proposals that do not find agreement to be dropped, and indeed this is an explicit element of the co-decision procedure.

As we saw in Chapter 2, the Council worked at a reasonable pace even in the mid-1980s with the then more limited availability of QMV (see Sloot and Verschuren, 1990; Golub, 1999). The pace increased after that, especially on issues subject to QMV in the Council and cooperation with the EP (Maurer, 1999). Rather more surprisingly, decision-making speed continued to increase, despite the introduction of the more complex co-decision procedure with the EP in 1993, and enlargement from EU-12 to EU-15 in 1995 (see Box 2.5 in Chapter 2). This reflects not only the effect of the possibility, introduced under the ToA, of concluding the co-decision procedure at the end of the EP's first reading (making for a shorter and speedier process), but also of a sort of co-decision reflex among practitioners, which facilitates the search for agreement. The CFE, meeting in 2002–3, was informed that over 70 per cent of all co-decision dossiers were agreed at their first reading (about 32 per cent) or their second reading (about 40 per cent), obviating the need for time-consuming conciliation.

Efficiency

Efficiency emerged in the mid-1990s as a key preoccupation, not least because of the prospect of serial enlargement, hence the succession of reform initiatives in the shape of the ToA, the ToN and the CT. Several aspects of efficiency have been drawn into the discussion and are examined below:

- the techniques and procedures of decision-making;
- the match between decisions taken and problems addressed (and, in the case of the second and third pillars and later the Lisbon Strategy, the limited results); and
- fears that extra numbers at the Council table would mean reduced efficiency.

Fritz Scharpf (1988) had argued from the evidence of the early 1980s that the Council was caught in a 'joint-decision trap'. By this he meant that there was a bias to produce decisions that protected the *status quo* and certain vested interests, and encouraged defensive bargaining. However, the picture since the early 1990s has been more varied between policy arenas, between pillars, and between member states, as well as according to political context.

Techniques and procedures

Here, contrasting patterns can be observed. Our study has highlighted a particular contrast between, on the one hand, Council work specific to particular subjects and, on the other, the grasp of the Council on the overall direction of EU policy and priorities. Especially in those areas of work that rest on an accumulation of practice over time, the Council process is quite streamlined in the way that dossiers are transmitted backwards and forwards, and up and down, the hierarchy of working parties, committees of senior officials and ministerial meetings; the budget procedure and standard trade policy matters are good cases in point. Decisions are reached on a reasonably expert basis, and they include policy extensions and innovations, as well as routine agreements. Large numbers of national officials are involved, and they are then locked into the process and engaged to follow decisions through. In newer areas, where the ground for common perspectives is less well established, and the relevant circles of national policy-makers and negotiators are less locked in, the procedures work in a clumsier fashion, and the results are more uneven.

The picture looks very different when one looks at the way in which the Council addresses strategic or overarching issues. Cross-Council coordination remains very hit-and-miss. The pronounced segmentation of work between policy areas and between Councils (and the working parties and committees that prepare ministerial meetings) impedes coherent decision-making and the consistent treatment of subjects. This echoes the way in which ministerial responsibilities are divided in the member governments; it reflects the equally striking dispersal of work between Commissioners and services inside the Commission; and it is accentuated by the volume of work in hand. These are all mutually reinforcing explanations, but not justifications, for the diffuse management of Council business. The disappointing progress towards the achievement of the targets of the 2000 Lisbon Strategy is probably the most frequently cited illustration in the current context.

The Council's methods of operation have themselves been a source of poor coordination. As we have seen in earlier chapters, both the Seville reforms and the provisions of the CT were intended to redress some of the problems: by an enhanced role for the European Council; by streamlining the work of the regular Council of Ministers (with its revised configurations); by allocating tasks more clearly to the GAERC; and by introducing much more systematic coordination across successive Council presidencies. Recent examples of weak coordination on strategic issues include the Lisbon Strategy, the difficulties encountered in dealing with the fiscal policy side of EMU, and continuing tensions between external economic relations and external political relations, or between overseas development policy and the common agricultural policy (CAP). So the recent reforms are indeed under test, and particularly in the enlarged EU, where both the Council and the Commission will be under pressure to deliver on both strategic issues and regular day-to-day business.

Another structural weakness has been the proliferation of procedures, or rather the proliferation of variations of the four main legislative procedures (co-decision; assent; cooperation; and advisory opinion) contained in the treaties. The 2002–3 CFE identified twenty-eight distinct procedures on the basis of the voting system required in the Council, Parliament's involvement (it had a role to play in twenty-one of the twenty-eight procedures) and the consultation of institutions or bodies other than the EP (see Box 1.5 in Chapter 1). The CT aimed to simplify these procedures substantially, by making co-decision (with QMV) the 'ordinary legislative procedure'. One might have expected the complexity arising from the proliferation of procedures to lead to legislative confusion or delay. Instead, the institutions have demonstrated a marked ability to adapt their working methods and behaviour to cope with this complexity. The best example of this is the co-decision procedure, where a rather smooth process of legislative deliberation has been set in place, and the Council has settled down into a kind of routine of co-decision (see Chapter 8). It is judged, in the eyes of its practitioners at least, to be efficient and to improve the quality of legislation.

Major changes have taken place over recent years in the way that the CFSP and, more recently, the ESDP are handled. Foreign ministers, supported by the new Political and Security Committee (COPS – see Chapter 3) and Coreper, spend an increasing amount of their time on CFSP and ESDP issues, operating in an external relations formation of the GAERC. The extension and upgrading of the Council Secretariat's role after the 1992 Treaty on European Union (TEU) already marked an effort to provide a more solid infrastructure for policy-makers (Chapter 4). The changed role of the Council's Secretary-General as primarily the High Representative of the Union for CFSP matters has made a huge improvement in the way foreign policy work is handled, in terms of efforts both to develop an intellectual coherence to policy, and to improve day-to-day operations. Critics argue that much more progress needs to be made at the procedural level, hence the provisions of the CT for creating the post of EU Foreign Minister (with a foot in both the Council and the Commission), and for developing the EEAS. These innovative arrangements would introduce new ways of working between the Council and the Commission, jointly acting as a kind of two-hatted executive for the CFSP. Certainly, the new provisions of the CT would make some important changes to current working methods, but even given the non-ratification of the CT there is some room for optimism that the practical improvements of recent years might prove to be robust.

In the 1990s, JHA suffered from extensive procedural deficiencies, its arrangements having been transposed from the CFSP domain without much thought being given as to their appropriateness in the area of justice and home affairs. A double hierarchy of parallel committees added to the confusion, and ministers and officials from the member states were not socialized into EU ways of working. A considerable learning process has occurred since then, pushed even further by the press of events on the JHA agenda. The 1997 ToA introduced some reforms, and practice has yielded further pragmatic changes to the way that policy is handled. The hard lines between the first and third pillars have softened considerably, and a kind of rhythm of productive work has been established.

In the first edition of this book, we noted the then rather stale debate on the reform of the Council, with the familiar calls for the Council Secretariat and/or the presidency to be more active coordinators; pleas to Coreper and the General Affairs Council (GAC) to take a firmer grasp of the overall management of Council business; and the assertion that greater use of QMV would expedite decision-making (see also Hayes-Renshaw and Wallace, 1995). We argued that these various anti-dotes would yield only limited efficiency gains, and suggested instead that the time had come for a fresher look at the Council, and for a more wide-ranging rearrangement of its vertical segments and horizontal layers. Our proposals included a call for fewer specialized configurations of the Council at both ministerial and official levels, through which related clusters of work could be addressed more coherently, strategic issues might be easier to identify, and the wider public might have a better chance of following the main lines of policy development. Our proposed clusters were as follows: external relations and CFSP; the broad macroeconomic, monetary and fiscal topics; microeconomic and sectoral issues (services, industry and agriculture); the development of physical resources and infrastructure (energy, transport and environment); and policies affecting the individual (labour market, education, citizenship and immigration). The reforms introduced in recent years go very much in this direction (Wallace and Hayes-Renshaw, 2003). On paper at least, they have much promise as ways of improving the Council's procedures and hence of yielding efficiency gains.

Matching solutions to problems

Here, it is much harder to produce a balance-sheet on the Council's effectiveness, since it is difficult to separate the effects of institutional practice from those of substantive policy agreements or disagreements among member governments, or from the impacts of policy contexts or external factors. One possible way of categorizing the different kinds of challenge to the efficiency of the Council would be to divide issues into three categories: policy reform; policy development; and new policy needs.

The *policy reform* challenges come, in particular, in the old-established areas of EU policy, where the policy *acquis* for one reason or another does not fit with the palette of needs of the enlarged EU, or of the changing policy context. Examples include the common agricultural and fisheries policies, the historical distribution of EU spending mechanisms, and the single market regulatory approach of the 1980s. In all these fields, there are some policy rigidities. Of course, these stem in part from the distribution of member states' preferences, especially those of the older member states. None the less, there is a good deal of evidence to suggest that some of the patterns of work within the Council reinforce these rigidities rather than soften them.

As regards *policy development*, one contributory factor to efficiency is how far there is an agreed view or set of ideas among member governments on the subject under discussion, whether it is to be addressed by legislative means or by a form of collective executive decision. Part of the success in taking EMU forward lies in the emergence of a predominant paradigm, at least as regards 'sound money', shared by a relevant epistemic community (McNamara, 2005). The introduction of public health and consumer-oriented legislation in the Council flows in part from the anchoring of the 'precautionary principle' as the reference point, albeit at the price of a good deal of tension with international partners, notably the USA. These examples are in line with explanations for the earlier success of the Council in driving forward the 1992 programme. In these areas, a shared paradigm has helped to drive forward procedural and process experiments that have delivered policy results. The thinner results of the Lisbon Strategy, or the more contested debates on the macroeconomic and fiscal dimensions of EMU, suggest both that there is a missing shared paradigm and that informal adaptations of procedures have not provided a solution. Thus, for example, the Sapir Report (2004) argued not only for policy changes but also that EU governance was part of the problem.

As regards *new policy needs*, in some ways the record since the mid-1990s is more encouraging than might have been expected. As we have argued at several points in this volume, the EU has become a good deal more adept at developing new policies in the fields of CFSP and JHA. Interestingly, these are fields in which the Council has had an important executive role. Non-treaty reform and evolutionary practice have generated significant outputs, with the Council Secretariat in a facilitating role, at least at the 'meso' level of policy.

Increased numbers

It is often argued that the solution to dealing with the larger number of member states in the EU is to adapt the voting rules, and to practise explicit voting more frequently. We dissent from this view. Voting rules may facilitate agreement, but they do not provide a panacea for disagreement. As indicated in Chapters 2 and 10, the availability of recourse to QMV, even if sparsely used formally, provides an additional collective discipline. It does not, however, obviate the need to build up agreements and to tie members into their endorsement. Even though we saw in Chapter 10 that formal safeguards such as the Ioannina compromise are rarely invoked (see Box 10.2 in particular), all member governments are sensitive to each others' substantive difficulties. In any case, QMV demands a high threshold of agreement, and the revised rules under the 2001 ToN and the CT did not lower the thresholds – quite the reverse, in fact. Paradoxically, the room for abstentions under the unanimity rule means in effect that decisions can (in theory at least) be agreed with a far lower number of 'yes-sayers' than under QMV. Our study cannot yet capture the impacts of the 2004 enlargement, or of the ToN voting rules, but early evidence has not yet indicated any changing patterns of general behaviour.

Legitimacy

Traditionally, the legitimacy of the Council has derived from the fact that its members are elected office-holders in their own countries. This has not, however, protected those legislating under the first pillar from the charge that their authority is contested, nor has it provided a basis of ready acceptance for member governments to transact business under the second and third pillars. There is declining esteem for the EU in general across the member states, as the EU's statistical publication, *Eurobarometer*, regularly records. While one obvious target of public criticism is 'Brussels bureaucracy', popularly interpreted to be the Commission, the fact remains that most of the examples of contested decisions have resulted from Council-endorsed legislation or other kinds of decisions. Those who contest the Council's legitimacy normally cite the lack of transparency of its procedures, problems associated with ratification, and the fact that it is not directly accountable.

Transparency

A general criticism of the Council in the past had to do with the opaqueness and complexity of its procedures. As we explained in Chapter 4, the Council's proceedings are now much more open to public access than they were, as a consequence of both formal changes to improve transparency and the advent of Internet access to documents. The skilful investigator can now, at the touch of a button, read agendas, press releases and minutes of Council meetings, or can, make a written request to have access to more specialized and detailed documents. Some parts of Council sessions, when the ministers are clearly 'legislating', are open to the public. This is not, however, quite the same thing as full access. Formal records tell only part of the story, and public sessions remain more public relations occasions than substantive events. After all, it should not be forgotten that the Council transacts confidential business. Defining negotiating mandates, for example, would not be better prepared if done more publicly – quite the reverse, in fact. The brokering of agreements among member governments on the details and principles of legislation would probably be harder under the direct public gaze. The pressures to take less flexible positions would increase, and the temptation would be strong to resort to small cabals to broker agreements. All in all, the result could well be to diminish, not to enhance, the atmosphere of mutual trust that we have repeatedly argued is an essential ingredient of Council cohesion. In short, there is a necessary trade-off to be made between openness and efficiency.

However, the main argument for improving the transparency of the Council was that it would produce not only better governance but also stronger legitimacy. There is no evidence that the measures introduced so far have increased the legitimacy of the Council in the eyes of ordinary citizens. Too little use seems to be made of the transparency provisions to improve reporting of the Council's work in either the national media or national parliaments.

Problems of ratification

Another sign of contested legitimacy is the emergence of more frequent problems of ratification. These occur when:

- governments assent to decisions in the Council and then fail to implement them, sometimes because opinion within the member states puts a brake on compliance (see Chapters 2 and 10); or
- governments refuse to assent and search for ways to evade the consequences.

QMV, by identifying dissenters overtly, can make it harder for those in the outvoted minority to deliver national compliance with the relevant new legislation. Contested decisions range from the minute detail of EU legislation to large and politically sensitive issues of state. Of these, only a minority are submitted to explicit votes that are published in the records of the Council. As we saw in Chapter 10, most of these explicitly-challenged EU decisions are on agricultural and fisheries issues, often at the operational level. Of the rest, many examples relate to apparently minor and parochial 'differences of taste' between countries: food standards, different approaches to animal welfare, or divergent policies on the daily life of the individual. Often national representatives have agreed to the relevant EU decision, but failed to carry the consent required at home for its implementation, or to appease a domestic advocacy group.

More important are the issues of high political salience for all member states, such as EMU, citizenship, and foreign and security matters. Here, the legitimation problem lies in the reluctance of citizens and parliaments in at least some member states to accept that their own governments should be committed to a collective EU process in these areas of public policy. The notion that a process that depended essentially on the Council might be accepted as more legitimate than one involving other EU institutions remains unproven. Indeed, an explicit strengthening of the Council *vis-à-vis* the Commission would leave the Council much more exposed in having to defend the legitimacy of its own proceedings. Subsidiarity may appear as a tempting catch-all remedy, by displacing on to national polities the legitimation of issues that cannot command consent at the European level. But this is unlikely to remove from the Community domain all the issues that disturb national electorates.

Quis custodiet custodes?

In any event, the recurrent problem in the discussion of the legitimacy deficit as regards the Council is to find a functioning antidote. So long as the Council remains an executive as well as a legislative body drawn from the representatives of the member states, the only systematic means of achieving accountability is through national mechanisms – that is, through national parliaments and tests of national political opinion. The pressures to move from implicit to explicit national controls have been accentuated in recent years, but the risk is that to do so would be to erode what collective identity has been achieved in the Council, to increase the individualism of each representative and, indeed, to make interest-based bargaining predominate over the development of shared values and norms. Incremental extensions of the EP's powers seem to have become a reflex of treaty reformers, and have gone some way to increasing the pressures on the Council to justify its legislative preferences, but this still falls short of producing wider political legitimacy for the process.

The balance sheet of reform

The pressures for institutional reform have increased, for three reasons: the enlargement of the EU's membership; more widespread contestation of European governance and its legitimacy; and the persistent tension between supranational and intergovernmental models of cooperation. In addition, two key contextual changes have made it harder for policy choices to be clearly defined, and thus for agreements to be reached, one to do with the political economy of Europe, the other geopolitical.

As regards the *political economy*, recent years have seen interesting developments. On the one hand, there is now a core consensus around the monetary part of EMU and the single currency regime, at least for the twelve member states within the euro-zone at the time of writing. On the other hand, however, there is no core consensus on the macroeconomic side of EMU, which remains subject to national policy actions, with an awkward relationship between the monetary and macroeconomic dimensions played out in difficult arguments within Ecofin, as we saw in Chapter 10 (see in particular Box 10.3). Similarly, there remains a span of divergent views and divergent national policies on the microeconomic and employment dimensions of the competitiveness agenda, which contrasts sharply with the consensus on market regulation that underpinned the Council's single market 'success'. It remains to be seen whether the Competitiveness Council configuration will achieve more purchase on these issues. It also remains to be seen how far the differing priorities of the new member states will affect the constellation of economic interests, and hence the policy debates, within the Council.

Similar observations can be made with regard to the *geopolitical* policy agenda of the enlarged EU. On the one hand, a redefined 'neighbourhood' by virtue of geography requires an adjustment within the Council to pay more attention to the views and experience of new member states. On the other hand, wider global issues, notably concerning the USA and the so-called war on terror, will certainly not make it easy to achieve cohesion of policy preferences and agreed policy responses.

However, it is hard to see how institutional reforms as such hold the solution to such challenges. Interestingly, proposals for decision mechanisms based around a core group or avant-garde have become less cogent than they seemed to some commentators a decade ago, other than in the obvious case of the Euro Group of single currency members. Here, we stress that our study shows no systematic cleavage between smaller and larger members. On the contrary, both winning and blocking coalitions are typically constructed from a range of member states, based primarily on affinities of interests and/or ideas (see Chapters 1, 2 and 10) rather than aimed at attaining a specific voting threshold. In the past, the delicate balances of influence have been constructed to protect small members against overweening larger partners, and to diffuse brute questions of power, political muscle and economic leverage. Thus, in our view, it will be just as important in the future to watch the patterns of evolution and experimentation in the Council via non-treaty incremental reform as to monitor the impact of formal rule changes by explicit treaty reforms. Therefore, in this context, the impact of the CT, if it were ratified, might be less of a *deus ex machina* than some commentators and protagonists suggest.

The first edition of this book appeared at a time when it was too early to have firm evidence regarding the impact of the new members joining the EU in 1995 (Austria, Finland and Sweden). The Twelve had decided that they could, or would, accommodate a few new members without making other than marginal changes to the institutions. In the event, the move from EU-12 to EU-15 did not make such a large difference to the functioning of the Council, although, of course, the new members brought with them different styles of work and alternative policy priorities – a greater emphasis on transparency, and social and environmental issues, were obvious cases in point (Bulmer and Lequesne, 2005). Their impact is also clear in the crystallization of the coalition of 'net-payers' into the EU budget. Perhaps even more significant is that the 1995 enlargement did not in any way impede the rhythm of progress towards EMU (despite Sweden's non-participation in the euro), or – even less expected – the evolution of the CFSP, in which the arriving new members, non-aligned in defence terms, did not hamper the development of the defence dimension of the common security policy.

The 2004 enlargement to an EU of twenty-five member states has been a bigger challenge to the system, both in terms of numbers at the table and in terms of the increased heterogeneity of member states' preferences to be accommodated. In addition, this group of new members has joined after experiencing a more paternalistic approach to their accession than had been the experience of the EFTA (European Free Trade Area) countries in the 1990s. There is as yet little consensus among practitioners as to how life will develop within the Council. Some speculate that, this time, the much larger number of members risks creating log-jams, while others are more sanguine. Much depends on how widely varied starting positions are, how deeply ingrained conflicting opinions turn out to be, and how far the members are social-ized into the process of developing consensus. For productivity to be sustained, a steady accumulation of habits of consensus-building and of effective partnership between the Council and the other institutions will be required, not least in order to cope effectively with further enlargements.

Chronology of the Evolution of the Council

Year	Treaties/Agreements	Structure	Powers	Voting
1951	Treaty of Paris (establishing the European Coal and Steel community – ECSC) Came into force July 1952; expired July 2002	Special Council of Ministers, work prepared by Cocor (*Commission de coordination du Conseil des ministres*)	Coordinates with governments Consulted by High Authority	Unanimity or weighted majority based on output of coal & steel Cocor – no power to vote
1957	Treaties of Rome (establishing the European Economic Community – EEC – and the European Atomic Energy Community – Euratom) Came into force January 1958	Council (of Ministers), work prepared by Coreper (Committee of Permanent Representatives)	Decides largely on basis of Commission proposal	Unanimity until 1970, then increased provision for qualified majority voting (QMV) Coreper – no power to vote
1958	Adoption of provisional internal rules of procedure of the Council (CRPs)			
1960	Intergovernmental decision	Creation of Special Committee on Agriculture (SCA)	Prepares work of agriculture ministers	
1962		Division of Coreper into Coreper I (Deputies) and Coreper II (Ambassadors)		
1965	Merger Treaty Came into force July 1967	Single Council (and Coreper) for the three communities		According to provisions in relevant treaties
1965–6	'Empty chair' crisis and Luxembourg compromise			Implicit veto retained

Year	Development	Decision-making / notes
1970 & 1975	Budgetary treaties	Shares budgetary authority with the European Parliament (EP)
1973	Accession of Denmark, Ireland and the UK; Expansion of Council & preparatory bodies (from 6 to 9 members); Adaptation of system of presidency rotation	Unanimity for principles, QMV for details; Adaptation of QMV system
1974	Decision of Paris Summit; Creation of the European Council	Purpose – to provide direction; Decisions taken by unanimity
1979	Adoption of official CRPs	
1981	Accession of Greece; Expansion of Council and preparatory bodies (from 9 to 10 members); Adaptation of system of presidency rotation	Adaptation of QMV system
1985	Single European Act (SEA) Entered into force July 1987; Formalization of European political cooperation (EPC), meetings prepared by the Political Committee (PoCo)	Cooperation Procedure with EP in some areas; Extension of QMV to many internal market issues
1987	Amendment of CRPs to provide for changes introduced by the SEA	
1986	Accession of Spain and Portugal; Expansion of Council and preparatory bodies (from 10 to 12 members); Adaptation of system of presidency rotation	Adaptation of QMV system

(*Continued*)

Year	Treaties/Agreements	Structure	Powers	Voting
1992	Treaty on European Union (Maastricht Treaty – TEU) Entered into force November 1993	Introduction of pillar structure European Council spans all three Common foreign and security policy (CFSP) issues prepared by Political Committee Justice and home affairs (JHA) issues prepared by K.4 Committee System of presidency rotation changed British opt-out on Social Chapter	European Council to coordinate Union policies Introduction of co-decision procedure with EP, including conciliation 1st pillar – cooperation and co-decision procedures with EP on basis of Commission proposal 2nd and 3rd pillars – Council decides and implements alone, but Commission can make proposals	1st pillar – extension of QMV to new areas 2nd and 3rd pillars – unanimity, possibility of moving to QMV at later date
1993	Amendment of CRPs to provide for changes introduced by the TEU			
1994	Ioannina compromise			Discussion to continue while blocking votes cast remain between certain thresholds
1995	Amendment of CRPs			
1995	Accession of Austria, Finland and Sweden	Expansion of Council & preparatory bodies (from 12 to 15 members) Adaptation of system of presidency rotation		Adaptation of QMV system

1997	Treaty of Amsterdam (ToA) Came into force May 1999	Secretary-General takes on additional role of High Representative for CFSP Post of Deputy Secretary-General of the Secretariat created Change in system of presidency rotation	Adaptation of co-decision procedure Provision for enhanced cooperation (flexibility) Opt-outs for United Kingdom (UK), Ireland and Denmark on Schengen Security and defence issues discussed as part of European security and defence policy (ESDP), work prepared by Political and Security Committee (COPS)	Extension of QMV to new areas
1997	Decision of Luxembourg European Council	Creation of Euro Group	Discusses matters of common interest to member states having adopted the euro	Members vote in Ecofin
1998 and 1999	Amendment of CRPs to provide for changes introduced by ToA			
1999	Conclusions of Helsinki European Council	Reduction in number of Council configurations (to 16)		
1999	Creation of register of Council documents (available on Council website) to facilitate public access to Council documents			
2000	Amendment of CRPs to provide for changes introduced by Helsinki conclusions			

(Continued)

Year	Treaties/Agreements	Structure	Powers	Voting
2001	Treaty of Nice (ToN) Came into force February 2003			New attribution of votes Adaptation of QMV system in advance of and following 2004 enlargement
2001	Adoption of joint regulation regarding public access to EP, Council and Commission documents			
2001	Adoption of code of good administrative behaviour for Council Secretariat in dealing with requests for access to documents			
2001	Amendment of CRPs (twice)			
2002	Conclusions of Seville European Council	Reduction in number of Council configurations (to 9) Creation of divisible General Affairs and External Relations Council (GAERC)	Certain parts of Councils to be open to the public	
2002	Amendment of CRPs to provide for changes introduced by Seville conclusions			
2003	Code of conduct approved by the Council			
2004	Amendment of CRPs (twice) *inter alia* to include provisions of the code of conduct			

Year			
2004	Accession of Cyprus, Czech Republic, Estonia, Hungary, Latvia, Lithuania, Malta, Poland, Slovakia and Slovenia	Expansion of Council and preparatory bodies (from 15 to 25 members) Allocation of places at meeting tables to new members	Adaptation of QMV system Triple majority required for QMV: QM threshold; cast by majority of member states; representing 62 per cent of total EU population (verification must be requested)
2004	Treaty establishing a Constitution for Europe (Constitutional Treaty – CT) Due to come into force only after ratification by all member states Rejected by France and the Netherlands in May and June 2005 Respectively	European Council to become official institution with elected President (2.5-year term) Explicit recognition of different Council configurations Division of GAERC into Foreign Affairs and General Affairs Councils Other configurations to be decided upon by the European Council EU Foreign Minister cum Commission Vice-President to be appointed for 5-year term by European Council	European Council given explicit representative role in foreign affairs Councils to have legislative, executive, policy-making and coordinating functions Co-decision procedure to become the 'ordinary legislative procedure' Councils to meet in public when deliberating and legislating Foreign Minister to chair Foreign Affairs Council and to conduct CFSP Introduction of team presidencies spanning 18 months	European Council to decide by consensus or QMV QMV to be default voting rule in Council Reform of QMV to introduce double majority: 55 per cent of member states; 65 per cent of total EU population
2004	Decision on new system of presidency rotation to cover period 2007–20	Places at Council table altered in line with new system of rotation	
2005	Signature of Accession Treaty with Bulgaria and Romania	Bulgarian and Romanian observers attend meetings of the Council and its preparatory bodies	Not allowed to vote

Appendix 2

Sources of Information on the Council

A variety of primary legal sources provide a description of the Council's **basic organization and activities:**

- the founding Treaties of Paris (establishing the European Coal and Steel Community (ECSC), 1951) and Rome (establishing the European Economic Community (EEC) and the European Atomic Energy Community Euratom, 1957);
- successive treaty amendments, in particular:

  - the Merger Treaty establishing a single Council and a single Commission (1965);
  - the Treaty amending certain budgetary provisions of the Treaties (1970);
  - the Treaty amending certain financial provisions of the Treaties (1975);
  - the Single European Act (SEA – 1986);
  - the Treaty on European Union (TEU – 1992);
  - the Treaty of Amsterdam (ToA – 1997);
  - the Treaty of Nice (ToN – 2001); and
  - the Constitutional Treaty (CT – 2004)

- the various Treaties of Accession ratifying successive enlargements, containing *inter alia* amendments of numbers for voting rules and presidency rotations;
- the Council's own internal rules of procedure (CRPs), updated when necessary in order to take account of changes introduced by treaty amendments and other agreements; they include specific provisions regarding public access to Council documents and a code of conduct governing working methods for an enlarged Council, available on the Council's website (see below);
- the Seville reforms, agreed at the Seville European Council of June 2002, and covering the organization of proceedings of the European Council and the structure and functioning of the Council (reproduced as Appendix 3 in this volume).

Information on the Council's **current organization and day-to-day activities** can readily be obtained from the Council's website (www.consilium.eu.int), an invaluable tool for the interested observer and inquisitive researcher (see below for an indication of the information it contains). The names and telephone numbers of EU officials can be obtained from the online inter-institutional directory (www.europa.eu.int/idea). The website of the current presidency (available via the Council website) is another useful source of information on work in progress.

Guide to the Council website (www.consilium.eu.int)
Information on the Council website is organized under seven different headings, as follows:

Press	Council	Policies	Constitution	Contacts	Javier Solana	Documents
• Press releases (Council, Secretary-General, CFSP, co-decision, etc.)	• Council configurations	• Council configurations	• Text	• Job offers	• Press releases	• Community policies
• Meetings and events (including agendas of Council meetings)	• European Council (including Presidency Conclusions since 1993)	• Co-decision (including a guide and current progress of dossiers)	• Signing ceremony	• Frequently asked questions (FAQs)	• Articles	• EMU
	• Next enlargement	• Foreign policy	• Intergovernmental conference	• External links	• Interviews	• Access to Council documents (public register*
• Audiovisual (including photographic library)	• Presidency websites (access to current and some previous websites)	• Security and defence	• European Convention	• Public events	• Press review	• JHA
• Information for the media	• President names (list of presidency foreign ministers since 1958)	• Fight against terrorism		• Information visits	• Speeches	• Council of the EU (including internal rules of procedure – CRPs)
• Documents (link to section on access to documents)	• Photographic library	• COST		• Who's who in the Council	• Reports	• CFSP
• Contacts		• Agreements		• Contact us	• Photos	• IGC
• Join our mailing list				• Procurement coordination unit (PCU)		• European Council
• Photos				• Order a publication		• Agreements
				• Traineeships office		• COST
						• ESDP
						• Fundamental Rights
						• Registration forms
						• Fundamental texts

Note:
* Including timetables and agendas, minutes of Council meetings and a monthly summary of Council acts. Note that some documents may only be available in French and/or English.

Areas Covered by the Council's Internal Rules of Procedure (CRPs)

Since the Council's internal rules of procedure (CRPs) are too long to include in this volume, we list below the areas that they cover. The 2004 version of the CRPs was published in the *Official Journal* OJ L 106 15/04/2004, pp. 22–45, and is available on the Palgrave book website (www.palgrave.com/politics/hayes-renshaw).

Article 1	Notice and venue of meetings
Article 2	Configurations of the Council, role of the General Affairs and External Relations Council and programming
Article 3	Agenda
Article 4	Representation of a Council member unable to attend
Article 5	Meetings
Article 6	Professional secrecy and production of documents in legal proceedings
Article 7	Cases where the Council acts in its legislative capacity
Article 8	Council deliberations open to the public and public debates
Article 9	Making public votes, explanations of votes and minutes
Article 10	Public access to Council documents
Article 11	Voting arrangements and quorum
Article 12	Written procedure
Article 13	Minutes
Article 14	Deliberations and decisions on the basis of documents and drafts drawn up in the languages provided for by the language rules in force
Article 15	Signing of acts
Article 16	Absence of the possibility to participate in the vote
Article 17	Publication of acts in the Official Journal
Article 18	Notification of acts
Article 19	Coreper, committees and working parties
Article 20	The Presidency and the businesslike conduct of discussions
Article 21	Reports from committees and working parties
Article 22	Quality of drafting
Article 23	The Secretary-General and the General Secretariat
Article 24	Security
Article 25	Duties of depositary of agreements and conventions
Article 26	Representation before the European Parliament

Chronology of the Evolution of the Council Secretariat

1952	Creation of small (10 officials) Secretariat for ECSC Special Council of Ministers, located in Luxembourg, to provide translation, minute-taking and legal advice facilities Christian Calmes (Luxembourg) appointed as Secretary-General
1958	Creation of General Secretariat for the European Coal and Steel Community (ECSC), European Economic Community (EEC) and European Atomic Energy Community (Euratom) Councils by means of Article 17 of the Council's internal rules of procedure. Located in Brussels (rue Ravenstein) Composed of 238 officials working in five Divisions Christian Calmes stays on as Secretary-General
1968	*Bureau de liaison* opens in Geneva, to deal with GATT (General Agreement on Tariffs and Trade) affairs
1971	Secretariat moves into Charlemagne building
1973	Accession of Denmark, Ireland and the United Kingdom (UK) – number of officials increases. Nicolas Hommel (Luxembourg) appointed as Secretary-General Reorganization – Divisions become Directorates-General (DGs A–E) Creation of DG F to deal with institutional questions
1980	Niels Ersbøll (Denmark) appointed as Secretary-General
1981	Accession of Greece – number of officials increases
1983	Creation of DG G (Economic and Financial Affairs)
1986	Accession of Spain and Portugal – number of officials increases
1987	Implementation of Single European Act (SEA) European political cooperation (EPC) Secretariat (headed by Giovanni Jannuzzi) located within but independent of the Council Secretariat
1993	Implementation of Treaty on European Union (TEU – Maastricht Treaty) EPC Secretariat incorporated into General Secretariat DG E takes on responsibility for the common foreign and security policy (CFSP) Creation of DG H (Justice and home affairs – JHA)
1994	Jürgen Trumpf (Germany) appointed as Secretary-General for five years

1995   Accession of Austria, Finland & Sweden – number of officials increases
         Creation of new DGs:
             DG I (Environmental policy, consumer policy, health)
             DG J (Social policy, employment, regional policy, education and youth)
             DG F given responsibility for co-decision with the EP and information
             policy
         Secretariat moves into Justus Lipsius building

1998   Schengen Secretariat incorporated into General Secretariat

1999   Implementation of Treaty of Amsterdam (ToA)

         Trumpf–Piris Report on reform of the Council taken up by Helsinki
            European Council
         Javier Solana (E) appointed Secretary-General and High
            Representative for the CFSP (SG/HRCFSP)
         Pierre de Boissieu (F) appointed as Deputy Secretary-General
         Creation of Political Planning and Early Warning Unit (Policy Unit)

2000 to   Reorganization of Secretariat:
2002   DG D disbanded – areas of responsibility divided up among other DGs
            Creation of DG MA (DG for Administrative Modernization), now the
            Department for General Administrative Affairs, directly attached to
            the Deputy Secretary-General
            DG F given responsibility for Press, Communications and Protocol
            DG J disbanded – areas of responsibility transferred to other DGs
         Responsibility for co-decision transferred to Legal Service

2001   Javier Solana becomes Secretary-General of Western European Union
            (WEU)
         Parts of WEU Secretariat incorporated into Council Secretariat
         New politico-military staff housed in secure building in Ave. Cortenbergh

2003 to   Implementation of Treaty of Nice (ToN)
2004   Refurbishment of Justus Lipsius building in preparation for enlargement
         Secretariat officials take over chairmanship of some working parties

2004   Appointment of Gijs de Vries as Counter-Terrorism Coordinator,
            reporting directly to the SG/HRCFSP
         Accession of Cyprus, Czech Republic, Estonia, Hungary, Latvia,
            Lithuania, Malta, Poland, Slovakia and Slovenia – number of officials
            increases
         Construction of LEX building begins; due to be completed in 2007
         DG MA expanded and transformed into Department for General
            Administrative Affairs
         Javier Solana and Pierre de Boissieu reappointed for five years

Chronology of the Council Presidency Rotation Systems, 1952–2006

(based on official language of each member state – see Table 5.1 in Chapter 5)

	Alphabetical			Alternating	Balanced
1952–72 ECSC & EC-6	1973–80 EC-9	1981–5 EC-10	1986–92 EC-12	1993–6/1998 EU-12	7/1998–2006 EU-15 & EU-25
Belgium	Belgium	Belgium	Belgium	Denmark	Austria
Germany	Denmark	Denmark	Denmark	Belgium	Germany
France	Germany	Germany	Germany	Greece	Finland
Italy	France	Greece	Greece	Germany	Portugal
Luxembourg	Ireland	France	Spain	France	France
Netherlands	Italy	Ireland	France	Spain	Sweden
	Luxembourg	Italy	Ireland	Italy	Belgium
	Netherlands	Luxembourg	Italy	Ireland	Spain
	United Kingdom	Netherlands	Luxembourg	Netherlands	Denmark
		United Kingdom	Netherlands	Luxembourg	Greece
			Portugal	United Kingdom	Italy
			United Kingdom	Portugal	Ireland
					Netherlands
					Luxembourg
					United Kingdom
					Austria
					Finland

Chronology of European Council Meetings, 1990–2005

Year	Date	Location	Presidency	Significance and topics discussed
1990	28–29 April	Dublin	Ireland	Discussion on German reunification
	25–26 June	Dublin	Ireland	Identification of main issues for IGCs on political union and EMU
	27–28 October	Rome	Italy	Agreement to convene IGC to pursue EMU; discussion on first Gulf War
	14–15 December	Rome	Italy	Decision on parallel IGCs on EMU and political union; financial aid for Soviet Union
1991	8 April	Luxembourg	Luxembourg	Decision on humanitarian aid for Kurds and Shiites in Iraq after first Gulf War
	28–29 June	Luxembourg	Luxembourg	Support for economic reform in the Soviet Union, including the Baltic States
	9–10 December	Maastricht	Netherlands	Signature of the Treaty on European Union (Maastricht Treaty)
1992	26–27 June	Lisbon	Portugal	Agreement on Lisbon Report to develop policy towards eastern Europe
	16 October	Birmingham	UK	Special European Council following September EMS crisis
	11–12 December	Edinburgh	UK	Response to Danish 'No' and Delors-2 budget package
1993	21–22 June	Copenhagen	Denmark	Conditions for eastern enlargement
	29 October	Brussels	Belgium	Extraordinary European Council to mark entry into force of the Maastricht Treaty
	10–11 December	Brussels	Belgium	Economy and employment – Delors' White Paper
1994	24–25 June	Corfu	Greece	Confirmation of 'EFTA' enlargement; Cyprus and Malta accepted as candidates
	15 July	Brussels	Germany	Extraordinary European Council to agree the candidate for Commission President
	9–10 December	Essen	Germany	Pre-Accession Strategy

Year	Date	City	Country	Description
1995	26–27 June	Cannes	France	Variety of economic and JHA issues
	22–23 September	Mallorca	Spain	(First) informal European Council to discuss IGC issues
	15–16 December	Madrid	Spain	Steps to EMU and agreement to convene new IGC
1996	29 March	Turin	Italy	Formal opening of the Intergovernmental Conference (IGC)
	21–22 June	Florence	Italy	Response to BSE crisis; discussions re: Yugoslav wars
	5 October	Dublin	Ireland	Informal European Council to discuss progress on the IGC
	13–14 December	Dublin	Ireland	Steps towards EMU, employment, Yugoslav wars
1997	23 May	Nordwijk	Netherlands	Informal European Council to discuss IGC matters
	16–17 June	Amsterdam	Netherlands	Adoption of Stability and Growth Pact; completion of IGC (Treaty of Amsterdam)
	24 November	Luxembourg	Luxembourg	Employment ('Jobs summit')
	12–13 December	Luxembourg	Luxembourg	Review of enlargement process, including discussion on Turkey
1998	15–16 June	Cardiff	UK	Employment policy and economic reform
	24–25 October	Pörtschach	Austria	Informal European Council
	11–12 December	Vienna	Austria	Passage to third stage of EMU
1999	24–25 March	Berlin	Germany	Agreement on Agenda 2000 budget package and steps to enlargement
	3–4 June	Cologne	Germany	Employment Pact; first CFSP 'common strategy'; decision on new IGC
	15–16 October	Tampere	Finland	First thematic European Council – Justice and home affairs
	10–11 December	Helsinki	Finland	Agreement on CFSP 'headline goals'
2000	23–24 March	Lisbon	Portugal	Agreement on Lisbon Strategy for economic and social reform
	19–20 June	Feira	Portugal	CFSP and Mediterranean issues
	13–14 October	Biarritz	France	Informal European Council – institutional issues from the IGC
	7–11 December	Nice	France	Longest ever European Council; agreement on Treaty of Nice
2001	23–24 March	Stockholm	Sweden	Annual spring meeting (Lisbon agenda); discussions with President Putin
	15–16 June	Göteborg	Sweden	Enlargement, economy and western Balkans issues
	21 September	Brussels	Belgium	Emergency meeting following September 11 terrorist attacks in the USA
	19 October	Ghent	Belgium	Informal mini-summit
	14–15 December	Laeken	Belgium	Laeken Declaration establishing the Convention on the Future of Europe

(*Continued*)

Year	Date	Location	Presidency	Significance and topics discussed
2002	15–16 March	Barcelona	Spain	Annual spring meeting (Lisbon agenda)
	21–22 June	Seville	Spain	Council reforms
	24–25 October	Brussels	Denmark	Enlargement
	12–13 December	Copenhagen	Denmark	Agreement on date of, and candidates to be accepted for, enlargement
2003	17 February	Brussels	Greece	Emergency summit on Iraq
	20–21 March	Brussels	Greece	Annual spring meeting (Lisbon agenda)
	16 April	Athens	Greece	Athens Declaration on future of EU
	19–20 June	Thessaloniki	Greece	Discussion of European Security Strategy; sets up IGC
	4 October	Rome	Italy	Extraordinary European Council to mark the opening of the IGC
	16–17 October	Brussels	Italy	Economic growth issues
	12–13 December	Brussels	Italy	No agreement of IGC text; adoption of European Security Strategy
2004	25–26 March	Brussels	Ireland	Annual spring meeting (Lisbon agenda)
	17–18 June	Brussels	Ireland	Agreement of text of Constitutional Treaty; appointment of Barroso
	4–5 November	Brussels	Netherlands	Appointment of Commissioners; Hague programme of JHA
	16–17 December	Brussels	Netherlands	Agreement on Bulgarian and Romanian accession; date for Turkish negotiations
2005	22–23 March	Brussels	Luxembourg	Annual spring meeting; revision of Stability and Growth Pact
	16–17 June	Brussels	Luxembourg	Financial perspectives and budget (failed to agree)
	27 October	Hampton Court	UK	Informal meeting of heads of state or government to discuss the opportunities and challenges of globalisation
	15–16 December	Brussels	UK	Agreement on financial perspectives and budget

Appendix 7

The Seville Annexes Regarding the Council and the European Council (Seville European Council, 21–22 June 2002)

Annex I   Rules for the Organisation of the Proceedings of the European Council

In order fully to exercise its role of providing impetus and of defining the general political guidelines of the Union in accordance with Article 4 of the Treaty on European Union, the European Council has agreed on the following rules for the preparation, conduct and conclusions of its proceedings:

Preparation

1.   The European Council shall in principle meet four times a year (twice every six months). In extraordinary circumstances, the European Council may convene an extraordinary meeting.
2.   European Council meetings shall be prepared by the General Affairs and External Relations Council, which shall coordinate all the preparatory work and draw up the agenda. Contributions by other configurations of the Council to the proceedings of the European Council shall be forwarded to the General Affairs and External Relations Council not later than two weeks before the European Council meeting.
3.   At a meeting held at least four weeks before the European Council, the General Affairs and External Relations Council, acting on a Presidency proposal, shall draw up an annotated draft agenda, distinguishing between:

   • items to be approved or endorsed without debate;
   • items for discussion with a view to the definition of general political guidelines;
   • items for discussion with a view to the adoption of decisions as described in paragraph 9;
   • items for discussion but not intended to be the subject of conclusions.

4.   For each of the items referred to in the second and third indents of paragraph 3, the Presidency shall prepare a brief outline paper setting out the issues, the questions to be debated and the main options available.
5.   On the eve of the European Council meeting, the General Affairs and External Relations Council shall hold a final preparatory session and adopt the definitive

362

agenda, to which no item may subsequently be added without the agreement of all delegations.

Except for urgent and unforeseeable reasons linked, for example, to current international events, no Council or committee may meet between the final preparatory session of the General Affairs and External Relations Council and the European Council meeting.

Conduct

6. In principle, the proceedings of the European Council shall last for one full day, preceded the day before by a meeting restricted to Heads of State or of Government and the President of the Commission, in line with current practice. The European Council meeting the next day shall continue until the end of the afternoon and shall be preceded by an exchange of views with the President of the European Parliament. Specific arrangements may be made if justified by the agenda.

7. Meetings in the margins of the European Council with representatives of third States or organisations may be held in exceptional circumstances only. They must not disrupt the normal conduct of proceedings of the European Council meeting and they must be approved at the same time as the draft agenda drawn up by the General Affairs and External Relations Council.

8. The Presidency shall ensure that business is conducted smoothly. To that end, it may take any measure conducive to promoting the best possible use of the time available, such as organising the order in which items are discussed, limiting speaking time and determining the order in which contributors speak.

9. In the context of enlargement and in exceptional cases, where an item is placed on the agenda of the European Council for a decision, the European Council shall discuss the item concerned. The political conclusions drawn from the positions emerging during the discussion shall be brought to the attention of the Council so that it may consider the implications for subsequent proceedings, in accordance with the applicable Treaty provisions.

10. Delegations shall receive summary briefings on the outcome and substance of the discussions on each item as proceedings continue. Such briefings shall be organised in such a way as to safeguard the confidentiality of discussions.

11. Each delegation shall have two seats in the meeting room. The total size of delegations shall be limited to twenty persons for each Member State and for the Commission. That number shall not include technical personnel assigned to specific security or logistic support tasks.

Conclusions

12. The conclusions, which shall be as concise as possible, shall set out policy guidelines and decisions reached by the European Council, placing them briefly in their context and indicating the stages of the procedure to follow on from them.

13. An outline of the conclusions shall be distributed on the day of the European Council meeting in good time for the start of proceedings. The outline shall distinguish clearly between those parts of the text which have previously been approved and which are not in principle subject to discussion and those parts of the text which the European Council is to discuss with a view to reaching final conclusions at the meeting.

Annex II   Measures Concerning the Structure and Functioning of the Council

1. With a view to improving the functioning of the Council in the run-up to enlargement, the European Council has adopted the following conclusions, which will be reflected to the extent necessary by the relevant amendments to the Council's Rules of Procedure, to be made by 31 July 2002.

A.   Creation of a new General Affairs and External Relations Council

2. The current General Affairs Council configuration shall from now on be called the 'General Affairs and External Relations Council'. In order best to organise proceedings with regard to the two main areas of activity covered by this configuration, it will hold separate meetings (with separate agendas and possibly on different dates and) dealing, respectively, with:

   (a) preparation for and follow-up to the European Council (including the coordinating activities necessary to that end), institutional and administrative questions, horizontal dossiers which affect several of the Union's policies and any dossier entrusted to it by the European Council, having regard to EMU operating rules;
   (b) the whole of the Union's external action, namely common foreign and security policy, European security and defence policy, foreign trade, development cooperation and humanitarian aid.

B.   List of Council configurations[1]

3. The following list of Council configurations shall be included in the Annex to the Council's Rules of Procedure:

   1. General Affairs and External Relations;[2]
   2. Economic and Financial Affairs;[3]
   3. Justice and Home Affairs;[4]
   4. Employment, Social Policy, Health and Consumer Affairs;
   5. Competitiveness ((Internal Market, Industry and Research);[5]
   6. Transport, Telecommunications and Energy;
   7. Agriculture and Fisheries;
   8. Environment;
   9. Education, Youth and Culture.[6]

   It is agreed that several Ministers may participate as full members of the same Council configuration, the agenda and the organisation of proceedings being adjusted accordingly.

   In the case of the General Affairs and External Relations Council, each government shall be represented at the different meetings of this new configuration by the Minister or State Secretary of its choice.

C.   Programming of Council activities

4. In keeping with the role conferred upon it by the Treaty of defining the general political guidelines of the Union, the European Council shall, on the basis of a joint proposal drawn up by the Presidencies concerned in consultation with the

Commission and acting on a recommendation by the General Affairs and External Relations Council, adopt a **multiannual strategic programme** for the three years to come. The first such strategic programme will be adopted in December 2003.

5. In the light of the multiannual strategic programme referred to above, an **annual operating programme of Council activities** shall be submitted to the General Affairs and External Relations Council in December each year. This programme shall be proposed jointly by the next two Presidencies in line and shall have regard, inter alia, to relevant points arising from the dialogue on the political priorities for the year, conducted at the Commission's initiative. The final version of the annual programme shall be drawn up on the basis of the General Affairs and External Relations Council's discussions.

    With a view to the earliest possible implementation of these arrangements and by way of derogation from the first subparagraph, the first annual operating programme of Council activities shall be drawn up in December 2002.

6. This programme shall be accompanied by a list of indicative agendas for the various Council configurations for the first six months of the year. The list of indicative agendas for the last six months shall be submitted by the Presidency concerned before 1 July, following the appropriate consultations, in particular with the following Presidency.

D. Measures relating to the Presidency

Cooperation between Presidencies

7. Where it is clear that a dossier will essentially be dealt with during the following six-month period, the representative of the Member State holding the Presidency during that six-month period may, during the current six-month period, chair meetings of committees (other than Coreper) and working parties at which the dossier is discussed. The practical implementation of this provision shall be the subject of an agreement between the two Presidencies concerned.

    Thus, in the specific case of the examination of the budget for a given financial year, meetings of Council preparatory bodies other than Coreper shall be chaired by a representative of the Member State holding the Presidency during the second six-month period of the year prior to the financial year in question. The same arrangement shall apply, with the agreement of the other Presidency, to the chairing of Council meetings at the time when the items in question are discussed.

8. For the preparation of meetings of Council configurations meeting once every six months, where such meetings are held during the first half of the six-month period, meetings of committees other than Coreper and working party meetings taking place during the previous six-month period shall be chaired by a delegate of the Member State which will chair the Council meetings in question.

Chairing of certain working parties by the General Secretariat of the Council

9. In addition to cases where the General Secretariat of the Council already acts as chairman, the following working parties shall be chaired by a member of the General Secretariat of the Council:

   * Working Party on Electronic Communications;
   * Working Party on Legal Data Processing;
   * Working Party on the Codification of Legislation;
   * Working Party on Information;
   * Working Party on New Buildings.

E.   Opening Council meetings to the public when the Council is acting in accordance with the procedure for co-decision with the European Parliament

10.   Council debates on acts adopted in accordance with the procedure for co-decision with the European Parliament shall be open to the public under the following circumstances:

- during the initial stage of the procedure: opening to the public of the presentation by the Commission of its main co-decision legislative proposals and the ensuing debate. The list of proposals concerned shall be drawn up by the Council at the beginning of each six-month period;
- during the final stage of the procedure: opening to the public of votes and explanations of votes.

11.   The debates shall be made public by providing the public with a room to which the deliberations of the Council will be transmitted live, including the indication by visual means of the outcome of votes. The public will be informed in advance by the appropriate means (for example, on the Council's Internet site) of the days and times at which such transmissions will take place.

F.   Conducting meetings

12.   The Presidency shall ensure that meetings proceed smoothly. It shall be the Presidency's responsibility to take any measure required to achieve the best possible use of the time available during meetings, including:

- limiting the time for which contributors may speak;
- determining the order in which contributors speak;
- asking delegations to present their proposals for amendment of the text under discussion in writing before a given date, together with a brief explanation if appropriate;
- asking delegations which have identical or close positions on any particular item to choose one of their number to express their joint position at the meeting or before the meeting in writing.

Notes

1.   The new arrangements regarding Council configurations will be applied by the Danish Presidency having regard to the constraints that may arise from the timetable of meetings already established.
2.   Including the ESDP and development cooperation.
3.   Including the budget.
4.   Including civil protection.
5.   Including tourism.
6.   Including audiovisual affairs.

Appendix 8

Statistical Data on Voting in the Council

This Appendix explains the data sets on explicit voting in the Council that have been used in this volume, as well as the techniques used to analyse them. In a further elaboration of the analysis in Chapter 10, we have also carried out a cluster analysis of the data in order to get a better picture of which member governments vote together in the Council and on what issues. We do not report this in detail here. A fuller version (including an account of the techniques used) appears in: Hayes-Renshaw, F., van Aken, W., and Wallace, H. (2006), 'When and Why the EU Council of Ministers Votes Explicitly', *Journal of Common Market Studies,* 44: 1. Data collection and collation, as well as statistical analysis, were carried out by Wim van Aken.

The data sets
The data sets can be broken down into two categories, according to their original source: (a) annual and monthly summary statistics of recorded votes per member state according to issue area and voting procedure collected by the Council Secretariat; and (b) roll-call voting statistics of explicit voting per member state collated from the Council press releases and minutes of individual Council sessions. The latter differ from the former as they allow an in-depth exploration of the nature of the votes cast and the corresponding roll-call votes without losing a general overview of the entire data sets.

1. Aggregate breakdown data set (1994–2004)
The sources for these data, aggregated for this volume, are:

* 1994 data from Hayes-Renshaw, F. and Wallace, H. (1997) *The Council of Ministers* (London: Macmillan, p. 54).
* 1995 data from Mattila, M. and Lane, J. E. (2001) 'Why Unanimity in the Council? Roll Call Analysis of Council Voting', *European Union Politics,* 2(1): 31–52. See the online database at http://www.valt.helsinki.fi/staff/mmattila/council/.
* 1996–2004 data from the Council Secretariat.

Note: The totals from Mattila and Lane (2001) for 1995 and 1996 appear high (344 and 340 recorded, respectively), relative to data in preceding and subsequent years, as well as data received from the Council Secretariat. No data are available from elsewhere for 1995.

2. Qualified Majority Voting (QMV) data set (1999–2004)
These data come from the Council Secretariat.
Note: No detailed data are available for 1994–8.

3.   Country breakdown data set (1994–2004)
The sources for these data are:

- 1994 data from Hayes-Renshaw and Wallace, *op. cit.*, p. 54.
- 1995 data from Mattila and Lane, *op. cit.*, online database, as above.
- 1996–2004 data from the Council Secretariat.

Note: Austria, Finland and Sweden were not members of the EU in 1994. Sweden voted 'no' 34 times in 1995 (Matilla and Lane, *op. cit.*), the highest number of the entire dataset (see above).

4.   Monthly Breakdown (1996–2004)
These data come from the Council Secretariat.

5.   Issue Areas – 1 (1998–2004)
These data come from the Council Secretariat.

6.   Issue Areas – 2 (1998–2004)
These data were collected by searching detailed records of individual Council sessions on the Council website (www.consilium.eu.int), in particular:

- Press releases (available under the heading 'press') and
- Council minutes (available under the heading 'Documents' and then 'Access to Council documents').

Note: Small discrepancies for some years appear to be related to some inconsistencies in the way that Council documents are formulated.

Statistical techniques
General descriptive statistics have been the main tool employed to analyse the data and to reach preliminary conclusions. The results allow for comparison between data sets along the lines of countries, issues areas, roll-call votes and voting procedures, or a combination of two or more of these. Initially, summary statistics revealed discrepancies related to different voting records as well as to coding issues. To remedy disagreement between datasets and different sources, the individual data have been subject to thorough comparison. Where discrepancies between data sets were substantial and persistent, individual data points were triangulated by issue area, member state and timing of the vote; that is, by year or month. Differences depended largely on the type of roll-calls and corresponding accounting methods used by the Council Secretariat and the authors. Only a very limited number of discrepancies continue to persist within a margin of error, and these appear to be related to the availability of the voting records, a problem that has become increasingly rare as the Council has become more systematic in operating its transparency policy in recent years.

The data-collection process has permitted the authors to build six internally and externally consistent data sets. The sets allow for detailed summary and descriptive statistics for a period of up to ten years (1994–2004), with annual and monthly voting records (detailing positive and negative votes and abstentions) per member state according to voting procedures, administrative sectors and type of roll-call. They provide us with a rather comprehensive insight into explicit voting.

Bibliography

Albert, M. (2003) 'The Voting Power Approach: Measurement without Theory', *European Union Politics*, 4(3): 351–66.

Albert M. (2004) 'The Voting Power Approach: Unresolved Ambiguities', *European Union Politics*, 5(1): 139–46.

Allen, D. (2005) 'Cohesion and the Structural Funds', in H. Wallace, W. Wallace and M. Pollack (eds), *Policy-Making in the European Union*, 5th edn (Oxford: Oxford University Press), 213–41.

Anderson, J. J. (2005) 'Germany and Europe: Centrality in the EU', in S. Bulmer and C. Lequesne (eds), *The Member States of the European Union* (Oxford: Oxford University Press), 77–96.

Arregui, J. (2004) *Negotiation in Legislative Decision-Making in the European Union* (Groningen: Rijksuniversiteit Groningen).

Avery, G. (1995) 'The Commission's Perspective on EFTA Association Negotiations', *SEI Working Paper* (Falmer: Sussex European Institute).

Axelrod, R. and Keohane, R. O. (1985) 'Achieving Cooperation under Anarchy: Strategies and Institutions', *World Politics*, 38(1): 226–54.

Baldwin, R. E. (1994) *Towards an Integrated Europe* (London: CEPR).

Ballmann, A., Epstein, D. and O'Halloran, S. (2002) 'Delegation, Comitology, and the Separation of Powers in the European Union', *International Organization*, 56(3): 551–74.

Beach, D. (2004) 'The Unseen Hand in Treaty Reform Negotiations: The Role and Influence of the Council Secretariat', *Journal of European Public Policy*, 11(3): 408–39.

Beach, D. (2005) *The Dynamics of European Integration* (Basingstoke: Palgrave Macmillan).

Best, E. (2001) 'The Treaty of Nice: Not Beautiful but It'll Do', *EIPASCOPE*, 1, 2–9.

Best, E. (2004) 'What is Really at Stake in the Debate over Votes?', *EIPASCOPE*, 1: 14–23.

Best, E., Gray, M. and Stubb, A. (2000) (eds) *Rethinking the European Union: IGC 2000 and Beyond* (Maastricht: European Institute for Public Administration).

Beyers, J. and Dierickx, G. (1996) *European Negotiations in the Working Groups of the Council of Ministers* (Leicester, UK: Centre for the Study of Diplomacy).

Beyers, J. and Dierickx, G. (1998) 'The Working Groups of the Council of the European Union: Supranational or Intergovernmental Negotiations?', *Journal of Common Market Studies*, 36(3): 289–317.

Börzel, T. (2003) *Environmental Leaders and Laggards in Europe. Why There Is (Not) a 'Southern Problem'* (Aldershot, Vt.: Ashgate).

Bossaert, D. (2003) 'Luxembourg: Flexible and Pragmatic Adaptation', in W. Wessels, A. Maurer and J. Mittag (eds), *Fifteen into One? The European Union and Its Member States* (Manchester: Manchester University Press), 298–314.

Bostock, D. (2002) 'Coreper Revisited', *Journal of Common Market Studies*, 40(2): 215–34.

Browne, E. C. and Franklin, M. N. (1973) 'Aspects of Coalition Pay-offs in European Parliamentary Democracies', *American Political Science Review*, 67(2): 453–70.

Budden, P. and Monroe, B. (1993) 'Decision-making in the EC Council of Ministers', paper presented to the European Community Studies Association (ECSA), Washington, DC.

Bueno de Mesquita, B. and Stokman, S. N. (1994) *European Community Decision Making*, (New Haven, Conn.: Yale University Press).

Bulletin of the EU (formerly *the EC*), published ten times a year by the General Secretariat of the Commission in French, English and German. Available online at www.europa.eu.int under 'Documents common to all the institutions'.

Bulmer, S. (1983) 'Domestic Policy and EC Decision Making', *Journal of Common Market Studies*, 21(4): 349–64.

Bulmer, S. (1985) 'The European Council's First Decade: Between Interdependence and Domestic Politics', *Journal of Common Market Studies*, 23(2): 89–104.

Bulmer, S. and Lequesne C. (eds) (2005) *The Member States of the European Union* (Oxford: Oxford University Press).

Bulmer, S. and Wessels, W. (1987) *The European Council* (London: Macmillan).

Buzan, B. (1981) 'Negotiating by Consensus: Developments in Technique at the United Nations Law of the Sea', *American Journal of International Law*, 75(2): 324–48.

Christiansen, T. (2002) 'The Role of Supranational Actors in EU Treaty Reform', *Journal of European Public Policy*, 9(1): 33–53.

Christiansen, T., Jörgensen, K. E. and Wiener, A. (eds) (2001) *The Social Construction of Europe* (London: Sage).

Clarke, M., May, J., Wallace, H. and Webb, C. (1977) *The European Community: An Exercise in Decision Making* (London: University Association for Contemporary European Studies).

Cloos, J., Reinesh, G., Vignes, D. and Weyland, J. (1994) *Le Traité de Maastricht: Genèse, Analyse, Commentaires* (Brussels: Bruylant).

Convention on the Future of Europe (2002) *Note on Legislative Procedures from the Praesidium to the Convention on the Future of Europe*, CONV 216/02, available on the Council website (www.consilium.eu.int).

Corbett, R., Jacobs, F. and Shackleton, M. (2003) *The European Parliament*, 5th edn (London: John Harper).

Corbett, R., Jacobs, F. and Shackleton, M. (2005) *The European Parliament*, 6th edn (London: John Harper).

Council of the European Union (1995) *Report on the Functioning of the Treaty on the European Union* (Brussels: OOPEC).

Council of the European Union, various documents; numbers cited in the text, available in the register of Council documents on the Council's website (www.consilium.eu.int).

Culley, P. (2004) 'The Agriculture and Fisheries Council', in M. Westlake and D. Galloway, (eds), *The Council of the European Union*, 3rd edn (London: John Harper), 143–55.

de Bassompierre, G. (1988) *Changing the Guard in Brussels. An Insider's View of the EC Presidency* (New York: Praeger).

de Ruyt, J. (1989) *Acte Unique Européen* (Brussels: Editions de l'ULB).

de Schoutheete, P. (1986) *La Coopération Politique Européenne* (Brussels: Nathan).

de Schoutheete, P. (1988) 'The presidency and the management of political cooperation', in A. Pijpers, E. Regelsberger and W. Wessels (eds), *European Political Cooperation in the 1980s: A Common Foreign Policy for Western Europe?* (Dordrecht: Martinus Nijhoff).

de Schoutheete, P. (2002) 'The European Council' in J. Peterson and M. Shackleton (eds), *The Institutions of the European Union*, 2nd edn (Oxford: Oxford University Press), 21–46.

de Schoutheete, P. (2006) 'The European Council', in J. Peterson and M. Shackleton, (eds), *The Institutions of the European Union*, 2nd edn (Oxford: Oxford University Press).

de Schoutheete, P. and Wallace, H. (2002) *The European Council* (Paris: Notre Europe).

de Zwaan, J. W. (1995) *The Permanent Representatives Committee: Its Role in European Union Decision-making* (Amsterdam: Elsevier).

Dehousse, R. (2003) 'Comitology: Who Watches the Watchmen?', *Journal of European Public Policy*, 10(5): 798–813.

Deloche-Gaudez, F. (2004) 'Le Secrétariat de la Convention Européenne: un acteur influant', *Politique Européenne*, 13: 43–67.

den Boer, M. (1996) 'Justice and Home Affairs: Attachment without Integration', in H. Wallace and W. Wallace (eds.) *Policy-making in the European Union* 4th edn. (Oxford: Oxford University Press), 389–410.

Deubner, C. (1995) *Deutsche Europapolitik: Von Maastricht nach Kerneuropa* (Baden-Baden: Nomos).

Deutsch, K., Burrell, S., Kann, R., Lee Jr., M., Lichterman, M., Lindgren, R., Loewenhaim, F. and Van Wagenem, R. (1957) *Political Community and the North Atlantic Area* (Princeton, NJ: Princeton University Press).

Dinan, D. (1999) *Ever Closer Union? An Introduction to European Integration*, 2nd edn (London: Macmillan).

Docksey, C. and Williams, K. (1994) 'The Commission and the Execution of Community Policy', in G. Edwards and D. Spence (eds), *The European Commission* (London: Longman), 117–45.

Dooge (1985) *Report to the European Council* (The Dooge Report), Ad hoc Committee for Institutional Affairs, Brussels: OOPEC.

Earnshaw, D. and Judge, D. (1993) 'The European Parliament and the Sweeteners Directive: From Footnote to Inter-Institutional Conflict', *Journal of Common Market Studies*, 31(1): 103–16.

Earnshaw, D. and Judge, D. (1996) 'From Co-operation to Co-Decision: The European Parliament's Path to Legislative Power', in J. Richardson, (ed.), *European Union: Power and Policy-Making* (London: Routledge).

Edwards, G. and Spence, D. (1997) (eds) *The European Commission* (London: Longman).

Edwards, G. and Wallace, H. (1977) *The Council of Ministers of the European Community and the President-in-Office* (London: Federal Trust).

Egeberg, M. (1999) 'Transcending Intergovernmentalism? Identity and Role Perceptions of National Officials in EU Decision-making', *Journal of European Public Policy*, 6(3): 456–74.

Egeberg, M. (2005) 'The EU and the Nordic Countries: Organizing Domestic Diversity?', in S. Bulmer and C. Lequesne (eds), *The Member States of the European Union* (Oxford: Oxford University Press), 185–208.

Ehlermann, C.-D. (1984) 'How Flexible Is Community Law? An Unusual Approach to the Concept of "two speeds"', *Michigan Law Review*, 82: 1274–93.

Elgström, O. (ed) (2003) *European Union Council Presidencies. A Comparative Perspective* (London: Routledge).

Elgström, O. and Jönsson, C. (eds) (2005) *European Union Negotiations. Processes, Networks and Institutions* (London: Routledge).

Elgström, O. and Smith, M. (2000) 'Introduction: Negotiation and policy-making in the European Union – Processes, System and Order', *Journal of European Public Policy*, 7(5): 673–83.

Eurobarometer, various issues. Available as a link from the Commission website (http://europa.eu.int/comm) under 'Public opinion analysis'.

European Commission (1995) *Report on the Functioning of the Treaty on the European Union* (Luxembourg: OOPEC).

European Parliament, *Activity Report of the EP Delegation to the Conciliation Committee*, various years, available on the EP's website (www.europarl.eu.int), following the links Activities, Conciliation, General information.

European Parliament (1999) *Activity Report of the EP Delegation to the Conciliation Committee, 1993–1999*, available as above.

European Parliament (2004) *Activity Report of the EP Delegation to the Conciliation Committee, 1999–2004*, available as above.

European Union Politics (2004) Special Issue, 5(1).

European Voice, various issues.

Eurostat available as a link from the Commission website (http://europa.eu.int/comm).

Evans, P. B., Jacobson, H. K. and Putnam, R. D. (eds) (1993) *Double-edged diplomacy: International Bargaining and Domestic Politics* (Berkeley, Calif.: University of California Press).

Farrell, H. and Héritier, A. (2003) 'Formal and Informal Institutions under Codecision: Continuous Constitution-Building in Europe', *Governance*, 16(4): 577–600.

Felsenthal D. S., Leech D., List C. and Machover M. (2003) 'In Defence of Voting Power Analysis: Responses to Albert', *European Union Politics*, 4(4): 473–97.

Felsenthal, D. S. and Machover, M. (1997) 'The Weighted Voting Rule in the EU's Council of Ministers, 1958–95: Intentions and Outcomes', *Electoral Studies*, 16(1): 34–47.

Financial Times, various issues.

Fisher, R., Ury, W. and Patton, B. (2003) *Getting to Yes: The Secret to Successful Negotiation* (New York: Random House Business Books).

Franck, C., Leclercq, H. and Vandevievere, C. (2003) 'Belgium: Europeanisation and Belgian Federalism', in W. Wessels, A. Maurer and J. Mittag (eds), *Fifteen into One? The European Union and Its Member States* (Manchester: Manchester University Press).

Galloway, D. (2001) *The Treaty of Nice and Beyond: Realities and Illusions of Power in the EU* (Sheffield: Sheffield Academic Press).

Garrett, G. (1995) 'From the Luxembourg Compromise to Codecision: Decision Making in the European Union', *Electoral Studies*, 14(3): 289–308.

George, S. (1994) *An Awkward Partner: Britain in the European Community*, 2nd edn (Oxford: Oxford University Press).

Gerbet, P. and Pépy, D. (1969) *La décision dans les Communautés Européennes* (Brussels: ULB).

Goetz, K. H. (2005) 'The New Member States and the EU: Responding to Europe', in S. Bulmer, and C. Lequesne (eds), *The Member States of the European Union* (Oxford: Oxford University Press), 254–84.

Goldstein, J. and Keohane, R. O. (eds) (1993) *Ideas and Foreign Policy: Beliefs, Institutions and Political Change* (Ithaca, NY: Cornell University Press).

Golub, J. (1999) 'In the Shadow of the Vote? Decision Making in the European Community', *International Organization*, 53(4): 733–64.

Gomez, R. and Peterson, J. (2001) 'The EU's Impossibly Busy Foreign Ministers: "No One Is in Control"', *European Foreign Affairs Review*, 6(1): 53–74.

Gonzalez Sanchez, E. (1992) *Manual del negociador en la Comunidad Europea* (Madrid: Oficina de la Informacion Diplomática).

Gonzalez Sanchez, E. (1994) 'La revolución de la Unión Europea: del sistema Quadripartito previsto en los Tratados Originarios a un Sistema Institucional Tripartito en la Perspectiva de la unificación Europea', *Revista de Instituciones Europeas*, 1: 85–115.

Granell, F. (1995) 'The European Union's Enlargement Negotiations with Austria, Finland, Norway and Sweden', *Journal of Common Market Studies*, 33(1): 117–42.

Grant, C. (1994) *Delors: Inside the House that Jacques Built* (London: Nicholas Brealey).

Haas, E. B. [1958] (2004) *The Uniting of Europe. Political, Economic and Social Forces 1950–57* (Stanford, Calif.: Stanford University Press; reprinted 2004, Notre Dame, Ind.: University of Notre Dame Press).

Haas, E. B. (1975) *The Obsolence of Regional Integration Theory* (Berkeley, Calif.: Institute of International Studies).

Hayes, F. (1984) 'The Role of COREPER in EEC Decision-making', *Administration*, 32(2): 177–200.

Hayes-Renshaw, F. (1990a) 'The Role of the Committee of Permanent Representatives in the Decision-making process of the European Community', Doctoral dissertation, London School of Economics.

Hayes-Renshaw, F. (1990b) 'Decision-making in the EC Council after the Single European Act', *European Trends*, 1: 74–80.

Hayes-Renshaw, F. (2006) 'The Council of Ministers' in J. Peterson and M. Shackleton (eds), *The Institutions of the European Union*, 2nd edn (Oxford: Oxford University Press).

Hayes-Renshaw F. and Wallace, H. (1995) 'The Council of Ministers: The Functions and Limits of Executive Power', *Journal of European Public Policy*, 2(4): 559–82.

Hayes-Renshaw, F. and Wallace, H. (1997) *The Council of Ministers* (London: Macmillan).

Hayes-Renshaw, F., Lequesne, Ch. and Lopez, P. M. (1989) 'The Permanent Representations of the Member States to the European Communities', *Journal of Common Market Studies*, 28(2): 119–37.

Hayes-Renshaw, F., van Aken, W. and Wallace, H. (2006) 'When and Why the EU Council of Ministers Votes Explicitly', *Journal of Common Market Studies*, 44: 1.

Heisenberg, D. (2005) 'The Institution of 'Consensus' in the European Union: Formal versus Informal decision-making in the Council', *European Journal of Political Research*, 44: 65–90.

Hoffman, S. (1966) 'Obstinate or Obsolete? The Case of the Nation State and the Case of Western Europe', *Daedalus*, 95: 862–915.

Hosli, M. O. (1994) *Coalitions and Power: Effects on Qualified Majority Voting in the European Union's Council of Ministers* (Maastricht: European Institute of Public Administration).

Hosli, M. O. and Machover, M. (2004) 'The Nice Treaty and Voting Rules in the Council: A Reply to Moberg (2002)', *Journal of Common Market Studies*, 42(3): 497–521.

Houben, P. H. J. M. (1964) *Le conseil de ministres des Communautés Européennes*, (Leyden: Sythoff).

Howorth, J. (2003) 'Foreign and Defence Policy Cooperation: European and American Perspectives', in J. Peterson and M. Pollack (eds), *Europe, America, Bush: Transatlantic Relations after 2000* (London: Routledge).

Humphreys, J. (1996) *A Way Through the Woods: Negotiating in the European Union* (London: Department of the Environment).

IDEA online, inter-institutional directory, available at www.europa.eu.int/idea.

Iklé, F. C. (1964) *How Nations Negotiate* (New York: Harper & Row).

Joerges, C. and Neyer, J. (1997) 'Transforming Strategic Interaction into Deliberative Problem-solving: European Comitology in the Foodstuffs Sector', *Journal of European Public Policy*, 4(4): 609–25.

Jones, A. and Clark, J. (2002) 'D'accord or Discord? New Institutionalism, Concordance, and the European Union Agriculture Council', *Environment and Planning C: Government and Policy*, 20(1): 113–29.

Jordan, A. (2002) *The Europeaniszation of British Environmental Policy. A Departmental Perspective* (Basingstoke: Palgrave Macmillan).

Journal of European Public Policy (2000), special issue, 715.

Jupille, J., Caporaso, J. A. and Checkel, J. T. (2003) 'Integrating Institutions: Rationalism, Contsructivism, and the Study of the European Union', *Comparative Political Studies*, 36(1–2): 7–40.

Kassim, H. (2005) 'The Europeanization of Member State Institutions', in S. Bulmer and C. Lequesne (eds), *The Member States of the European Union* (Oxford: Oxford University Press), 285–316.

Kassim, H., Menon, A., Peters, G. and Wright, V. (eds) (2001) *The National Co-ordination of EU Policy. The European Level* (Oxford: Oxford University Press).

Kassim, H., Peters, G. and Wright, V. (eds) (2000) *The National Co-ordination of EU Policy. The Domestic Level* (Oxford: Oxford University Press).

Kauppi, H. and Widgrén, M. (2004) 'What Determines EU Decision Making? Needs, Power or Both?', *Economic Policy*, 19(39): 221–66.

Keohane, R. O. (1986) 'Reciprocity in International Relations', *International Organization*, 40(1): 1–28.

Kirchner, E. (1992) *Decision-making in the European Community. The Council Presidency and European Integration* (Manchester: Manchester University Press).

Kohler-Koch, B. and Eising, R. (eds) (1999) *The Transformation of Government in the European Union* (London and New York: Routledge).

Kok, W. (2004) *Facing the Challenge: The Lisbon Strategy for Growth and Employment*, Report from the High Level Group chaired by Wim Kok (Brussels: Council of Ministers).

König, T. and Bräuninger, T. (2004) 'Accession and Reform of the European Union', *European Union Politics*, 5(4): 419–39.

König, T. and Proksch, S.-O. (2005) 'Voting and Exchanging: How to Model Council Decision Making', Paper presented at the EUSA 9th Biennial International Conference, Austin, Texas.

Korkman, S. (2004) 'The Ecofin Council and the Eurogroup', in M. Westlake and D. Galloway (eds), *The Council of the European Union*, 3rd edn (London: John Harper), 83–101.

Laffan, B. (2000) 'The Big Budgetary Bargains: From Negotiation to Authority', *Journal of European Public Policy*, 7(5): 725–43.

Laffan, B. and Lindner, J. (2005) 'The Budget', in H. Wallace, W. Wallace, and M. A. Pollack, (eds), *Policy-making in the European Union*, 5th edn (Oxford: Oxford University Press), 191–212.

Laffan, B. and Shackleton, M. (1996) 'Making and Managing Budgets', in H. Wallace and W. Wallace (eds), *Policy-making in the European Union* (Oxford: Oxford University Press), 71–96.

Laffan, B. and Shackleton, M. (2000) 'The Budget', in H. Wallace and W. Wallace (eds), *Policy-Making in the European Union*, 4th edn (Oxford: Oxford University Press), 211–41.

Lavenex, S. and Wallace, W. (2005) 'Justice and Home Affairs', in H. Wallace, W. Wallace and M. Pollack (eds), *Policy-Making in the European Union*, 5th edn (Oxford: Oxford University Press), 457–80.

Leibfried, S. (2005) 'Social Policy', in H. Wallace, W. Wallace and M. A. Pollack (eds) *Policy-Making in the European Union*, 5th edn (Oxford: Oxford University Press), 243–78.

Lenschow, A. (2005) 'Environmental Policy', in H. Wallace, W. Wallace and M. A. Pollack (eds), *Policy-making in the European Union*, 5th edn (Oxford: Oxford University Press), 305–27.

Lewis, J. (1998a) 'Is the "Hard Bargaining" Image of the Council Misleading? The Committee of Permanent Representatives and the Local Elections Directive', *Journal of Common Market Studies*, 36(4): 479–504.

Lewis, J. (1998b) 'Constructing Interests: The Committee of Permanent Representatives and Decision Making in the European Union', Doctoral dissertation, University of Wisconsin-Madison, Department of Political Science.

Lewis, J. (2002) 'National Interests: Coreper', in J. Peterson and M. Schackleton (eds), *The Institutions of the European Union* (Oxford: Oxford University Press), 277–98.

Lewis, J. (2003) 'Institutional Environments and Everyday EU Decision Making: Rationalist or Constructivist?', *Comparative Political Studies*, 36 (1–2): 97–124.

Lewis, J. (2005) 'The Janus Face of Brussels: Socialisation and Everyday Decision Making in the European Union', *International Organisation*, 59(4): 937–71.

Lewis, J. (2006) 'National Interests – COREPER', in Peterson, J. and Shackleton, M. (eds) *The Institutions of the European Union* (Oxford: Oxford University Press).

Lindberg, L. N. (1963) *The Political Dynamics of European Economic Integration* (Stanford, Calif.: Stanford University Press).

Lindner, J. (2005) *Conflict and Change in EU Budgetary Politics* (London: Routledge).

Loth, W., Wallace, W. and Wessels, W. (eds) (1995) *Walter Hallstein: Der vergessene Europäer?* (Bonn: Europa Union Verlag).

Ludlow, P. (2002) *The Laeken Council* (Brussels: Eurocomment).

Ludlow, P. (2004) *The Making of the New Europe: The European Councils in Brussels and Copenhagen* (Brussels: Eurocomment).

Ludlow, P. (2005) *Dealing with Turkey, Briefing Note* (Brussels: Eurocomment).

Majone, G. (1996) (ed.) *Regulating Europe* (London: Routledge).

Majone, G. (2000) 'Two Logics of Delegation: Agency and Fiduciary Relations in EU Governance', *European Union Politics*, 2(1): 103–22.

Majone, G. (2005) *Dilemmas of European Integration: The Ambiguities and Pitfalls of Integration by Stealth* (Oxford: Oxford University Press).

Mattila, M. (2004) 'Contested Decisions: Empirical Analysis of Voting in the European Union Council of Ministers', *European Journal of Political Research*, 43,(1): 29–50.

Mattila, M. and Lane, J.-E. (2001) 'Why Unanimity in the Council? A Roll Call Analysis of Council Voting', *European Union Politics*, 2(1): 31–52.

Maurer, A. (1999) *What Next for the European Parliament?* (London: Federal Trust).

Maurer, A. (2003a) 'The Legislative Powers and Impact of the European Parliament', *Journal of Common Market Studies*, 41(2): 227–47.

Maurer, A. (2003b) *Auf dem Weg zur Staatenkammer. Die Reform des Ministerrats der EU* (Berlin: SWP Studie).

McDonagh, B. (1998) *Original Sin in a Brave New World: The Paradox of Europe: An Account of the Negotiation of the Treaty of Amsterdam* (Dublin: Institute of European Affairs).

McNamara, K. R. (2005) 'Economic and Monetary Union', in H. Wallace, W. Wallace and M. A. Pollack (eds) *Policy-Making in the European Union*, 5th edn (Oxford University Press), 141–60.

Metcalfe, D. (1998) 'Leadership in European Union Negotiations: The Presidency of the Council', *International Negotiation*, 3(3): 413–34.

Meunier, S. (2000) 'What Single Voice? European Institutions and EU–US Trade Negotiations', *International Organization*, 54(1): 103–35.

Meunier, S. and Nicolaidis, K. (1999) 'Who Speaks for Europe? The Delegation of Trade Authority in the EU', *Journal of Common Market Studies*, 37(3): 477–501.

Milton, G. and Keller-Noëllet, J. (2005) *The European Constitution. Its Origins, Negotiation and Meaning* (London: John Harper).

Milward, A. (with the assistance of Brennan, G. and Romero, F.) (2000) *The European Rescue of the Nation-state*, 2nd edn (London: Routledge).

Mittag, J. and Wessels, W. (2003) 'The "One" and the "Fifteen"? The Member States between Procedural Adaptation and Structural Revolution', in W. Wessels, A. Maurer and J. Mittag (eds), *Fifteen into One? The European Union and Its Member States* (Manchester: Manchester University Press), 413–54.

Moberg, A. (2002) 'The Nice Treaty and Voting Rules in the Council', *Journal of Common Market Studies*, 40(2): 259–82.

Monar, J. (2002) 'Justice and Home Affairs', in G. Edwards and G. Wiessala (eds), *Journal of Common Market Studies: Annual Review of the EU 2001/2002*, (Oxford: Blackwell Publishers Ltd), 121–36.

Monar, J. (2004) 'Justice and Home Affairs', in L. Miles (ed.), *The European Union: Annual Review of the EU 2003/2004* (Oxford: Blackwell Publishers Ltd), 117–33.

Moravcsik, A. (1991) 'Negotiating the Single European Act: National Interests and Conventional Statecraft', *International Organization*, 45(1): 19–56.

Moravcsik, A. (1998) *The Choice for Europe: Social Purpose and State Power from Messina to Maastricht* (Ithaca, NY: Cornell University Press).

Neligan, D. M. (1999) 'The Council of Ministers', in J. Dooge and R. Barrington (eds), *A Vital National Interest': Ireland in Europe 1973–1998* (Dublin: Institute of Public Administration), 77–88.

Newhouse, J. (1967) *Collision in Brussels: The Common Market Crisis of 30 June 1965* (London: Faber).

Nicoll, W. (1984) 'The Luxembourg Compromise', *Journal of Common Market Studies*, 21(1): 35–43.

Nicoll, W. (1993) 'Note the Hour – and File the Minute', *Journal of Common Market Studies*, 31(4): 559–66.

Nilsson H. (2004) 'The Justice and Home Affairs Council', in M. Westlake and D. Galloway (eds), *The Council of the European Union*, 3rd edn (London: John Harper), 113–42.

Noël, E. (1967) 'The Committee of Permanent Representatives', *Journal of Common Market Studies*, 5(1): 219–51.

Noël, E. and Etienne, H. (1971) 'The Permanent Representatives and the "Deepening" of the Communities', *Government and Opposition*, 3: 422–47.

Norman, P. (2005) *The Accidental Constitution*, 2nd edn (Brussels: Euro Comment).

Nuttall, S. (1992) *European Political Cooperation* (Oxford: Clarendon Press).

Nuttall, S. J. (2000) *European Foreign Policy* (Oxford: Oxford University Press).

Official Journal of the European Union, various issues; accessible via the Europa website (www.europa.eu.int), following the links 'European law', 'EUR-LEX' and then 'Official Journal'.

O'Nuallain, C. (ed.) (1985) *The Presidency of the European Council of Ministers* (London: Croom Helm).

Palayret, J.-M., Wallace, H. and Winand, P. (2006) *Visions, Votes and Vetoes: Reassessing the Luxembourg Compromise 40 Years On* (Brussels: Peter Lang).

Patterson, L. A. (2000) 'Biotechnology Policy', in H. Wallace and W. Wallace (eds), *Policy-making in the European Union* 4th edn (Oxford: Oxford University Press), 317–43.

Peterson, J. (1995) 'Decision-making in the European Union: Towards a Framework for Analysis', *Journal of European Public Policy*, 2(1): 69–93.

Piris, J.-C. (1994) 'After Maastricht, are the Community Institutions More Efficacious, More Democratic and More Transparent?', *European Law Review*, 19(5): 449–87.

Pollack, M. A. (2005a) 'Theorizing EU Policy-making', in H. Wallace, W. Wallace and M. A. Pollack (eds) *Policy-Making in the European Union*, 5th edn (Oxford: Oxford University Press), 13–48.

Pollack, M. A. (2005b) 'Theorizing the European Union: International Organization, Domestic Polity, or Experiment in New Governance?', *Annual Review of Political Science*, 8: 357–98.

Pollack, M. A. and Shaffer, G. C. (2005) 'Biotechnology Policy', in H. Wallace, W. Wallace and M. A. Pollack (eds), *Policy-making in the European Union*, 5th edn (Oxford: Oxford University Press), 329–51.

Puchala, D. J. (1977) 'Worm Cans and Worth Taxes: Fiscal Harmonisation and the European Policy Process', in H. Wallace, W. Wallace and C. Webb (eds), *Policy Making in the European Communities* (Chichester: Wiley), 249–72.

Putnam, R. D. (1988) 'Diplomacy and Domestic Politics: The Logic of Two-level Games', *International Organization*, 43(2): 88–110.

Quaglia, L. (2004) 'Italy's Policy Towards European Monetary Integration: Bringing Ideas Back in?', *Journal of European Public Policy*, 11(6): 1096–111.

Raunio, T. and Wiberg, M. (1998) 'Winners and Losers in the Council: Voting Power Consequences of EU Enlargements', *Journal of Common Market Studies*, 36(4): 549–62.

Rhodes, M. (2005) 'Employment Policy', in H. Wallace, W. Wallace and M. A. Pollack (eds), *Policy-making in the European Union*, 5th edn (Oxford: Oxford University Press), 279–304.

Richardson, J. (1982) *Policy Styles in Western Europe* (London: George Allen & Unwin).

Rieger, E. (2005) 'Agricultural Policy', in H. Wallace, W. Wallace and M. A. Pollack (eds) *Policy-making in the European Union*, 5th edn (Oxford: Oxford University Press), 161–90.

Risse, T. (2004) 'Social Constructivism and European Integration', in A. Wiener and T. Diez, (eds) *European Integration Theory* (Oxford: Oxford University Press), 159–76.

Rometsch, D. and Wessels, W. (1994) 'The Commission and the Council of Ministers', in G. Edwards and D. Spence (eds), *The European Commission* (London: Longman), 202–24.

Rosamond, B. (2000) *Theories of European Integration* (Basingstoke: Palgrave) Macmillan.

Ross, G. (1995) *Jacques Delors and European Integration* (Cambridge: Polity Press).

Ruggie, J. G. (1993) *Multilaterism Matters: The Theory and Practice of an Institutional Form* (New York: Columbia University Press).

Rummel, R. (1982) *Zusammengesetzte Außenpolitik* (Kehl am Rhein: N. P. Engel Verlag).

Salmon, J. A. (1971) 'Le Comité des Représentants permanents', in M. Virally, P. Gerbet and J. A. Salmon (eds), *Les missions permanentes auprès des organisations internationales* (Brussels: Bruylant).

Sapir, A., Aghion, O., Bertola, G., Hellwig, M., Pisani-Ferry, J., Rosati, D., Vinals, J. and Wallace, H. (2004) *An Agenda for a Growing Europe: Making the EU Economic System Deliver*, Report of an Independent High Level Study Group chaired by André Sapir (Oxford: Oxford University Press). Originally published online by the Commission, 2003.

Scharpf, F. (1988) 'The Joint-decision Trap: Lessons from German Federalism and European Integration', *Public Administration*, 66(3): 239–78.

Scharpf, F. (1994a) 'Community and Autonomy: Multi-level Policy-making in the European Union', *Journal of European Public Policy*, 1(2): 219–42.

Scharpf, F. (1994b) *Optionen des Federalismus in Deutschland und Europa* (Frankfurtam Main: Campus).

Scharpf, F. (1997) *Games Real Actors Play. Actor-Centered Institutionalism in Policy Research* (Boulder, Col.: Westview Press).

Schmitter, P. C. (1992) 'Interests, Powers and Functions: Emergent Properties and Unintended Consequences in the European Polity', unpublished paper, Stanford University.

Schofield, N. and Laver, M. (1985) 'Bargaining Theory and Portfolio Pay-offs in European Coalition Governments, 1945–83', *British Journal of Political Science*, 15(2): 143–64.

Schulz, H. and König, T. (2000) 'Institutional Reform and Decision-Making. Efficiency in the European Union', *American Journal of Political Science*, 44(4): 653–66.

Sedelmeier, U. (2000) 'East of Amsterdam: The Implications of the Amsterdam Treaty for Eastern Enlargement', in A. Wiener and K. H. Neunreither (eds), *European Integration after Amsterdam: Institutional Dynamics and Prospects for Democracy* (Oxford: Oxford University Press), 218–35.

Shackleton, M. (1990) *Financing the European Community* (London: Pinter).

Shackleton, M. (2002) 'The European Parliament', in J. Peterson and M. Shackleton (eds), *The Institutions of the European Union* (Oxford: Oxford University Press), 95–117.

Shackleton, M. and Raunio, T. (2003) 'Codecision since Amsterdam: A Laboratory for Institutional Innovation and Change', *Journal of European Public Policy*, 10(2): 171–88.

Sherrington, P. (2000) *The Council of Ministers: Political Authority in the European Union*, (London/New York: Pinter).

Sie Dhian Ho, M. and Van Keulen, M. (2004) *The Dutch at the Helm – Navigating on a Rough Sea: The Netherlands 2004 Presidency of the European Union* (Paris: Notre Europe).

Skog, R. (2002) 'The Takeover Directive – an Endless Saga?', *European Business Law Review*, 13(4): 301–12.

Sloot, T. and Verschuren, P. (1990) 'Decision-making Speed in the European Community', *Journal of Common Market Studies*, 29(1): 75–85.

Smith, M. (2005) 'The European Union and the United States of America: The Politics of "Bi-multilateral" Negotiations', in O. Elgström and C. Jönsson (eds), *European Union Negotiations. Processes, Networks and Institutions* (London: Routledge), 164–82.

Solana, J. (2002) 'Report by Mr Javier Solana, Secretary General of the Council, on "Preparing the Council for Enlargement"', presented to the Barcelona European Council, 15–16 March.

Spence, D. (1991) 'Enlargement without Accession: The EC's Response to German Unification', London: RIIA Discussion Paper.

Stark, C. (2002) 'Different Types of Meetings of the EU Heads of Government, Contribution to the Convention on the Future of Europe', http://europa.eu.int/constitution/futurum/conathacad-2-en.htm.

Steinberg, R. H. (2002) 'In the Shadow of Law or Power? Consensus-based Bargaining and Outcomes in the GATT/ETO', *International Organization*, 56(2): 339–74.

Stubb, A. (2002) *Negotiating Flexibility in the European Union. Amsterdam, Nice and Beyond* (Basingstoke: Palgrave Macmillan).

Taggart, P. and Szczerbiak, A. (eds) (2006a) *Opposing Europe? The Comparative Party Politics of Euroscepticism: Vol. 1: Case Studies and Country Surveys* (Oxford: Oxford University Press).

Taggart, P. and Szczerbiak, A. (eds) (2006b) *Opposing Europe? The Comparative Party Politics of Euroscepticism: Vol. 2: Comparative and Theoretical Perspectives* (Oxford: Oxford University Press).

Tallberg, J. (2003) 'The Agenda-shaping Powers of the EU Council Presidency', *Journal of European Public Policy*, 10(1): 1–19.
Tallberg, J. (2004) 'The Power of the Presidency: Brokerage, Efficiency and Distribution in EU Negotiations', *Journal of Common Market Studies*, 42(5): 999–1022.
Teasdale, A. (1993) 'The Life and Death of the Luxembourg Compromise', *Journal of Common Market Studies*, 31(4): 567–79.
Thomson, R., Boerefijn, J. and Stokman, F. (2004) 'Actor Alignments in European Union Decision Making', *European Journal of Political Research*, 43(2): 237–61.
Thomson, R., Stokman, F. N., Achen, C. H. and König, T. (forthcoming) (eds) *The European Union Decides* (Cambridge: Cambridge University Press).
Tiilikainen, T. (2003) 'Finland: Smooth Adaptation to European Values and Institutions', in W. Wessels, A. Maurer and J. Mittag (eds), *Fifteen into One? The European Union and its Member States* (Manchester: Manchester University Press), 150–65.
Tizzano, A. (1989) 'The Permanent Representations of the Member States to the European Communities', *Public Administration and Europe '92* (Rome: Scientifica), 519–48.
Tortora da Falco, F. (1980) *Il Comitato dei rappresentanti dai Trattati istitutivi alla prassi comunitaria* (Naples: Giannini).
Trondal, J. and Veggeland, F. (2003) 'Access, Voice and Loyalty: The Representation of Domestic Civil Servants in EU Committees', *Journal of European Public Policy*, 10(1): 59–77.
Tsebelis, G. (1990) *Nested Games* (Berkeley, Calif.: University of California Press).
van Schendelen, M. (1996) '"The Council Decides": Does the Council Decide?', *Journal of Common Market Studies*, 34(4): 531–48.
van Schendelen, R. (2003) *Machiavelli in Brussels: The Art of Lobbying the EU* (Amsterdam: Amsterdam University Press).
Vibert, F. (1994) *The Future Role of the European Commission* (London: European Policy Forum).
von der Groeben, H. (1982) *Aufbaujahre der Europäischen Gemeinschaft. Das Ringen um den Gemeinsamen Markt und die Politische Union (1958–66)* (Baden-Baden: Nomos).
Wallace, H. (1971) 'The Impact of the European Communities on National Policy-Making', *Government and Opposition*, 6: 520–38.
Wallace, H. (1973) *National Governments and the European Communities* (London: Chatham House/PEP).
Wallace, H. (1996) 'The Institutions of the EU: Experience and Experiments', in H. Wallace and W. Wallace (eds), *Policy-making in the European Union*, 3rd edn (Oxford: Oxford University Press), 37–70.
Wallace, H. (1997) 'At Odds with Europe', *Political Studies*, 45(4): 677–88.
Wallace, H. (1999) 'The Domestication of Europe: Contrasting Experiences of EU Membership and Non-Membership', Sixth Daalder Lecture, Leiden University Department of Political Science.
Wallace, H. (2002) 'The Council: An Institutional Chameleon?', *Governance*, 15(3): 325–44.
Wallace, H. (2005) 'An Institutional Anatomy and Five Policy Modes', in H. Wallace, W. Wallace and M. A. Pollack (eds), *Policy-Making in the European Union*, 5th edn (Oxford: Oxford University Press), 49–90.
Wallace, H. and Edwards, G. (1976) 'European Community: The Evolving Role of the Presidency of the Council', *International Affairs*, 52(4): 535–50.
Wallace, H. and Hayes-Renshaw, F. (2003) *Reforming the Council: A Work in Progress* (Stockholm: SIEPS).
Wallace, H. and Wallace, W. (1995) *Flying Together in a Larger and More Diverse European Union* (The Hague: Scientific Council for Government Policy).

Wallace, W. (2005) 'Foreign and Security Policy', in H. Wallace, W. Wallace and M. A. Pollack (eds), *Policy-Making in the European Union*, 5th edn (Oxford: Oxford University Press), 429–56.

Webb, C. (1983) 'Theoretical Perspectives and Problems', in H. Wallace, W. Wallace and C. Webb (eds), *Policy-Making in the European Community*, 2nd edn (Chichester: John Wiley).

Werts, J. (1992) *The European Council* (Amsterdam: North-Holland).

Wessels, W. (1991) 'The EC Council: The Community's Decision Making Center', in R. O. Keohane and S. Hoffmann (eds), *The New European Community. Decisionmaking and Institutional Change* (Boulder, Col.: Westview Press), 133–54.

Wessels, W. (1992) 'Staat und (westeuropäische) Integration: die Fusionsthese', *Politische Vierteljahresschrift*, 23(99): 36–61.

Wessels, W., Maurer, A. and Mittag, J. (eds) (2003) *Fifteen into One? The European Union and Its Member States* (Manchester: Manchester University Press).

Westlake, M. and Galloway, D. (2004) *The Council of the European Union*, 3rd edn (London: John Harper).

Widgrén, M. (1994) 'Voting Power in the EC and the Consequences of Two Different Enlargements', *European Economic Review*, 38: 1153–70.

Wiener, A. and Diez, T. (2004) *European Integration Theory* (Oxford: Oxford University Press).

Willocks, E. (2003) 'Enlargement of the European Union – the Council Process', in M. Hoskins and W. Robinson (eds) *A True European: Essays for Judge David Edward* (Oxford: Hart Publishing), 99–115.

Woolcock, S. (2005) 'Trade Policy', in H. Wallace, W. Wallace and M. A. Pollack (eds) *Policy-Making in the European Union*, 5th edn (Oxford: Oxford University Press), 377–99.

World Bank (2002) *World Development Indicators*.

Young, A. (2005) 'The Single Market', in H. Wallace, W. Wallace and M. A. Pollack (eds), *Policy-Making in the European Union*, 5th edn (Oxford: Oxford University Press), 93–112.

Zartman, I. W. and Berman, M. (1982) *The Practical Negotiator* (New Haven, Conn.: Yale University Press).

Zimmer, C., Schneider, G. and Dobbins, M. (2005) 'The Contested Council: Conflict Dimensions of an Intergovernmental EU Institution', *Political Studies*, 53(2): 403–22.

Index